D0603697

POP CULTURE
CHINA!

Other titles in ABC-CLIO's series

Popular Culture in the Contemporary World

Pop Culture Germany! Media, Arts, and Lifestyle, Catherine C. Fraser and Dierk O. Hoffmann

Pop Culture India! Media, Arts, and Lifestyle, Asha Kasbekar

Pop Culture Russia! Media, Arts, and Lifestyle, Birgit Beumers

Pop Culture Latin America! Media, Arts, and Lifestyle, Lisa Shaw and Stephanie Dennison

Pop Culture Arab World! Media, Arts, and Lifestyle, Andrew Hammond

POP CULTURE

CHINA!

Media, Arts, and Lifestyle

Kevin Latham

Santa Barbara, California Denver, Colorado Oxford, England

Library of Congress Cataloging-in-Publication Data
Latham, Kevin, 1964-
Pop culture China! : media, arts, and lifestyle / Kevin Latham.
p. cm. — (Pop culture series)
ISBN 978-1-85109-582-7 (hard copy : alk. paper) — ISBN 978-1-85109-587-2 (ebook)
1. Popular culture—China. I. Title.
DS727.L358 2007
306'.0951—dc22
2007009706

11 10 09 08 07 1 2 3 4 5 6 7 8 9 10

This book is also available on the World Wide Web as an ebook.
Visit http://www.abc-clio.com for details.

Production Editor: Alisha Martinez
Editorial Assistant: Sara Springer
Production Manager: Don Schmidt
Media Editor: Jason Kniser
Media Resources Coordinator: Ellen Brenna Dougherty
Media Resources Manager: Caroline Price
File Manager: Paula Gerard

ABC-CLIO, Inc.
130 Cremona Drive, P.O. Box 1911
Santa Barbara, California 93116–1911

This book is printed on acid-free paper ♾™
Manufactured in the United States of America

For Silvia, Alessandra and Matteo.

Contents

Chronology

1644	The Qing dynasty starts. This is to be the last of China's imperial dynasties.
1841–1842	The first Opium War with Britain leads to the cession of Hong Kong Island to the British in perpetuity under what the Chinese government calls one of the "unequal treaties."
1856–1860	The second Opium War with Britain leads to another "unequal treaty," under which Kowloon and Stonecutters' Island are additionally ceded to the British.
1885	Taiwan becomes a province of the Qing empire.
1895	China is defeated in the Sino-Japanese war, leading to the cession in perpetuity of Taiwan to the Japanese.
1898	The New Territories of Hong Kong are leased to the British for ninety-nine years.
1900	Largely Christian rebels lead the Boxer Rebellion against the Manchu Qing dynasty. The rebellion is suppressed by foreign troops in Beijing whose governments subsequently call for heavy compensation from the Chinese government.
1905	Sun Yat-sen sets up the *Tongmenghui* ("Alliance Society"), the forerunner of the *Guomindang* (usually written Kuomintang or KMT).
	The imperial examination system is abolished.
	China's first film, a Beijing opera film called *Dingjun Mountain,* is produced in Beijing.
1911	The Xinhai Revolution overthrows the Qing dynasty. Sun Yat-sen becomes the first president of the Republic of China.
1912	Former Qing official Yuan Shikai takes over as president of the Republic.
1916	Yuan Shikai dies and China descends into localized warlordism.

1919 Student protests on May 4 against the Treaty of Versailles and its reallocation of colonial territories in China to the Japanese lead to what is subsequently known as the May 4th Movement. The May 4th Movement is the name that becomes attached to a loose grouping of intellectuals calling for radical cultural reform.

1921 The Chinese Communist Party (CCP) is set up in Shanghai.

1923 The nationalist KMT, led by Sun Yat-sen and Chiang Kai-shek, establishes contacts with the Soviet Union leading to "united front" operations with the Chinese Communists.

1925 Sun Yat-sen dies.

1927 Chiang Kai-shek launches attacks against the Chinese Communists, seizes control of Shanghai, and effectively starts the civil conflict between the two sides that continues intermittently until the communist victory in 1949.

1928 Chiang Kai-shek sets up the KMT Nationalist government with its capital in Nanjing.

1931 Japan annexes Manchuria.

1932 Japanese planes bomb Shanghai, and the CCP declares war on Japan. The KMT Nationalist government seeks peace with the Japanese.

1934 Following a series of military defeats by the KMT in Jiangxi, Mao Zedong leads CCP forces on the Long March to Yan'an in northwest China.

1935 The Long March ends and Mao Zedong sets up the CCP's guerrilla base in Yan'an.

Shanghai film star Ruan Lingyu commits suicide.

1936 In the Xi'an Incident, warlord Zhang Xueliang captures Chiang Kai-shek and persuades him to do more to resist Japanese occupation.

1937 China officially starts its Anti-Japanese War of Resistance. The Japanese take over Shanghai and kill tens of thousands of civilians in the Nanjing Massacre.

1938 The KMT government is forced to move to a new base, in Chongqing in Sichuan Province in western China.

1941 The Japanese take over Hong Kong.

1942	Mao makes his landmark *Talks to the Yan'an Forum on Literature and Art*, which effectively define the relationship between politics and cultural production for the next forty years.
1945	World War II ends. The defeat of the Japanese brings about also the end of the anti-Japanese war in China. Taiwan returns to Chinese sovereignty, and Hong Kong returns to Britain.
1946	The civil war between the KMT and the CCP starts.
1947	Russian Soviet forces retreat from Manchuria, allowing the Communists to take it over and refocus their attacks on the KMT from the north.
1949	The CCP wins the civil war, the People's Republic of China is established on October 1, and Chiang Kai-shek retreats to Taiwan with the remnants of the KMT military and nationalist government.
1950	Land reform is introduced across China, redistributing land to peasant farmers from former landlords.
	The Korean War starts and China takes over Tibet.
1953	The Korean War ends. The CCP publishes its first five-year plan.
1956	Mao and the CCP encourage open criticism of the Party and its policy in what becomes known as the One Hundred Flowers Movement, which makes reference to a poem with the line "Let a hundred flowers bloom; let a hundred schools of thought contend."
1957	The Anti-Rightist Campaign sees many of the intellectuals who had dared to speak out in the One Hundred Flowers Movement the previous year condemned, arrested, and sent to prison or work camps.
1958	The Great Leap Forward is officially launched.
1959	The height of the Great Leap Forward is reached.
1960–1961	Famine in the Chinese countryside as a result of the miscalculated policies of the Great Leap Forward, combined with bad weather, kills an estimated 20 to 40 million people.

1962 The Great Leap Forward ends, and partial marginalization of Mao from power occurs with Liu Shaoqi and Deng Xiaoping taking on greater responsibilities.

1963 Mao launches attacks on Liu Shaoqi in what turns out to be the lead-up to the Cultural Revolution.

Mao's wife, Jiang Qing, starts to promote theatrical reform that over the next few years will see the sidelining of the established repertoire in favor of revolutionary model operas.

1965 A newspaper article co-written by Jiang Qing critical of Wu Han's play *Hai Rui Dismissed from Office* begins a heated intellectual and political exchange that culminates in the Cultural Revolution.

1966 The Great Proletarian Cultural Revolution launches.

1968 The Cultural Revolution officially ends, although the social disruption associated with it continues until Mao's death in 1976. The People's Liberation Army (PLA) helps restore order to a country thrown into chaos by Mao's Red Guards.

1969 Liu Shaoqi dies in prison.

1971 Lin Biao, Mao's presumed successor, dies in a mysterious plane crash. The PRC is recognized rather than Taiwan as the legitimate representative of China at the United Nations.

1972 U.S. President Richard Nixon makes a historic and symbolic visit to China.

1975 Chiang Kai-shek dies in Taiwan.

1976 Zhou Enlai dies in January, Mao dies in September, and the Gang of Four is toppled in October. Hua Guofeng becomes premier and party chairman.

1978 Deng Xiaoping re-emerges as a key power broker after the Third Plenum of the Eleventh CCP Central Committee and starts the process of gradually introducing economic reforms.

The Democracy Wall protests start.

The United States under President Carter establishes diplomatic relations with the PRC rather than the ROC on Taiwan.

1979 Democracy Wall is closed down.

1980 Zhao Ziyang, reform-minded protégé of Deng Xiaoping, takes over as premier from Hua Guofeng.

1984 The first Fifth Generation films, *The One and Eight* and *Yellow Earth*, are completed.

1989 Former general secretary of the CCP Hu Yaobang dies, triggering a wave of commemorative protests among students in particular. Urban workers and intellectuals join protests that culminate in martial law being imposed in May and the violent removal of protesters from Tiananmen Square on the night of June 3–4, with thousands of people killed and injured.

Zhao Ziyang is forced to step down.

1992 Deng Xiaoping makes a tour of southern China that revitalizes economic reform throughout the country.

1993 China's bid to host the 2000 Summer Olympic Games fails in favor of Australia.

1994 Chinese computer networks link up with the Internet.

1997 Deng Xiaoping dies. Hong Kong is returned to China.

1999 Macau is returned to China.

2001 China wins its bid to host the 2008 Summer Olympic Games and finally joins the World Trade Organization in December.

2002 China participates in the soccer World Cup finals for the first time.

2003 Hu Jintao becomes president of China.

2004 The SARS (severe acute respiratory syndrome) crisis hits Guangzhou, Beijing, and other cities in China.

2005 Zhao Ziyang dies in January.

2006 China's Internet users, mainly located in the cities, number more than 10 percent of the population for the first time.

1

Understanding Popular Culture in China

This book offers an introduction to the development of China's contemporary popular cultural landscape and the rapid changes it has undergone in recent decades. China has undergone rapid change since the 1980s, when it started the process of economic and social reform that has seen a version of capitalism largely take over from the state socialism established in preceding decades. Anyone revisiting China after a period as short as two or three years is likely to find many aspects of the country changed: buildings, roads, and other infrastructure appear and disappear; new technologies bring new opportunities; social attitudes and behavior are constantly being transformed and reinvented; and new social and cultural practices emerge while others fade away.

As China plays an increasingly prominent part in world politics and economics, there is ever more incentive to learn more about the country and its people. Considering, however, that China—whose territory occupies 3.7 million square miles (nearly one-fourth of the Asian continent)—has been home to one of the world's greatest civilizations for millennia, to acquire a working understanding of this land requires no small effort. Chinese people often proudly proclaim 5,000 years of history and point to more than 3,000 years of literature, poetry, and philosophical scholarship. Over that extensive timespan, China has been constantly changing, despite the persistence of various important institutions such as imperial rule, the imperial official examination system (until 1911), and cultural and philosophical traditions such as Confucianism, Buddhism, and Taoism. Yet under scrutiny even these relatively fixed features of Chinese society and culture turn out to be less constant than they seem. Confucianism has been constantly evolving; Buddhism, imported into China long ago from India, has been transformed into something considered by many to be fundamentally Chinese; and Taoism, itself a philosophy of change, has inspired a range of popular religious practices that have always differed in detail throughout the land, even from one village to the next.

Hence, however fast and far-reaching the current changes may appear to be to both Western and Chinese eyes, it is important to view these changes against a historical backdrop that is no stranger to change. Not only was there change and diversity in the long Imperial period, the twentieth century was also a major period of upheaval and transformation for China. It saw the collapse of imperial rule and subsequent decades of civil war, Japanese occupation and resistance against it, the emergence of new political ideologies from nationalism to communism, the massive social and political revolution that accompanied the establishment of the People's Republic of China (PRC) in 1949, the violence and upheaval of the Great Proletarian Cultural Revolution, and the changes following the death in 1976 of Chinese Communist Party (CCP) Chairman Mao. By the early twenty-first century, Chinese popular culture is nothing if not accustomed to change.

Mao Zedong was the leader of the People's Republic of China from 1949 to 1976, having led the Chinese Communist Party since the 1930s. A great visionary and revolutionary, Mao was also to become one of history's most uncompromising authoritarian rulers. (The Illustrated London News Picture Library)

This book must therefore aim to be only a partial introduction to contemporary Chinese popular cultural practices. Due to its limitations of size, it will stress some aspects of popular culture more than others. Doubtless some aspects will be left out of the discussion entirely, and inevitably some new ones will emerge shortly after the publication of this book. The intention behind this volume is to offer a handbook covering the main areas of popular cultural practice with sufficient historical and cultural background to make understandable both contemporary practices and at least some of those that will develop from them in years to come. The future of television and other media, for instance, will continue to be shaped by the opposing pressures of commercial market forces on the one hand and government and Party notions of the media's political responsibilities on the other. One may not be able to predict exactly what will come next, but one can attempt to understand the landscape in which Chinese popular culture evolved and exists today.

This book is intended to be most useful for students who already have some familiarity with China or Chinese culture and society; however, it is also intended to be accessible as an introduction to Chinese popular culture for those with little or no prior knowledge in this area. It takes a broadly anthropological approach to its subject matter, even though it does not presume any particular previous familiarity with anthropological principles. To achieve these goals requires some preliminary attention, in this introductory chapter, to the fundamental historical and social issues that will figure at various times throughout this volume: the Chinese Communist Party, Chairman Mao, the civil war, the anti-Japanese war, Deng Xiaoping, economic reform, and so on. To cover some of these basics, for readers without previous knowledge of China I have included a section entitled "Historical Orientation" in this chapter; those already familiar with the key issues in recent Chinese history may choose to skip it.

The remainder of the chapter following the historical orientation briefly sets the scene in terms of the different political territories of contemporary China and their relationship to each other, Chinese language issues, and how we should attempt to understand China and notions of Chineseness. Some basic understanding of Chinese language is useful, if not crucial, for understanding Chinese popular culture. Similarly, some familiarity with the basic social characteristics of contemporary China is important if readers with little other experience of China are to be able to contextualize and situate the account in following chapters.

Finally, there is the issue of "popular culture" itself. Although most people tend to have some idea of what is meant by this phrase, they are uncertain of any exact definition. In the context of this volume, the question also has to be asked in relation to the specifics of Chinese history, politics, economics, and social development. How popular culture is often conceptualized in academic study on China is not necessarily the same as for other parts of the world.

Historical Orientation

It is impossible to condense a history of China into a few pages, and that is not what I set out to do in this section (for fuller accounts and useful introductions to modern Chinese history see Grass, Corrin, & Kort 1997; Phillips 1996; Spence 1983; and, for an anthropological overview of much of the PRC period, Potter & Potter 1990). The aim here is to point out key historical issues and events that have a bearing on the chapters that follow. In particular, I will focus on the period from the late nineteenth century to the present day. Although I will deal with issues generally in chronological order, I will present them under issue headings rather than in a continuous historical narrative, in order, as much as possible, to emphasize the selective nature of this orientation and to avoid a temptation to read this as a comprehensive history.

Opium

Although it may at first seem odd, opium offers a good place to start this historical contextualization of contemporary Chinese popular culture. This is not least because opium, imported by the British from India in exchange for Chinese tea destined for the bourgeois teacups of Europe, was a fundamental feature of nineteenth-century Chinese popular culture. Indeed, opium addiction started to become such a massive problem, one that crossed boundaries of social class, that the Chinese authorities of the Qing dynasty (1644–1911) outlawed the drug in 1836 and attempted to restrict foreign opium imports. Despite opium's being outlawed in Britain also, the British continued to trade the drug in China, regardless of the devastating social and economic effects China's opium dens were having on the Chinese population.

Chinese efforts to stop the opium trade, however, resulted in the so-called Opium Wars of the 1840s and 1850s. These began when in 1841 a Chinese official named Lin Zexu stood up resolutely to corruption among British traders and Chinese officials to enforce the long-circumvented ban on the opium trade. Eventually Lin led a flotilla of ill-equipped junks to turn away British opium vessels from the key southern port of Guangzhou (Canton); however, in the sporadic war that followed, the imperial British navy, then one of the supreme nautical and military powers of the world, humiliated unprepared and poorly trained Chinese troops. The Chinese were defeated; subsequently they were forced to concede, among other things, trading access to several ports along the eastern coast, which became known as the Treaty Ports.

Another part of the resolution to the conflict was the cession to the British of the barely inhabited island off the southern coast of Guangdong Province called Xianggang, later more familiarly known as Hong Kong. As discussed in later chapters, contemporary Hong Kong popular culture has been an important influence in the development of mainland Chinese popular culture, in the post-Mao reform period in particular. Further military action and a second Opium War in the 1850s saw China make further "treaty port" trading concessions to Britain, France, Russia, and the United States.

Indirectly, opium also contributed to the modernization of China through a series of political and social reforms. The repeated defeats suffered at the hands of the European powers in the Opium Wars and in the Sino-Japanese war of 1895, which led to Taiwan becoming a Japanese colony, were seen as a major humiliation by Chinese government officials, the Chinese imperial household, and Chinese intellectuals alike. Asking how it was that China, with its rich history of cultural, scientific, and technological innovation, could have fallen behind the rest of the industrializing world, a range of Chinese intellectuals proposed various wide-reaching social, economic, and structural reforms to core Chinese institutions including the military, education, transport, communications, and eventually also even the bureaucracy and the imperial exam system used to recruit government officials. Key figures leading the so-called Self-strengthening Movement from the 1860s to the 1890s included former military men turned scholar-officials Li Hongzhang (1823–1901) and Zuo Zongtang (1812–1885). The Wuxu or Hundred Days Reform, which shifted attention from military, scientific, and technological reform to social and political reform after the defeat at the hands of the Japanese in 1895, was promoted by famous and influential reformers including Liang Qichao (1873–1929) and Kang Youwei (1858–1927), both of whom called for a constitutional monarchy and had to flee to Japan to avoid arrest and execution as a result. Toward the turn of the century, proponents of such reforms began to include more radical revolutionaries, people for whom the problem was not just the various institutions of the imperial system but the very system—the monarchy—itself. It is possible to argue that were it not for the widespread use of opium in nineteenth-century China, the course of subsequent Chinese history could have been quite different.

Revolutions

In the twentieth century, China underwent two major political revolutions. The first of these was the Xinhai, or 1911, Revolution (*Xinhai* being the way of identifying the year 1911 in the traditional Chinese calendar), which started on October 10 of that year and culminated in the inauguration of the Republic of China (ROC) on February 12, 1912. The revolution was carried out by a mixture of different political dissident groups, who shared little strong political vision for China's future aside from the fact that it should be without the ethnically Manchu, as opposed to Han Chinese, Qing dynasty. Consequently, the key tenets of the revolution often became anti-Qing and anti-Manchu, even if that is a large simplification of the dynamic complexity of the political maneuvering that accompanied the revolution in the years before and after 1911. The most prominent political groups involved included the Tongmenghui, which was the forerunner of the Kuomintang (KMT), the nationalist party founded by Sun Yat-sen (Sun Zhongshan) and subsequently led by Chiang Kai-shek (Jiang Jieshi), whose nationalist government transferred to Taiwan on losing to the CCP in the civil war in the 1940s. Other groups involved in the revolution included the Xingzhonghui (Revive China Society); the Gongjinhui (Society for Public Advancement); the Wenxueshe (Literature Society); the Huaxinghui (China Revival Society); and the Guangfuhui (Bright Restoration Society). These groups were only loosely linked to each other, and although there was some coordination among them they were largely working in geographically separate parts of the country. The Tongmenghui, for instance, had its power-base in Southern China, centered in Guangdong Province; the Huaxinghui worked largely in the Hunan area of central southern China; and the Guangfuhui operated in Shanghai, Zhejiang, and Jiangsu in eastern China, while the Gongjinghui operated further up the Yangtze River. The 1911 Revolution was significant for several reasons, not least because it saw the overthrow of the Qing dynasty. Chinese dynasties have come and gone over the centuries, so what was ultimately more important was less the fall of a dynasty than the fact that the revolution did not install a new one but rather saw the launch of the Republic of China based in theory on democratic ideals and principles. Sun Yat-sen was, for a few months in late 1911 and early 1912, its first president. He agreed to step down in February 1912 in order to allow former Qing official Yuan Shikai to head up the first Nationalist government. Yuan had strong and influential links to a range of different players in the revolution—the intellectual revolutionaries, the military and political establishments, wealthy gentry and businessmen—and consequently was seen as the only person likely to bring some unity to the fledgling republic without throwing the country into civil war. It was to be discovered that Yuan had ambitions of becoming the next emperor. He reneged on agreements with his revolutionary partners and presided over a chaotic period of Chinese political history characterized by division, social and political fragmentation, and warlordism until his death in 1916. The confusion lasted until 1927, when Chiang Kai-shek, leading the Kuomintang, unified the country in the name of the nationalist Republic of China, based in Nanjing.

The second major Chinese revolution of the twentieth century was that which brought the Chinese Communist Party to power in the whole country for the first time and saw the founding of the People's Republic of China in 1949. The 1949 Revolution resulted from the victory of the CCP over the Kuomintang in their long-running struggle against the nationalist government forces while both sides were also resisting Japanese occupation. On October 1, 1949, Chairman Mao Zedong declared the founding of the PRC in front of a massive crowd in Tiananmen Square outside the gates to the former imperial Forbidden City in the heart of Beijing. Unlike its 1911 predecessor, however, the 1949 Revolution did lead to almost immediate massive social, political, and economic changes.

A defining feature of the Chinese Communist Revolution was that it was principally orchestrated from the countryside. Having been driven out of the large cities by Chiang Kai-shek's forces in the 1920s and 1930s as well as the Japanese occupation of most of eastern, central, and northern China from the late 1930s, the CCP established its military and political headquarters in the small town of Yan'an in the northeastern province of Shaanxi. Consequently, the Chinese Communists, led by the pragmatic Mao Zedong, effected a strategy of winning over peasants in the surrounding countryside, the vast majority of whom were poor, before moving into the nationalist-held cities. This was to leave an enduring mark on the Chinese Revolution, with the category of peasants included alongside the more regular socialist categories of workers and soldiers as the most exalted social groups. In part this also reflected the fact that China was, and still is, predominantly rural and the majority of the population consists of peasant farmers, even if in recent decades there has been rapid urbanization.

The particular importance of the 1949 Revolution for Chinese popular culture was enormous. The politicization of art—including literature, film, and painting—was a marked feature of cultural production in Yan'an and the other Communist-controlled parts of the country from the early 1940s on. After 1949, however, the obligatory political motivation for all kinds of cultural production was extended to the whole country and, importantly, also became state policy; however, artistic production from the 1950s through the 1970s was not as monolithically homogeneous as is sometimes assumed. At least before the Cultural Revolution, which started in 1966, there were variable periods of greater and lesser flexibility and tolerance on the part of the Party monitors. Nonetheless, artistic production was centrally directed and was expected to follow key dogmatic principles about the superiority of socialism, the right of the Party to govern, the role of art and the media in supporting the Party, and the need to serve the people. Consequently, variation occurred within tight Party-imposed limits on what was acceptable.

This obligatory political role of cultural production also meant that the media and other forms of art and popular culture reflected the broader social, political, and economic changes afoot in society—rural land reform, nationalization of industry and commerce, family and marriage legal reform, and the general re-evaluation of social categories and hierarchies. As we will see in subsequent chapters (e.g., on theatre or cinema), pre-1949 popular culture did not necessarily disappear, but it did become more narrowly focused. Traditional Chinese operas—Beijing opera, for instance—continued to be performed and continued to be popular, but certain pieces in the classical repertoire were either banned or rewritten to fit with the political doctrine of the day. By comparison, the direct popular cultural effect of the 1911 Revolution was far more subtle and restrained. Indeed, one might argue that the revolution itself had little noticeable effect, even if broader political and intellectual currents of the time were posing some fundamental challenges to popular cultural production of different kinds.

May 4, 1919

One of the most important dates in twentieth-century Chinese cultural history is May 4, 1919. This is the day that is remembered for a spate of patriotic demonstrations, led by students and intellectuals, chiefly in large cities such as Beijing and Shanghai, objecting to the Treaty of Versailles. In the treaty, signed in Europe as a resolution to the First World War, the victorious powers in the conflict divided up German assets among themselves, including the Chinese Treaty Port of Qingdao in Shandong Province, home to the now world-famous formerly German brewery. Qingdao, along with other German concessions in China, was to be handed over to the Japanese, and the demands of the Chinese representatives at the talks were ignored. Consequently, the treaty came to be seen not only as a symbol of foreign imperial disrespect for China, its territory, and its people but also as a symbol of the weakness and ineffectiveness of the Beijing government struggling to keep control of the political and military situation close to home, not to mention overseas.

Anger about the treaty, chiefly among Beijing university students, triggered a protest with around 3,000 demonstrators in Beijing's Tiananmen Square. The protest was at times violent, and the home of a prominent diplomat, Cao Rulin, was burned down by angry students. The government intervened and made dozens of arrests. These events triggered further student strikes and protests in Beijing, garnered broader support among intellectuals, and within a month spread to other cities in China, notably Shanghai, where students, workers, and businessmen went on strike and staged further protests.

The lasting significance of what has since come to be known as the May 4th Movement, however, was not so much for its political demands as for the long-lasting effects that it had on Chinese cultural and intellectual activity up to the present day. The May 4th Movement was not one organization but is a loose term used to refer to the broad groupings of students, political activists, and intellectuals supporting and in agreement with the demands and ideals of those organizing the protests. In this regard, the May 4th Movement tapped into other intellectual and political sentiments that had been expressed in less striking ways for years, if not decades. Indeed, the roots of the movement in some ways can be traced back to the nineteenth-century imperial reformers who demanded the modernization of the political system.

Intellectuals of the time were not only asking for political reform, often along the lines of Western-style democracy, they were calling for cultural reform. In short stories, essays, novels, plays, and other literary and artistic forms, leading intellectuals such as Hu Shi, Lü Xun, Chen Duxiu, and Li Daming along with other writers such as Mao Dun, Lao She, and Yü Dafu launched scathing, but sophisticated, attacks on what many considered to be core elements of traditional Chinese intellectual culture—classical Chinese language and Confucian and Neo-Confucian–inspired notions of gender and family, for instance. They called for literature to be written in vernacular Chinese rather than the extremely difficult, terse, and elite-oriented classical Chinese that had been the standard written form for centuries. May 4th intellectuals saw cultural reform as a fundamental stepping-stone to broader social and political reform. How could ideas of democracy be entertained while the very Chinese language itself separated an intellectual ruling elite from the often illiterate working masses?

The May 4th Movement was broadly left-leaning in its politics and advocated a strong cultural nationalism, albeit alongside radical cultural reform, and its influences spread across cultural production from literature to film. The name of May 4th continued to be used for decades to come to refer to literary and cultural production, as well as other intellectual activities, broadly inspired by or in line with the critical cultural objectives of the movement. The influence and importance of the May 4th writers and intellectuals has never really diminished. The broad objectives of the movement were not entirely incompatible with those of Communist Party intellectuals—indeed, several leading May 4th writers, such as Lao She and Mao Dun, also became prominent CCP members. Subsequently, apart from the extraordinary Cultural Revolution period when some May 4th writers suffered severely along with other intellectuals, the historical importance of the movement continued to be valued after the founding of the PRC. Indeed, in some ways the level of significance attached to the movement is a result of the communist victory in 1949. Due to their left-wing associations, many May 4th writers were far less appreciated, or were even banned, by the Kuomintang.

Another reason the May 4th Movement has had enduring significance is that many of the core questions being asked by May 4th writers at the beginning of the last century have never been totally resolved. Indeed, many of them were also being asked by the post–Cultural Revolution intellectuals of the 1980s and 1990s. Film, literature, television, drama, and other 1980s and 1990s forms of expression that we will consider in this book were once again questioning the enduring, restraining, and limiting nature of China's culture, its oppressive effects on women's roles in society, its relation to the West and Western culture, and the role of the individual in relation to broader cultural and political processes.

The Chinese Communist Party

The Chinese Communist Party (CCP) was founded in 1921 by a small group of reform-minded left-wing intellectuals in a small house in Shanghai. These intellectuals included Li Dazhao and Chen Duxiu, both of whom had been active and prominent participants in the New Culture Movement that followed the 1911 Revolution (New Culture Movement was the name adopted by its proponents for the outward-looking critical questioning of Chinese culture and Confucianism that eventually came to underpin the May 4th Movement). The first CCP congress was held on July 20, 1921, with twelve Chinese people in attendance and two Russians. Among the twelve Chinese was a young Mao Zedong.

The CCP was set up under the supervision of the Comintern, which had great influence over policy and direction in the early years of the Party's history. However, the Soviet influence also led to a fundamental split in the Party, between those loyal to Moscow and those with a more pragmatic eye on the local Chinese context. Among the latter, Mao Zedong emerged as a prominent personality. Against Comintern directions, Mao ran a very successful recruitment drive among peasants in the central Chinese provinces of Hunan and Jiangxi in the late 1920s that eventually led to the establishment of the Jiangxi Soviet and the Fourth Red Army under a young communist called Zhu De who was to go on to become one of the CCP's best known and highest-ranking military officials and army generals. Despite the early success of Mao's wing of the CCP, however, the Soviet line was that the revolution would eventually have to come from the urban proletariat, not the rural peasantry. The Moscow-backed faction of the CCP focused on organizing urban worker unrest and attempted urban uprisings, with little success. Consequently, the activities of the Jiangxi Soviet's leaders were tolerated for their relatively impressive achievements.

In 1934, however, the Kuomintang (KMT), with whom the CCP had been in open conflict since 1927, inflicted a series of military defeats on the CCP, which was forced to flee its Jiangxi base. This led to what has since become known as the Long March, a 6,000-mile trek from Jiangxi to Yan'an in the northwest. More than 100,000 people, most of them soldiers, set out to make this journey in October 1934. One year later, 8,000 survivors arrived in Yan'an, where Mao, who had along the way established himself as the Party's leader, was to establish his wartime power-base and revive the CCP and its army.

From Yan'an, Mao built up the Communist forces, established a military and political refuge and headquarters, and started the arduous process of winning over the country to the communist cause. Building upon his successful experiences in Jiangxi and Hunan, Mao and his forces set about generating support for the Party among the peasantry who were later to form the power-base that would support Mao in the civil war, the war against the Japanese, and eventually the founding of the People's Republic. The CCP set up a new soviet society and formulated many of the policies and strategies that would inform its rule in the post-1949 PRC.

Mao Zedong

Chinese Communist Party leader Mao Zedong, often referred to as Chairman Mao, became a twentieth century icon not only in China but many parts of the world. Partly as a consequence of this iconic status, opinion of Mao has been polarized: He has often been either deified as a revolutionary hero or vilified as an evil, authoritarian, egoistic dictator. There are elements of truth supporting both of these views, but neither is sufficient or satisfactory for an objective understanding of the greatest figure in modern Chinese history. Indeed, the complex and sometimes contradictory nature of Mao's character defies a simple summarization. For that reason, what I can offer here is inevitably limited and partial. I do not attempt a thorough, detailed account of Mao's life, political thought, or political career—rather, I will present some points key to a basis for understanding this intriguing and staggeringly influential figure in Chinese and global political history.

Mao was born on December 26, 1893, to a financially comfortable, though not wealthy, peasant family in Hunan Province. He received both a classical and a modern education as a child and had early military experience in Hunan at the time of the Xinhai Revolution. He met Li Dazhao while working as an assistant curator at the library of the National Beijing University and subsequently became involved in the intellectual and revolutionary movements that surrounded the May 4th Movement and eventually the founding of the CCP. He worked in collaboration with the KMT in the early 1920s, during the period of cooperation between the two parties before their split and open conflict in 1927. By 1926, Mao was directing the KMT's Peasant Movement Training Institute and helping to organize peasant associations and unions. After the KMT-CCP rift, Mao led what has become known as the Autumn Harvest Uprising in his home province of Hunan. He instigated a peasant revolt against landlords and the KMT, but the latter's stronger military forces quashed the uprising relatively easily. Mao's troops were forced to split up, and he fled with many of them to Jiangxi Province, where he and fellow communist Zhu De organized the peasants into what was to become the Soviet Union of China, which consisted of ten soviets, in Jiangxi Province, with an army of around 80,000 to 100,000 soldiers. The success of the Jiangxi Soviet, as it became known, was a cause of concern for Chiang Kai-shek and the KMT, because it posed a real threat to the power of the nationalist government. KMT forces surrounded and attacked the CCP forces, who subsequently embarked on the Long March to Yan'an.

Yan'an was a very important place for Mao. Following the Long March, he was left in undisputed command of the Party and its army, and Yan'an provided the refuge for him and the CCP to recuperate their energies, to consolidate their defenses, and to establish a working socialist community that recruited followers from among the Chinese peasantry. Some came from other parts of the country to join the CCP in Yan'an; others came from the surrounding area. Although Yan'an was relatively remote and the influence of the CCP was marginalized by the civil war with the KMT and the Japanese occupation of eastern and central China, this rural retreat gave Mao and the Party the breathing space and the opportunity to put their ideas into action, to develop policy, and to demonstrate to themselves and others what the Party could do and what it stood for.

Mao retained his grip on the CCP after the founding of the PRC in 1949, although it was weakened in the 1960s, leading to the Cultural Revolution in which Mao once again consolidated power. Supported by his powerful third wife, Jiang Qing, and his at one time nominated successor, Lin Biao, Mao built up a strong personality cult among the Chinese population—young people in particular—for whom he was a genuine national hero. He managed to dispose of, outwit, or sideline all internal opposition from within the Party through acts of political cunning or outright violent repression.

Until the late 1970s, Mao was unreproachable in China. After his death in 1976 and the start of economic reform, the open-door policy, and gradual political liberalization introduced by Deng Xiaoping, however, Mao's position in Chinese history was publicly revised. For the first time, some of his major mistakes started to be criticized, most notably the Cultural Revolution in the late 1960s and the Great Leap Forward of the late 1950s, which brought massive social disruption and suffering to millions of people around the country. The Great Leap Forward was an attempt to mobilize the Chinese people to impossible levels of production to make a massive economic "leap forward"; ill-conceived and misguided, the campaign resulted in failed harvests, massive waste, and the death by famine of tens of millions of peasants in the early 1960s. The Cultural Revolution (see below) threw the country into complete chaos while Mao maneuvered to remove his political enemies from the scene. From the late 1970s on, Mao became publicly fallible—officially his deeds are considered to have been 70 percent good, 30 percent bad—although to this day he retains the status of a national hero, admired and respected by hundreds of millions of Chinese.

The Cultural Revolution

The Great Proletarian Cultural Revolution, usually referred to simply as the Cultural Revolution, was one of the most complex series of events in recent Chinese history. Scholarly opinion is still divided on the best way to interpret and understand what went on in China during the ten years beginning in the summer of 1966, and this is not the place to resolve those debates. The Cultural Revolution clearly has an immediate pertinence in the context of this volume, however. The Cultural Revolution not only saw all aspects of China's cultural tradition reviled, criticized, and in some cases destroyed, but it also had many enduring effects on cultural production in the decades that followed, from the "misty" poets of the late 1970s and early 1980s, through the "fifth generation" filmmakers, to television, drama, and other media production.

The Cultural Revolution also has its roots in what in many other parts of the world might seem like a fairly abstract debate about a play written six years earlier. The play was called *Hai Rui Dismissed from Office* and was written by the deputy mayor of Beijing at the time, a man named Wu Han. The play told the story of a virtuous imperial official fired by a corrupt emperor. The play was originally praised by the Party and even Chairman Mao himself; however, in 1965 Mao's wife, Jiang Qing, in collaboration with one of her supporters, Yao Wenyuan, wrote an article for a Shanghai newspaper condemning the play and its author. The article was subsequently reproduced by other newspapers around the country. In short, it accused that the corrupt emperor in the play was an allegorical representation of Mao, who had fired Peng Dehuai, a popular army general and veteran of the Long March, after his criticism of Mao's handling of the Great Leap Forward. The heated wrangling over Wu's play and its supporters, which was effectively an effort by contending groups within the CCP leadership to denigrate their opposition, continued into 1966 and rolled into the launch of the Great Proletarian Cultural Revolution in early August of the same year.

Ostensibly the Cultural Revolution was a continuation of the earlier Communist Revolution, but it sought to push revolutionary action a step further. Its rationale was that although class differences had been addressed by land reform, the nationalization of industry, and other post-1949 policies, the ideology of imperialism and the bourgeoisie had not been crushed. Hence, the Cultural Revolution targeted temples, works of art, and other cultural artifacts that now stood for the decadent, imperialist, feudal, or bourgeois past. Although the damage to buildings and artifacts was enormous, the real damage inflicted by the Cultural Revolution was on people. The revolution evolved as a series of actions whereby Mao manipulated young people throughout the country to target his enemies, particularly among the intellectual classes. At the top level, the principal targets and victims of the Cultural Revolution were Liu Shaoqi and Deng Xiaoping, who had taken over much of the daily running of the nation following the disastrous years of the Great Leap Forward and whom Mao had started to view as a threat to his leadership. Mao's perception was not entirely without justification—Liu was known to be planning to try to sideline Mao from real power while allowing him to retain his position as a national figurehead. Mao had reacted with a series of political attacks on Liu from 1963 onward. In that year Mao also launched the Socialist Education Movement, also known as the Four Cleanups Campaign, which aimed to clean up politics, the economy, organization, and ideology by flushing out reactionary elements—that is, Mao's enemies—within the Party and government. The campaign had little immediate effect but had important mobilization effects among schoolchildren, who were subject to the campaign. Some analysts say this was crucial for Mao when it came to the Cultural Revolution because he was able to mobilize young people quickly and efficiently as Red Guards, the key grassroots-level players in the Cultural Revolution.

Mao's famous Red Guards were basically schoolchildren and students who were loosely mobilized to implement the objectives of the Cultural Revolution. They ransacked buildings and property and subjected millions of their peers and elders to public humiliation and terrifying verbal bullying, in which accused imperialists or counterrevolutionaries were insulted, threatened, and abused before crowds of jeering onlookers. On many occasions such actions became violent. Millions of people were beaten, imprisoned, killed, or driven to suicide as the country slipped into years of chaos. Schools, universities, factories, offices, and other public institutions were forced to close for months if not years.

Officially the Cultural Revolution ended in 1968, but the term is generally used to refer to the entire ten-year period between 1966 and Mao's death in 1976, because the heightened political atmosphere continued and new policies maintained the emphasis on political re-education and rooting out bourgeois influence. The Red Guards were brought under some control by the military in 1968, and some partial normality returned to everyday life, but the political atmosphere was still highly sensitive, people still lived in fear of becoming the victim of whatever the next ideological campaign might be, and the operation of schools, factories, and offices was still disrupted.

In 1968, Mao also launched the campaign to send urban youth "down to the countryside." Some have argued that this was in part a way of bringing Red Guards, who no longer served Mao's political purposes, back under some degree of control. The public reasoning was that privileged urban youth and intellectuals needed better to understand the lives of working peasants. Consequently, millions of young people were forced to live and work in rural villages distant from their homes and families. Most of them remained in the countryside until the late 1970s, when they were allowed to return. This down-to-the-countryside campaign was to have a profound effect on future cultural production in China, because nearly all of the artists, filmmakers, and other intellectuals who came to the fore in the 1980s shared experiences of nearly a decade working with peasants in the countryside or having been in the army while also having missed out on years of education.

Following a failed military coup by Mao's nominated successor, Lin Biao, in 1971, which ended with Lin's death in a mysterious plane crash over Mongolia, Mao turned once again for support to the veteran politician Premier Zhou Enlai, who had somehow survived the political turmoil of the Cultural Revolution relatively unscathed. Ironically, one of the most high-profile victims of the Cultural Revolution, Deng Xiaoping, who had been heavily criticized, removed from power, and sent to work in a factory, was brought back into government on Zhou's advice. Liu Shaoqi was less fortunate. He was sent to a prison camp early in the Cultural Revolution, where he died in 1969.

The Cultural Revolution period came to an end in 1976. The year started with the news that Zhou Enlai, who had become one of the key contenders to be Mao's successor, had died. Political wrangling and maneuvering followed as the other contenders jostled for position. There were six key players in the running: Mao's wife, Jiang Qing; three of her close supporters, Wang Hongwen, Zhang Chunqiao, and Yao Wenyuan, who together with Jiang were later to become known as the Gang of Four; Deng Xiaoping, in the weakest position after the death of his supporter Zhou; and Hua Guofeng, the then relatively unknown minister of public security. Jiang and her supporters had been attacking Zhou and Deng since 1974 with limited success, but together the Gang of Four soon succeeded in moving Deng out of the way. Nonetheless, somewhat unexpectedly, Mao named Hua Guofeng to succeed Zhou as premier and eventually also himself as Party chairman. Hua did not have long to wait—Mao died on September 9, 1976.

The official Chinese version of subsequent events reports that the Gang of Four attempted a coup, which failed, although it is difficult to know whether that was actually the case. Nonetheless, Hua moved quickly to have the Gang of Four arrested. They were blamed for the Cultural Revolution, which came to a final end with their arrest, and eventually came to trial in 1981.

The Open-Door Policy and Economic Reform

The battling among China's political leadership did not come to an end with the fall of the Gang of Four. Hua Guofeng was pressured to bring Deng Xiaoping back into the government, which he did in July 1977. Deng was an experienced political survivor, and with his own band of young, reform-minded supporters, notably Hu Yaobang and Zhao Ziyang, was able to present an alternative vision of China's future to the retrospective Soviet-informed approach being offered by Hua.

The Third Plenum of the Eleventh CCP Congress, held in Beijing in December 1978, was a groundbreaking event in the history of the PRC. Deng managed to introduce the first of his economic reforms that started to move China in an entirely different direction of development. Deng was a pragmatist. He is famously remembered for saying that it does not matter whether a cat is black or white, a good cat is the one that catches mice. This pragmatic attitude was to change the fundamentals of the Chinese economy with the important factor becoming not class, as it had been under Mao, but economic development. Class struggle, which had dominated the political, social, and economic landscape for so long, was suddenly pushed aside, and economic development started to take center stage.

The economic reforms started in the countryside, where fundamental changes to land tenure and labor organization were introduced. Central to these was the launch of the household responsibility system, which replaced the former collective farming. The new system returned land to individual households, who became responsible for making quota contributions to the collective, but for the first time with the possibility of selling any excess production on the also newly established open market. Households became responsible for organizing their own work, rather than having that done for them by the collective work unit as in the past, and they could engage in various kinds of side production including extra crop production, handicrafts, or even taking up employed work elsewhere. In the early 1980s, these reforms transformed the countryside and saw massive increases in agricultural output and growth in household income.

Economic reforms in the cities came a little later in the 1980s, and although they had a less immediately visible effect they were just as consequential as those in the countryside. The fundamental principle that changed was that private capital and enterprise became not only legal but increasingly encouraged as the reforms went from strength to strength. Private business started with individual market traders in the 1980s and developed from there until twenty years later there were hundreds of thousands of dollar-millionaire businessmen in China. By 2004, official Chinese statistics reported that there were more than 236,000 Chinese citizens with more than $1 million in financial assets, excluding home real estate. China is awash with multimillion and multibillion dollar businesses, both state-owned and private. Nonetheless, China's economy still bears the marks of its state-planned past. A large proportion of the economy is still state-owned, even if this proportion has been in steady decline. China has re-imported capitalism after decades of socialism, but it is a capitalism with Chinese characteristics.

In the long run, economic reform has brought considerable wealth and a much higher standard of living to hundreds of millions of Chinese, and Chinese cities have been physically transformed by economic development. Communism, Mao, and even the Cultural Revolution, which started only forty years ago, mean little or nothing to the younger generation that grew up in the reform era and have become increasingly distant memories for those who lived through them. It used to be that the work unit, as well as being an employer, was where most people encountered and interacted directly with the state: It was through the work unit that citizens received payments, welfare, education, housing, and other services, and the work unit was the principal arena for all government policy implementation. Economic reform decentralized the role of the work unit in people's lives. It encouraged greater individual and family independence and has fostered new forms of consumerism, individualism, and independence completely unimaginable just thirty years ago, even with highly personal areas of people's lives still regulated by the state, such as family planning with the one-child policy.

This brings us to two other key reforms important for understanding contemporary Chinese popular culture. One is the open-door policy; the other is the one-child family policy. The open-door policy refers to the way that Deng Xiaoping not only opened up the economy but opened up the country to the rest of the world. Under Mao, China was not entirely isolated, having various relationships—good and bad—with other communist nations around the world including North Korea, Vietnam, the Soviet Union and its Eastern European satellite states (at least until the early 1960s), and various communist or socialist countries in Africa. The Chinese population was almost entirely cut off, however, from the capitalist outside world, principally represented by the United States, Western Europe, Australia, Canada, Japan, Southeast Asia, and South America. With Deng's reforms this started to change. Foreign businesses and businesspeople were gradually welcomed into China, as were more and more foreign tourists and students. Chinese people, particularly in the large cities, gradually got used to seeing foreigners around and later talking to them, doing business with them, and even making friends with or marrying them.

The change was not instant. For instance, even up until the early 1990s, foreigners were supposed to use an entirely different currency called foreign exchange certificates (FEC) as opposed to the "people's money," or *renminbi*, that ordinary Chinese used. The former could only be used in large, specially designated stores and hotels, while the latter often could not. By the mid- to late 1980s, though, a thriving black market and relaxation of shopping restrictions on both Chinese and foreigners meant that the dual currency became increasingly pointless. Similarly, through the 1980s, various forms of state rationing and allocation persisted for key foodstuffs including grains, flour, and oil. In these ways, for at least the first decade, there were various, layered economies working one on top of the other with interaction between them. Foreigners did not operate in entirely the same economy as ordinary Chinese, who also increasingly operated in what Charles Stafford has called a "ritual economy," a *guanxi* network of friends, relatives, and acquaintances based on gifts, favors and reciprocity (Stafford 2006; see also Yang 1994; Yan 1998).

The country did open up to the outside world quickly and steadily, however. Restrictions on foreign media involvement in Chinese media markets persist to the present day, although China's accession to the World Trade Organization (WTO) in late 2001 did start to open up previously closed areas of the economy to at least some foreign participation. In terms of popular culture, however, probably the most important consequence of the open-door policy has been a broadening of the horizons and everyday experiences of ordinary Chinese citizens. By the early 2000s, many Chinese people, particularly urban Chinese, were taking overseas vacations, studying abroad, and interacting with foreigners at work, at study, and in the street. Through these changing and developing contacts, Chinese people's understanding and appreciation of themselves has also been changing and developing.

The one-child family policy was introduced in the late 1970s, although other forms of strict family planning had been in place before that. Through the 1980s, the policy gradually evolved, to some degree adapting itself to changing circumstances while often tightening up implementation. The policy has always been differently implemented in the cities compared to the countryside. In the former, it has been much more rigidly enforced, to the point where it is fairly strange to find anyone under the age of twenty-five who has a sibling. In the countryside, by contrast, the policy has been implemented much more sporadically, and even by the late 1980s in some rural areas peasants could still get permission to have a second or even third child if the first one or two were girls.

The Chinese cultural preference for boys and its impact on the one-child policy has been widely publicized overseas and often condemned for its consequences. The preference arises from the fact that according to Chinese tradition, girls are married out from their biological families and go to live with and become a member of the husband's family. Particularly in rural areas, this has significant economic consequences. Not only does the bride's family have to spend money on a good dowry, but, more importantly, they lose a valuable worker in the family economic unit. The husband's family, by contrast, gains an extra worker plus the potential for children and descendants. Given that ancestor worship is a fundamental aspect of popular Chinese religious beliefs and practices, great importance is attached to having children—that is, sons—who will continue the family line and ensure future generations of the family to care for the ancestors after their deaths.

The consequence of this traditional male-child preference has been millions of aborted pregnancies where the fetus was known to be female. What is more, the long-term effects of this practice have now started to become evident in some parts of rural China where villages have a massive imbalance of young men and women, with many of the former unable to get married simply because there are not enough women available.

Tiananmen Square 1989

One of the most important and most talked-about dates in recent Chinese history is June 4, 1989. That was the day that the Chinese authorities finally sent in troops to clear student demonstrators from Beijing's Tiananmen Square following weeks of a highly visible public standoff between the government and the protesters. A full explanation of all the events running up to June 4, 1989, is beyond the scope of this introduction; however, some basic appreciation of what happened is essential for anyone trying to understand contemporary China. The story of the events that occurred in Beijing in June 1989 starts several years earlier in Shanghai. In December 1986, students in the city organized public demonstrations calling for more participatory politics and improvements in the standard of living. Similar demonstrations also sprang up in Beijing. The demonstrations continued for several days before the students were persuaded to return to their campuses; however, the country's political leadership was pleased neither with the fact that the demonstrations had taken place nor with how they had been handled. Consequently, in January 1987 the General Secretary of the CCP, Hu Yaobang, was forced to resign and make a public self-criticism of his failings.

Hu was seen by many people around the country as a scapegoat. He was a popular figure in the country and one of the key reformers, along with Zhao Ziyang, of the post-Mao period and had been particularly open in his criticism of the mistakes of the Mao period. Everyone knew that behind the scenes Deng Xiaoping and other old-guard politicians held the real power in the country, even if they no longer officially held the senior positions in the Party. Hu's resignation was therefore seen by many, particularly the students involved in the protests, as being unjust.

Hu died suddenly of a heart attack on April 15, 1989, an event which seemed to touch a raw nerve among Chinese students. Waves of demonstrations in the large cities throughout the country started out as commemorative acts of respect for Hu but soon became embroiled with calls for Hu's full rehabilitation, a renewal of the calls for more democracy and political participation from 1986, and open questioning of the Chinese leadership. There were also vocal demands to end, or at least tackle, corruption and nepotism in public office. Subsequently, the protests grew and developed in Beijing, Shanghai, Chengdu, Guangzhou, and other large cities throughout the country. Students went on hunger strike and set up a makeshift camp in Tiananmen Square, the symbolic center of the Chinese capital where Mao had addressed millions of Chinese people declaring the foundation of the People's Republic in 1949 and Red Guards during the Cultural Revolution. Mao's mausoleum is located in the middle of the square, and the Great Hall of the People stands on its western flank. From April 1989 onward, however, a large proportion of the massive open space of the square—at 880 meters long and 500 meters wide, the largest public square in the world—filled with tents, blankets, sleeping bags, and thousands of student demonstrators. The demonstrations also built up a broader popular momentum and included factory workers, office workers, journalists, and Party members. Consequently, although the movement is often thought of as a student movement, by May a wide cross-section of the urban population was involved.

The demonstrations significantly coincided with the historic first visit to China by a Soviet leader—Mikhail Gorbachev—since Sino-Soviet relations ruptured in the early 1960s. Consequently, Beijing was packed with foreign journalists, primarily there to report on Gorbachev's visit but naturally eager to come away with news of the unfolding demonstrations and protests. The Chinese authorities in Beijing declared martial law on May 20, but troops sent into the city were blocked by local residents on the outskirts. There then followed a fortnight of tense standoff and uncertainty before eventually two tank divisions from outside of Beijing were ordered into the city to clear the square on the night of June 3–4. The soldiers met fierce resistance from Beijing residents in many parts of the city before arriving in Tiananmen Square itself early on the morning of June 4. Indeed, many soldiers as well as civilians died in the disturbances that night. It is very difficult to say how many people were killed in the clampdown, and estimates range from a few hundred to many thousands. A fairly widely agreed figure is around 3,000 people killed with thousands more injured, although the official figures released at the end of June that year said that only 200 people were killed, with 3,000 civilians and 6,000 soldiers injured, and the

Chinese government has always rejected higher estimates of casualties.

In the following months, the Chinese media, which in April and May had fairly openly reported on the student protests, their demands, and the latest developments, launched a barrage of propaganda condemning the unrest and the "hooligan" elements that had instigated them. A national manhunt was launched for student leaders and others involved in the protests. Thousands of people were arrested across the country, and many were given lengthy prison sentences or even executed for their involvement in the unrest. Some of the most prominent student leaders managed to escape to overseas. It has become political taboo in China to discuss the events of May and June 1989: They are rarely mentioned publicly, and the Chinese government has always stuck to its line that the crackdown was necessary to maintain order.

In terms of Chinese popular culture, the effects of the Tiananmen Square protests have been multiple. The events themselves have become a feature of Chinese popular culture outside of the mainland, in Hong Kong, Taiwan, and overseas. The famous image of a lone demonstrator standing before a line of tanks has become an internationally recognized image, and human-rights groups and others worldwide refuse to forget what happened that summer.

A Chinese man stands alone to block a line of tanks during a pro-democracy demonstration in Tiananmen Square in Beijing on June 5, 1989. The man was subsequently pulled away by bystanders, and the tanks continued on their way. The Chinese government crushed a student-led demonstration for democratic reform and against government corruption, killing hundreds or perhaps thousands of people. Ironically, the name Tiananmen means "Gate of Heavenly Peace." (AP/Wide World Photos)

Within China itself, however, the effects of 1989 were to usher in a period of tighter political restrictions and greater political caution. In the 1980s, the Chinese media had gradually reformed in two broad directions: commercialization on the one hand and behind-the-scenes political relaxation on the other. For years following the events of 1989, however, the media became far more sensitive about political issues, wary of overstepping political boundaries, and cautious about upsetting the political leadership. The commercialization of the media and the introduction of new technologies continued apace, as we shall see in later chapters, but it was not until the late 1990s that media industry professionals once again started gently questioning the political role and definition of the media in professional journals and conferences (see Zhao 1998).

In the 2000s, for most Chinese the events of 1989 are a long way in the past. Those of the younger generation, in particular, often have no recollection of the events and little if any awareness of what happened. Particularly for urban Chinese, there are other things with which to occupy themselves—swaths of media and entertainment opportunities, work, careers, families, home improvements, the Internet, and so on, while for many rural Chinese the events of 1989 were often a far more remote experience even in 1989, let alone nearly twenty years later. The Chinese government would argue that it is only because it took the bold move to end the 1989 demonstrations and restore social and political stability to the major cities that the robust economic growth and improvements in disposable income, standards of living, and lifestyle opportunities that have characterized the subsequent decade and a half for millions of Chinese have been possible. Those who remember 1989, were involved personally in the demonstrations, or had relatives killed, injured, or imprisoned may beg to differ.

The ROC, the PRC, Taiwan, Hong Kong, and Macau

China's complex history over the last couple of centuries has left its legacy on the political map of Chinese territories. Consequently, the word "China," although often used to refer to the mainland PRC, also refers to the island of Taiwan, even though it has its own distinct elected government; Hong Kong, which was a British colony for a century and a half until 1997; and Macau, which was a Portuguese colony for hundreds of years, up until December 20, 1999.

The Republic of China (ROC) is the political entity that was founded in 1912 following the Xinhai Revolution. In the late 1940s, as the nationalist forces of the KMT were starting to lose the civil war against Mao's CCP troops, Chiang Kai-shek ordered a retreat from mainland China to the island province of Taiwan, itself only recovered from fifty years of Japanese colonial rule in 1945 and which has consequently retained the name of the ROC to the present day. One of the few items of policy that united the KMT government on Taiwan and the CCP government on the mainland, even through the decades of cold war and the occasional hostile military exchange across the Taiwan Strait, was the principle that Taiwan is part of China. Where they differed was in whom they considered to be the legitimate rulers of the country. For years the KMT continued to refer to the mainland as being held by "bandits"—the communists.

Since the open-door policy and economic reform in mainland China in the 1980s, tensions between the two Chinese territories have gradually eased. In the late 1980s, Taiwanese people were allowed for the first time since 1949 to go to the mainland to visit relatives. From that time, there were also increasing levels of Taiwanese economic investment in the mainland, particularly in neighboring Fujian Province across the sea from Taiwan. Since Taiwan lifted the martial law in 1987 that had been in effect since 1948, the island has undergone a political transformation. After decades of one-party rule, new political parties sprang up, eventually leading to the first open election of the president of the Republic of China in 1996. The 1996 elections saw the KMT retain power, but in 2000 the elections were won by Chen Shui-bian of the pro-Taiwan Independence Democratic Progressive Party. Chen also won, by a hair's breadth, again in 2004.

The open-door policy in the PRC also saw Taiwan make an unprecedented contribution to Chinese popular culture. The political differences between the governments of the two regions has meant a great deal of caution on both sides with regard to what they see as potentially disruptive or dangerous ideological propaganda. Consequently, there are no direct media links or broadcasts allowed between the two. From the 1980s onward, however, various elements of Taiwanese popular culture, particularly pop music and pop stars but also including television drama, film, and some literature, attracted a strong following in mainland China, both legal and illegal.

The other important Chinese popular cultural influence from outside mainland China has been that of Hong Kong, with a lesser contribution coming from Macau. Like Taiwan, both of these former colonies existed in near total isolation from their communist neighbor for decades—up until the 1980s, when Hong Kong cinema, pop music, popular cultural novels, and later television programs and Internet portals started to attract interest among the mainland Chinese population.

The island of Hong Kong was originally handed over to the British under what the Chinese called "the unequal treaties" signed after the first Opium War. The island was largely uninhabited and of negligible economic importance to the Chinese; however, it turned out to have fundamental importance for the expansion of foreign, particularly British, trade in and with China, including the trafficking of opium. In 1860, a second treaty ceded the Kowloon Peninsula—the territory on the mainland immediately opposite Hong Kong Island—and Stonecutters' Island to the British, while the New Territories—a larger swath of land beyond Kowloon and including more than 200 other islands—was leased in 1898 for 99 years. It was this lease that ultimately ensured the return of the whole of the territory of Hong Kong to Chinese sovereignty in 1997, since Hong Kong Island would not have been a viable entity on its own, dependent as it was on the New Territories and mainland China, for instance, for much of its electricity and water supply.

Before the establishment of the PRC in 1949, Hong Kong lived largely in the shadow of Guangzhou, or Canton, the provincial capital of neighboring Guangdong Province. The territory had its own vibrant popular cultural markets, with newspapers, entertainment—including Cantonese opera and cinema—art, and literature. Yet it was considered largely a commercial center and also a foreign colony and, as such, less important as a center of Chinese cultural excellence. After 1949, however, Hong Kong found itself rapidly isolated from the mainland, but it saw millions of immigrants arrive from all over China, including a large number of culture industry professionals and businessmen from Shanghai, Beijing, and Guangdong. Hong Kong's popular culture came into its own over the following decades, feeding both local and export markets to Southeast Asia in particular. In the 1980s, Hong Kong cinema, popular literature, pop music, and television played a role at the forefront of Chinese popular cultural transformation.

Neighboring Macau, which is famous as a regional gambling mecca, being much smaller and less economically powerful than Hong Kong has always been a net consumer of Hong Kong popular culture and much less an arena of popular cultural production. However, the physical, economic, and social proximity of the two former colonies means that people from Macau have often made important contributions to Hong Kong cultural production.

Chinese Language Issues

Chinese is a complex language that works differently from European languages in various ways. The full complexity of the language cannot be summarized here, but it is important to have some understanding of the key principles underpinning Chinese use. Chinese is written using characters. Each character can be thought of as a word in English, but Chinese characters are often combined in pairs, known as binomes, to make up the equivalent of English words. So, for instance, the character *diàn* means "electric" or "electricity," and the character *shì* means "to look at," "to watch," or "vision." Each character can be used in various ways as an individual word in itself; however, the binome *diànshì* means "television"—literally, "electric watch."

Chinese characters are made up of several components that in some cases relate to the meaning of the characters. Every character has what is called a "radical" component. According to the contemporary system used in the PRC, there are 227 radicals, which can either be used as characters on their own or be combined with other components to create other characters. So, for instance, the symbol 木, *mù*, means "tree" or "timber," but it is also the "tree" radical. Hence, 林, *lín*, means "wood" or "forest," and many characters denoting plants or trees have the "tree" radical on their left-hand side—for example, 梅, *méi*, "plum," 柳, *lǐu*, "willow," and 松, *sōng*, "pine." Other common radicals include "man" and "woman" radicals, the "water" radical, and the "fire" radical. The word for "mother," 妈, *mā*, has the "woman" radical on the left, as does that for elder sister, 姐, *jiě*. The word for "sea," 海, *hǎi*, has the "water" radical (three comma-like dots) on the left, and "hot," 热, *rè*, has the four dots of the "fire" radical underneath.

Chinese is also what is called a "tonal" language. Standard Chinese—that is, Putonghua, or Mandarin, as it is often known—has four tones: a flat tone with a level pitch, a rising tone with a rising pitch, a dipping tone whose pitch goes down and then up again, and finally a falling tone with falling pitch. In English and other nontonal languages, although accent and emphasis can change the meaning of a word in the context of a sentence, there is no change in meaning of a particular word,

Girl in front of Chinese characters on a commemorative plaque to past resistance against foreign imperialism in Shanghai. The text includes reference to the May 4th movement, the Opium Wars, and China's "liberation" that came with the founding of the PRC. (Corel)

such as "horse," if said with a rising versus a falling voice—either way the word "horse" still refers to the four-legged animal. In Chinese, the sound *ma* refers to the four-legged animal that we call a horse, but, importantly, only if it is said with a third, dipping tone: *mǎ*. Meanwhile *mā*, with a first tone, means "mother," usually as the binome *māma; má*, with second tone, means "flax" or "sesame"; and *mà*, fourth tone, means to curse or swear. Consequently, it is very important in Chinese to get the right tone for the word you want to say—otherwise you may find yourself saying something you did not intend to, or you may simply not be understood.

Putonghua is the official language of both the PRC and Taiwan (where it is referred to as *guóyǔ*—"national language"), although standard pronunciation does differ slightly between the two regions. However, there are also more than 2,500 dialects in China. These vary enormously in pronunciation and mutual intelligibility: Many have different pronunciation from Putonghua but are nonetheless largely understandable by Putonghua speakers. Others, such as Cantonese and Shanghai dialect, are so different from standard Chinese as to be unintelligible to the average Putonghua speaker. Cantonese, for instance, has nine tones instead of four and often quite different pronunciation for characters in common as well as its own vocabulary and usage. One might say that Cantonese is as different from Mandarin as French or Spanish is from English. Despite such diversity in spoken Chinese, written

Chinese is the same for all dialect regions. A written text could be read using either Putonghua or dialect pronunciation, but the characters would generally be the same. Standard written Chinese approximates standard spoken Chinese, but again there are some differences between the way people would say things and the way they might express the same thought in writing. This means that for literate Chinese, it does not matter which dialect they speak, they can always communicate with other Chinese people in writing should their dialects differ to the level of mutual unintelligibility.

Defining the Field: What Is China and What Is Chinese?

What is China and what is Chinese are two surprisingly difficult questions to answer. As we have seen with the political history of the PRC and Taiwan, for instance, it is sometimes difficult even to find political consensus as to what constitutes China among Chinese people themselves. What counts as Chinese has different answers depending on whether one is considering political definitions, linguistic definitions, cultural definitions, or social definitions. A Tibetan is internationally recognized as a citizen of the PRC, even if he or she may protest cultural, linguistic, and social differences from the majority of other PRC citizens. In fact, China has fifty-six officially recognized "nationalities," of which the Han Chinese majority is just one; many people claim to be from yet other distinct non-Han minority nationalities, even if their claim is not recognized by the Chinese government.

Taiwanese people are internationally recognized as citizens of the Republic of China and not the PRC—they travel on ROC passports, for instance—even if the PRC insists the island is still one of its provinces and only the PRC is recognized by the United Nations. Yet most people in Taiwan are also Han Chinese, giving them considerable cultural and linguistic overlap with many of their mainland neighbors. These issues, and many more, define an area of intense scholarly debate about how best to understand China and notions of Chineseness (see, e.g., Tu 1994; Ang 2001; Chow 2000). Furthermore, both Hong Kong and Taiwanese popular culture deserve separate volumes of their own. For the purposes of this volume I generally take "China" to refer to the PRC and specify when it is necessary to distinguish other political Chinese territories such as Hong Kong and Taiwan. There are also strong arguments that the large Chinese diaspora, particularly in Southeast Asia, Europe, and the United States, constitutes a fundamental and influential group of Chinese people when it comes to identifying and understanding Chinese cultural issues. Again, for the purposes of this book, I refer to the diaspora, where appropriate, in a similar way to Hong Kong and Taiwan.

This narrowing of the field, however, does not entirely resolve the problem. Given the size of China and its population—around 1.3 billion people—it is often impossible to generalize for the whole of China and its people. There is, in fact, a long scholarly tradition in different areas of China Studies that has constantly sought to deal with the conundrum of what is usually categorized as "unity and diversity" (see, e.g., Liu & Faure 1996). The kinds of questions involved include to what extent is China a cultural unity, as suggested by the largely common written language or similar understandings of Confucian, Buddhist, and Taoist traditions or other popular religious activities, for example? Or to what extent is it important to consider the many regional and local diversities that have always characterized Chinese cultural practices? Again, this book is not the place to resolve these issues, but it is of fundamental importance that readers divest themselves of simplistic notions of universal Chinese cultural practices, including popular cultural practices. For this reason it is necessary to indicate some of the principal sources of diversity in contemporary China.

A good starting point is regional cultural diversity. This is partly reflected by the number of Chinese dialects discussed above; however, Chinese regional cultural diversity extends beyond language. For instance, as we will see later, there are wide variations in regional cuisine, with broad differences between a rice-eating south and a more wheat-oriented north or very distinctive, spicy offerings in Sichuan and Hunan, for instance, compared to the plainer flavors of Guangdong. There are also other cultural differences in the way people traditionally get married, bury their dead, and carry out other important life-cycle or community rituals. There are also regional variations in dress, architecture, music, farming, theatre, and much more.

Many of these differences can be traced back centuries or even longer. There are also more recent important regional differences that have emerged in the economic reform period. Most notable among these is the difference between the eastern coastal provinces such as Shandong, Zhejiang, Jiangsu, Fujian, and Guangdong and the western hinterland provinces and autonomous regions such as Yunnan, Tibet, Sichuan, Xinjiang, Gansu, Shanxi, Shaanxi, and Guizhou. The eastern coastal provinces and directly ruled metropolitan centers, such as Shanghai and Chongqing, have been the main beneficiaries of economic reform. A lot of the new factories and businesses that have driven economic development over the last two to three decades have been set up in the large principal cities in the east—Guangzhou, Shanghai, Tianjin, Beijing, Shenzhen—and the surrounding provinces. As a consequence, economic development in this part of China is generally a long way ahead of the western region, and this has led to ever-widening gaps in terms of communications infrastructure—from roads to telephone lines—job opportunities, salaries, levels of disposable income, educational opportunities, the development of the leisure and entertainment industries, or the availability of consumer goods. Many of the more recent developments in Chinese popular cultural practices, particularly those that involve new information and communications technologies, are led by people in the east of the nation and in the cities in particular.

In addition to regional diversities, one of the most fundamental differences to have emerged in contemporary China is between rural and urban areas. The relationship between rural and urban China is multifaceted and complex; however, for the purposes of this discussion it can be simplified to some degree. As with the east-west divide mentioned above, the rural-urban divide is to a large degree driven by disparities in economic and infrastructural development. Cities, particularly provincial capitals, tend to benefit from new technologies first, tend to attract more state, foreign, and private investment, tend to be the places that new enterprises and investors choose to set up new factories, offices, or research and development centers and consequently tend to have wealthier, better-educated, higher-earning, higher-spending, and more influential citizens.

Chinese citizens all have a fundamentally important household registration *(hukou)*, which designates their officially recognized home. People's household registration dictates where they can live, work, and have access to education, health care, and other welfare services; it also influences their marriage prospects and life and career opportunities. In general, urban registration is considered far preferable to rural registration, because it gives the holder the right to live in the city, with all its consumer, entertainment, employment, educational, and health care opportunities as well as access to superior government services, housing, and transport.

The rural-urban boundary is much more fluid than it was in the past. In the Mao period and the early reform period, the division between the rural and urban populations was rigidly enforced. It was virtually impossible to move one's residence from one place to another without permission, and permission was rarely forthcoming. Even regular travel to Beijing or other large cities was rare and difficult. However, under reform, restrictions on travel and work were gradually relaxed. At the end of the 1980s this resulted in millions of mainly rural residents traveling to the large cities in search of work and other opportunities. This had the effect of creating what is known in China as the *liudong renkou*, "floating population." In the late 1980s the number in the floating population was estimated to be tens of millions. By 2005, some estimates put it as high as 200 million. Consequently, although the household registration system remained in operation, it became increasingly possible for peasant farmers to move to the cities, at least on a temporary basis. This has resulted in an urban underclass of millions of migrant workers working for lower wages than any urban resident would accept and doing difficult and dirty work such as construction, trash collection, and factory work. Young women from the poorer parts of the country often move to the more economically developed cities such as Shenzhen, Shanghai, Guangzhou, Beijing, and Tianjin, where some will find factory jobs, often working long shifts in tough conditions and living in packed workers' dormitories. The less fortunate ones may end up prostitutes or homeless. Despite greater freedom of movement, however, the household registration system still severely restricts rural migrants' access to government services in the cities. Their entitlement to education for their children, health care, and other social services remains in the countryside where their household registration is. This means that millions of Chinese families have been split up in recent decades, with one parent (or both) moving hundreds or thousands of miles to cities for work and one parent (or perhaps only grandparents or other relatives) staying at home with the child or children.

All of this means that although there are still stark contrasts between rural and urban China, there is increasing mixing, interaction, and juxtaposition of the two ways of life, particularly in urban contexts. There is also an accentuation of the contrasts between the two. City dwellers regularly see and encounter peasants from the countryside, but often in ways that accentuate their "otherness" or difference.

The peasant may be waiting alongside a road looking for casual employment, for instance, something most urban residents would never think of themselves doing. Migrant workers live in visible but separate dormitory blocks, and for construction workers in particular these are often only temporary structures made of bamboo. Consequently, the rural-urban divide is not just one of different populations and different physical living contexts but one of perceptions, ideas, and understandings. Rural migrants hold stereotypes and preconceptions of city dwellers, and vice versa.

Other important social differences that must be taken into consideration in order to understand contemporary China in general as well as its popular culture are those of gender, age, and class. Women often have very different life experiences, expectations, and opportunities from men. There is much useful literature detailing the nature of these different experiences both traditionally or historically and in contemporary China (see, e.g., Evans 1996; Stacey 1983; Wolf & Witke 1975; Wolf 1985; Tao, Zheng, & Mow 2004; Li 1992; Johansson 1998; Zhong, Zheng, & Di 2001; Croll 1995; Honig & Hershatter 1988) and clearly we cannot do justice to the topic here; however, a few simple examples would include the effects of the one-child policy, women's historical exclusion from taking the imperial exams or holding office, and the fact that women are traditionally married out into another family, while men "marry in" a wife.

There are many traditional Chinese practices relating to family and kinship that distinguish between generations. Confucian teaching instructed Chinese to respect their parents and ancestors totally, for instance, and old people have generally been venerated for their knowledge and experience. More recent Chinese history and personal life experiences have probably done more than even such traditional teachings to identify and distinguish divisions or distinctions between age groups or generations of Chinese, however. Lisa Rofel, in her book *Other Modernities* (1999), for instance, identifies three different generations of women in the economic reform period, each having grown up in periods identified by very different political environments. One generation came to political awareness in the 1950s on the wave of the enthusiastic optimism that swept the new China. Another generation matured at the time of and experienced or participated in the upheavals of the Cultural Revolution, and the other generation grew up in the reform period, with little or no first-hand experience of Mao's China, the Cultural Revolution, or the previous extent of the reach of China's state socialism. These three closely tied successive generations have very different outlooks, expectations, and understandings of the world depending upon their experiences of the state, the Party, economic reform, and family and personal life.

In relation to popular culture in particular, Chinese of the younger generation have only known the relatively liberal times of the economic reform period. They have grown up with an increasingly wide spectrum of new media and communications technologies, from the audio cassette player, the television set, and the video recorder in the 1980s to broadband Internet, third-generation mobile phones, and MP3 and MP4 players in the 2000s. It is sufficient to point out that according to official Chinese statistics, around 80 percent of China's Internet users are under the age of thirty-five, and the majority of these are under thirty. Consequently, there is a significant difference in approaches to and understandings of technology between the younger and the older generations.

The younger generation is also distinguished from previous generations by the one-child family policy, which, although not uniformly implemented throughout the country, has nonetheless meant that the vast majority of younger Chinese, and urban Chinese in particular, have no brothers and sisters. This generation has also therefore been subject to a range of previously relatively unimportant social practices. In particular, parents and grandparents have only one child on whom to focus all their attention, leading to what has been dubbed the "little emperor" phenomenon: more-or-less spoiled single children accustomed to being the center of attention. As family incomes have grown steadily for many in this period, young Chinese have also had more toys, more treats, more fast food, and more television than any of their predecessors. At the same time, however, this generation has been subject to much greater pressures from family and parents: The only child is expected to do well in school, find a good job, make money, support the family, and look after his or her parents in their old age (see, e.g., Fong 2004).

Another important vehicle for social differentiation in China is class. Given the centrality of the Communist Revolution to recent Chinese history, it is not surprising that class, in a Marxist sense, has featured prominently in the making of contemporary China. There is much literature on class and social differentiation in communist China (as a starting point see, e.g., Watson 1984) and we can only cover several basic points here. First, in the Mao era, everyone in China had a class designation and class was a fundamental category that affected people's everyday lives as well as their career or marriage prospects and their experiences of China's various political campaigns. The most valued classes according to the system were peasants, workers, and soldiers. These were categorized as good class categories. Bad class categories, by contrast, included various kinds of bourgeoisie, landlords, and capitalists. The latter suffered most in political campaigns, from land reform in the early 1950s, when millions of landlords were executed, to the Cultural Revolution. One's class label was inherited from one's father, which meant that later generations of Chinese who may have grown up entirely in the PRC and never have known the old society or had anything to do with the actions of their ancestors could still be condemned for their bad class background.

In the early 1980s, Deng Xiaoping's economic reforms downplayed class in Chinese politics, and gradually one's class label became less and less important. Indeed, within less than a decade, the issue would rarely come up in everyday social interaction, and by the 2000s, this kind of class system is alien to the younger generation. That does not mean that class is no longer important in understanding contemporary China, however. The vocabulary of class from the past is rarely used, but economic reform has led to the emergence of huge contrasts in wealth. Ironically—after several decades in which class definition could strongly affect personal destiny, even though the contrasts between rich and poor, or even politically privileged and unprivileged, were in material terms relatively small—now that class is no longer politically important the country is more markedly stratified into economic classes than ever before. China now has a class of super-rich multimillionaires, largely made up of businesspeople and private entrepreneurs; a growing middle class that numbers in the hundreds of millions; and still hundreds of millions of people who live below internationally recognized poverty levels.

What Is Popular Culture?

It might at first seem unnecessary to ask what is popular culture; indeed, many people when asked this question could readily answer with a list of various aspects of consumption and consumerism, technology, music, film, books, newspapers, magazines, Web sites, and so on. Although it is relatively straightforward to identify social practices that can be regarded as constituting popular culture, however, it is rather more difficult to pin down any kind of definition of popular culture. The word "popular," for instance, is itself a rather vague term—popular for whom? Who decides what counts as "popular?" Does it have to be popular with a majority of the population? How do you measure popularity? These are general questions for consideration, but there are also specific questions about popular culture in relation to China, where we find that scholars have attempted to define the term in ways that would not necessarily apply in other parts of the world.

To start with, the literature on Chinese popular culture covers a wide range of subject matter. One recent edited volume on Chinese popular culture (Link, Madsen, & Pickowicz 2002) included, among others, chapters on the NBA and basketball culture, corruption, gender inequality, satirical sayings, tabloids, magazines, private letters, job-hunting, beggars, homosexuality, and home furnishing. Now although some of these—newspapers, magazines, basketball, home furnishing—clearly relate to common perceptions of what popular culture is, others—job-hunting, begging, and corruption—are less obvious. At the same time, one has to ask why some of these issues—gender inequality and homosexuality—might be included as "popular" culture, rather than as aspects to be investigated as components of Chinese culture more generally. An earlier volume by the same editors (Link, Madsen, & Pickowicz 1989) raises the same kinds of questions. It includes papers on hand-copied fiction, popular cinema, divorce, peasant operas, home furnishing, the Catholic church, ethnic identity and prejudice, visual representations of Confucian "propriety," and private entrepreneurs and personal values. In other words, the chapters covered the broader topics of religion, ethnicity, morality, entertainment, and marriage, all of which, apart perhaps from entertainment, one might expect to investigate under the more general heading of Chinese culture. The editors of another volume on popular culture in late Imperial China agreed that "popular culture comprises an enormous range of phenomena, from domestic architecture to millenarian cults, from irrigation projects to shadow plays" (Johnson, Nathan, & Rawski 1985). All this shows how the term "popular culture" has tended to be loosely used in writing on the subject in relation to China.

It is impossible to produce a perfect definition for Chinese popular culture that will cover all eventualities and satisfy all scholars and authors. One author, however, has usefully attempted to put forward a working definition of popular culture in the contemporary Chinese context that in many ways reflects and reveals some of the key assumptions made by others dealing with the subject, even if it would not easily stretch to cover all the topics listed above. Tom Gold has written:

> I use "popular culture" to refer to cultural products produced for the mass market, which reflect market-determined popular taste and are for enjoyment. This is in contrast to more elite or high culture which has a much narrower appeal and poses more of an intellectual challenge to the consumer. It is also in contrast to politically contrived directed culture. (Gold 1993: 908)

In this summary, there are several key characteristics of Chinese popular culture identified: the importance of the mass market and market forces, the contrast with higher culture, and its being often "unofficial." The latter, in fact, is what led the editors of one of the volumes mentioned above (Link, Madsen, & Pickowicz 1989) to give their book the title "Unofficial China."

Let us take each of these factors briefly in turn. The mass market and market forces are clearly important features of much of what follows in this book. There are two factors here: the market and the masses. China's media markets in particular have had to deal increasingly with market forces and commercial competitive pressures. "The market" is also seen by many as what decides the fate of many of China's media and consumer products. This volume is not only about market-driven culture, however; we will also consider aspects of ritual, traditional theatre, martial arts, food, and music, to name just a few things, that are not market-driven and in some cases survive despite opposing market pressures.

The notion of the masses in China is very heavily laden with historical and political connotations. The masses were at the center of Mao's politics, and the term *dazhong*—used to refer to the masses—even today in China has the connotations of socialism, workers, peasants, and soldiers, the key working categories of communist China. It is ironic, therefore, that many features of the contemporary "mass market" popular cultural products in China—from video-on-demand and SMS information services to home improvements and fashion, for example—actually push toward greater individualism and personalization of consumption patterns and consumer behavior.

This draws our attention to some of the difficulties of translating the term "popular culture" into Chinese. There are several possibilities, but each of these has a different range of connotations and none of them overlaps exactly with the flexible and wide-ranging English term. For instance, one common translation is *liuxing wenhua*, with *wenhua* being the conventional translation for "culture." *Liuxing* is usually translated as "fashionable," hence in *liuxing wenhua* the sense is "transiently or contemporarily popular but possibly passing as a fad or fashion." Another translation is *tongsu wenhua*, where *tongsu* means "popular" in the sense of "widespread among the people" but can also have some connotations of vulgarity, low value, or common-ness. Other, less common, translations include *dazhong wenhua* and *minjian wenhua*. The former—"mass culture"—cannot escape the connotations of the Maoist past mentioned above, and the latter—"among the people culture"—is more like "folk" culture and tends to conjure up ideas of folklore, folk songs or music, dance, myths, and legends.

The contrast of Chinese popular culture with high culture is again useful up to a point. Much of what we will discuss in the following chapters—television, pop music, instant messaging, mobile phone downloads—does not generally qualify for consideration as high culture. In China, notions of high culture are more commonly associated with traditional watercolor painting, poetry, literature, philosophy, calligraphy, and some kinds of music and theatre. We will deal with some of these in the following chapters, even if the central focus of the book is often on more recent cultural pastimes. Defining popular culture against high culture may offer a useful shortcut that bridges apparent similarities between notions of culture common in the West with those in China; it may also be misleading, however.

To begin with, a full understanding of Chinese popular culture has to incorporate understandings of at least some forms of art, theatre, and music that would probably be considered high culture. Then there are also many areas of popular cultural production that straddle the boundary between high and low or mass culture—take cinema, for instance. Cinema is generally considered an important feature of mass and popular culture. Yet the new Chinese cinema of the 1980s, some of which was popularly viewed in China at the time and has since been very widely viewed on video and DVD, was produced by young intellectuals engaging in fairly intellectual and scholarly debates about cinematic production, film aesthetics, and the nature of and possibilities for Chinese national cinema as well as the impact and legacy of CCP politics and the twentieth century more generally on Chinese culture. The same could be said of the massively popular 1989 television series *Heshang*, or *River Elegy* (see chapter on television).

Similarly, forms of traditional Chinese theatre have always been broadly popular with the masses, but they have also, at different times and in very different contexts, pleased audiences across social classes, from illiterate peasants to high-ranking officials and emperors. Categorizing such theatre as either high or low culture does not seem particularly useful or appropriate. Similarly, should one consider Chinese martial arts as high or low culture? Hong Kong kung-fu movies, for many people, would be clearly the latter, but the cultivation of military and fighting skills, alongside and as a complement to literary and artistic skills, has been valued among the Chinese elite for thousands of years. Such appealing terms as high and low culture therefore need to be used with some caution in Chinese contexts.

There are some similar difficulties to deal with when considering the issue of "politically contrived directed culture" in China. There have been various debates in recent years that have asked to what degree economic reform in China has brought about the emergence of civil society or a public sphere, recalling the work of Habermas (1989) (see, e.g., Huang 1990; Rowe 1990; Davis et al. 1995). Some scholars argue that economic liberalization and the various other social, cultural, and to some degree political liberalizations that have accompanied it in China have opened up new spaces, real and metaphorical, for

Chinese people to express themselves openly and freely, to circulate and interact free of state intervention or control, and even (to a limited degree) to stand up to, criticize, or oppose certain state practices. The editors of the *Unofficial China* volume state their aims as follows:

> The chapters in this book define popular culture in a way that centers around the most salient problem in modern China—the tension between state and society. . . . Popular culture, as the term is used here, consists of ideas, beliefs, and practices that have origins at least partially independent of the state . . . [it] includes any kind of culture that has its origin in the social side of the tension between state and society. (Link, Madsen, & Pickowicz 1989: 5)

This is a very tempting frame of analysis, and one cannot deny the greater freedoms and new opportunities that millions of Chinese people enjoy today that they could not even have dreamed of in the past. Closer inspection of many of these new opportunities, however, often reveals a less clear-cut picture in terms of the role of the state than a simple state-society divide tends to assume.

The Internet is a useful example. It has enabled Chinese people to interact by e-mail, through instant messaging, through SMS text messaging, in chat rooms, and on bulletin boards. Chinese have access to a breadth of news and information unimaginable just twenty years ago. They can shop online, buy foreign vacations, arrange university places overseas, and much more. Yet, at the same time, China has one of the most rigorous and effective Internet filtering and monitoring systems in the world. There is still no absolute freedom of speech or expression in China, and anyone found posting online content considered politically sensitive is likely to face years in prison. It is therefore not so easy to say categorically that there is a new public sphere emerging in China. The key issue is the role of the state.

The days when "politically contrived directed culture" was ubiquitous and when nothing reached the general population without first going under the lens of the CCP are in the past, but that does not mean that the state and the Party do not still successfully seek to direct cultural production and consumption. Indeed, many scholars would argue that they have become all the more sophisticated in the ways that they seek to do it, in reaction to the development and spread of new technologies and the changing nature of Chinese society (see, e.g., Barmé 1999). In post-Mao China, compared to the past, there are many new freedoms, including religious freedoms, freedoms to display and celebrate ethnic identity, and freedoms to write, publish, make films, and engage in forms of criticism. Yet all of these "freedoms" have their politically defined limits. Religions and ethnicities have to be state-recognized and celebrated as the Party deems appropriate, and freedom of speech does not extend far beyond the individual and personal level. The state is not omnipresent in people's lives as it was in the Mao era, but it is rarely very far away from almost any aspect of everyday life.

Consequently, it is difficult to define popular culture as existing in a realm of society as opposed to the state. In fact, as many of the following chapters will make clear, understanding Chinese popular culture very often requires careful attention to how precisely the state is involved in and related to forms of social and cultural activity and practices. Popular culture does not exist outside of or in contrast to the state but very often in a constant and evolving dialogue with it.

Scope and Limitations of This Book

The preceding discussion of China's recent history and the increasing fragmentation and differentiation of the Chinese population should give the reader an idea of the limitations of this volume. It is impossible in a work of this size to give equal attention to all sectors of the population and to all the different parts of China in relation to all of the topics covered. Related to the kinds of wealth and economic development differentials outlined above, it is inevitable that urban China and the eastern coastal provinces in particular tend to lead the way in many forms of new popular cultural production and consumption; consequently, this volume tends to focus more heavily on these areas. I have tried to give attention, where appropriate, to important differences between urban and rural contexts or between wealthier and poorer parts of the country; however, it has to be remembered that many of the poorest people in rural China, who number in the hundreds of millions, may have poor television reception, very limited access to newspapers or magazines, and even more limited access to telecommunications networks and the Internet. More than 66 percent of China's Internet users used broadband in 2006, yet broadband networks are almost entirely restricted to urban areas.

Returning to our discussion of how to define contemporary Chinese popular culture, we therefore have to remember that what is presented in this volume is an introductory and partial answer to the question. Many things discussed in this book may be enjoyed by tens or hundreds of millions of Chinese people, but given the size of the population, there may be still more for whom these things have no significance whatsoever. Given the way that I have chosen to identify elements of Chinese popular culture, this volume also deals in several chapters with issues that concern young people much more than older people, such as pop music, mobile phone downloads, and the Internet. This volume also focuses almost entirely on Han Chinese popular culture, at the expense of ethnic minorities. All of these limitations are predominantly driven by the practical issues of space. Other topics that might have been legitimately included in the following chapters would include travel and tourism; visual and fine arts such as painting, sculpture, and various more contemporary forms of artistic representation; literature; and poetry. A larger volume might also devote more attention to topics such as popular religion, state-controlled religion, ethnicity, sexuality, and advertising, to name but a few.

The aim of this volume is therefore to offer an introductory overview to a broad selection of some of the key areas of contemporary Chinese popular cultural production and consumption. New technologies and new consumer opportunities as well as changing regulatory, political, and social contexts mean that new popular cultural practices are emerging all the time, while some of those discussed in this volume will in the relatively near future become outdated—this fact is unavoidable when dealing with such a rapidly developing and constantly changing country, people, and society as that of contemporary China.

References and Further Reading

Ang, I. 2001. *On not speaking Chinese: Living between Asia and the West.* London: Routledge.

Barmé, G. 1999. "CCPTM & ADCULT PRC." In *In the red: On contemporary Chinese culture.* New York: Columbia University Press.

Chow, R. 2000. "Introduction: On Chineseness as a theoretical problem." In R. Chow (ed.) 2000. *Modern Chinese literary and cultural studies in the age of theory.* Durham and London: Duke University Press.

Croll, E. 1995. *Changing identities of Chinese women: Rhetoric, experience, and self-perception in twentieth-century China.* London: Zed Books.

Davis, D. S., Kraus, R., Naughton, B., & Perry, E. J. (eds.) 1995. *Urban spaces in contemporary China: The potential for autonomy and community in post-Mao China.* Cambridge: Cambridge University Press.

Evans, H. 1996. *Women and sexuality in China: Dominant discourses of female sexuality and gender since 1949.* Oxford: Polity.

Fong, V. 2004. *Only hope: coming of age under China's one-child policy.* Stanford, CA: Stanford University Press.

Gold, T. 1993. "Go with your feelings: Hong Kong and Taiwan popular culture in Greater China." *China Quarterly*, No. 136 (December 1993), 907–925.

Grass, J., Corrin, J., & Kort, M. 1997. *Modernization and revolution in China.* Revised edition (first edition 1991). Armonk, NY: M. E. Sharpe.

Habermas, J. 1989. *The structural transformation of the public sphere.* Trans. T. Burger with the assistance of Frederick Lawrence. Cambridge: Polity.

Honig, E. & Hershatter, G. 1988. *Personal voices: Chinese women in the 1980s.* Stanford, CA: Stanford University Press.

Huang, P. (ed.) 1990. *Symposium: "Public Sphere"/"Civil Society" in China.* Special Issue of *Modern China:* Vol. 19, No. 2. Paradigmatic Issues in Chinese Studies III.

Johansson, P. 1998. *Chinese women and consumer culture: Discourses on beauty andidentity in advertising and women's magazines 1985–1995.* Stockholm: Stockholm University, Institute of Oriental Languages.

Johnson, D., Nathan, A. J., & Rawski, E. S. (eds.) 1985. *Popular culture in late imperial China.* Berkeley, CA: University of California Press.

Li, Y. (ed.) 1992. *Chinese women through Chinese eyes.* Armonk, NY and London: M. E. Sharpe.

Link, P., Madsen, R., & Pickowicz, P. G. (eds.) 1989. *Unofficial China: Popular culture and thought in the People's Republic.* Boulder, CO: Westview Press.

———2002. *Popular China: Unofficial culture in a globalizing society.* Lanham, MD: Rowman & Littlefield Publishers Inc.

Liu, T. T. & Faure, D. (eds.) 1996. *Unity and diversity: Local cultures and identities in China.* Hong Kong: Hong Kong University Press.

Phillips, R. T. 1996. *China since 1911.* New York: St. Martin's Press.

Potter, S. H. & Potter, J. 1990. *China's peasants: The anthropology of a revolution.* Cambridge: Cambridge University Press.

Rofel, L. 1999. *Other modernities: Gendered yearnings in China after socialism.* Berkeley, CA: University of California Press.

Rowe, W. 1990. "The public sphere in modern China." *Modern China*, Vol. 16, No. 3 (July 1990), 309–329.

Spence, J. D. 1983. *The gate of heavenly peace: The Chinese and their revolution.* Harmondsworth, UK: Penguin Books.

Stacey, J. 1983. *Patriarchy and socialist revolution in China.* Berkeley, CA: University of California Press.

Stafford, C. 2006. "Deception, corruption and the Chinese ritual economy." In K. Latham, S. Thompson, & J. Klein (eds.) *Consuming China: Approaches to cultural change in contemporary China.* London: RoutledgeCurzon.

Tao, J., Zheng, B., & Mow, S. L. 2004. *Holding up half the sky: Chinese women past, present, and future.* New York: Feminist Press at the City University of New York.

Tu W. (ed.) 1994. *The living tree: The changing meaning of being Chinese today.* Stanford, CA: Stanford University Press.

Watson, J. L. (ed.) 1984. *Class and social stratification in post-revolutionary China.* Cambridge: Cambridge University Press.

Wolf, M. 1985. *Revolution postponed: Women in contemporary China.* Stanford, CA: Stanford University Press.

Wolf, M. & Witke, R. (eds.) 1975. *Women in Chinese society.* Stanford, CA: Stanford University Press.

Yan, Y. 1998. *The flow of gifts: Reciprocity and social networks in a Chinese village.* Stanford, CA: Stanford University Press.

Yang, M. 1994. *Gifts, favors and banquets: The art of social relationships in China.* Ithaca, NY: Cornell University Press.

Zhao, Y. 1998. *Media, market, and democracy in China: Between the party line and the bottom line.* Urbana and Chicago, IL: University of Illinois Press.

Zhong, X., Zheng, W., & Di, B. (eds.) 2001. *Some of us: Chinese women growing up in the Mao era.* New Brunswick, NJ: Rutgers University Press.

2

Mass Media in China

Government, Communication, and the Media: Basic Principles

The most commonly known, and possibly the most commonly misunderstood, feature of Chinese mass media is its relation to and control by the Chinese Communist Party (CCP). Most people are aware of China's one-party political system dominated by the CCP, and most people are aware of the lack of independent media in the country. Within certain limits, however, the media can, and do, regularly offer critical analysis of Party policy and even direct criticism of Party and government officials and departments. Many media outlets are financially independent of either the Party or the government and generally operate in a highly competitive market driven by audience figures and advertising revenue. This does not mean that there is a "free press" in China, nor does it mean that there is total freedom of speech. It does mean that Party control of the media is a rather more complicated and multifaceted affair than Western media stereotypes usually concede. For this reason it is fundamentally important to understand and interrogate this complexity properly to understand how Party control of the media works and what it entails.

Indeed, it is important to question what the notion of "'control" itself actually entails. In China, Party control of the media is effectively implemented by a combination of what can be called the "Party Principle'" of the media, which stipulates that all media have a responsibility to function as the mouthpiece of the CCP, restrictions on media ownership, and a system of self-censorship that nonetheless in recent years has incorporated gradually increasing degrees of editorial flexibility.

The Party Principle

The Party Principle (*dangxing yuanze*) lays the foundation for the relationship between the Party and the media. Since the founding of the CCP in 1921, the Party has historically defined the role of the media as its mouthpiece—in Chinese *houshe,* literally throat and tongue—following Leninist notions of propaganda. This has meant that all media under control of the Party should therefore (1) accept the leading role of the Party both in society in general and in media production in particular and (2) promote Party policies, campaigns, and directives as their own. Within a few years of the communist victory in 1949 that saw the establishment of the People's Republic of China, all media organizations in the country—at that time principally newspapers, radio stations, film studios, and cinemas—came under the control of the Party and hence became subject to the expectations and obligations of the Party Principle.

Chairman Mao shown reading a proclamation of the founding of the People's Republic of China on October 1, 1949 on the Tiananmen Gate rostrum. (Corbis)

It is important to note, however, that the CCP is also founded upon the principle, in theory at least, of being the party of the people. It is made up of a hierarchical structure of committees reproduced at different levels of national organization from villages through townships, counties, cities, and provinces up to the national or central level of government. In the philosophy of the CCP this is not simply an administrative or bureaucratic structure, it is a system of communication. In China, the Party structure itself is a medium that should facilitate two-way communication between the people and the central authorities.

Consequently, the CCP philosophy known as the Mass Line, upon which the operation of the party is based, envisions the opinions, needs, and ideas of ordinary people being communicated up the party structure to the central level, where policy is formulated. Subsequently, policy is communicated back down the party structure, from one committee to the next, for implementation at the different levels. In this process, which is conceptually epistemological as much as administrative or political (see Blecher 1983), the role of the media is paramount to the dissemination of information, instruction on policy implementation, explanation of policy rationales and principles, and, most importantly, encouraging the active participation of the people. It is in this way that the Chinese media have to be seen as the mouthpiece of the Party. Such work is conceived not simply as a matter of indoctrination and coercion but as an important mechanism within a larger system of administration and governance that is predicated upon a philosophy of government and communication by and for the people.

Media Ownership

The key role of the media in the running of government and the implementation of Party policy requires two related criteria to be fulfilled to make the system work. First, the people must not have access to alternative sources of information or opinion. From the Party's point of view, there is no merit in allowing media to report critically on government policy or to undermine the authority of the Party if the media bear some of the responsibility for the successful implementation of such policy. That is why the Party Principle is considered to be so important.

Second, for the Party to ensure that all media are accurately conveying the information appropriate for the implementation of policy, it is considered easiest to ensure control through ownership. This also has to be seen in relation to communist thinking that, in contrast to private ownership under capitalism, emphasizes the importance of public ownership. The media should be owned by the people and operate on behalf of and in the interests of the people, and the CCP considers itself to be the leading representative of those interests. For this reason, under China's nominally communist system it is difficult to contemplate the private ownership of media production.

Under Mao, Party ownership of the media had far-reaching implications for both sides. On the one hand, the newspapers, radio, and later television stations were tightly restricted as to what they could print or broadcast, with much of the content dictated more or less directly by Party propaganda committees, often ultimately headed by Mao himself. On the other hand, however, funding for the media came from government sources. To the present day, the restriction on ownership of broadcasting or publishing enterprises remains, even if some media production is now permitted by privately owned enterprises (for instance, television drama production and distribution can be carried out by private companies). Crucially, though, what have changed are the funding arrangements of media production. Now, media organizations generally have to rely on their own income from sales and advertising, which introduces the logic and pressures of the competitive market into the sector.

Censorship and Self-censorship

The control of media content in China by the Party and the government is predominantly achieved through a combination of self-censorship by senior editors and producers, accompanied by continuing media surveillance by the appropriate-level Party propaganda committees. Basically how this works is that all those involved in media production have, as indeed do most ordinary people in the population, a reasonable idea of what the Party will or will not accept in terms of political or critical content and representations of social morality including sex and violence. For the most part, therefore, journalists, television or radio producers, and others involved in media production, much like their counterparts in other parts of the world, follow their instincts as to what is and is not acceptable.

It is then the responsibility of senior editors and broadcasting executives to review media content before it is published or transmitted, looking out for anything that they think could be problematic for whatever political, economic, or moral reason. In general, media content is not otherwise checked by Party officials prior to publication or broadcast; however, if subsequently a report or program were to be deemed inappropriate by senior members of the relevant Party propaganda committee, the offending organization would be contacted immediately and warned not to repeat the mistake. In most cases that would be the end of the issue; however, in more serious cases the media organization could face a range of penalties, from enforced personnel changes to outright closure.

Self-censorship, as opposed to censorship, is therefore at the heart of the system relying upon the dual role of senior editors as both journalists and Party officials. Crucially, the hierarchical structure of the Party, with everyone held responsible for what they do by someone above them and the possibly serious personal consequences of making mistakes, traditionally ensured that media production stayed within the confines of Party acceptability. In the post-Mao period, however, this dual role of senior editors has become a triple role with the introduction of market forces into China's media worlds. The pressures to be commercially competitive and at the same time at least sustainable if not profitable have created an additional role, that of business executive, for these key decision-makers in the media production process (see, e.g., Latham 2001, 2006; Zhao 1998; Liu 1998).

This added responsibility makes a fundamental difference to the daily operation of media organizations. Whereas once, senior editors had to think simply about the combination of journalistic professionalism and maintaining the appropriate political line, now editors in these positions have to think also about making a profit. In a nutshell, this entails pleasing readers, viewers, listeners, or Web site visitors by offering lively, entertaining, interesting, and popular media content, whether it be entertainment programming or news production. In relation to news, for instance, this means that media executives and producers can no longer be satisfied with dull but safe stories about Party meetings, production figures, or leaders' visits to factories, because these stories tend to make readers turn the page and viewers reach for the remote control. They therefore often seek out more sensational stories with greater human interest or immediate social relevance for readers.

In relation to television dramas, to give a different example, this means that producers can no longer be satisfied with formulaic plots and characters that carry a pre-digested message of socialist values. Again, although such values may readily and genuinely be incorporated into television dramas—particularly those of China Central Television (CCTV), for example—the producers and executives nonetheless have to exploit other dramatic devices and strategies to ensure they hold their audiences and compete realistically with less politically motivated viewing available on other channels.

Hence, in contemporary China there is always a compromise and a balance being sought between politically acceptable and popular media production (see Lynch 1999). With the pressure of market forces and fierce competition in all media sectors, senior editors and producers find themselves with both the incentive and the crucial strategic position within the system of self-censorship to enable them to regularly test the limits of Party control of the media.

Pushing the Limits

It is important when thinking about how the Chinese media gently push the limits of Party control to pay attention to which limits are being pushed and how. Some limits are still untouchable—journalists cannot directly or openly attack or criticize senior leaders, question the legitimacy of CCP rule, or reveal state secrets, for instance. Over the last two decades, however, many limits have become more flexible.

During the 1989 student demonstrations and democracy movement that culminated in the brutal suppression of protesters in Tiananmen Square, prior to the imposition of martial law in the second half of May there was widespread media coverage of the hunger strikes, of street demonstrations, of banners and posters critical of the government, and of calls for political change. Indeed, some of the student leaders on hunger strike famously interrogated Party leaders in the Great Hall of the People on national television.

Although the subsequent clampdown on the media was harsh—for months afterward, the news was filled with condemnatory reports of "hooligans" being brought to justice, and journalists became very wary of what they reported for several years to come—the degree of openness in initially reporting the demonstrations showed the extent to which Chinese media had changed in the short space of a decade since Deng Xiaoping came to power. Through the 1980s there were growing calls among very senior journalists, editors, and Party officials for media reform. The crucial and symbolic link between the Party and the media was even openly questioned on a number of occasions. This was a period of great intellectual excitement and optimism. Following the Cultural Revolution, the intellectual classes, including journalists, found themselves enjoying unprecedented freedom of expression and opportunities to debate and investigate social, cultural, and to some degree even political issues of the day in previously unthinkable ways.

Following the events of 1989, the early years of the 1990s were, by contrast, times of renewed concern, anxiety, and caution. However, after a famous tour of Southern China by Deng Xiaoping, which stimulated economic optimism throughout the country, the atmosphere of media production also lightened, and journalists, television producers, and media executives gradually started to relax and experiment slightly more freely once again. This atmosphere was certainly different from the 1980s, when intellectuals had channeled considerable enthusiasm into the possibilities of some kind of political reform including media reform. In the 1990s, political aspirations were toned down. Instead, the media industries found themselves facing up to a completely different future. Technology was changing by the day with the emergence of cable and satellite television, the use of computer technologies in media production, digital broadcasting, and the Internet. At the same time, a consumer boom in Chinese society promoted new forms of media consumption, like VCDs (video compact discs) and mobile phones. The market for media products over the decade flourished.

The media industries therefore channeled their energies more into commercially driven changes than politically driven reform. Nonetheless, this saw journalists and media producers constantly pushing the limits of what was acceptable in media production, whether it was by emulating or importing Hong Kong or other foreign programming; making news reporting more sensational; probing the causes and effects of social problems such as unemployment, crime, or poverty; or making greater use of pretty, and possibly slightly more scantily clad, young women in films, advertisements, and television shows.

At the same time, regulations governing the media have gradually been relaxed in many areas. The realm of political content remains sacrosanct, but what counts as "political" has been gradually reduced. For instance, economic news reporting, television drama or entertainment production, television program distribution, advertising, and various other sectors of the media industries are now considered nonpolitical. This had far-reaching implications as, toward the end of the decade, it meant that private or non-media capital could be invested in these sectors, the governmental and Party surveillance regime became slightly more relaxed, and there were new opportunities for innovation and experimentation.

Foreign Media, Chinese Media, and the WTO

In recent years, international media companies, particularly the large transnational corporations such as AOL Time Warner, Bertelsmann, Rupert Murdoch's News Corp, Viacom, and Disney, have started eyeing Chinese media markets with some enthusiasm. As China has opened up during the reform period, Chinese audiences have become increasingly familiar with, and in some cases enthusiastic about, foreign media content. Foreign access to Chinese media markets has always been tightly regulated, however. Overseas television channels have been generally restricted to luxury hotels and selected residential compounds, principally targeting expatriate foreign workers. Foreign newspapers and magazines are generally only available in foreign languages and in luxury hotels and at comparatively high prices. Meanwhile, foreign films are imported within tight quotas even though pirated Hollywood and Hong Kong films are readily available on the streets.

China's eventual entry to the World Trade Organization (WTO) in December 2001 did not immediately alter this state of affairs, but, importantly, it did set a number of timetables for increasing foreign involvement in different media sectors, particularly telecommunications and audio-visual product distribution. Also in December 2001, AOL Time Warner's China Entertainment Television and News Corp's Hong Kong-based Star TV obtained unprecedented permission to transmit directly into people's homes in relatively open-minded and economically developed Guangdong Province near Hong Kong. Meanwhile, Warner Brothers, Kodak, Hong Kong's Golden Harvest, and other international cinema operators have become involved in running cinemas through Sino-foreign joint ventures. In the early 2000s, Hong Kong's influential Internet portal operator (Tom.com) and multimedia company the Tom Group gradually acquired an impressive range of advertising and television–related businesses on the mainland, in many ways paving the way for others to follow. China has been gradually opening up to foreign media competition.

Although this process of opening up still has a way to go and many areas of Chinese media remain closed to foreign involvement, the effect of foreign media on Chinese mass media and popular culture has been significant. Hong Kong and Taiwanese popular music in particular have become enormously popular in the PRC since the 1980s. Hong Kong television dramas have also proven popular in many parts of China, particularly in the south, and Hong Kong, Taiwanese, and international advertising and marketing techniques have been widely copied, adapted, and adopted, even by the CCP itself (Barmé 1999). At the same time, the Internet; new possibilities for foreign travel; studying overseas; interaction with foreign tourists, students, and businesspeople; and the telecommunications revolution—which has dramatically transformed international communication with friends, colleagues, and relatives—have all opened up China's media landscape in ways that have made the CCP's principles for controlling and limiting media content look distinctly anachronistic.

Media, the Party, and Control

Understanding Chinese mass media requires resisting the temptation to stereotype or think of things in terms of black and white. It is clearly not adequate to think solely in terms of a totalitarian state controlling every aspect of media production and indoctrinating unwitting audiences. Nor is it possible to think of Chinese media in terms of press freedom and Western-style liberal democracy. Nor is it possible to see them entirely in terms of free-market capitalism. There are elements of all these influences at play in the complex configuration of political, economic, social, and cultural practices that make up the Chinese media landscape.

There is still an obligation for many media organizations to report unpopular news stories such as Party meetings or leaders' visits. They are still required to maintain party line positions on social and political issues specified by the Party. The nature and urgency of this obligation, however, varies from one medium to another and also among different media organizations within any particular sector.

Central-level media organizations such as CCTV, the *People's Daily*, and *China People's Radio* are closely monitored and, being the national and international mouthpieces for the Party and the government, unsurprisingly have less leeway for innovation and experimentation than other organizations. Once one moves down the media hierarchy to the provincial, city, county or township level, however, the picture becomes more complicated by far.

Newspapers, for example, are generally considered less politically sensitive than television, but they vary widely in their content and degree of adherence to Party directives. All titles may be occasionally obliged to carry key speeches or editorials dictated by the central government; yet, whereas some publications are strongly obliged to promote the party line, there are other categories and kinds of newspapers that are able to avoid or marginalize this unpopular content. Meanwhile, local-level television and radio stations can focus on local news, which is generally popular, and issues that directly interest their audiences, such as provision of education or health care, unemployment, or crime. Local media organizations may also find themselves able to criticize and investigate government departments or officials lower than themselves in the official hierarchy. This can lead to the exposure of corruption, malpractice, incompetence, or errors that makes for highly popular reading, listening, or viewing. At the same time, local-level cadres are more likely to have vested interests in the commercial success of local media under their supervision, which can sometimes lead to a more relaxed attitude toward media content. All these factors make the issue of media "control" a complicated and multifaceted affair.

In the chapters that follow, we will consider the different forms of mass media in China—television, radio, newspapers, magazines, cinema, the Internet, and telecommunications—and see how these various general principles of Chinese media, as well as economic and political developments, affect these different sectors in different ways as each plays its part in shaping China's contemporary popular cultural landscape.

References and Further Reading

Barmé, G. 1999. "CCPTM & ADCULT PRC." In *In the red: On contemporary Chinese culture.* New York: Columbia University Press.

Blecher, M. 1983. "The mass line and leader-mass relations and communication in basic-level rural communities". In G. C. Chu & F. Hsu (eds.) *China's new social fabric.* London: Kegan Paul International.

Cell, C. P. 1983. "Communication in China's mass mobilization campaigns". In C. Godwin, Chu, & F. Hsu (eds.) *China's new social fabric.* London: Kegan Paul International.

Latham, K. 2001. "Between markets and mandarins: Journalists and the rhetorics of transition in southern China." In B. Moeran (ed.) *Asian media productions.* London: Curzon/ConsumAsian.

———2006. "Powers of imagination: The role of the consumer in China's silent media revolution." In K. Latham, S. Thompson, & J. Klein (eds.) 2006. *Consuming China: Approaches to cultural change in contemporary China.* London: RoutledgeCurzon.

Liu, H. 1998. "Profit or ideology? The Chinese press between party and market." *Media, Culture & Society,* Vol. 20, No. 1, 31–41.

Lynch, D. C. 1999. *After the propaganda state: Media, politics, and "thought work" in reformed China.* Stanford, CA: Stanford University Press.

Zhao, Y. 1998. *Media, market, and democracy in China: Between the party line and the bottom line.* Urbana and Chicago, IL: University of Illinois Press.

3

Television

Watching television is the most popular leisure activity in contemporary China. Even in the countryside, more than 90 percent of the population has access to a television set, and in the cities the figure is close to 100 percent. Chinese people watch on average between two and five hours of television every day; it is their primary, most often used, and most widespread source of news, entertainment, and information and constitutes a major feature of most Chinese people's daily lives. According to official statistics, in 2005, to meet this demand, China had 2,234 terrestrial television stations, most of which doubled as radio stations, broadcasting an average 242,146 hours of programming every week to a potential audience of nearly 1.25 billion people. On top of this, there were around 1,300 cable television stations, with just under 128.42 million subscriber households. That amounts to more than 400 million cable viewers generally enjoying a choice of twenty to thirty channels including relays of terrestrial and provincial satellite channels. Television is therefore a fundamental component of contemporary Chinese culture and society.

In the post-Mao reform period, a number of factors contributed to the development and expansion of television in China. With economic reform, consumer desire and spending power grew rapidly. The Chinese government also recognized and promoted television as the most convenient and modern form of mass communication, which led to a proliferation of television channels broadcasting throughout the country. At the same time, as manufacturers increased and improved production, television sets gradually became more readily available to Chinese people, even if they were still very expensive in the 1980s. In the 1990s, the television revolution went even further as cable television spread rapidly throughout metropolitan areas, satellite television was launched (later in the decade), and new technologies moved television consumption toward the era of digital, broadband, and online broadcasting.

A woman carries a television set in a rural part of China's southwestern province of Sichuan in 2005. Television sets became prestige consumer goods in the 1980s but have now become a part of everyday life for most Chinese. (AFP/Getty Images)

The reform period also saw a number of fundamentally important social changes that contributed to the increasing popularity of television. People became more individualistic, became more consumer-oriented, and enjoyed greater freedom of choice in how they spent their increasing amounts of personal and family-centered leisure time. In the Mao era, leisure time was generally limited in a number of ways. Due to six- or even seven-day workweeks; the requirement to attend political classes, meetings, or rallies outside of work; the organization of collective social and leisure activities by the work unit; and the time-consuming nature of manual domestic chores, people enjoyed relatively little individual leisure time. In the post-Mao period, by contrast, there was a general depoliticization of everyday life, with far less obligation to attend political meetings or classes. Toward the end of the 1980s and into the 1990s, many people also saw their workweek reduced to five days, and work units became less and less involved in organizing leisure activities for their workers. At the same time, a rise in consumerism—encouraged by the government—accompanied economic reform and fostered desire for material goods including televisions, radios, and video recorders as well as other household appliances. In fact, the greater availability and affordability of time- and labor-saving consumer goods such as washing machines, refrigerators, sewing machines, and bicycles also increased the amount of free time in people's everyday lives.

Television fitted neatly into this changing social environment. Television sets conveyed social status, and television programming could provide (a) a complement to family mealtimes, (b) background noise for socializing, (c) a readily available time-filler, (d) easily and quickly digested news, (e) free, lively, and novel forms of entertainment, and (f) new sources of information and education. Television had the potential to change people's lives, but it also comfortably accompanied changes in society, attitudes, and lifestyles that were already afoot.

Television therefore makes two key contributions to contemporary Chinese popular culture: the television programs themselves and the social consumption of television in terms of notions of modernity, status, prestige, and material culture. Both of these aspects of television concern us here.

This chapter will first give an overview of the development of television in China,

Chinese workers assembling television sets at a line of the TCL Corp's Chengdu plant in Southwest China's Sichuan Province, 2006. TCL was, until 2006, a partner with France's Thomson SA in the world's biggest television set production venture. (AP/Wide World Photos)

looking particularly at the economic, political, and technological changes of the 1980s and 1990s that enhanced the position of television in society. It will then discuss television as an object of consumption in the new China before going on to introduce Chinese television stations, channels, and programming; however, television cannot be understood simply in terms of objects or programs—it has also to be seen as sets of social practices. Television is a part of how people lead their lives, and it is important therefore to think about audiences, viewing contexts, and ways of viewing or engaging with television programs. These issues are dealt with in the penultimate section of this chapter.

The rapid development of television in China over the last two decades is also continuing apace. New technologies are changing the realities and potential of television in China almost daily. The government is implementing a policy of digitization that should have all of China's television networks broadcasting digitally within the next ten years. Broadband technologies are increasingly popular, bringing the possibility of video-on-demand, online broadcasting, and the convergence of television, telecommunications, and computer networks. These and other technological advances are multiplying the number of television channels and may revolutionize television-viewing habits. In the final part of the chapter, we will therefore consider the future of television in China, focusing in particular on the way that changes in broadcasting, technology, and social attitudes are combining to fragment the national viewing audience with multiple niche channels, regionalism, and new conceptualizations of more personalized home entertainment.

The Development of Chinese Television: An Overview

The Early Years

Chinese television was born in the late 1950s with the help of Soviet expertise and technology. Initial experiments were carried out in 1956 by the Central Broadcasting Science Research Factory and the Beijing Broadcasting Equipment Factory, leading to the first experimental broadcasts by Beijing Television on May 1, 1958. Regularly scheduled programs started in September of that year, broadcasting four times a week for two to three hours each time (Li 1991: 340). Within a couple of years, a handful of other Chinese cities had also launched television stations. These early broadcasts were limited, however, not only in terms of time on air but in terms of audience reached. Beijing Television in the late 1950s had one transmitter, which covered no more than the Beijing area, and there were less than a thousand television sets to receive its signal.

The early 1960s brought some tough times for China and for its budding television industry. The Chinese-Soviet split of 1960, which saw the withdrawal of Soviet technicians and made spare parts very hard to come by, along with severe economic conditions following the disastrous Great Leap Forward, virtually halted the development of Chinese television until the end of the decade (Howkins 1982: 27). In 1962, all but five (Beijing, Shanghai, Tianjin, Guangzhou, and Shenyang) of China's fledgling television stations were closed down. The chaos of the Cultural Revolution starting in 1966 then forced further closures for periods of months at a time, and in effect Chinese television stood at a standstill until the early 1970s (Li 1991: 340–341; Howkins 1982: 28).

Programming at this time was dominated by Mao-centered news and political education with reporting of political rallies and meetings. Entertainment was, at times, reduced to the handful of revolutionary, model operas that were approved by Mao's wife Jiang Qing.

In the early 1970s, Chinese television resumed moving forward. By 1972, there were more than thirty television stations in the country, with one for every province, autonomous region, or municipality apart from Tibet. Research into color television led to the first experimental broadcasts, once again at Beijing Television, on May 1, 1973. Tianjin and Shanghai television stations also broadcast in color in the same year, and by the early 1980s all central and provincial broadcasts were in color.

In 1978, China Central Television (CCTV) was launched as the new national broadcaster, with its programs relayed by regional television stations. It has to be remembered, however, that through the 1970s, television sets were still relatively few and far between. A national network of stations developed with central and regional programming, but it was not until the 1980s, when the effects of Deng Xiaoping's economic reforms kicked in, that ordinary Chinese people started to become accustomed to the idea of watching television as a daily practice.

The 1980s: Television Revolution

The 1980s saw a massive growth in television. The number of television stations

A Chinese security person walks past the logo for China Central Television, the biggest television broadcaster in China. (AP/Wide World Photos)

exploded, and ordinary people started to think of television sets as attainable household appliances, though ones expensive and difficult to obtain. According to official statistics, in 1983 the number of television stations in China had grown to 52; by the end of 1988 the number had shot up to 422. The mid-1980s also saw China acquire telecommunications satellite capacity to transmit programs regularly on two national channels. By the end of 1985, television coverage was up to 68.4 percent of the population, already higher than radio coverage. By 1988, just under half of Chinese households had a television set, compared to less than 2 percent in the late 1970s, and by the beginning of the next decade television coverage was up to 79.4 percent of the population. At the close of the 1980s, China was also producing around 25 million television sets per year, with about 40 percent of those color.

In short, even though television had been broadcast in China for more than twenty years, it was in the 1980s that television really arrived in ordinary people's homes throughout the country. This was the decade of China's television revolution. Suddenly television became a new feature of everyday life. It took over people's conversations; it accompanied their daily routines and offered them new opportunities to see their political leaders and to receive educational broadcasts. This "television revolution" can be seen in two opposing ways: Some would argue (see, e.g., Lull 1991) that it gave people new opportunities to form opinions about and to privately contest Party and government policy, while others would say that it brought into people's homes a propaganda tool more effective than ever before.

In the 1980s, television also played its part in changing Chinese people's everyday habits and social practices. The television became an accompaniment to mealtimes, a topic of conversation, and a new focus of sociality. Watching television became a new family and community practice.

Before television became ubiquitous, people flocked to neighbors' homes, crowded around windows, or packed restaurants or other places for the chance to watch television. Particularly in rural areas, but also to some degree in towns and cities, watching television could be an activity for the whole community.

Once television sets became more common, they offered a new focus for domestic life. Families sat around the television for the national news and other popular programs, and less interesting programs became aural wallpaper to accompany everyday chores or casual conversation. As television and television viewing became more sophisticated—with more channels, more choice, better programming, and better reception—viewers became more active in their engagement with television. They started to be more selective in their viewing, more critical and judgmental of program quality, and more independent in their appreciation or acceptance of content.

Television changed not only everyday life but some of the most traditional of Chinese customs and traditions. Chinese New Year, for instance, was transformed from an occasion passed with family and friends in domestic surroundings to being at least in part celebrated along with nearly a billion other Chinese as CCTV's New Year's variety entertainment show drew the highest audience ratings and became an expected accompaniment for New Year's Eve celebrations.

Even at the end of the 1980s, though, most Chinese people were still watching in black and white. Color sets cost three times as much as black and white—a year and a half's pay for a worker earning average wages. Nonetheless, the attraction of and importance attached to television was demonstrated in the fact that people did aspire to own a color set and they considered the financial sacrifice worthwhile. This left China, at the end of the 1980s, ready for the next phase of the country's television revolution: the technological revolution.

The 1990s: Technological Revolutions

Terrestrial television staked a solid claim to its place in Chinese history in the 1980s, but in the following decade, television was to race through a series of technological revolutions at breakneck speed.

First, as the cost of television sets came down—partly driven by intense price wars among Chinese manufacturers—and average earnings and disposable income rose steadily, more and more families achieved their dream of owning a color television set. Televisions got bigger and better, and more and more families also acquired videocassette recorders and other domestic video equipment.

The second, and more fundamentally important, technological revolution hit Chinese cities in the early 1990s: cable television. Throughout the country, cable television networks were set up by the local television authorities, offering relayed terrestrial television plus extra channels, such as in Guangdong Province, those from Hong Kong television. Cable fees have always been low, costing between Rmb4 and Rmb10 yuan per month, which has meant little income through subscriptions for the network operators; however, affordability was crucial for the rapid spread of the technology as a common means of receiving television. Cable networks also dramatically improved reception for millions of homes.

The third technological revolution started in the mid-1990s and brought about even more fundamental change. This was the satellite television revolution. Until 2006, satellite broadcasts in China were not legally received through privately owned satellite dishes, as was the case in many other parts of the world. Rather, satellite channels had to have government approval and were relayed through cable television networks. All the satellite channels commonly received in people's homes are Chinese channels, including the sixteen CCTV channels, provincial satellite channels, and others such as Hong Kong–based Phoenix Satellite Television. In 2006 there were also approximately thirty licensed foreign satellite channels, including CNN, BBC World, HBO, ESPN, Star Sports, National Geographic, MTV, Channel V, and CNBC; however, these were only licensed to broadcast in luxury hotels (three-star and above) and select residential compounds, particularly those with large numbers of expatriate workers.

Chinese relax under a satellite dish which was set up in Beijing's Tiananmen Square Sunday June 29, 1997, in preparation for TV coverage of the Hong Kong handover ceremonies. (AP/Wide World Photos)

The Chinese authorities are wary of loosening too much their grip on people's viewing, and satellite television is, as in many other parts of the world, regarded as a potential threat from outside. Part of this threat is political. The authorities do not want viewers watching foreign news reports that might be unfavorable toward China (e.g., in terms of human rights issues)—Taiwanese satellite channels are a particular concern because they broadcast in standard Mandarin Chinese and despite a relaxation in relations across the Taiwan Strait since the late 1980s that has seen enormous levels of Taiwanese business investment on the mainland, Taiwan is still considered by the CCP to be a potential enemy, a renegade province, and a political and military threat.

It should also be emphasized that the government's fears of foreign broadcasts are not only political. The Chinese communist authorities are also keen to restrict access to pornography, violence, and unmonitored religious content, which are also considered to be potential sources of moral degeneration and social disorder.

The social and cultural importance of the emergence of satellite television in China should not be underestimated. Even though it is still a relatively young technology in the country, it has once again remapped the conceptual television landscape. Satellite relays have brought dozens of channels from distant provinces into people's homes. This not only increases the choice of viewing but presents viewers with alternative conceptualizations of the Chinese nation space.

As China's television industry moved into the twenty-first century, it found itself facing a host of further technological revolutions, including the introduction of digital television, mobile television, cellphone television, broadband Internet access, and so-called three networks convergence—the integration of television, telephone, and computer networks. These are dealt with below.

Television as an Object of Consumption

When thinking about television in China as part of contemporary Chinese popular culture, it is important to consider not only the kind of programming that people are broadcasting and watching but how the actual television set itself fits into social and cultural contexts as an object of consumption, a marker of prestige, a symbol of modernity, and an object of desire, aspiration, and social status.

In the Chinese film *Ermo* (1994), directed by Zhou Xiaowen and starring Mongolian actress Alia as a peasant woman in a poor region of western China, the physical and social significance of the television set as an object of desire and consumption in 1980s China is made abundantly clear. The film is a semi-humorous commentary on China's consumer revolution brought about by the open-door policy and economic reforms of the 1980s; it tells a story of jealousy and rivalry between two neighbors. To keep up with the woman who lives next door, Ermo (Alia) becomes determined to work all hours possible and to save every penny in order to buy the largest and most expensive television set available in the local town's main department store. In the film, the television set comes to symbolize many things: modernity and social change, financial means, social standing and popularity in the village, foreign culture, exoticism, consumer desire, egoism, and social tensions.

In this particular film, although the strangeness of some portrayed television content is used to highlight the novelty of television's arrival in remote parts of China, the key focus is not on television programs but on the television set itself. Ermo is little interested in what is on television—indeed, when she finally obtains the television set, everyone else in the village is keen to watch it but she herself pays little attention. For Ermo, the important thing was to have the television set and to have a television bigger and better than that of her neighbor. Her obsession with this quest is used to show how the economic reforms and the material changes that came with them were changing society, social values, social interaction, and the everyday lives of ordinary Chinese people.

In the post-Mao period, television sets, along with washing machines and refrigerators, became one of the three most sought-after household appliances. In the 1980s and 1990s, the social importance associated with television sets was also clearly demonstrated in their inclusion among desirable dowry items. Wealthy urban families in the late 1980s would commonly seek to give their daughters combinations of modern furniture, bicycles, electric fans, sewing machines, washing machines, and television sets. Ideally the television set should have been an imported color set with as large a screen as possible.

Japanese brands such as the ones mentioned generally dominated the high end of the television market with the more prestigious being Sony, Panasonic, and Hitachi. Chinese-made televisions were cheaper than Japanese-made but for many years were also of poorer quality and less reliable. They were also thought less stylish and less prestigious. Hence, a status gap emerged between imported and domestic televisions.

This status gap points to an evolving spectrum of consumer desire in relation to television sets. In the early 1980s, few people could afford a color set, and imported sets were hard to obtain. The norm, among those that had televisions, was a Chinese-made black and white set. (At this time there was also differentiation between more and less prestigious Chinese brands.) However, as television became more and more popular, at least in the cities, color televisions became more widespread and by the 1990s were quite normal features in Chinese homes. Official Chinese figures show that in 1985 only 17.2 percent of urban households owned a color television, but just one decade later in 1995 this had risen to a fraction under 90 percent, and by 2001 there were more than 120 television sets for every 100 urban households, which would point to two-set households becoming increasingly common.

In the countryside, by contrast, the growth in number of color sets was rather less dramatic but nonetheless significant. In 1985, there were only 0.8 color television sets per 100 households. This rose to just under 17 percent in 1995 and then more sharply to 48.74 percent and 54.41 percent in 2000 and 2001, respectively. It is important to note, however, that the consumer divide in China is not just between urban and rural areas but also between different parts of China. In 2001, for instance, the prevalence of color television sets in rural areas of the poorer, less economically developed western provinces of China was only just over

Shooting a television commercial in Shanghai, China. (Corbis)

42 percent—more than 12 percent lower than the national average and lower still compared with the wealthier coastal provinces and large metropolises.

Statistics do not tell the whole story, but they give a clear indication of how color television sets went, over the relatively short period of one decade, from being relatively few and far between (less than one in five urban households had one in 1985) to being virtually ubiquitous in the cities and meanwhile went from being rarities in the countryside to finding their way into every other rural household by the end of the century.

With this growth in color television sales, there was a shift in the prestige value of different kinds of sets. By the late 1990s, color sets were the norm in urban areas, and black and white sets had become old-fashioned—indeed, they were only third best, after foreign and Chinese-made color sets. It was not that the consumer prestige of television sets disappeared, however, so much as that it continued to transform itself. As standard color sets became more common, new technologies introduced the next generation of sought-after models. In the early 2000s, wide-screen, high-resolution digital, and flat-screen televisions all created new consumer demands for expensive sets that not only offered better viewing quality but made statements about the taste, spending power, and social status of their owners.

It has to be emphasized, however, that the significance of having a flat-screen television in 2003, when they were very new, was not the same as having even a black and white television in 1983—the social context changed dramatically over these two decades. The novelty, impact, and interest generated by the first television sets to appear in people's communities in the early 1980s was much greater than the arrival of a new form of television twenty years later. Indeed, by 2006, flat-screen television sets were already relatively common top-range consumer products. The significance and social importance of television as an object of consumption has been transformed over the years with changes in historical, social, economic, and cultural circumstances. Television has evolved from being one of the key symbols and markers of the novelty of economic reform, modernization, the open-door policy, and improving standards of living to a common, even granted, feature of everyday life and contemporary Chinese consumerism.

Stations, Networks, and Channels

Television stations in China are hierarchically organized in a manner that parallels the structure of the Party and government. There are four levels of television: central (i.e., national), provincial, municipal, and local. In 2005, there was a total of 2,234 terrestrial television stations, the majority of which were at the city or county level. The fact that Chinese television stations reproduce the government and Party structure in their organization is a reflection of the fundamental conceptualization of television as a mouthpiece of the Party: a tool of government, having a core propaganda function.

The hierarchy of television channels also replicates the hierarchy of supervisory structures. All television broadcasting comes under the jurisdiction of the State Administration for Radio, Film and Television (SARFT), which generally operates as an independent government body but ultimately comes under the control of the Ministry of Information Industries (MII). SARFT operates at the central or national level but then has regional and local branch offices or administrations at the lower levels in the hierarchy that oversee television production in their area. So, for example, Guangdong Television is directly answerable to the Guangdong Province Administration for Radio, Film and Television (GPARFT), which in turn is responsible to SARFT. Meanwhile, the television stations in the larger Guangdong cities such as Shenzhen, Zhongshan, Foshan, Zhaoqing, Chaozhou, and Jiangmen come under the local administration in those cities, which in turn come under GPARFT. Provincial capitals, such as Guangzhou in Guangdong, are graded separately and considered higher than other cities but still under the provincial administration for radio, film, and television.

There are basically three types of mainstream television broadcasting in China—terrestrial, cable, and satellite—and all three fit into this hierarchical structure. All three kinds of television are not reproduced at all levels of the structure, however. At the central level there is China Central Television (CCTV), which in 2006 had sixteen channels most of which were generally available on terrestrial and cable television throughout the country—this included China's first 24-hour news channel, launched in 2003 as one of a number of planned subscription channels contributing to the station's expansion, commercialization, and preparation for digital broadcasting. CCTV-4 and CCTV-9, the Mandarin and English culture and news channels, largely aimed at foreign audiences, are also transmitted via satellite and have viewers in Europe and the United States.

Lower down the television hierarchy, to continue with the Guangdong example, there are two provincial-level terrestrial television stations: Guangdong Television and Guangdong Southern Television, both based in Guangzhou, which is also home to Guangzhou Television. In terms of terrestrial television, there are then twenty-three city-level stations throughout the province, including two educational stations and seventy-five county-level stations. Most of the city-level administrations also run cable television networks, but there is no provincial cable television network. In terms of satellite television, there is only a handful of channels, run by the two provincial-level stations and Guangzhou Television.

Terrestrial Television

Terrestrial television still constitutes the backbone of Chinese television broadcasting and accounts for the vast majority of Chinese television stations. Terrestrial stations at all levels of the television hierarchy broadcast news, educational, and entertainment programs and also bear the responsibility for broadcasting local news and information. Indeed, the further down the hierarchy a station is, the greater the emphasis on locally oriented programming.

CCTV's sixteen channels are as follows:

- CCTV-1, the main news and entertainment channel
- CCTV-2, the economic channel
- CCTV-3, the general arts and information channel
- CCTV-4, the international Chinese-language channel, aimed principally at overseas Chinese viewers
- CCTV-5, the sports channel
- CCTV-6, the movie channel
- CCTV-7, the youth, agricultural, and military affairs channel
- CCTV-8, the television drama channel
- CCTV-9, CCTV International, the English-language channel, aimed principally at overseas viewers
- CCTV-10, the science and education channel
- CCTV-11, the traditional theatre channel, with performances of Beijing and other regional operas as well as classical Chinese music
- CCTV-12, originally launched as the western China channel, aimed at the poorer and less-developed parts of the country, which also have large minority nationality populations, but transformed into a legal affairs channel at the end of 2004.
- CCTV News Channel (launched in 2003), broadcasting national and international news around the clock
- CCTV Children's Channel (also launched in 2003)
- CCTV Music Channel (also launched in 2003)
- CCTV-E&F (launched on October 1, 2004), the Spanish and French channel, aimed principally at overseas viewers

Provincial-level channels in many ways compete with CCTV and generally try to carry a high-quality mix of news, dramas, sports, and general entertainment programming. Their regional sphere of operation is less clearly defined and of less immediate appeal than the local responsibilities of city- and county-level stations. Audiences are generally less interested in provincial news than they are what is going on either in their own immediate vicinity or nationally and internationally.

For city- and county-level stations, by contrast, their local focus is one of their main strengths. Most do not have the financial resources to compete with the larger provincial or national stations in terms of television dramas or entertainment programming; however, they have both the resources and the responsibility to report on local affairs, from politics to environmental issues, sports, education, and crime. It is these issues, particularly in the form of local news programming, that attract some of their largest audiences. Many smaller television stations, for instance at a rural township level, also only broadcast for limited hours daily. They run on relatively small budgets, with fewer personnel, and rely more heavily on local government subsidy than their larger counterparts.

By far the most popular and commonly watched terrestrial television nationally is CCTV; however, to understand the nature of terrestrial television viewing in China, the lower-level channels are equally important for the contribution they make to the range of viewer choices available in any particular area. The distinctively localized nature of lower-level television stations also means that such viewer choice is different in different parts of the country.

Satellite Television

Satellite and cable television have played a crucial role in the development of Chinese television in recent years. Not only have they shaped the present, but they will have a fundamental influence on the future development of China's television culture. More than half of China's television-viewing households are now watching via cable networks that rely heavily upon satellite channel relays for much of their content. This central broadcasting role has given cable and satellite television influential parts to play in the transformation of Chinese popular culture.

"Satellite television" in China is not what the term often brings to mind in other contexts throughout the world. Until recently, with the exception of some remote rural areas beyond the reach of terrestrial signals, direct-to-home (DTH) satellite television viewing with an individual satellite dish was illegal in China. This is at least in part due to the CCP's caution about opening Chinese homes to satellite channels produced outside their jurisdiction. There are around thirty-five mainly provincial-level Chinese satellite television stations, however, with some broadcasting multiple channels.

Due to the ban on DTH reception of satellite channels, the usual way of viewing them has been as relays through local cable networks. In other words, satellite channels are generally watched on cable television, and precisely which satellite channels are available in any particular area depends on which channels the cable network chooses to carry. In fact, as a result of this arrangement there is often some degree of local protectionism as local television authorities seek to shield their own local channels from external competition.

This situation looks set to change in the next few years, as in October 2006 DTH reception became legal as part of SARFT's plans for the introduction of digital television in China. Broadcasting capacity has been cleared on a dedicated satellite to carry all the Chinese satellite television channels and enable them to be broadcast on one digital platform. This will make a considerable difference to Chinese television viewers, who should no longer have their range of channels pre-selected by the local television authority. It may also make it easier to illegally receive foreign satellite television channels.

As mentioned earlier, in 2006 around thirty foreign satellite channels had permission to broadcast in China, under strict limits. An important exception to these limits was made in late 2001 when permission was given for Hong Kong–based Star TV, a subsidiary of Rupert Murdoch's News Corp., to broadcast a new satellite channel in Guangdong Province through cable television networks. They launched the channel, Xing Kong Satellite Television, in April 2002. At the same time, similar permission was given to another Hong Kong–based channel, China Entertainment Television, then owned principally by AOL Time-Warner and subsequently sold to the Tom Group (owned by Hong Kong tycoon Li Ka-shing). This was the first time that the Chinese authorities had agreed to allow foreign television channels to broadcast directly into Chinese homes, although the Hong Kong–based Phoenix Satellite Television Chinese Channel had become popular with cable viewers in many parts of China in the late 1990s and in 2006 claimed 140 million viewers in mainland China.

In fact, Phoenix in many ways set the model agenda for Chinese satellite television stations. Aware of the political sensibilities in the China region and aiming at audiences in Hong Kong, Taiwan, and mainland China, Phoenix from the outset focused on entertainment programs and not news, with a heavy diet of dramas, soap operas, films, and variety entertainment and music shows. This is a model that the more successful Chinese satellite television stations, such as Hunan Satellite Television, have followed. Phoenix was launched in the mid-1990s by principal shareholders Chinese businessman Liu Changle, who also became the company's chairman and CEO, and Rupert Murdoch's Hong Kong–based Star TV—between them, these two owned more than 75 percent of the publicly listed company. In 2006, the Chinese authorities gave the go-ahead for the sale of a 20 percent share in Phoenix by Star TV to Chinese mobile phone operator China Mobile. This was the first time that a telecommunications company had been allowed a shareholding in a television station broadcasting into China.

Cable Television

The Chinese authorities started installing cable television networks in the early 1990s, enabling Chinese television viewers, principally in the cities, to enjoy multiple channels on an unprecedented scale. Importantly, these networks came under the direct control and supervision of local or regional offices of the then Ministry of Television and Radio (MTR), the predecessor of SARFT.

This had two important consequences. First, because these offices had a supervisory role and were ultimately responsible for all broadcasting in their region, they were able to offer viewers retransmissions of all the competing television stations in their region (city- or county-level stations and provincial-level stations as well as the relay of national CCTV broadcasts). Cable networks were not owned or controlled by any one television company or station. Second, this meant that cable television networks were built up from the local level and not imposed or controlled by higher-level central authorities.

This was also the time that television, in major urban centers at least, was becoming a highly lucrative enterprise, with television advertising at a premium. This meant that the local offices of the MTR also found themselves with their own new valuable financial resource. Combined with the two factors above, this produced a locally driven and often protectionist set of cable television networks.

In the early years of cable television, one of the main problems was a lack of content. The networks had the capability to carry dozens of channels, but there were not that many channels to be relayed. This was to change in the mid-1990s with the successful development of satellite television, which led to an explosion of television channels available at the local level. In 2005, more than 128 million households subscribed to cable television in China, amounting to more than 400 million viewers.

The ban on DTH satellite television reception in China meant that an important relationship of codependence developed between cable and satellite television operators whereby cable networks are dependent upon satellite stations for the provision of channel content while satellite operators are dependent upon the cable networks to get their programming into people's homes.

The start of the twenty-first century also saw SARFT looking to bring greater unity to the Chinese television system, particularly the cable networks. In 2002, it finally launched an ambitious project, after some years of planning, to integrate and unify cable television networks throughout the country. SARFT was keen to tackle the relatively fragmented and locally organized nature of cable television in order to take advantage of the country's extensive cable television networks for new forms of national broadcasting. One of the key problems that it faced was a certain resistance and reluctance on the part of local cable television managers (i.e., regional offices of SARFT) because these offices had substantial political and economic interests vested in retaining control over their cable television networks. As a result, the project proved difficult because of the prohibitive cost of trying to buy up the networks in their entirety, and even by 2006 the project was only airing a few hours a day of unified broadcasting across several networks scattered throughout the country.

Television Networks, National Identity, and Popular Culture

Benedict Anderson (1983) famously introduced the notion of imagined communities to conceptualize the social processes through which people come to think of, or imagine, themselves as members of a broader national community. A key tenet of Anderson's theory was the idea that readers of newspapers, for instance, as well as journalists and editors, conceptualized the community of readers of the same newspaper as being coterminous with the nation-state. At the heart of his account is the role that the media can play in constructions of nationalism or notions of national identity.

The Mao period in mind, this notion can be useful, particularly considering the homogeneity of the media, the messages, and the social conditions of media reception. In the early post-Mao period the idea also has some force. With satellite television, however, things look rather different. When there was just CCTV, the idea of the nation—a more or less similar collection of individuals united behind the notion of being citizens of the same country—again held more sway. In particular, popular national broadcasts such as the New Year's

Eve extravaganza and the national CCTV news could work to portray and perpetuate the notion of a united population. With diverse satellite stations broadcasting in some cases in incomprehensible dialects or languages and presenting locally produced content with clear elements of local flavor, and hence difference, audiences have come to be faced with subtle forms of diversity within the idea of the nation-state.

To think of such a situation in terms of imagined communities, one is faced with a far more complex array of possible imaginings, including disjunctive or contradictory ones, that if anything work against the notion of the nation and its imagining as a unity of similar people engaged in similar media practices.

Cable and satellite television, for instance, have come to play a significant part in the remapping of Chinese popular culture and a re-imagining of the Chinese nation-state. Prior to cable and satellite television, with only a very few notable exceptions television viewing was restricted to the one to five national CCTV channels plus in most cases one or two provincial channels and one or two local (city or county) channels. In many rural areas, only some of these could be received, if any at all, and in remote mountainous regions, such as parts of Tibet, Yunnan, and Guizhou, even today terrestrial television reception is impossible.

A Chinese shopkeeper watches the Shenzhou VI space rocket launch during a live television broadcast in Beijing on October 12, 2005. National CCTV news helps perpetuate the notion of a united population in China, although CCTV is increasingly facing challenges from audience fragmentation and technological diversification. (AP/Wide World Photos)

In the 1980s and early 1990s, local television was often also restricted to a limited amount of locally produced programming, chiefly local news and documentary reports, with much airtime taken up with programming supplied by CCTV or old films. Meanwhile, all channels relayed the seven o'clock CCTV evening news report. This meant that audiences were presented with a fairly unified picture of the nation, centered in Beijing and supplemented by the complementary perspective provided by local television channels. With the arrival of cable and satellite television, this all changed.

First there was a new proliferation of channels. Provincial television stations launched satellite channels in addition to their existing terrestrial broadcasts, and many soon developed multiple satellite channels. At the same time, these channels became increasingly available through expanding cable television networks, whose audiences were therefore presented with greater choice and who became inevitably more fragmented in their viewing. The emergence of provincial-level satellite television channels while regional and local-level stations also became more financially successful also saw greater resources going into local-level program production. As a result, local and provincial channels were able to enhance their own identity and

Homes with terrestrial television antennas in rural China. Television reaches more than 95 percent of the country, but in very remote areas only a few channels are sometimes available. Satellite television is increasingly filling these gaps. (iStockPhoto.com)

characteristics. Indeed, as local (particularly provincial-level) stations came to compete with each other for nationally distributed audiences, a degree of uniqueness helped stations stand out in what has become a highly competitive market environment.

This increased "localization" of television programming has had two related, though contradictory, effects: It has helped stations establish their own specific identities, but it has also accentuated the diversity among Chinese audiences. It is not simply a matter of local news or documentary reports but also a matter of linguistic and cultural diversity. Confronted on their television screens with Uighur-language dramas from the northwestern province of Xinjiang, where the majority population is made up of Turkic Muslim peoples, viewers in coastal Guangdong or Shanghai, for instance, have become all the more aware of cultural and linguistic differences between themselves and other Chinese citizens. With Cantonese, Shanghainese, and other dialects used in television broadcasts, also unintelligible to people in other regions of China, the imagined Chinese community of national television audiences is being daily undermined at the local level while the significance and influence of national CCTV channels slowly diminishes.

The development of cable and satellite television, whereby Chinese television culture has at once both diversified and become more widely available in its diversity to Chinese television audiences, has therefore fundamentally affected the area of Chinese popular culture. The significance and understanding of Chinese national identity through the mutual understanding and appreciation of a centralized television culture has been fundamentally reconfigured and in some ways undermined.

This trend continued in the early 2000s as Chinese broadcasters at national and provincial levels in particular moved toward the development of niche television channels such as sports, travel, history, news, and shopping channels, all of which further fragment Chinese television audiences. As Chinese television progresses down the road to digital broadcasting and even further proliferation of channels, it is clear that specialized channels will increasingly become the norm.

Television Programs

A few basic statistics give some idea of the scale of Chinese television broadcasting and production. In 2001, Chinese television stations broadcast an average 183,789 hours of programming every week. About two-thirds of this (122,690 hours) comprised in-house productions. This makes a total of more than 9.5 million hours of television broadcasts in the year. By 2005, this was up to 242,146 hours per week, or 12.6 million hours per year. Chinese television also covers a broad range of programming including dramas, movies, cartoons, news, youth programs, entertainment and variety, documentaries, and educational programs.

Dramas are by far the most popular kind of television program in China. In the early 2000s, dramas accounted for between one-quarter and one-third of total television viewing; the next most popular categories were cartoons, movies, entertainment, and news, which each claimed between 10 and 20 percent.

Dramas

The most popular kinds of drama are imperial action costume dramas, other historical costume dramas, contemporary social dramas, and soap opera–type dramas. Dramas make an important contribution to contemporary Chinese popular culture because of their popularity, their success as an engaging and relaxing diversion for the populace, and at times their ability to provoke and participate in social or political debate and reflection.

This latter quality, however, should not be exaggerated. As Richard Dyer (1991) has pointed out, there is often a tendency in media and cultural studies to overlook the fact that much television and film production is actually "only entertainment." There is a strong tendency in analyses of China, and Chinese media in particular, to overemphasize their political, resistive, or critical qualities when in fact the vast majority of popular media production and consumption is for most people apolitical. Hence, although it is important to consider examples that deal with politics, it is important not to overlook the dominant role of entertainment that television drama principally fulfills.

Historical action dramas are generally set in a fairly distant imperial past somewhere between the Tang dynasty (618–907) and the last Chinese imperial dynasty, the Qing (1644–1911), with the Song (960–1279), Ming (1368–1644), and Qing dynasties providing common dramatic landscapes. These dramas feature court intrigues, gallant warriors, conspiring government officials, evil usurpers, upright magistrates, and a host of other fairly clearly identifiable character types, something which is reminiscent of traditional Chinese theatre. One of the additional attractions of such dramas is their martial-arts content, giving rein to a certain amount of Hong Kong movie and television–style stunts and special effects using trampolines and cable suspension.

The stories are often based on well-known real or mythical figures from Chinese history, literature, and folklore, although the plots often take considerable license with traditional storylines and characters. Other historical costume dramas are often set in the early twentieth century, in part at least because of the turbulent historical backdrop of the period but also because it was the crucial period that saw the formation and growth of the Chinese Communist Party and culminated in the founding of the People's Republic of China. Chinese movies made in the 1950s and 1960s often also dealt with this period, but the television dramas of the 1990s and 2000s adopted a far less politicized, predictable, and stereotyped picture of the past. In the cinema of the 1960s, this period, littered with stories of civil war between communists and nationalists, of fighting the Japanese, and of warlords, entrepreneurs, labor disputes, social upheaval, refugees, and decadence was exploited to motivate class struggle and justify the existence and political position of the CCP. In contemporary China, the same themes have come to have a stronger entertainment than educational function. They set the parameters of what is possible in terms of plot, but the focus of attention has shifted to the storyline itself rather than the political messages that the plot might be used to convey.

The Western-style soap opera, with its open-endedness and gradually evolving "rolling" plot lines, is relatively new to Chinese television, with many people seeing *Joy Luck Street*, a collaboration between Beijing Television and the United Kingdom's Granada Television (launched in

1999), as the first of its kind. There are clearly similarities between soaps and Chinese long-series dramas. Indeed, one of the most common formats for television dramas of different kinds is a one-hour episode either daily or five or six times a week, with a series consisting of somewhere between thirty and fifty episodes.

However, there are also differences between the two. Chinese dramas tend to be more episodic than soaps, with more condensed stories and often a completed storyline within each episode. There is also less sense of being a fly on the wall of "ordinary life" in Chinese dramas than there is in many Western soaps. On the contrary, many Chinese television producers work on the assumed need to have extraordinary events to drive stories along and give them a sense of purpose. The format of a long series with daily episodes also gives a certain intensity to the social experience of a successful television drama in China, as it can become a major talking point and focus of attention both in the media and in daily conversation for months.

Contemporary social dramas have turned out to be some of the most widely discussed and controversial forms of television drama. Certainly one of the attractions of historical dramas, particularly those set in a distant imperial past, is that they can be made that much more politically neutral. There is scope for mild political allegory at times, but that is rarely on the minds of television producers who want to avoid problems with the authorities and make commercially successful and popular television.

Modern-day dramas, on the other hand, cannot avoid dealing with issues that affect people in their everyday lives, including socially sensitive issues such as unemployment, state enterprise reform, education, social welfare, health care, the differences between rich and poor, and the role of government. In these areas, television producers have a fine line to tread between their audiences and the authorities. On one hand, bland, predictable, straight party-line propaganda is now very difficult to make attractive to audiences and therefore commercially successful. On the other hand, there are clearly limits to what the Party will accept in terms of social commentary that might also be considered politically sensitive.

Over the last couple of decades, a number of contemporary dramas have drawn attention both within and outside China for their social commentary and timely perspectives on social and political change in China. Two in particular stand out as having generated discussion not only among the population at large but among intellectuals, politicians, and foreign scholars and commentators.

One of these was called *New Star* (*xin xing*) and was broadcast in China in 1986, telling the story of a young, reform-minded Party cadre who overcame the resistance and obstructivism of conservative elements in the Party and tackled the inefficiencies of the old bureaucratic structures. The series was immensely popular in China and drew massive national audiences, at times virtually bringing the country to a standstill. This was a drama that managed to tap into the spirit of the times. The country had been undergoing an enormous economic, social, and political transformation that fundamentally affected and changed the lives of virtually everyone living in China. This drama took those changes as its focus of attention and dared to criticize aspects of the established political structures that

Yearnings

Yearnings (*kewang*), or *Aspirations,* was first broadcast in Nanjing in late 1990 but soon became a national craze carried by more than 100 television stations throughout the country. Some cities reported the program claiming as much as a staggering 98 percent of audience share, and in Beijing it reached 27 percent, far outstripping any other program of the time.

The series told the story of two Beijing families, the Wangs and the Lius, from the time of the Cultural Revolution through the economic reform period of the 1990s. The Wangs were sophisticated intellectuals living in a modern flat in the late 1980s, while the Lius were workers living in a traditional Beijing family compound. The upheaval of the Cultural Revolution played a key role in bringing these two very different families together, which ultimately led the son of the Wangs to marry the daughter of the Lius. The series then played out a succession of complicated storylines that explored the relationships between the two families, with the Wangs generally coming off as uncaring and arrogant compared to the working-class simplicity and straightforwardness of the Lius, most notably the utterly virtuous and self-effacing daughter, Liu Huifang.

Some commentators have sought to emphasize political themes in the series, such as the disillusionment of the Cultural Revolution's lost generation, its frustrated ambitions, and sense of loss or the differences between intellectuals and manual workers (see, e.g., Wang 1999; Zha 1995: 25–54). In some ways, though, what was striking about the series was its focus less on politics than on entertainment. The celebrated author Wang Shuo, who was one of the series' writers, once said of the concept behind the program: "Make somebody as good as is possible and then let them be done over really badly. It's easy for people to sympathize with their fate; and then you have a show" (quoted in Barmé 1999: 104).

Unlike *New Star,* however, *Yearnings* did not deal overtly with political issues but concentrated on the love stories, rivalries, disputes, and other human elements of the relationship between the two families. This gave it a stronger soap-opera feel and made it gripping viewing for hundreds of millions of Chinese. The show was an unexpected success, and the authorities were somewhat taken by surprise by it, although once they realized the degree of popularity of the program they were quick to praise it and offer their own version of its social relevance and the messages it carried.

had been untouchable for decades, even if at the same time it supported the dominant reform-minded sections of the Communist Party led by Deng Xiaoping (see also Lull 1991: 92–126).

In hindsight, *New Star* looks rather dated—simply produced and still heavily laden with Party messages—however, in its time it was groundbreaking television daring to deal with sensitive issues of social and economic reform in ways that less than ten years previously would have been unimaginable. It was one of China's key television series that changed the character, orientation, and social and political role of Chinese popular culture from simply a vehicle for education and propaganda to a stimulus for discussion, debate, and self-reflection.

In early 1991, Li Ruihuan, then the member of the Politburo responsible for ideological work, praised the series for the warm and positive reception that it had generated among the people and the "new model of relationships" that it offered. However, he also praised it for what it taught the Party about ideological work: A good television program needs first of all to entertain if it hopes to educate people. In this sense, *Yearnings* can be taken as a turning point in attitudes toward politics and entertainment in contemporary Chinese popular culture. Indeed, it is widely recognized that from the early 1990s the Party has adopted a much slicker, softer, more subtle approach to the educative role of the media.

In the late 1990s and early 2000s, historical costume dramas started to dominate Chinese television drama, although high levels of copycat production and some poor production standards caused the genre to lose favor with audiences and administrators alike. This may explain in part why in the early 2000s Chinese audiences started looking farther afield for new television drama interests. In particular, from 2004 onward, imported South Korean television dramas became very popular with Chinese audiences, even though they were restricted to nonpeak viewing times by Chinese television regulations. The fashion for Korean dramas even saw some of the better-known actors and actresses invited to China to work in Chinese television drama productions.

News

Television news is of fundamental importance in understanding Chinese popular culture, for a number of reasons. First, Chinese people generally have a genuine thirst for news and information, which makes news media extremely popular. Second, television is the most commonly used source of news and information in China. Third, television news can be one of the quickest and simplest ways of understanding what the government is thinking and doing. Chinese television news is therefore one of the most important influences on how people come to understand the world around them, whatever the particular combination of compliance, acceptance, and critique any individual may bring to what he or she sees on the television screen.

Chinese television news has a reputation, particularly but not solely outside the country, for being bland, self-centered Party propaganda with endless reports of political meetings, state visits, and the activities of the top leadership and rose-tinted views of production, the positive contribution of the Communist Party to society, and the stalwart strength of working people. Chinese television news has also often been noted for its prescribed quota—around 70 percent—of "positive" as opposed to "negative" news of the type that tends to dominate Western news bulletins. For many years, this would have been a fair account of Chinese television news, and it is not totally inaccurate even today, but recent developments in television at different levels of production have made such a representation at best incomplete and at worst misleading.

CCTV's flagship news program, the seven o'clock national news (*xinwen lianbo*), which has traditionally always attracted the largest daily national audience, is still recognizable in this description although it is slicker and more adventurously presented than in the past. Many other news programs across the country could also be described this way; however, the increasing array of news and information now carried on television in other news bulletins or more analytical news programs has been gradually changing even this most politically sensitive of media genres.

Chinese television news professionals are very aware of the need not only to inform people and to support government policy but to maximize viewing figures, to offer professional critical journalism as far as is possible, and to get closer to their audiences. This has led them to question the content of news, the style of presentation, reporting techniques, and the whole notion of commercial branding in television news. As a result, reports of political meetings are often kept to a minimum, live reporting has increased, presenters have become more personable, and reports of social, economic, and business news have increased.

The ability, will, and means to popularize television news vary from one television station to another. For instance, central television is under very close supervision by the top leadership, thus its journalists enjoy comparatively little flexibility in their work. For CCTV it is much harder to reduce the amount of meetings or leaders news. With massive resources compared to other stations in China, however, workers at CCTV have far more opportunity to use innovative techniques, technology, and modes of presentation such as live satellite links during bulletins, deployment of their own foreign correspondents, and more sophisticated use of graphics and editing technologies.

Meanwhile, local-level stations can often leave out some of the less important local political meetings and can more easily focus on issues that are close to people's hearts—education, health care, transport, the local economy, and so on—and yet also fulfill their news responsibilities. In fact, for audiences local news is one of the most attractive features of local television programming.

At the national level, the development of a number of groundbreaking investigative news reports in the 1990s made a massive impact on the image of television news in the public eye. Perhaps the most famous of these has been *Key Issue Forum* (*jiaodian fangtan*), broadcast every night immediately after the seven o'clock evening news and taking as its subject matter current issues of concern. These are usually social issues related to China's rapidly changing society and often deal with the negative manifestations of economic reform such as dishonest traders, the plight of laid-off workers, and differential funding of schools and hospitals. What is important, however, is that these critiques are made less often from a conservative traditional communist position, which one would expect to criticize privatization and the development of capitalism, and more often from the point of view of the legitimately concerned consumer. Such programs are not able openly to criticize government policy or leadership, but by focusing on these issues they do nonetheless constitute a critical force in the formation of Chinese social consciousness.

Another development in television news particularly since the arrival of cable and satellite broadcasting is the emergence of specialized news programs such as business and economic news. The importance of such programs is that they are generally considered less politically sensitive and therefore have slightly more leeway to experiment with format and presentation as well as incorporate analysis and comment. CCTV-2 is an economic channel, and other satellite channels carry extended economic news broadcasts. In 2003, CCTV also launched China's first 24-hour dedicated news channel, initially available to cable viewers but intended to form part of a future pay-TV package.

CCTV has also used major national, international, or global events to experiment with new forms of reporting. The Hong Kong handover in 1997 was one such event, with the country's first round-the-clock live broadcast from the territory. Reporting of the celebrations for the fiftieth anniversary of the founding of the People's Republic in 1999 were also used as a platform for enhanced live broadcasting. In 2003, the reporting of the second Iraq war broke the molds for Chinese international, live, and war reporting. The Beijing 2008 Olympics are also planned to showcase the country's digital television platform, with interactive coverage and also some degree of cellphone reception.

Although none of these developments in Chinese television news individually amounts to a revolution, and even combined they do not overtly threaten the political role of television news in the country, nonetheless they do combine as a manifestation of changing attitudes within the industry and some sectors of the administration and of increasing commercial pressures in the television sector.

Entertainment Programs

Entertainment programming covers a wide range of genres including game shows and quizzes, song shows, variety shows, karaoke, fashion, comedy, music, and entertainment industry news. One of the most popular entertainment television genres is the variety show, with a spectrum of individual singers, choirs, traditional Chinese musicians, acrobats, and comedians making appearances in turn.

The largest and most spectacular of these shows is the CCTV Chinese New Year's Eve extravaganza, which has at times claimed more than 90 percent audience share and broken all viewing records. Since the mid-1980s, this show, with its full array of pop stars, celebrated army singers, comedians, film and television actors, and presenters and various other performing artists such as dancers, acrobats, lion dancers, and traditional musicians, has become a national feature of New Year's celebrations.

The program has also performed the role of concretizing China's televisual imagined community (Zhao 1998). This was still the case in the early 2000s, when the program continued to attract phenomenal, if slightly reduced, audiences despite competition from a plethora of alternative channels. However, the nature of this imagined community has become increasingly transient and momentary, with the variety show drawing together the nation for the passing hours of New Year's Eve only to see it dissolve into more dispersed viewing once the festive period is over.

In this way, entertainment television is generally becoming increasingly fragmentary in terms of audience appeal—MTV-style programs appeal to the young, while the variety shows become increasingly middle-aged viewing, and principally the elderly watch traditional theatre programs. With multiple channels, these alternatives no longer follow on one from another but are available simultaneously, and with multiple television sets in many urban homes at least, entertainment viewing is becoming more and more socially divisive.

Filming of Chinese game show *Win in China*. The 1990s and early 2000s saw an increase in game and quiz shows in China. (AP/Wide World Photos)

There has also been a general diversification and transformation of entertainment programming over the last couple of decades. Broadly speaking, one can identify four phases of Chinese television entertainment programming evolution. The first phase was the kinds of variety arts and entertainment programs mentioned above, particularly popular in the 1980s. This was followed by a game-show phase and a quiz and knowledge contest phase in the 1990s through the early 2000s. Then in 2004 there was an explosion of reality television programs, particularly following the success of China's own version of a *Pop Idol*–like reality show (like *American Idol* in the United States) called *Supergirl's Voice*, which drew massive national audiences—around 400 million tuned in for its 2005 finale.

Popular Movies, Documentaries, and Children's Television

The movies shown on Chinese television are predominantly Chinese films, with some generally cheap foreign imports from the United States, Europe, Hong Kong, and other parts of Southeast Asia. International blockbusters usually take several years to get onto the small screen apart from in DVD format, and even then they are few and far between.

The Chinese films shown include old war films from the 1950s and 1960s telling of the heroic fight against the nationalists and the Japanese. Chinese films from the 1980s and 1990s also get a regular airing. Broadcast television is not where most people look for movies, however, considering the very widespread popularity of VCDs and DVDs, with thousands of films

Reality TV and *Supergirl's Voice*

Reality TV really started in China in 2000, when Guangdong Television (GDTV) launched a survival travel program inspired by a Hong Kong–Japanese television collaboration several years earlier. The development of the reality TV genre in China can be broadly thought of as in two phases. The first phase, from 2000 to around 2003, started with experimentation and the launch of the first programs. These were almost entirely survival-type programs in which participants in the shows were subjected to various kinds of physical difficulties and strategic challenges. The second phase, from 2003 onward, saw the diversification of the genre into many different types as well as the proliferation of reality series across the country's television channels.

The first reality TV program in China is generally agreed to have been GDTV's *Great Survival Challenge* (*shengcun da tiaozhan*), broadcast in June 2000. The program selected three participants from more than 500 applicants all over the country. The three then had to complete a journey taking in Guangxi, Yunnan, Tibet, Xinjiang, Inner Mongolia, Heilongjiang, Jilin, and Liaoning–effectively a complete tour of the country's western and northern border provinces–with very limited supplies and money. The participants completed the more than 20,000-mile journey in 195 days. *Great Survival Challenge* was widely followed by the Chinese media around the country, and the three participants enjoyed a short period of media fame following the completion of their journey. The program spawned a second series which, coinciding with the eightieth anniversary of the founding of the Chinese Communist Party, chose to commemorate the event by retracing the Long March from Jiangxi to Yan'an in the 1930s. However, the series also adopted an elimination format following the lead of CBS's *Survivor* program in the United States. The series started with twenty participants, who were gradually whittled down to a final winner.

Great Survival Challenge initiated a wave of other reality programs on national and

available on disk and hundreds of pirated foreign films, including the latest Hollywood releases, readily available on Chinese streets. There are, however, now a number of specialized movie channels, including CCTV-6, which shows principally Chinese films throughout the day and much of the night.

In 2003, CCTV-6 broadcast around seventeen hours per day, showing six or seven movies in that time. The channel also sees itself has having a significant role to play in supporting the Chinese film industry and purchases copies of most Chinese films produced each year. In 2003 this was about 100 films. With the future development of digital television in China, however, CCTV-6 will find itself with more rival movie channels springing up around the country.

Documentary films on Chinese television cover many issues and topics—history, anthropology, wildlife, current social affairs, and so on. Many documentaries are Chinese-made, but there is also an increasing proportion of imported films, particularly on wildlife and geography. Documentary film, however, has a relatively long history in China that predates the rise of television in the 1980s.

provincial television emulating the model it had lain down. With the exception of a couple of beauty contest-type programs, this early phase of development was dominated and largely characterized by survival reality programming.

From around 2003 onward, China's reality TV market started diversifying away from the survival challenge-type format and including indoor reality programs, performance-based programs, work-based programs, and beauty and education programs, among others. There was a strong burst of growth in 2005 when Hunan Satellite Television, one of the country's most commercially innovative provincial broadcasters, launched the third series of *Supergirl's Voice*, a reality TV-style girls' singing talent show.

The program attracted 150,000 participants in twelve cities around the country including Beijing, Shanghai, Changsha, Chengdu, and Guangzhou. One reason for the success of the program was the fact that the competition was literally open to any woman, of any age, of any ability, and from anywhere in China. There were no entrance requirements or limitations, and there was no preselection of participants. The finale of the whole series in late August 2005, in which the overall winner was selected by text-message voting, drew an audience of more than 400 million viewers across the country and achieved an average of 29.54 percent audience share in the thirty-one provincial capitals and directly governed municipalities, as high as 50 percent in Wuhan. These were unprecedented figures for a program from a provincial-level station and even rivaled the CCTV Spring Festival entertainment gala. Direct revenues from the 2005 *Supergirl's Voice* were reported to have reached more than Rmb60 million. In addition, value-added service revenues from short messaging services (SMS) voting were reportedly worth Rmb30 million. The eventual winner of the show, twenty-one-year-old Li Yuchun from Sichuan, was voted winner with 3.5 million SMS text messages. In all, more than 8 million SMS votes were counted on the night of the finale alone.

The enormous success of the program encouraged dozens of copycat programs to be made over the next few years, helping reality TV shows become one of the most popular entertainment genres in China.

The CCP has always recognized a key educative role in filmmaking. This meant that many documentary and educational films were made during the Mao period, covering topics from agriculture, animal husbandry, and guerrilla warfare to ethnography of minority peoples, Communist Party history, and industrial production. Consequently, documentary filmmaking has always been a part of establishment media production and has similarly been a permanent feature of television since its early days.

In the late 1990s and early 2000s, partly as a result of new compact digital video technologies that made filming simple and discreet, new possibilities for independent, or semi-independent, documentary filmmaking emerged. In fact, many of the filmmakers who started producing their own individual films were also employees of television stations. Some of these films have been seen abroad as constituting new forms of social and political criticism, winning prizes in a number of international documentary film festivals. In China, however, although noncritical independent films have been bought and broadcast by regional and local television stations, the impact of more controversial films is

Heshang

There is one Chinese documentary film that has stood out more than any other over the last couple of decades for its impact and social significance. *Heshang,* often translated as *River Elegy,* was a series of films contemplating China's cultural and historical heritage and the influence it had had on contemporary Chinese attitudes, politics, society, and culture. The series made use of many metaphors and analogies but nevertheless made a clear statement criticizing China's traditional, conservative closedness, including under the influence of Marxism-Leninism. The program strongly promoted the reform agenda of leaders like Zhao Ziyang who wanted China to open up more to the outside world. It famously used the analogy of China having a land-bound, introverted history that needed to be thrown aside in favor of an outward-looking culture rooted in the idea of the sea, commerce, and openness to the outside world.

The program was shown twice—in 1988 and 1989—on CCTV and is widely seen as having contributed to the intellectual environment that led up to the democracy movement and the Tiananmen Square protests in May and June 1989. Although the program was a collective effort produced at CCTV by a group of academics, television producers, and writers and was broadcast on national television not just once but twice, it nonetheless was dealt some severe criticism from the authorities, particularly after the events of June 1989 and the political demise of Zhao Ziyang.

When first shown, *River Elegy* got a mixed reception. It was widely applauded in the press and by intellectuals, but its criticism of traditional symbols of Chinese identity such as the Great Wall and the Yellow River were too much for many viewers, who condemned the unpatriotic attitude of the program. After the events in Tiananmen Square in 1989, the program was widely condemned for its historical inaccuracies and for its part in inciting the protests and demonstrations. Nonetheless, in its short life as a television program it brewed up a political, cultural, and intellectual storm unprecedented in Chinese television and one the influence of which was felt for years to come.

always limited by the lack of opportunities for them to be seen.

Children's television in China includes some dramas, animal programs, documentaries, and educational programs as well as music television. The most popularly watched children's television programs, however, are cartoons, which account for between 15 percent and 20 percent of total television viewing in many parts of the country. Although there are many Chinese animations made and broadcast every year, many cartoons are imported, particularly from Japan. This is one of the ways, in addition to cartoon books and other general consumer merchandise that carries Japanese cartoon characters, in which Japanese popular culture is successfully becoming part of China's contemporary popular cultural scene. However, in 2005 and 2006, the popularity of foreign cartoons—Japanese, U.S., and others—also saw SARFT introduce a number of measures limiting airtime for foreign cartoons along with a range of measures to support the Chinese animation industries.

Television Audiences and Popular Culture

In thinking about television as a feature of contemporary popular culture it is important to consider television not simply as a collection of channels and programs but as arrangements of social and cultural practices. That is to say, television is not an array of artifacts but a range of things that people do and talk about. Exploring popular culture requires attention to dynamic social practices and discursive contexts. We therefore have to consider not just what is watched but how it is watched and by whom. We have to consider discourses of television that circulate in society, and we have to consider the changing nature of Chinese television audiences.

Changing Television Audiences

Chinese television audiences have not stood still. They have been continually developing and shaping themselves since the early days of television in China, but changes became ever more rapid and radical after the start of the television revolution in the 1980s. China's television audience evolved from being a very small elite to becoming a national mass audience numbering in the hundreds of millions, with families at the heart of viewing practices. As Chinese television developed into the late 1990s, however, this national family-centered audience has become increasingly fragmented and individualized.

Talking about fragmentation of the television audience is a convenient shorthand for a number of trends, processes, and changes that have affected Chinese audiences. These principally include the development of multiple and specialized channels, increased channel choice through cable and satellite broadcasting, enhanced exposure to regional broadcasting with the use of regional dialects, and the continuing diversification of Chinese society.

As we have seen, cable and satellite television in particular have broadened the choice of channels available to many Chinese households, particularly in the cities and more economically developed eastern coastal provinces but also elsewhere. In the last two decades, CCTV has evolved from being a single-channel national broadcaster to one with sixteen channels and a growing collection of pay-TV subscription channels in the pipeline. At the same time, city and provincial television stations have in many cases developed multiple channels broadcast both locally and nationally via satellite. Considering this trend in CCTV alone makes it clear that China's once largely unified television audience has now been split and divided according to viewing taste and personal interests. This effect is only multiplied by the various regional options available, producing in the end not one Chinese television audience but a plethora of television audiences, even if they are at times overlapping and intermingled with each other. More recent general developments toward niche television channels (history, sports, economics, fashion, etc.) and pay-TV enhance this effect even further.

As the number of channels has increased and the national audience has become increasingly divided, so too have local and regional variations emerged in television-viewing preferences. To begin with, local channels have increased the amount of dialect broadcasting. In the early to mid-1980s, much local television broadcasting was restricted to a few hours of programming, plus news. If there was any broadcasting in the local dialect, it would be little more than an hour of news slipped in between predominantly Mandarin programming. As television became more and more popular, widespread, and successful, however, local channels started broadcasting more and more in dialect, until in the late 1980s there were channels broadcasting almost entirely in dialect. This clearly contributed to the fragmentation of the national television audience.

The developing television environment of the 1990s also saw differences of regional taste for programming emerge, a trend which was even more marked in the early 2000s. For instance, viewing figures from the early 2000s comparing audiences in China's major cities showed considerable variation and regional loyalty in people's viewing preferences around the country. The most popular dramas in the major cities like Beijing, Shanghai, Guangzhou, Chengdu, Wuhan, Shenyang, Nanjing, Hangzhou, Fuzhou, and Tianjin were usually dramas broadcast on the local networks rather than CCTV. Not all of these dramas were local products, and there would always be a small amount of overlap among the lists of most popular dramas for each city, but the differences were more notable than the similarities. The fact that people watched dramas on local networks rather than national ones also means that even if they were watching the same programs, they would quite often be watching them at different times.

There were similar variations with other genres of television. For instance, in 2000, the top news programs in both Fuzhou and Tianjin were the CCTV weather forecast and the national CCTV evening news; however, whereas in Tianjin these programs claimed 18.8 percent and 10.7 percent of the audience, respectively, in Fuzhou they attracted only 7.3 and 6.3 percent. Meanwhile, in Shanghai, four Shanghai Television news programs each claimed 13.8 percent, 12.3 percent, 11.1 percent, and 10.5 percent of audience share, with only one of the top ten news programs not being on the same channel, and even that was from another Shanghai station (figures from ACNielsen).

There are also various special cases throughout the country, most notably television viewing in Guangdong Province, which is dominated by Hong Kong television relayed through local cable networks. With their strong linguistic, cultural, historical, and economic links to Hong Kong, most Cantonese are generally watching completely different channels and programs than the rest of the country is. Meanwhile, in the far northeast near the Korean peninsula, many people, including the region's many ethnic Koreans, can and do receive some Korean broadcasting. In 2006, SARFT launched a dedicated Korean-language satellite television channel, aimed at remote ethnically Korean communities in the Korean border regions.

The changes in television audiences over the last couple of decades are interrelated with the social changes of the same period. As society in general changes, inevitably the audience and television both change with it; at the same time, television is in some ways changing society. Television production, now with strong commercial imperatives as well as political ones, has become individual and consumer-focused. It is largely driven by pleasing audiences, which means adapting and catering to an array of social tastes and interests. Yet television has also powered new forms of consumption through advertising; it has opened up new opportunities for social debate and discussion with series such as *Yearnings* and *River Elegy;* it has helped transform leisure activities and family interactions; it has fueled new expectations for information and entertainment and has opened millions of Chinese eyes to at least mediated visions, however partial or distorted they may be, of the world outside China. In these various ways, television has become a new actor on the Chinese social and cultural scene. It is not simply a medium for but a participant in cultural production.

Ways of Watching

Thinking about the ways that television has changed Chinese society helps to highlight the importance of considering not just television content but ways of watching. This includes both the physical and the social practices of watching—such as where, when, and with whom—as well as issues of cultural sensibility such as critical interpretation, value judgment, and artistic appreciation.

In terms of viewing habits, the most common way to watch television in China, as in many other parts of the world, is at home in the evening with family. Television is often a backdrop to mealtimes, which means that it is watched sporadically between and around conversation. At times it can of course also dominate domestic social space and silence conversation. At other times it certainly provokes and stimulates it.

Domestic viewing, however, has also gradually transformed over the last two decades. In the late 1980s, in the large cities, even when most households had their own television set, there would be a fair degree of neighborly interaction and viewing together. As housing conditions have improved, with fewer shared facilities, better security, more privacy, and air-conditioning (which makes people close windows and doors in the summer), some domestic social interaction has disappeared behind closed doors, erecting barriers to the kinds of neighborly intimacy that used to be a compulsory feature of most people's lives. This is also something that varies from city to city, however, as the nature and quality of housing depends on regional wealth, the historical architectural styles of the city, the width of streets, the attitudes of government planners, the degree of modernization of the city landscape, and the regional climate.

Suzhou, for instance, is an old city of narrow streets, canals, and traditional housing. Like other cities it has its areas of modern development blocks, not least since becoming one of China's leading IT manufacturing centers. The old parts of the town, however, still impose a certain degree of intimacy onto social relations. Guangzhou is also traditionally a city of narrow streets and shops and restaurants. However, swaths of old, densely packed, low-rise housing has been demolished in recent years to make way for new roads, bridges, and office blocks, and with an unbearably hot and humid climate, the domestic air-conditioner has contributed greatly to closing up the domestic television-viewing space. Similarly, many of Beijing's famous alleys of courtyard houses have been swept away in the name of modernization to be replaced by modern concrete apartments. All these factors affect the social nature of the television-viewing experience.

In the late 1990s, particularly in wealthier and urban homes, it has also become increasingly common for households to have a second television set, often in one of the bedrooms. This also marks the trend toward television viewing becoming a more individualized and less social practice, even within families.

In the poorer parts of China where television sets are still not ubiquitous, however, television viewing is often a more broadly sociable experience. In the 1980s, as many villages, for instance, got their first television sets, neighbors and other villagers would crowd into the living room of a house with a television, watching also from outside through the windows and doorways. As television has become more common, such scenes have become less so; however, it is still common practice in many parts of China to watch television at a neighbor's home. China's hundreds of millions of migrant workers living in temporary accommodation or dormitories, as well as the millions of university students across the country, also watch television far more commonly in a public, semi-public, or communal space.

These features of television viewing are important, as they fundamentally affect the nature of the experience. Public spaces tend to be more male-dominated, and dormitories are almost universally single-sex. The village home invaded by neighbors to watch the television is opened up as a temporary public space even if it bears the trimmings of domesticity. Public and semipublic viewing spaces also affect issues of program choice, understanding, freedom of interpretation, satisfaction, and advertising impact, to name but a few. As wealthier Chinese move toward more individualized and personalized television viewing, poorer Chinese are often watching in the most social of contexts. This points out once again the fragmentation and diversification of Chinese television audiences.

In terms of cultural sensibilities, clearly one of the key influences has been the effect of the CCP, the one-party state, and its conceptualization of the role of the media. This is important not simply to indicate ideological domination, which is often hard to measure, but because it points us toward a range of attitudes that affect people's viewing. Indeed, rather than being susceptible to indoctrination, one could argue that the full awareness among Chinese people of the relationship between the Party and television has in many cases nurtured a heightened critical awareness, sensitivity to political nuances, and strong skepticism in their viewing.

Here there is a crucial difference between Western media and Chinese media that must be remembered. With Western media there is usually the *aim* of being impartial, particularly in news reporting. Many media studies critiques of Western media have therefore shown how in fact they are usually far from impartial and tend on the whole to support the ideological status quo (see, e.g., Fiske 1987: 281–308; Hall, Critcher, Jefferson, Clarke, & Robert 1978). The question then arises as to how far, if at all, Western audiences are seduced by the ideological position of the media. In China, by contrast, the link between the Party, the government, and the media is well known and well understood. The pro-Party bias of the media is not hidden or denied; on the contrary, it is expected. This fundamentally affects the way that people engage with television. Every individual will have his or her own opinions and attitudes toward Party media, but they all start from a position of some degree of awareness of its political role.

Nonetheless, for most Chinese viewers, most of the time, watching television is not a political activity. Western media and intellectual attention to Chinese television invariably focuses on the political—the degree of "indoctrination" of or "resistance" by audiences, the degree and nature of propaganda, the Party's continuing control of television organizations, and so on. Yet Chinese television in the 2000s, in terms of both content and preferred viewing, is often principally a vehicle of entertainment rather than propaganda. Of course the two cannot always be separated, and the former is sometimes used for the purposes of the latter, but Chinese viewers are generally more than capable of identifying, reflecting upon, and passing judgment on the political messages that some of their entertainment carries.

Discourses of Television

Chinese television is the subject of numerous social conversations and debates among viewers, producers, journalists, intellectuals, and politicians. The ways people talk and write about television in China are what we might call China's discourses of television. These discourses are potentially countless in that they would have to include discussion, thoughts, and ideas about television in relation to a limitless range of possible social issues—gender, education, child care and the family, the arts, the economy, politics, nationalism, and so on.

However, we can focus on four linked areas of television discourse: television as part of other media commentary, professional debates about television, intellectual debates about television, and everyday conversation about television.

Other media commentary about television is an important feature of Chinese television experiences. In terms of Chinese popular culture, television does not stand isolated but exists in a milieu of cross-media references and interaction. Television presenters, actors, actresses, and other stars form part of the staple diet of entertainment journalism in newspapers, in magazines, and on the Internet. Radio stations may also discuss popular contemporary television programs and personalities. Many daily newspapers have entertainment pages, if not special pullout television or entertainment sections. There are also daily and weekly specialized entertainment or television papers and a plethora of magazines dealing with similar materials. Hence, for many Chinese the cultural phenomenon of television involves more than just broadcasting and entails use of a wider mix of media sources.

Television stations or television bureaus produce many television papers or magazines themselves, and in addition to providing full television listings these try to promote their home station's programs. Television journalism covers a large range of issues, including the latest and upcoming events in key drama serials; interviews with stars, writers, and producers; prelaunch publicity for new series; background reports on the making of programs; actors' and actresses' lives; and other general television information. This journalism helps create a heightened awareness of programs and stars in the realm of public media reality.

The Internet is an increasingly important forum for television. China's most popular portals devote considerable attention to entertainment news, with television a predominant feature. There are also dedicated television magazine Web sites, professional and technical Web sites, and Web sites run by television stations themselves.

The magazine Web sites carry articles, interviews, and background news and information about television programs and stars, similar to their printed counterparts. Their main advantage, however, is their speed and interactivity. They can update news stories more quickly, and they invariably offer viewers the chance to participate in bulletin-board discussions or chat rooms. With the growing popularity of short messaging services (SMS), there are also opportunities for people to get television and entertainment news updates sent directly to their mobile phones. Entertainment channels of Internet portals are broadly similar.

Television station Web sites in the early 2000s varied enormously in terms of quality, technical sophistication, and range of services offered; however, generally they had one or both of two broad aims. The first was to publicize the station's own programming with schedules, news, articles, and interviews supporting their output. In this way, the Web site was an extension of the marketing and publicity work of the station itself, and most television station Web sites included this in one form or another. The second aim was to make the Web site function as a commercial entity in itself, usually focusing on news or aiming to compete with the leading Internet portals. This made the Web site a very different kind of project and was done in one of two ways. In some cases, several media organizations, such as television stations, radio stations, newspapers, and magazines, have pooled resources to produce a general news portal. Others have decided to work alone.

The CCTV Web site is a useful example to consider. In 2003, CCTV upgraded and redesigned the site in an attempt to combine these two broad aims in one site. The site adopted newspaper-style headlines and layout for its lead news stories, which took prominence on the homepage. The site then had two large sets of links that facilitated the dual functioning of the site. There was one set of links for each CCTV television channel, with more than twenty extra links for the most popular CCTV programs, presenters, and genres of programming. The other set of links was similar to that found on many other general portals and included channels for news, economy, technology, education, sport, military affairs, and lifestyle. The site clearly sought to exploit and enhance the well-known brand names from CCTV's broadcasting as well as set itself up as an online news and information provider. In such cases, the role of television in popular culture is starting to spread and diversify beyond the realm of broadcasting.

Professional discourses of television are generally less public, even if they are often readily accessible to anyone interested enough to pursue them. Professional television journals publish articles reflecting on the latest trends in television production, covering technical equipment issues, editing software, audience research, the politically defined Party-television relationship, and issues relating to news, television dramas, documentaries, or general reform of the industry. Some of this discussion is also to be found online.

This is an important realm of debate for understanding contemporary Chinese television, not least because it reveals the contrasting attitudes in the industry between reformers and traditionalists, between those who openly question the political definition of Chinese media and those who defend it. The significance of these debates is not in what they say, however, but simply in the fact that they occur at all. In the past, it would have been unimaginable, not to mention personally dangerous, for television professionals to question the relationship between their medium and the Party. In the early 2000s, such sentiments could be readily expressed within the limited circulation of professional debate.

There is some overlap between the professional discourses and other intellectual debates surrounding television in China. Some of the key protagonists in such debates are university academics. There is also often a close relationship between professional intellectuals involved in television production, including in particular producers and scriptwriters, and other academics. This has produced two contradictory trends in intellectual attitudes toward television. On one hand, some intellectuals have lauded the rise of the television serial drama as a way for ordinary people, many of whom lack a high level of education, to circumvent the traditionally elitist notion of cultural production, which has valued high cultural genres of literature, poetry, and art. On the other hand, the popularity of television drama has played directly into the hands of such elitist intellectuals, who see it as catering to the lowest common denominator.

This intellectual dichotomy is not unfamiliar in other parts of the world. However, in China it carries its own particular resonances with political and intellectual discourses in the past. First, there is a particular history of "the masses" in China so that antielitist understandings of popular culture slip comfortably into the well-worn discursive grooves that have valorized workers, soldiers, and peasants throughout the history of the PRC. For those putting forward these arguments this can be a good thing and a bad thing. It is a good thing because they are able to present arguments that are unlikely to be seen as subversive by the Party and which can draw upon established rhetorical connotations and language to make new points. It is a bad thing because their arguments may also run the risk of being swallowed up by those same stale rhetorical associations, not to be taken seriously and to be written off as old-fashioned Marxism.

Nonetheless, some of the more interesting intellectual analyses of television and popular culture have come from the antielitist end of the spectrum. Radical Chinese thinkers have drawn some inspiration from Western cultural studies to re-evaluate the position of television in contemporary Chinese society, giving it a heightened status and significance in the public realm. A common line of argument has been that, with the ideological void left by the dilution of Chinese socialism, the role of moral and ethical leadership that has traditionally been fulfilled by intellectuals from imperial times through the May 4th Movement in the early twentieth century and subsequently by the CCP is now being fulfilled by various forms of popular culture, with television at the forefront. The immediacy and ubiquity of television, combined with the skepticism and interpretive flexibility demonstrated by audiences, makes it a prime mover in the negotiation of moral and ethical values in contemporary society (see, e.g., Keane 1998; Dai 1997).

Clearly, everyday conversation about television is linked to all three of the other areas of television discourse. Apart from the relation with intellectual discourses outlined above, other media commentary prompts, guides, influences, and participates in the way that people talk and think about television. Professional debates about television often focus on what precisely the relationship between television and its audiences actually is or should be; what power, if any, it actually has; and how television producers need to react to the changing social context. Hence, professional debates often entail those who work in and run television reflecting upon what they understand everyday conversations on the topic of television to be about, upon intellectual debates about and critiques of what they do, and upon how effectively they communicate with their audiences.

Nonetheless, everyday conversation as a television discourse is probably the most difficult to identify and verify with any certainty. We have already seen how audiences are diversifying and fragmenting. Consequently, public opinions are also diversifying. Television stations and advertisers increasingly resort to market surveys, people-meter audience measurement techniques, and viewing figures as a means of trying to understand their audiences and what they like to watch; however, these are notoriously inaccurate ways of understanding what people really think about television.

Clearly, people's everyday conversations vary enormously and cannot be summarized in a few paragraphs, but from the point of view of Chinese popular culture it is worth noting a few key features of such conversations. First, although politics is important to many Chinese, everyday conversation about television between Chinese people does not generally dwell upon issues of Party control, propaganda, and freedom of speech. Far more commonly, conversation relates to the entertainment aspects of television—whether a program makes good viewing, whether it is well made, who is performing in or presenting it, whether it is funny, moving, or informative, and so on. Conversation also often picks up on social issues and themes raised in programs, particularly dramas, such as unemployment, changing social values and institutions, education, welfare, youth, the elderly, migrant workers, and gender and rural-urban differences. It is for this reason that some intellectuals see television as having taken the lead in discourses of morality in Chinese society.

The Future of Chinese Television

The future of Chinese television will be shaped by two key factors: technological change and social change. Both of these indicate further audience fragmentation; personalization of television viewing; a weaker relationship between television, politics, and national identity; and the greater commercialization of the whole industry.

From the technological point of view, the key developments will be digitization; the development of broadband Internet access with the possibility of three networks convergence (telecommunications, television, and computers); direct-to-home satellite television; mobile television, particularly on public transport; and different kinds of cellphone television. The most important of these is the movement toward digital television, which will see the number of channels multiply with more niche and specialized channels, greater viewing choice, and some degree of interactivity.

In 2003, the Chinese authorities laid out a clear timetable for the development of digital television in China. According to the plan, between 2003 and 2005 China would see the handful of digital television trials already operating expand and multiply in a period of technological experimentation and development. By the end of this period a projected 30 million households would be watching digital television, and broadcasting in some of the large key cities like Guangzhou, Shanghai, and Shenzhen would be entirely digital. The following three years, between 2006 and 2008, would then see the market mature, with the spread of established technologies into the remaining large cities and moving from developed to less developed parts of the country. All cable and satellite broadcasting was expected to be on digital platforms by 2008, in time for the Beijing 2008 Olympics, and it was envisioned that the greater part of Chinese television broadcasting by 2010 would be digital, with the analog signal to be switched off in 2015.

In actuality, at the end of 2005 digitization was falling behind schedule, with only 3.97 million digital cable households. Certainly, in some cities, such as Shanghai and Guangzhou, the degree of digitization was fairly well advanced, but the figures show just over a tenth of the digital audience compared to the original plan. What is more, technical delays in developing a digital terrestrial standard and launching DTH digital satellite television all showed that the digitization process was proving more difficult in practice than originally anticipated.

Nonetheless, the impact of digital television will be to increase the number of channels coming into Chinese people's homes several-fold, putting added pressure on broadcasters and content providers to fill the massive increase in airtime. It is likely that imported programs will meet at least part of this increased demand and niche channels will multiply. Digital television will also introduce viewers to differing degrees of interactivity, enabling greater personalization of the viewing experience through increased viewing options. Digital television also heralds the arrival of pay-TV in China as television stations seek to recoup some of their expenses through subscription channels and pay-per-view events and movies. According to SARFT statistics, by the end of 2005 there were 1.26 million digital pay-TV-subscribing households throughout the country.

The growth of broadband Internet access brings new viewing opportunities, such as video-on-demand, either through much quicker downloads or through streaming video technologies. At least up until 2003, however, the most common form of broadband provision was through telecommunications providers, with the rival cable television operators lagging some way behind. With vicious rivalry between the telecommunications and cable television sectors, this almost certainly prevented the full exploitation of the potential for cable operators and television stations to provide content for broadband. Nonetheless, in the future broadband will be a key feature of Chinese television viewing, and with high interactivity becoming a crucial factor in developing ever more personalized television services.

Such a vision is closely linked to the often referred to but rarely progressed idea of three networks convergence. The problem in this area is once again the rivalry between telecommunications and cable television operators, who for years considered themselves competitors rather than potential collaborators. Although both ultimately come under the jurisdiction of the Ministry of Information Industries (MII), SARFT is more than semi-autonomous and in the late 1990s and early 2000s fought a number of internal battles with the telecommunications-friendly leaders of the MII. Cable television operators long begrudged their being banned from entering the lucrative telecommunications business and coveted the high revenues of their telecommunications counterparts. It is for this reason that broadband holds the key to the future of converged networks as both telecommunications and cable television operators are allowed to participate in the sector.

In fact, in 2005, various trials of Internet protocol television (IPTV) in Shanghai in particular, but also Beijing and a few other large cities, saw the formation of previously unlikely alliances between telecommunications companies and television and radio broadcasters. In late 2006, Shanghai's IPTV service—a collaboration between Shanghai Telecom and the Shanghai Media Group—was officially launched. With broadband Internet user numbers rising fast, IPTV is set to become an important feature of Chinese television's future. The launch of DTH satellite television broadcasting will also clearly transform China's television landscape. This will also contribute to the proliferation of channels that people can receive and circumvent some of the local protectionism that currently restricts viewer choice.

In terms of social change, the trend is in the same direction as that outlined earlier. In the foreseeable future, Chinese society will continue to become more socially divided, with increasing gaps between eastern and western provinces, between rural and urban areas, and between generations, genders, and social classes. The emerging mainly urban middle classes will become more and more prominent in society and will play a key role in the future development of television for they will be some of the main consumers of the new technologies. Their disposable income, for instance, will be largely relied upon to make pay-TV commercially viable and to attract advertisers. This in turn will affect the kind of programming that the platforms carry as they seek to appeal less to the lowest common denominator and more to the aspirational values of middle-class families.

For the development of Chinese popular culture, all these factors, social and technological, point toward Chinese television becoming more internally differentiated, more personalized, and more focused on special-interest groups and individual consumers. This will also involve greater audience interactivity, often involving cross-media technologies such as telephone hotlines, SMS text message voting, and program input as well as use of the Internet.

A to Z

An Zaijiu. A Korean actor who came to fame in imported Korean dramas in the mid-2000s before going on to play in Chinese-produced television drama.

Aspirations. See *Kewang*.

Audiences. Chinese television audiences are constantly changing and evolving; however, understanding audiences is key to understanding Chinese television and its role in Chinese popular cultural production. In the 1980s, audiences expanded quickly but remained largely national in character, with CCTV the most popular and influential broadcaster, whose programming was supplemented by local television stations. In the 1990s, however, as the number of television channels multiplied, television production became ever more commercially astute and sophisticated. Technological developments transformed the way people watched television; audiences started to become more fragmented and individualized. This is a trend that has continued to the present day with the emergence of video-on-demand, mobile television, cellphone television, and greater audience participation and interactivity in programs.

Beijing Television. One of China's largest and most influential local-level television stations. Beijing Television was also responsible for China's first ever television broadcast, on May 1, 1958, making it the country's oldest television station. In the 2000s, the station has become a successful commercial operation, producing popular programming sold to other stations around the country.

Blue Life and Death Love (lanse shengsilian). An imported Korean television drama very popular with Chinese viewers in 2005.

Cable television. Introduced in towns and cities in the early 1990s, cable television transformed television viewing for millions of people around the country. In particular it ensured better reception for many and greatly increased the extent of channel choice. Due to the ban on direct-to-home satellite television reception, cable television has also been crucial for bringing provincial satellite television channels into people's homes.

Cai Lin. A Korean actor who came to fame in imported Korean dramas in the mid-2000s before going on to play in Chinese-produced television drama.

Che Renbiao. A Korean actor who came to fame in imported Korean dramas in the mid-2000s before going on to play in Chinese-produced television drama.

China Central Television (CCTV). China's national television station, based in Beijing and broadcasting sixteen channels of entertainment, news, and information programming.

Digitization. A long-term process of transferring Chinese television broadcasting from analog to digital formats. In the 1990s, SARFT laid down a national timetable for digitization that expected to see most of the large cities predominantly digital by 2008 and most of the other towns and cities by 2010. The plan is to switch off the analog signal by 2015. By 2006, China had around 4 million digital television households, much less than originally anticipated, suggesting that the whole process could take longer than originally planned. Digitization is being implemented first in cable television, second with DTH satellite television, and finally with terrestrial broadcasting.

DTH. Direct-to-home satellite television reception has been illegally adopted by several million viewers in China since the 1980s, particularly in remote parts of the country where terrestrial reception is poor. For the majority of the population, however,

DTH viewing has generally been off-limits. In late 2006, SARFT allowed DTH viewing legally for the first time. The market is expected to develop most strongly again in remote parts of the country, particularly as other forms of reception—cable, terrestrial, and broadband in particular—will offer strong competition in the cities and more developed parts of the country.

Educational television. Instructional television programming produced largely for schools and other educational institutions. Many of China's regular television stations produce or broadcast educational programs both for schools and for individual, personal education. Some of the most common and popular of these are for language learning, English in particular; however, China also has a range of specifically educational television stations and channels devoted entirely to educational broadcasting. Unlike other channels, these come under the jurisdiction of the Ministry of Education rather than SARFT.

FocusMedia. China's largest nondomestic television advertising agency in the early 2000s. The company has been largely responsible for introducing television monitors into public spaces such as lift lobbies, shopping malls, and office block foyers. Along with mobile television, this kind of advertising has seen television start to transform the experience of public space in China's large cities.

Gehua. The shortened name for Beijing Gehua CATV Network Co. Ltd., the operator of Beijing's cable television network. Gehua is a member of the Beijing Radio, Film and Television Group, which also includes Beijing Television Station and Beijing People's Radio Station. The Shanghai Stock Exchange–listed company is primarily responsible for relaying and transmitting cable television programs; constructing, developing, managing, and maintaining the Beijing cable television network; and selling advertising for satellite channels relayed through its network.

Glass Shoe (boli xie). An imported Korean television drama very popular with Chinese viewers in 2005.

Heshang. Translated as *River Elegy* or *Song of the River*, a controversial and much-discussed documentary program broadcast in 1989 on the eve of the Tiananmen Square protests and military crackdown. The program presented an account of Chinese history and culture as strongly "earthbound" (i.e., static, rooted, introverted, and difficult to change) compared to Western cultures being seafaring, open, adventurous, and experimental. The program urged greater opening-up to foreign ideas and thinking.

Hunan Satellite Television. A provincial satellite television station like others in China, but one that has helped break new ground in commercial entertainment television in the country. The station was one of the first Chinese television stations to raise money in private capital markets, floating on the Shenzhen Stock Exchange in 1999. The station has a strong focus on entertainment programming, including dramas and variety performance shows. In 2005, the station's *Pop Idol*–style reality TV show, *Supergirl's Voice*, attracted hundreds of millions of viewers around the country, for the first time attracting audiences to a provincial-level station that truly challenged, in terms of numbers of viewers, even the most popular of CCTV broadcasting.

Interactivity. An increasingly important aspect of Chinese broadcasting. Interactivity has been achieved in several ways, largely using telecommunications to enhance the standard television format. Phone-in participation has often been used in quizzes and game shows, but since 2000, the use of short messaging services (SMS) text messaging has greatly increased. The most prominent use of SMS has been in reality TV voting, but it is also used for including viewers' opinions and ideas and for competitive participation in programs. With digitization, broadband Internet, and IPTV becoming increasingly popular, interactivity is also entering a new phase of development that will see much greater interactivity through viewers' television sets or computers.

IPTV. Internet protocol television. Coming to the fore in 2005 as a new development in Chinese television, IPTV has attracted great attention in the Chinese press. IPTV is effectively television watched over a broadband Internet connection, offering video-on-demand, greater program interactivity and choice, and new viewing possibilities. In China, IPTV has been institutionally groundbreaking because it brings together telecommunications operators and broadcasters to provide both networks and content. These two areas have been deliberately kept strictly separate in China until now, to avoid fierce cross-sector competition.

Jiaodian Fangtan. Literally *Key Issue Forum*, *Jiaodian Fangtan* is one of the most popular Chinese television broadcasts. Aired every night immediately after the seven o'clock evening news (*xinwen lianbo*) on CCTV, the program offers a short investigative report on an issue of contemporary concern such as dishonest traders, the plight of laid-off workers, or differential funding of schools or hospitals. It usually deals with social issues related to China's rapidly changing society and often with the negative manifestations of economic reform. The program is not able to openly criticize government policy or leadership, but by focusing on sensitive consumer and citizenship issues it does nonetheless constitute an important critical force in China's contemporary media landscape.

Kewang. A Nanjing Television drama series, later broadcast also on CCTV, that attracted massive national audiences in 1990. The fifty-episode series dealt with the fate and fortunes of two families—one intellectual and one of regular working people—from the Cultural Revolution period into the economic reform period. The series was generally nonpolitical, dealing with love stories, rivalries, disputes, and other human elements of the relationship between the two families.

LCD television sets. Liquid crystal display televisions, along with other flat-panel technologies such as plasma, took China by storm in the mid-2000s as prices came down and the Chinese population became wealthier and conscious once again about fashion in relation to television. The boom was helped by the fact that most of the world's flat-panel televisions started being made in China by Chinese manufacturers. In 2006 alone, Chinese flat-panel television sales were around 500 million units.

Mermaid (renyu xiaojie). An imported Korean television drama very popular with Chinese viewers in 2005.

Mobile television. Identified by the Chinese television industry as one of the important developments of the future, mobile television refers to the development of television watchable on the move, usually on public transport (buses, trains, boats, planes, taxis) but also in private cars. Already deployed in many of the country's major cities, it has started changing the experience of public space and television viewing.

New Star. An influential and groundbreaking television drama series broadcast in the late 1980s. The program dealt with a young Communist Party cadre and his efforts to introduce change, often against the wishes of more conservative-minded colleagues and superiors. The series attracted very large national audiences and became a major talking point throughout the country.

Oriental Television. See *Shanghai Oriental Television.*

Phoenix Satellite Television. A Hong Kong–based satellite television station widely watched in many parts of China, though not available everywhere. The station helped establish a model of nonpolitical entertainment programming that many other Chinese satellite television stations have sought to emulate with a strong diet of dramas, soap operas, films, and variety entertainment and music shows. Phoenix was launched by a Chinese businessman, Liu Changle, in the mid-1990s in conjunction with Rupert Murdoch's Hong Kong–based Star TV. In 2006, approval was given for telecommunications operator China Mobile to buy a 20 percent share in the company, the first time that a telecommunications company had been allowed a shareholding in a television station broadcasting into China.

Reality TV. A popular television format dominating Chinese entertainment television in 2005 and 2006 but with a history dating to the late 1990s. Often emulating internationally established models of reality television like *Pop Idol*, *Survivor*, *The Apprentice*, and *Big Brother*, reality TV has spawned dozens of different kinds of programs, often adapted slightly to suit the Chinese context. These have included music and performance shows, cosmetic surgery makeovers, education shows, legal shows, outdoor survival shows, and business shows. Of these, *Supergirl's Voice* set new records in terms of audience share in 2005 and clearly established SMS text voting as a standard component of the elimination format adopted by many.

River Elegy. See *Heshang.*

SARFT. The State Administration for Radio, Film, and Television. SARFT is the government body that overseas all television broadcasting in the country. It is structured along the usual Chinese government lines of a central, national-level office and then branch offices at the different regional levels—provincial, city, and county. SARFT is responsible for formulating and implementing regulations covering most of the country's television broadcasting, production, and reception.

Satellite television. Some of the country's most popular television channels are broadcast by (mainly provincial-level) satellite television stations. Until 2006, direct-to-home satellite reception was illegal in China and most satellite television was watched through cable network relays. Some of the most innovative entertainment channels, such as Phoenix Satellite Television and Hunan Satellite Television, have been satellite channels.

Shanghai Oriental Television. Set up by Shanghai Television in the mid-1990s, Shanghai Oriental Television soon became a leading innovator in viewer-centered commercial programming. A subsidiary advertising company of Shanghai Oriental Television was also floated on the Shanghai Stock Exchange, breaking new ground in television finance. A member company of the influential Shanghai Media Group (SMG), the station is very popular with Shanghai audiences and popular to a lesser degree in other parts of the country.

Technology. Has played a crucial role in the development of television in China and will be equally important in the future. The way that cable and satellite television have been deployed in the past has fundamentally changed Chinese people's viewing habits. Technological developments, from digitization to the mobile phone and broadband Internet access, will play their part in shaping the way that people watch and engage with television in the future.

Weixing dianshi. The Chinese term for satellite television, often abbreviated as *weishi.*

Xinwen Lianbo. The early evening news program broadcast daily on CCTV at seven o'clock. From its early days, this has been one of the most watched and most important anchor programs in Chinese television's history, and even in today's much more competitive television climate it maintains very high audience share. It is the main televised news, information, and propaganda vehicle of the Chinese government and Communist Party.

Yearnings. See *Kewang.*

Youxian dianshi. The Chinese term for cable television, literally "having cable television."

Zhongyang dianshitai. The Chinese name for China Central Television, CCTV. See *China Central Television (CCTV).*

References and Further Reading

Anderson, B. 1983. *Imagined communities: Reflections on the origins and spread of nationalism.* London: Verso.

Barmé, G. 1999. *In the red: On contemporary Chinese culture.* New York: Columbia University Press.

Dai, J. 1997. "Wenhua dixingtu di qita." *Dushu,* 2: 7–12.

Dyer, R. 1991. *Only entertainment.* London: Routledge.

Fiske, J. 1987. *Television culture.* London: Routledge.

Hall, S., Critcher, C., Jefferson, T., Clarke, J., & Robert, B. 1978. "The social production of news." In *Policing the crisis: Mugging, the state and law and order.* London: Palgrave Macmillan.

Howkins, J. 1982. *Mass communication in China.* New York: Longman.

Keane, M. 1998. "Television and moral development." *Asian Studies Review,* Vol. 22, No. 4.

Li, X. 1991. "The Chinese television system and television news." *China Quarterly,* No. 126 (June 1991), 340–355.

Lull, J. 1991. *China turned on: Television, reform and resistance.* London: Routledge.

Wang, Y. 1999. "Intellectuals and popular television in China: Expectations as a cultural phenomenon." *International Journal of Cultural Studies*, Vol. 2, No. 2 (August 1999).

Zha, J. 1995. *China pop: How soap operas, tabloids and bestsellers are tranforming a culture.* New York: New Press.

Zhao, Y. 1998. *Media, market, and democracy in China: Between the party line and the bottom line.* Urbana and Chicago, IL: University of Illinois Press.

4

Radio

Over the last twenty years of the twentieth century, radio lost its dominant position in China's media landscape. Prior to the early 1980s, radio was the most important medium in China. People were more likely to listen to radio than to engage with any other mass medium (with newspapers in second place and television in third). Radio was also, for most people, their primary source of news and information. Since the 1980s, this priority has gradually reversed as television became the dominant medium, and in the early twenty-first century the relative ranking would be television, newspapers, and then radio. According to official statistics from 2004, 85.4 percent of the population were most likely to receive their news from television, 51.6 percent from newspapers, and 37.5 percent from radio.

Although the relative popularity of radio has diminished compared to television in recent years, its importance in terms of Chinese popular culture should not be underestimated. As the dominant medium up until the 1980s, radio has a historical and political significance that cannot and should not be ignored. For the first three and a half decades of Communist rule, radio was the quickest, most widespread, most important, and most direct form of mass communication between the government or Party and the Chinese people. Furthermore, in the 1980s radio was at the forefront of broadcast media commercialization, pushing ahead of television in its pace of change in relation to content and format and its relationship to its audiences.

The significance of radio as a medium in the countryside and in the poorer and more remote regions of China should also not be underestimated. China's very visible metropolitan population lives in a highly mediated world with multimedia mobile telecommunications, the Internet, dozens of television channels, multiplex cinemas, and on-tap sources of audio and video home entertainment from broadband viewing on demand to DVDs and online gaming. The vast majority of China's population, however, does not live in the cities and does not have full access to all of these forms of media and entertainment. At the beginning of the twenty-first century, even though the urban population continued to rise, China was still demographically nearly 64 percent rural. At the same time, even if there is only 37.5 percent of the population listening to radio, this is still somewhere around 500 million listeners.

The nature of radio's contribution to contemporary Chinese popular culture is also different from that of television. Due to the nature of the medium, it is listened to in quite different ways from how television is watched. One key issue, for instance, is its mobility. Whether it is received on a portable personal radio, a car radio, or coming through speakers inside a train, radio is a traveling medium that accompanies people on their journeys. For the large numbers of people in China living or working away from home, often living in dormitory or temporary accommodation, radio is also a far more practical and readily accessible medium than television.

Compared to television, radio in China, particularly in the post-Mao period, developed a more personal and interactive relationship with its audiences. For instance, many radio stations in the increasingly commercial media environment of the 1990s turned to popular phone-in programs, dealing with local, personal, and everyday life issues, as well as competitions and prizes as ways of attracting and expanding audiences.

In a similar fashion, radio has found its niche in particular as a local mass medium. Radio has found itself better situated to respond to certain localized demands and needs of audiences for news, information, and debate. These include on-the-spot, live, local news broadcasts, local sports reporting, travel news, local social news, and information about local events. Some of these, such as travel bulletins, for instance, are much better suited to radio than any other medium. Television, newspapers, and the Internet cannot compete with radio for providing information about traffic jams and road accidents. Local television news programs are also very popular with audiences, but local radio has much greater scope for extended discussion with invited experts, interactive discussion with listeners, and rapid response to breaking and rapidly changing news stories.

Having been forced to face up to competition with television, radio has therefore adapted over the last twenty years to develop its own special role in the contemporary Chinese media landscape. This has entailed finding niche audiences and social functions for itself in the gaps left vacant by television and other media. This means that radio, although less conspicuous than television, is an important feature of contemporary Chinese popular culture and should not be overlooked.

Radio and Television: Similarities and Differences

There are some broad similarities between Chinese radio and television as the two principal broadcast media in China. For instance, the relationship between radio, the Party, and the state is defined in the same way as for television. There are no private radio stations in China, and at this time private shareholding or investment in broadcasting organizations is not permitted by the Chinese authorities. The role of radio as a vehicle for the Party and government to inform the populace about policy, to mobilize public opinion and support, and to function generally as a mouthpiece for their general political purposes is defined in the same way as that of television.

Radio also experienced the same broad transition throughout the post-Mao reform period from the state-planned economy to a largely market-driven economy combining elements of both state ownership and control on one hand and commercialized market forces on the other. Like other media, including television and newspapers, radio stations increasingly had to pay their own way through advertising and sponsorship deals, which meant a radical change in mindset from the days of state-operated Maoist propaganda to those of consumer demands, audience ratings, and advertising rates.

Some of the more recent experiences of radio stations, as China's commercial media environment matures, have also led to developments in radio similar to those that are happening in television. For instance, television has seen the fragmentation of audiences and the general move toward specialized television channels of various kinds such as news channels, movie channels, and travel channels. Similarly, in recent years the leading Chinese radio stations have moved from one- or two-channel broadcasting to multiple-channel broadcasting on different frequencies, with news radio, travel radio, music radio, economic radio, sports radio, arts radio, and other special interest channels.

Although there are clearly similarities and overlaps between the operation and experiences of radio and television, there are also differences worth noting. One fundamental difference, for instance, is the general trajectory that radio and television have taken as they have negotiated the vagaries of China's emerging quasi-market economy. In the 1970s, whereas television had a high profile in the sense of being known *about*, it was watched by only a tiny proportion of the population. This then changed rapidly in the 1980s as the medium came out of effectively nowhere to become the most popular and politically significant form of mass media in the country in the space of a few years.

By contrast, radio has undergone a transition in the same period from being the dominant medium in the Mao period to being a secondary medium with a relatively low profile by the time it reached the second decade of the reform period. It has seen a shift from being the main broadcast medium, responsible for the communication of all kinds of news and information, to being a medium with a far more circumscribed sphere of operation.

In the past, radio also enjoyed a ubiquity that television even now has yet to achieve. From the 1950s onward, radio was broadcast not only over the airwaves but also via wired networks over systems of loudspeakers. This meant that radio accompanied Chinese people into every corner of their lives. Even peasants working in the fields in remote parts of rural China could find themselves planting and harvesting to the crackling sound of political speeches, news, and rousing revolutionary music. Television will never really be able to match this kind of exposure, in part at least because of the nature of the medium.

In the early twenty-first century, remnants of this era of radio dominance can still be found. The loudspeakers in the paddies are long gone, but it is still common for students to walk around campus accompanied by the tones of university or other forms of radio. Passengers on long-distance trains still awake to the stirring sounds of revolutionary marches, and although it is increasingly rare, some large state enterprises still have wired radio in the streets of their residential zones. Hence, radio has a rather different social distribution profile from television. Although it is part of private space in the domestic sphere, radio has also more commonly than television been a feature of public space and in more diverse and flexible ways.

Historical Background

In the 1920s and 1930s, numerous radio stations representing various economic and political interests were set up in China's main cities, such as Shanghai, Beijing, Tianjin, and Guangzhou. Some private stations were set up by foreign investors using foreign capital, while others were founded upon Chinese private capital. Politically motivated broadcasting stations were also set up by the various warlords and their local regimes, the Kuomintang government in Nanjing, and the invading Japanese forces during the Japanese war and period of occupation. The contemporary era of Chinese broadcasting, however, emerged from the Yan'an retreat of the CCP, with the launch of its own radio station during the war.

On December 30, 1940, Yan'an Xinhua Radio—the first CCP broadcasting enterprise and the predecessor of the Central People's Broadcasting Station (CPBS)—officially transmitted for the first time. The station used Soviet equipment powered by an ad hoc generator and was able to broadcast for only a couple of hours a day. The fragility of the outfit was clearly demonstrated when a valve blew in 1943 and could not be replaced because of the isolated location of the CCP headquarters and put the station out of action for two years.

Yan'an Xinhua Radio (also later known as Northern Shaanxi Xinhua Radio) resumed broadcasting in August 1945 and continued until March 1949 when it followed the victorious Communist Party to Beijing and started its transformation into China's national broadcaster. On October 1, 1949, the station became the Central People's Broadcasting Station (CPBS), which is still the main national radio broadcaster. Meanwhile, in 1947, the CCP had also launched its first English-language service from a small village in Hebei Province as its first attempt to bring its message to a broader, international audience.

When the communists took over China in 1949, there were forty-nine government-operated radio stations in the country, seventeen of which were newly founded. There were also thirty-three privately owned stations that were temporarily allowed to continue broadcasting under the supervision of the CCP; over the next few years, however, these private stations were gradually taken over by the government's people's radio stations. By the end of 1953, there were no longer any privately owned radio stations in operation.

In the 1950s, CPBS broadcast around fifteen to sixteen hours per day—50 percent news, 25 percent public education, and 25 percent culture and entertainment (Chang 1989: 155). This division of labor clearly indicates the priorities of the authorities at the time for public information, or propaganda, broadcasting. These priorities are also apparent from consideration of the

Chinese peasants receive a gift of radio broadcasting equipment from a group of Chinese steel workers in Chongqing, ca. 1950. Radio was to play a key role in CCP governance in the early decades of the PRC. (Corbis)

nature of broadcasting and, importantly, reception in China from the 1950s and 1960s onward.

Before the television boom of the 1980s—and even for some time following—the CCP always had a preference for radio above any other medium as a means of communicating with the people and hence explaining, promoting, and implementing government policy. Radio had distinct advantages: It was relatively easy to spread throughout the country, even into rural areas; it brought the voices of leaders directly to the population; and, unlike newspapers, it faced no barrier of high levels of illiteracy.

There was a steady growth in the number of radio stations in China through the 1950s and 1960s. By 1958, there were 97 radio stations, and by the end of 1959 there were 122 stations operating under the supervision of the Central Bureau of Broadcasting Affairs. By 1961, the Bureau was overseeing 151 stations (Chang 1989: 155). In 1965, official statistics suggested that there were around 11.5 million radio receiving sets in the country, which amounted to only 1.6 radios per 100 people; this ratio, however, needs to be considered in light of the fact that for most people, listening to radio did not involve sitting around a personal or family receiver.

Unlike today—where radio consumption is for the most part a matter of personal choice—for decades of the People's Republic period, listening to radio in China was an unavoidable feature of everyday life due to the wired networks of loudspeakers set up by the relevant level of government authorities from rural villages to large cities. In this way, the government's messages were often hard to avoid.

Wired radio networks consisted of local radio base stations, which basically received off-the-air broadcasts (often from the central level) and retransmitted them through networks of loudspeakers distributed in the streets, people's homes, factories, mines, canteens or restaurants, fields, dormitories, parks—indeed, almost any imaginable public space. The system operated in conjunction with teams of monitors selected from the local population specifically assigned the responsibility of listening to central broadcasts and reporting their content. These monitors could also be responsible for introducing speeches by key leaders or talks by top social scientists and for organizing audiences within their work units.

The strength of wired radio networks was their ability to reach into even the most remote parts of the country. They also overcame the problem of a lack of radio sets enough for all the population. As far as the Party was concerned, the system's strength was also in bringing its voice right into the countryside, where over-the-air reception could be limited and there were few resources for conventional radios. The significance of wired radio in Chinese popular culture, however, goes beyond the straightforward transmission of government news, information, and propaganda to the people. Rather, wired radio established a strong radio culture on one hand and offered opportunities for grass-roots interactivity with the media on the other. This is a feature of radio that, as we shall see, has taken on new forms in the post-Mao era.

It is easy to imagine that Chinese people would have tired of the inescapability of radio broadcasts as a result of wired radio, and for sure it was at times a strain for many; however, many people also became attached to their wired radio and started to think of it as an indispensable feature of their lives. This was not simply because of political news broadcasts but more fundamentally because of the practical informational role that it played. Wired radio was used to offer advice on agricultural issues, to give weather forecasts, and to inform workers and peasants of new quota systems, government commodity prices, and production methods. It also provided entertainment to a populace with little alternative access to music, literature, or theatre. Nonetheless, probably the feature of wired radio networks that particularly endeared them to listeners was the degree of local content based on input from workers and peasants themselves.

Apart from relaying CPBS broadcasts and leaders' speeches, wired radio networks also had daily local news bulletins of between thirty and sixty minutes in length, possibly several times a day. They would also put together their own locally produced programs on arts, music, literature, and other cultural productions. These programs would often be based upon news, information, and feedback that came from networks of part-time reporters or news-gatherers who were often peasants or workers themselves. This kind of input to the networks' broadcasting could therefore include readers' letters, feedback on programs broadcast earlier, agricultural advice, short stories or poetry, and straightforward local news stories—usually related to production in some way. These aspects of wired radio networks were therefore crucial for establishing and maintaining a sense of them being the "people's" networks, even if programs were obviously monitored closely for their political and ideological content.

Radio broadcasts of all kinds were quite widely disrupted between 1966 and 1968, during the Cultural Revolution. In the 1970s some degree of normality was returned, and the expansion of radio broadcasting recommenced. Official figures in the early 1970s claimed that wired radio networks covered as much as 98 percent of production brigades and 87 percent of production teams in the country, and by the early 1980s estimates put the number of loudspeakers throughout China at nearly 100 million.

The 1980s, however, were to start to change radio in China just as they changed other media across the country. The new decade saw radio facing commercialization, market competition, and a new level of rivalry from television and other media that had not existed before.

Commercialization and Cross-Media Competition

The 1980s brought a marked change of direction in the popularity, importance, and production style of Chinese radio, particularly at the local level in the larger metropolises. In 1983, the Party started discreetly suggesting within the profession that all broadcasters—television and radio—should, if they were not doing so already, start considering alternative sources of revenue to the government subsidies that they had always enjoyed and operated on. Toward the end of the decade this had become explicit Party policy, and radio stations, as well as television stations, had to rely to a greater or lesser extent on ways of raising money to stay on the air. In short, this meant introducing or increasing advertising revenue, which in turn meant reappraising radio's position in the overall Chinese media marketplace.

This reappraisal started taking shape in the mid- to late 1980s but became ever more pressing in the 1990s as television not only stabilized its dominant position in China's mediascape but branched out with new technological developments such as cable and satellite broadcasting. The basic imperatives facing radio stations at this time were

- to develop or re-establish close relationships with their audiences;
- to negotiate and redefine their territory, as their once-dominant role was rapidly appropriated by television; and
- to attract advertisers and sponsors.

For some years, particularly in the early to mid-1980s, radio retained its strong presence in rural areas, because many peasants had little money and had to save for some time to buy expensive television sets. This meant that radio clung more tenaciously to its traditional position in the poorer parts of China where television took slightly longer to take hold. That is not to say that radio disappeared from the urban popular cultural landscape, but it did have to rediscover its strengths and weaknesses and turn them into new, market-driven

Pearl River Economic Radio

PRER was launched by Guangdong People's Radio on December 15, 1986, as a direct result of intense competition from Hong Kong broadcasters. In the more relaxed political environment of the 1980s under economic reform, people in Guangdong Province started watching television from neighboring Hong Kong and listening to Hong Kong radio, even though strictly speaking it was still illegal. Hong Kong radio stations, which generally broadcast in Cantonese, offered listeners in Cantonese-speaking Guangdong lively program formats and content in a familiar cultural idiom that made their own state broadcasters seem stilted and dull by comparison.

In terms of program formats, for instance, Hong Kong radio variously offered round-the-clock music broadcasting, current affairs and lifestyle phone-ins, listener competitions, relaxed and informal presentational styles, and live news reporting. In terms of content, it also offered the latest Hong Kong and Taiwanese pop music as well as a high proportion of lifestyle-oriented programming dealing with food, entertainment, entertainment industry gossip, health issues, family issues, and personal relationships (Zhao 1998: 96–97).

Guangdong Radio already had a Cantonese-language channel, but it could not compete in its existing format with the more exciting and enticing broadcasting coming from Hong Kong. As a result, the station saw its audience share throughout the Pearl River Delta slipping rapidly. The station therefore applied for permission to re-launch its Cantonese-language channel as PRER, adopting the livelier and more relaxed formats of Hong Kong radio and reinventing its content to appeal to emerging audience tastes. As far as mainland Chinese broadcasting was concerned, PRER was a groundbreaker, and it proved an enormous success with local listeners in Guangdong.

Its pioneering format emulated the style of Hong Kong broadcasters but also had the advantage of offering local news, travel, and other information of greater immediate relevance to their listeners than that on Hong Kong radio. The new PRER style was above all listener-focused and listener-friendly. It aimed at broadcasting what audiences wanted, not just what the government decreed (Zhao 1998: 96).

Although PRER was born out of a very particular situation relating to Hong Kong competition for Guangdong listeners, the success of the new channel held up an example to other mainland broadcasters of how to attract audiences. Indeed, radio stations across the country subsequently copied many of PRER's ideas and innovations.

strategies. In this area, Pearl River Economic Radio, launched in Guangdong Province in 1986, was to become a nationally emulated model of broadcasting reform.

Guangdong Province in southern China was at the forefront of economic reform from the beginning of the 1980s, and it has often found itself also at the forefront of media reform in the country (see Vogel 1989). The province has always had greater exposure to foreign media, particularly from Hong Kong, than other parts of China, and the launch of Pearl River Economic Radio (PRER) came as a direct result of that exposure. The channel was in the vanguard of media reform that came from professionals in the industry. It introduced livelier formats and content that was depoliticized and had greater immediate relevance to Guangdong people's everyday lives. The channel also clearly showed to other Chinese broadcasters the commercial potential for depoliticized media production and is an example of how the market and competition has changed Chinese media over the last two decades.

Radio Commercialization and the Broadcasting Divide

By the early 2000s, running radio stations as commercial enterprises, though retaining their political and propaganda obligations, had become standard practice throughout China, although to a more advanced degree in the larger cities and more economically developed parts of eastern China. Advertising and sponsorship had become a fundamental aspect of broadcasting, and much of what radio stations did was driven directly or indirectly by audience figures. This included the diversification of programming and the development of special-interest broadcasting (see below). The commercialization of radio has also created a growing gap between the more successful and wealthier radio stations and their poorer contemporaries.

Radio stations throughout the country have experimented over the last two decades with different forms of advertising and sponsorship collaboration. These include

- the straightforward selling of advertising slots within or between programs;
- the selling of sponsorship for particular programs;
- "infomercials" or indirectly contracting out airtime and content to different organizations; and
- selling editorial involvement to companies and government departments.

For instance, some radio stations have invited senior executives from local companies or heads of government departments to supply content on a regular basis for a fee or to have a place on a specially formed editorial board for particular programs or sections of programming. Companies also sponsor regular programs, listener competitions, and other promotions. In effect, through commercialization in these various ways, radio stations have developed much closer relationships with advertising companies—often subsidiary companies of broadcasting organizations—and advertisers.

For the commercially successful radio stations, this has meant a massive boost in revenues and complete financial independence from government. Radio stations still receive government subsidies, but the relative size and importance of the subsidy has decreased steadily for many stations, particularly in eastern China. Even in the early 1990s, self-generated income at successful stations was likely to equal ten or twenty times income from government subsidies. Ten years later, for some this could now have multiplied several times over (Zhao 1998: 68).

In 2005, the top six radio stations by advertising revenue—Beijing Radio, Guangdong Radio, Shanghai Radio, Shenzhen Radio, Zhejiang Radio, and Tianjin Radio—all reported advertising income in excess of Rmb100 million (approximately US$14 million). Beijing Radio topped the list, with advertising revenues of nearly Rmb300 million (US$42 million). For the Central People's Broadcasting Station (see below), the main national broadcaster, the figure is a relatively modest Rmb100 million. At the same time, however, a large gap had opened up between these top-earning radio stations and their poorer counterparts in other parts of the country. Provincial-level stations in the poorer parts of western China had advertising revenues in the same year of less than 1 percent those of Beijing Radio.

Such differences in wealth and income obviously have consequences for the kind of service being offered by the stations. They have also had significant effects on rural broadcasting services. Since the introduction of market competition to the radio sector, government subsidies have declined. This has had a greater effect on radio stations and broadcasting authorities in the poorer parts of China, which have not enjoyed massively inflated advertising revenues. As a result, investment in maintaining broadcasting infrastructure in these parts of China has suffered.

Particularly hard-hit have been wired-radio networks in rural areas, many of which have closed down completely. The spread of television has not helped matters. As television has become the principal source of news, information, and entertainment throughout the country, full radio coverage has become a lower priority for the Chinese authorities than it once was. By the late 1990s, in fact, most wired radio networks in the country had been taken out of service. In poorer and more remote parts of China where it is not possible to receive terrestrial television broadcasts, some villages relied entirely on their wired radio networks, and when these closed down, they were left less connected and informed even than in the pre-reform era.

Radio Stations

Radio stations in China, like television stations, are organized according to the four-layer structure of government (national, provincial, municipal, and local). Their broadcasting is also overseen by branch offices of the State Administration for Radio Film and Television (SARFT) at the appropriate level. In 2001, there were 301 radio stations in all, including 2 national-level stations and 34 provincial-level stations.

The two national-level stations are the Central People's Broadcasting Station (CPBS) and China Radio International (CRI), both of which come directly under SARFT supervision and are also constituent members of the China Radio, Film, and Television Group set up in 2003, which includes among its members also China Central Television (CCTV) and the China Film Corporation.

Central People's Broadcasting Station

CPBS remains the main central government propaganda station and along with CCTV and CRI comes under the editorial board of SARFT. CPBS in 2006 broadcast on eight channels and had a comprehensive news Web site (www.cnradio.com) with national, international, and categorized news stories. The eight radio channels were as follows:

CPBS-1: the main news-focused Mandarin channel, broadcast nationally

CPBS-2: "The Voice of the Economy," a mixed channel focusing on economic, science and technology, and lifestyle news, broadcast nationally in Mandarin

CPBS-3: "The Voice of Music," a national music channel

CPBS-4: "The Voice of the Capital," featuring programming centered around life in Beijing

China Radio International

In 2006, CRI was principally the Chinese equivalent of the Voice of America or the BBC World Service, and it broadcast around 220 hours of programming every day in forty-three different languages. About two-thirds of this programming was in English. Like CPBS, CRI has therefore also been heavily government- and propaganda-focused; however, its principal target audiences are foreigners overseas, rather than Chinese either at home or abroad. That said, the CRI English-language service does also operate a domestic service, broadcasting mainly music to major cities throughout the country.

In keeping with this range of responsibilities, CRI airs a broad mix of Chinese and international news and current affairs, Chinese cultural and arts programming, and Chinese government policy and opinion as well as music, sports, entertainment, business, science, and technology programming. The station, whose main broadcasting is on short-wave, also has a number of agreements with broadcasters around the world to relay programs locally on FM and AM frequencies.

CRI also has a comprehensive multilingual Web site offering news, cultural information, and transcripts of CRI programs and reports as well as practical information about frequencies, schedules, reception, and other station details.

Although CRI is a radio station principally aimed at overseas and foreign listeners, it has its own significant place in contemporary Chinese popular culture. There are two aspects to this. First of all, as the radio station is one of the key voices of the Chinese government overseas, it plays an important role in defining what Chinese culture is or at least what the mainland authorities would like it to be. Second, the radio station also claims millions of listeners for its domestic service. Many of these are young people wanting to learn or improve their English—and English learning should not be overlooked as a feature of contemporary Chinese popular culture. The domestic service also plays a lot of music, both Chinese and foreign, and this also attracts young people.

CPBS-5 and CPBS-6: featuring programming aimed at Taiwan

CPBS-7: "The Voice of China," a channel broadcasting to Hong Kong, Macao, and the Pearl River Delta in southern China

CPBS-8: Minority nationalities radio, featuring programming in five national minority languages

CPBS, as the national radio broadcaster, has unrivaled status in China. However, that does not necessarily mean that it is the most popular radio station. In fact, the range of channels makes evident the government and propaganda-oriented nature of the station's programming. The CPBS early morning news program, broadcast nationally from 6:30 to 7:00 and carried on other networks around the country, has an iconic status somewhat like the 7.00 evening news on CCTV; apart from this, though, many listeners prefer the easier and more lively listening offered by more locally and regionally based radio stations.

Provincial-, Municipal-, and Local-Level Stations

In general, the effects of commercialization have been felt more strongly at the lower levels of radio broadcasting than at the national level. CPBS competes with regional and local radio stations throughout the country, but it is the only domestically focused national-level broadcaster. It therefore has no direct competitors. That is not to underestimate the stiff competition faced in some areas where local stations are particularly strong. However, the rivalry between CPBS and local stations is of a different order from that between local stations. CPBS, as the national government broadcaster, on one hand does not face financial hardship and yet on the other hand has its political and propaganda responsibilities more strictly dictated.

At the lower levels of the radio hierarchy, competition can be intense. This is competition not only with other radio stations but with other media—television, newspapers, and the Internet in particular. The key to competition for many lower-level radio stations is exploiting their proximity to their audiences. This can be either in the sense that radio can follow people around closely in their daily lives—whether via car radios, portable radios, Walkman devices, or wired radio—or in the sense that being locally based, they can be quick to report local issues and events and establish a presence in the communities they serve. Nonetheless, what a radio station can achieve also depends importantly on the funds it has at its disposal.

Smaller and poorer lower-level stations—from provincial to county level—have had far less opportunity to innovate, experiment with new formats and content, or invest in new broadcasting technologies. There are still areas in which they can compete and find their own niche, however, most notably in terms of local news reporting and travel news for drivers. Local radio journalists can often arrive more quickly on the scene of a breaking story than their television rivals and with the aid of a simple mobile phone can report direct from the scene within minutes. Local people will also often call in to their local radio station with news items, issues of social concern, information about local events, and other matters of interest to local people. In this way, local radio stations, particularly municipal and county-level stations but also to some degree provincial stations, have continued to exploit their close relationships with the local community established in the time of wired radio.

The larger and wealthier stations like Beijing Radio and Guangdong Radio have gone much further in seeking to change the nature of Chinese radio broadcasting in recent years. A good example, as well as PRER, is Shanghai Oriental Radio (SOR—also known as Shanghai East Radio).

Shanghai Oriental Radio

Shanghai Oriental Radio (SOR) (*shanghai dongfang guangbo diantai*) was launched in 1992 in the newly developed Pudong business district of Shanghai along with Shanghai Oriental Television, under the supervision of the Shanghai Radio and Television Bureau. The station is a good indication of likely future trends in Chinese radio. Like PRER, it was launched with strong commercial and competitive motives, being completely financially independent and forced to pay its own way. Also like PRER, the station therefore aimed to get closer to its audience with livelier, friendlier, and more personal program formats and content.

Institutionally, SOR is different from PRER in that it was set up to compete directly with Shanghai People's Radio, breaking the general rule at the time that one administrative district should have just one radio station. PRER, by contrast, was one channel under Guangdong People's Radio, not an organizationally separate institution.

In the early days, the station rapidly earned a reputation for being innovative, forward-looking, and audience-centered. In particular it became well known for its radio phone-in and talk-show programs offering advice, discussion, and opinion on a broad range of issues. Its news reporting was immediately seen by local people as quicker, slicker, and more akin to Western news reporting than the traditional Chinese bulletin heavily influenced by government business. SOR was also one of the first Chinese radio stations to introduce 24-hour broadcasting, aiming at a new audience of sleepless listeners. Up until 2002, the station broadcast two channels: an AM channel concentrating on news, current affairs, and general interest issues, including many of its phone-in programs; and an FM channel focusing on music. In 2002, the Shanghai Radio and Television Bureau redistributed local frequencies, giving SOR extra channels. This enabled the station to divide up its content in a more focused manner. Subsequently, the station operated five channels—two on AM and FM and three other FM channels:

- News 104.5
- City 792, the general interest channel
- Pop Music, on FM101.7
- The classical music channel, on FM103.7
- The Economic Channel, on FM97.7

The Economic Channel incorporates the Voice of Pujiang, an older radio station launched in 1988 and revamped in 2002. With target audiences particularly in Taiwan, the station has a four-hour evening slot on FM97.7.

The effect of SOR on the Shanghai broadcasting scene was almost immediate. Within months, Shanghai People's Radio had changed its news programs to emulate the SOR style; after that it launched new programs intended to compete directly with SOR favorites. SOR was an immediate success with audiences and a major stimulus for the transformation of both local and national media.

Programs

Radio Programming in the Mao Period

Chinese radio programs cover a broad range of formats and content. Historically, the center of gravity of radio broadcasting has been in news and information broadcasting because of the relationship to government and the Party. In the Mao era, there were also music, arts, and literature programs, but they accounted for a relatively small proportion of overall programming and were considered as supplementary to the core informational content. In the Mao era, radio was also seen as having a strong educational role, which, when it came to political education, clearly also overlapped with its informational and propaganda roles.

The main news programming was heavily centralized, with local stations required to rebroadcast programs from CPBS and to read out speeches from Party leaders or important editorials from the *People's Daily* (see Chapter 5). National and international news was all collated and compiled at the center. Local radio stations, however, including the wired-radio operators, also produced local news programming. To some degree this was also driven by central agendas, even if the actual news was local. For instance, during any national mass-mobilization campaign aimed at implementing government policy (such as collectivization, productivity drives, or political or thought education) the local news agenda would include the latest steps and achievements of local work units, production brigades, or production teams toward meeting those ends.

At this time, most news was related in some way to politics, the economy, and production; hence local news would report the meeting or setting of production targets, political meetings, and commodity prices. Particularly in rural areas, there would also be a good deal of airtime dedicated to new agricultural production and farming methods or techniques such as in planting, seed selection, harvesting, and animal husbandry; if appropriate, depending on the area, this could also extend to forestry, fisheries, hunting, and other rural activities.

Much entertainment programming consisted of music; however, which music and how much of it varied according to the political climate. To provide the most severe example, the only music heard during the Cultural Revolution period would have been from the eight model operas (see Chapter 13). At other times, also allowable was Chinese classical music or other revolutionary and military songs. Specially selected folk songs, which being seen as a voice of the peasantry have a special place in CCP history (see Chapter 14), were also often broadcast.

Post-Mao Programming

In the late 1970s and 1980s, restrictions on radio content were gradually lifted as the more relaxed attitude of the post-Mao reform period took hold. The directly political, propaganda, economic, and production-oriented programming decreased, and entertainment programming, particularly music, increased at this time.

In the 1980s, CPBS programming on its main national channels was roughly 15 percent news, 60 percent entertainment, 20 percent features, and 5 percent advertising, trailers, announcements, and so on (Chang 1989: 170). Entertainment covered a wide variety of programming including music, drama, traditional theatre, literature, and the arts, while features were broadly educational programs covering science, history, health, sports, language-learning, or agriculture. Much of this programming would not have been out of place on lower-level radio stations in the 1980s, although the further down the hierarchy the more local and less ambitious the content became. Such programming also continues to the present day. As the 1990s approached and market forces and the commercialization of broadcasting started becoming a lived reality for broadcasters, new programming formats and content emerged, particularly from the innovative and groundbreaking stations like PRER and SOR.

This started with fairly simple innovations like pop music request shows, which were new to China at the time. Hong Kong and Taiwanese pop music had not been allowed in China under Mao but rapidly became a part of everyday popular culture in the 1980s. Homemade pop stars like singer Cui Jian (see Chapter 14) also became household names. This created a new pop music market in terms of sales of records and cassettes but also in terms of popular listening on radio. Although music had constituted a significant proportion of broadcasting in the later Mao period and the early 1980s, it was based upon a fairly stolid diet of revolutionary, classical, and folk music.

Some of the really substantive changes to radio programming came with highly innovative programming for China, such as radio hotline phone-in programs, interactive talk shows, and listener competitions. Some SOR news programs also included live calls from selected listeners as a regular part of the format. PRER introduced phone-ins in response to their popularity with Guangdong listeners used to Hong Kong stations, and SOR took this a step further, making them virtually the station trademark in the 1990s. They have since been adopted by other radio stations throughout the country and remain a highly popular form of programming to the present day.

Phone-ins cover a wide range of topics and issues—town-planning, transport, education, health, show business, music, public utilities, consumer issues, marriage guidance, family planning, sexual health, relationship advice, and so on. These programs broke the mold of top-down broadcasting and offered a kind of personal immediacy and interactivity, real or apparent, that television could not match. Phone-ins have been and are sometimes broadcast live, although stations have also at times been ordered to work from recordings and to vet callers before putting them live on air. Nonetheless, phone-ins have on different occasions given listeners the opportunity to air grievances, vent disappointments, and make criticisms of the authorities within the limits acceptable to the CCP. It should also be noted, however, that the most popular phone-ins are not particularly politically sensitive and are more likely to deal with personal issues such as sexuality, marriage problems, or health.

Phone-ins and other forms of interactive programming that have turned radio into a public forum for discussion, debate, criticism, and comment have been seen by some commentators as signs of an emerging public sphere—a realm of social debate and critique relatively independent of the state (see Chapter 1)—or as steps toward greater freedom of speech and Western-style democracy. The importance of such programming in this regard should not be underestimated in China, where for decades the concept of ordinary listeners speaking their mind live, uncensored, and uncontrolled over the radio would have been unimaginable. Indeed, this is one area in which radio has been at the forefront of changing the acceptable limits of Chinese media practice and the ground rules of public cultural interaction. Nonetheless, real limits to what the Party will accept still exist, and these phone-ins have to be understood also in terms of how they may control public debate and criticism as much as enable it.

At SOR, these Party limits were occasionally pushed as far as they would go. In the early 1990s, phone-ins became a vehicle for almost direct and immediate complaint that could sidestep layers of time-consuming and obstructive bureaucracy. The knowledge that millions of local people could be listening to complaints about large companies or organizations at times proved a remarkable stimulus for corrective action. Within the radio station's first year, it was ordered by the authorities to stop broadcasting phone-ins live, and it switched instead to a system whereby listeners could call in at any time during the day and have their comments recorded and considered for use in the program. At the same time, this gave the radio station the chance to get a response from the relevant organizations to the complaints made (see Erwin 2000 for more details).

Such restrictions clearly changed the nature of the programs entirely and removed their potentially critical edge; however, even with live phone-ins there are ways in which they can be used to reinforce Party ideology as much as, if not more than, question it. For example, phone-ins often involve a resident or visiting expert in the studio whom listeners ask for advice on the topic of the day. Such experts, however, are often Party appointees or civil servants who have a vested interest in reiterating government positions. Indeed, it can be argued that the apparent openness of a phone-in situation only adds weight to the Party-approved messages, which the programs end up being the vehicles to convey (Erwin 2000; cf. Zhao 1998: 98). For this reason it is too simplistic to equate this newly found voice of the people with straightforward democratization.

Channel Specialization

In the early twenty-first century, an important trend in the organization of radio programming has been the movement toward specialized channels. The trend is important because, as with television, it indicates the emergence of a far more fragmented and divided audience than used to exist. It also means that at a glance, a broadcast schedule for radio stations in the 1980s can look quite different from those of the early 2000s.

In the 1980s and into the 1990s, radio channels still often had generally defined responsibilities to provide news, information, education, entertainment, and other broadcasting, all on one or two channels. This was still the case in many parts of China in 2004. Particularly at the larger, more successful radio stations like Beijing Radio, Shanghai People's Radio, SOR, and Guangdong Radio, however, the trend was toward more focused channels. These would commonly be news channels, lifestyle and general-interest channels, economic or business channels, popular and classical music channels, youth channels, travel channels, sports channels, educational channels, and arts channels.

Channel specialization has broadened the choice of programming available to listeners and made it easier for them to select more precisely which programs they want to hear and also to avoid programs that do not interest them. This is increasingly important in a maturing commercial and competitive environment, as there are now always alternative entertainment, information, and listening options available. At the same time, it presents broadly preselected audiences to advertisers. For instance, sports-channel listeners will be more likely customers for sports-related products than classical-music-channel listeners, and the latter are more likely to be good customers for compact discs or other musical goods.

Radio Audiences

As radio and Chinese society have changed over the years, clearly the audience has changed with them. In the Mao period, the Chinese radio audience comprised the vast majority of the population. As we have seen, however, over the twenty years of the post-Mao period, many people have turned their attention to television, and radio audiences have gone into decline. Just over one-third of the population listened to radio on a regular basis in 2004, compared to 80 to 90 percent of the population regularly watching television. Nonetheless, radio still maintains its appeal for many listeners. Audience surveys have also revealed that as well as the predictable attractions of news, information, and entertainment that radio offers, many listeners' key reasons for liking radio included also its companionship and its interactivity. These are characteristics of radio that the other main media—television and newspapers—cannot provide in the same way.

In the Mao period, radio covered the whole spectrum of society, and of course radio audiences are still comprised of people from all around the country and from all sectors of society. One of the key differences in radio audiences between the Mao period or the early 1980s and the early 2000s, however, is that in the early 2000s, key audience groups had become more specifically identifiable. For instance, key listeners of many radio stations, particularly those in the cities, are drivers of different kinds—taxi drivers, bus drivers, official or company chauffeurs—who spend

Taxis waiting along a busy street in Shanghai, China. Taxi drivers are some of China's keenest radio listeners. Not only does it help pass the time while in their cars, but radio also provides useful travel and traffic information. (iStockPhoto.com)

long hours in their cars with little distraction but to listen to the radio; they also listen to the radio specifically for traffic reports and travel news. The recognized importance of drivers as listeners is indicated by the fact that stations as large as SOR or Beijing Radio have dedicated travel and transport channels.

Other key listeners are music fans of different kinds, as radio offers the latest popular music for free as well as news and information about new music releases, concerts, books, and videos, industry gossip, and other related issues. Radio holds a similar attraction for classical Chinese or foreign music fans. This reminds us of the effects of channel specialization that has taken place in recent years and how that has changed audiences and their listening habits. With specialized channels, including some very popular music channels, it is that much easier for audiences to tune in to gratify their specific interests. No longer are music or sports programs, for example, obscured amid large quantities of other programming; audiences can tune in to a music or sports program at virtually any time of the day.

Students and young people are also key listeners in the cities, and audience surveys in the early 2000s suggested that radio audiences were getting younger, even though with new technologies including the Internet, online gaming, television, and broadband to contend with, there is a lot of competition for their attention. However, young people and students still generally remain among the poorer members of society and may often live in dormitory accommodation where television and other media may not be available. Young people also demonstrate a clear enthusiasm for music programs and have an inquisitiveness and adolescent curiosity for the kinds of lifestyle discoveries that advice hotlines and phone-ins, for instance, can often offer.

Other key listeners in the cities include travelers, migrant workers, and others living in dormitory, shared, or confined accommodation. In the countryside, local radio in particular is still popular with many peasants, even if they have access to television, for the advice and information it offers on the weather as well as agricultural, forestry, fishing, and other rural issues.

The Future of Radio

As with television, some key factors affecting the future of radio are closely related to the development of new technologies. These can bring both challenges and opportunities. For instance, trials of digital audio broadcasting (DAB, or digital radio) were launched in the late 1990s in a number of selected towns and cities. Foshan Radio in Guangdong Province, for instance, sent technicians to work with the BBC in the United Kingdom and learn more about the use and implementation of the technologies from the U.K. experience. They started digital broadcasts in 1997 as one of the first DAB pilot projects in the country.

DAB has the potential to revolutionize radio in China, as elsewhere. It could see a massive proliferation of channels, including more and more specialized channels, much better sound quality, and better interconnectivity with other new digital technologies such as cable television, both narrowband and broadband Internet access, and digital satellite broadcasting. Indeed, such new ways of receiving radio are likely to be important in the development of the medium in China, as in the short-to-medium term there is likely to be little interest or enthusiasm for buying an expensive digital receiver if an old analog receiver works perfectly well. Most consumers would welcome finding extra radio channels available on their computer or cable television as a bonus. Indeed, radio stations offer online broadcasts or downloads of key programs, such as news bulletins, to people with computers or MP3 players.

Nonetheless, the same technologies that present new opportunities also represent growing competition for radio. For instance, with fast-growing use of the Internet and its increasing popularity as a source of news and information, it is likely to pose an ever greater challenge to radio in the future. Radio stations have risen to this challenge, however, and are increasingly incorporating the Internet into their broadcasting activities. Large and wealthy radio stations operate sophisticated portal-style Web sites with comprehensive news coverage as well as station information. They also increasingly make their programs available online.

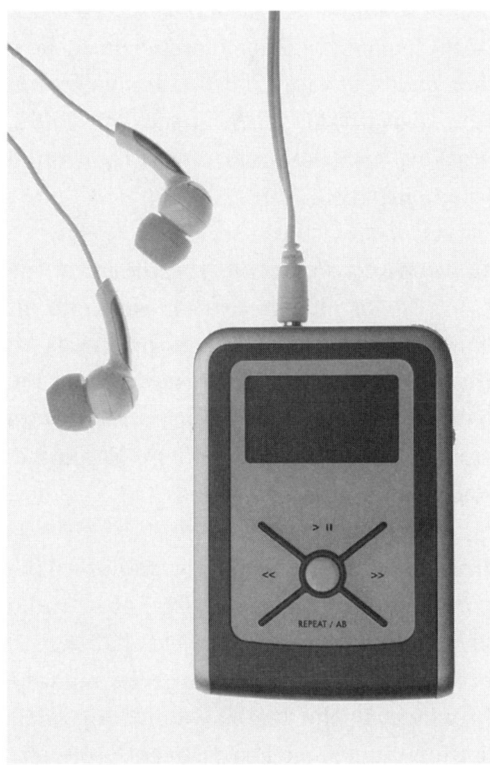

The introduction of MP3 players has presented competition for radio by offering online broadcasts or downloads of popular programs. (iStockPhoto.com)

That radio has a future in China is not in doubt, yet success in radio broadcasting is going to be increasingly dependent on the ability to work with new technologies, to change formats and content along with consumer trends and customer demands, and to continue to seek out and exploit areas of broadcasting where radio has a natural advantage over other media. These challenges are also some of the main forces that have shaped the heart of radio's unique contribution to contemporary Chinese popular culture.

A to Z

Advertising. As radio stations have moved from their broadly propaganda-defined roles to becoming commercially viable and even profitable, advertising has become the principal source of revenue for many radio stations.

Beijing City Management Radio. A specialized channel set up in 2005, devoted to news and information related to building projects, transport, city planning, and management in the capital. Although essentially a public information channel, it has been set up and run with the awareness that to make it effective in that role it will also need to be popular, be close to people's lives, expectations, and experiences, and not take a lecturing stance.

CPBS. The Central People's Broadcasting Station is China's radio equivalent of CCTV, the main national television broadcaster. The station operates eight channels with different specializations and different target audiences (see text).

CRI. China Radio International is China's equivalent of the Voice of America or the BBC World Service. Although about two-thirds of the programming is in English, the station broadcasts in more than forty languages. Broadcasting mainly on shortwave, CRI airs a broad mix of Chinese and international news and current affairs, Chinese cultural and arts programming, and Chinese government policy and opinion as well as music, sports, entertainment, business, and science and technology programming.

DAB. Digital audio broadcasting is at the forefront of technological change in Chinese radio. After initial trials run in the late 1990s, radio stations have gradually increased their DAB service provision. The technology will enable a massive proliferation of channels, much better sound quality, and better interconnectivity with other new digital technologies.

Diversification. At the heart of the reform and transformation of Chinese radio in the 2000s, diversification includes the development of cross-media platforms, including with newspapers and magazines, as well as developing new opportunities with advertising, music production or distribution, publishing, e-commerce, SMS content services, IPTV, and online gaming. Diversification principally aims to find other sources of revenue, develop a stronger brand presence in broader markets, and raise funds for investment.

Economic radio. The name used by many of the more innovative, experimental and commercially oriented radio stations set up in the economic reform era, particularly from the 1990s onward. Many of these have directly or indirectly followed the model laid down by Pearl River Economic Radio.

Foshan Radio. Although a relatively small and little-known local radio station outside of its immediate Guangdong vicinity, Foshan Radio was the first Chinese radio station to run DAB trials in the late 1990s, working in collaboration with the United Kingdom's BBC.

Guangdong Province. Has been at the forefront of change in Chinese radio, at least in part because of its proximity to Hong Kong, which stimulated the establishment of innovative commercial radio stations such as Pearl River Economic Radio in the 1980s.

Hong Kong radio. Indirectly stimulated the commercialization of Chinese radio through its influence upon and challenge to broadcasters in neighboring Guangdong Province. In the 1980s, Guangdong radio stations, such as Pearl River Economic Radio, largely emulated Hong Kong radio styles and formats as a starting point for developing more popular, audience-centered commercial radio.

Interactivity. As part of their moves toward more popular radio programming that is close to the people, many Chinese radio stations have introduced forms of interactivity, from phone-ins to SMS text messaging. At the heart of the strategy is the effort to make audiences feel more involved with their radio stations.

IPTV. Internet protocol television is an example of radio diversification. In 2005, Beijing Radio linked up with the capital's telecommunications operator Beijing Netcom to move into this new broadband Internet broadcasting format.

Local news and information. These have become the strengths of many Chinese radio stations in an increasingly competitive media market. Radio journalists often have a degree of operational flexibility that can help them be first to report local news items. Radio stations also draw upon strong networks of local knowledge and contacts.

Music. Has been an important part of Chinese broadcasting since its early days. In the post-Mao era, it has often been the ability of radio stations to keep up with popular music fashions that have enabled them to survive or thrive. Pop music is an important part of most radio stations' broadcasting.

New technologies. As with television, new technologies hold some of the important keys to the future of radio, with digital broadcasting, convergence with computer and telephone networks through the Internet, and portable music devices from laptops to MP3 players. As television becomes ever more mobile, however, the traditional competitive feature of radio—its ease of access almost anywhere—may come under threat.

Online broadcasting. Many of the more successful Chinese radio stations offer online broadcasting options or program downloads. As broadband Internet use becomes ever more popular this will become an increasingly important form of radio broadcasting and reception in China.

Pearl River Economic Radio. PRER was one of the first Chinese radio stations to experiment with new program styles and formats in the late 1980s.

Phone-ins. A common and popular feature of post-Mao radio, particularly from the 1990s onward. The format encourages a sense of radio programs being inclusive, being close to the people, and dealing with real people's problems and opinions. Some of the most popular programs deal with personal relationships.

SARFT. The State Administration for Radio, Film, and Television. SARFT is the government body that oversees all radio broadcasting in the country. It is structured along the usual Chinese government lines of a central, national-level office and then branch offices at the different regional levels—provincial, city, and county. SARFT is responsible for formulating and implementing regulations covering most of the country's radio broadcasting, production, and reception.

Shanghai Oriental Radio. One of Shanghai's most innovative and popular radio stations which has been at the forefront of the transformation of radio broadcasting in the city from the early 1990s onward.

The station offers a range of phone-ins, news, music, and information programming.

Specialization. With increasing competition and movements toward more radio channels, specialization is an increasingly important feature of contemporary radio. There are already specialized radio channels for different kinds of music, news and information, economics and business, travel, and much more. With digitization, there will be even more specialized channels in the future.

Taxi drivers. Some of China's keenest radio listeners. Not only does it help pass the time while in their cars, radio provides useful travel and traffic information. Many radio stations, keenly aware of this niche audience, target their travel channels largely at taxi drivers and offer taxi-oriented programming and news.

Wired radio. One of the most important media in China in the 1950s, 1960s, and 1970s. Before people had television, radio was one of the most important sources of news and information for the whole country. Wired radio, carried on a network of loudspeakers located in people's homes, the streets, shops, offices, and even the fields, was one of the most common and popular ways of listening to radio. It also often had a very local character, with locally produced and targeted programs. By the late 1990s, most wired radio networks in the country had been taken out of service.

Yan'an Xinhua Radio. Later known as Northern Shaanxi Xinhua Radio, Yan'an Xinhua Radio was the predecessor of the Central People's Broadcasting Station. It was the main Communist broadcaster operating from Mao's wartime base in Yan'an, Shaanxi Province. On October 1, 1949, the station became the Central People's Broadcasting Station (CPBS).

References and Further Reading

Bishop, R. L. 1989. *Qi Lai! Mobilizing one billion Chinese: The Chinese communication system.* Ames, IA: Iowa State University Press.

Chang, W. H. 1989. *Mass media in China: The history and the future.* Ames, IA: Iowa State University Press.

Erwin, K. 2000. "Heart-to-heart, phone-to-phone: Family values, sexuality, and the politics of Shanghai's advice hotlines." In D. S. Davis (ed.) *The consumer revolution in urban China.* Berkeley, CA: University of California Press.

Howkins, J. 1982. *Mass communication in China.* New York: Longman.

Lynch, D. M. 1999. *After the propaganda state: Media, politics, and "thought work" in reformed China.* Stanford, CA: Stanford University Press.

Vogel, E. 1989. *One step ahead in China: Guangdong under reform.* Cambridge, MA: Harvard University Press.

Zhao, Y. 1998. *Media, market, and democracy in China: Between the party line and the bottom line.* Urbana and Chicago, IL: University of Illinois Press.

5

Newspapers

China is a country of avid newspaper readers, and newspapers are a fundamental feature of contemporary Chinese popular culture. In 2005, there were 1,931 different newspaper titles published in China, with a total of 41.26 billion copies printed throughout the year with a total sale value of Rmb26.1 billion (around US$3.3 billion). This means that in that year, China produced around 116 million copies of newspapers every day, or one newspaper per twelve Chinese people per day. Consumer surveys in the early 2000s showed that around 50 percent of the population read a newspaper on a regular basis, and newspapers generally ranked second only to television as people's main source of news.

Certainly, one of the main reasons for buying or reading a newspaper is to keep up-to-date with the latest news. However, the significance of newspapers for understanding contemporary Chinese popular culture extends beyond their role as providers of news and information. They also play an important articulatory role in relation to other media and other popular cultural activities from television, radio, cinema, and the arts to consumerism, music, show business, and sports. Newspapers are important multipurpose cultural artifacts in contemporary Chinese society. They not only report on the everyday life of Chinese people but facilitate it, contribute to it, and help constitute it in ways that make them much more than simply pieces of printed paper or sources of news. Newspapers have a real social existence of their own, in the sense that they enter into and play a key part in people's social relationships. Hence, in addition to reporting news, newspapers also

- contribute to making the political system work;
- play a propaganda role for the government;
- stimulate and participate in debate on social issues such as education, health, employment, transport, planning, crime, injustice, and corruption;
- facilitate and promote other leisure activities such as sports, shopping, reading, watching television, moviegoing, dancing, dining, martial arts, music, tourism, museum attendance, and art appreciation;

- stimulate consumption and inform consumers of their rights;
- help produce and maintain notions of community;
- engage readers with culture and entertainment through short stories, serialized literature, photography, and art; and
- connect sports and music fans to their favorite teams, bands, musicians, or idols, keeping them up-to-date, informed, and feeling in touch.

All of these different functions are important for understanding newspapers in relation to contemporary Chinese popular culture.

Newspapers have also played a key role in transforming Chinese media and journalism over the two and a half decades of economic reform. Compared to the broadcast media (particularly television, which is considered more politically sensitive than other media by the Chinese authorities), newspapers have often had greater freedom to experiment with new content and styles of reporting, to push the limits of Party and government control, and to operate on a strongly commercially driven basis. Like other media, newspapers have undergone a massive transformation in the post-Mao era and developed new forms shaped by the contending pressures of political obligation to government and the Party on one hand and the imperative to be competitive and to make a profit on the other. Yet newspapers have adapted to and experimented with the possibilities offered by China's changing cultural and

A newspaper vendor at her stand at one of Beijing's main shopping streets near Tiananmen Square reflects the growth and increasing independence of the Chinese news media. (Corbis)

political environment more than other media have.

Chinese newspapers are not by any means a homogeneous set of publications. Indeed, an understanding of the differences between kinds of newspapers is crucial for understanding the ways that the Chinese press has developed over the last two decades, how newspapers position themselves in the contemporary Chinese popular cultural scene, and how they have been able to negotiate the opposing pressures from the Party and the market.

In this chapter we will therefore first consider the historical background of Chinese newspapers, which is still very important for understanding the present. We will then consider how newspapers have changed in the post-Mao period, what typical newspapers are like in terms of content, and how they figure in contemporary Chinese popular cultural practices.

Historical Background: The Mao Era and Before

Writing has played a key role in Chinese civilization for millennia, and there is a long history, reaching far back into imperial times, of chronicling court events and imperial proceedings and keeping close historical records. Some court bulletins and monthly journals date back to at least the eighth century or even the Han dynasty (206 BC–AD 220), and from at least the seventeeth century China had national systems of communication that can be seen as the forerunners of contemporary print journalism. In the Qing dynasty (AD 1644–1911) there were regularly produced gazettes called *Jing Bao* that enjoyed circulation in the tens of thousands. These journals collated government documents and edicts and were distributed throughout China. There were also provincial gazettes reporting local government affairs and various occasionally produced newssheets published commercially in the large cities to report important or extraordinary events (Lee & Nathan 1985: 362).

Government gazettes were principally read by government officials, while newssheets were read more widely. It was in the second half of the nineteenth century, largely on the initiative of foreign businessmen and missionaries, that China developed a real newspaper industry, one which took aim more at the general population. This new industry was based in the treaty ports, and the largest and best-known of the new Chinese-language newspapers was the *Shen Bao*, also known as the *Shanghai Gazette*, launched in 1872 and which grew to a circulation of around 15,000. With a readership largely comprising businessmen, these early newspapers had a strong commercial news content. They also tended to veer away from politics for fear of upsetting readers or, perhaps more importantly, the government.

The end of the nineteenth century and the first decades of the twentieth century were volatile political times in China, however, and various key historical events, such as China's defeat in the Sino-Japanese War of 1895 and the May 4th Movement of 1919, greatly boosted the circulation of the existing treaty-port newspapers and triggered the launch of various more politically oriented titles. These politically motivated journals soon outnumbered their commercial predecessors, although they often had short lives and there was a rapid turnover of titles.

The broader significance of all these newspapers and journals from the mid- to late-nineteenth century onward cannot be underestimated. For instance, the emergence of this lively political journalism is often associated with the spread of liberal and reformist ideas that eventually led to the 1911 Revolution and the end of the Qing dynasty. Furthermore, with the development of these journals China also saw the emergence of what would become the largest mass media audience in the world. At the time under discussion, the circulation of newspapers and journals relative to the overall population was still small; little more than 1 or 2 percent of the population read newspapers even in the first couple of decades of the twentieth century (Lee & Nathan 1985). Yet, for the first time, there were relatively large numbers of people reading much of the same news and starting to imagine themselves as a community of readers, with common interests, linked through their media consumption (cf. Anderson 1983).

Accurate statistics are not available for this period, but by the early twentieth century, newspaper readership was probably between 2 and 4 million people, including multiple readers and illiterate people who had newspapers read to them. This is also the time when newspaper reading started to change from being an entirely elite practice to something more widespread. In the late nineteenth century, newspapers were printed in a form of classical Chinese called "easy *wen-li*," intended to make newspapers easier to read. However, newspaper readers were still concentrated among the urban elite, the wealthy, government officials, educated businessmen, and students. Toward the turn of the century, even though readership was still fundamentally urban, more and more newspapers were finding their way out of the treaty ports, where the majority were published, to smaller cities and towns and even into the countryside. Newspapers printed in Japan by overseas students and reformers even found their way to fairly remote rural villages.

By the 1930s, literacy rates were also rising among the lower classes, and there were various titles catering to urban readers across the social spectrum. Newspapers now also became largely commercially, rather than politically, motivated, with the fundamental aim of reaching as large a readership as possible and turning a profit, although that did not mean that newspapers necessarily became nonpolitical.

The Republican period (1911–1949) was one of political instability and turmoil in China, with the war against the invading Japanese, the civil war between the communists and the nationalists, and massive social upheaval throughout the first half of the century. Newspapers were almost inevitably embroiled in the politics of the period, and two key characteristics of the Chinese press later in the century emerged during this time. First, newspapers operated under clear political patronage—whether from the nationalist Kuomintang, the communists, or one of the numerous warlords who controlled parts of China—throughout this period. It was very difficult, if not impossible, for newspapers to survive without the appropriate political (and often ultimately military) protection of whoever held local power (MacKinnon 1997: 8). Second, newspapers also therefore became mouthpieces for those various political powers. Censorship and the incorporation of propaganda into the news became a standard feature of the Chinese press during this period. In the People's Republic under Mao, both of these features of Chinese newspapers were institutionalized to a previously unseen degree. There was now only one political patron—the CCP—and all newspaper production soon came firmly under its control.

The CCP had been publishing Party newspapers for several decades; the *Red Flag Daily* and the *Red China Daily*, published in Shanghai and Jiangxi Province, respectively, were in print from the late 1920s through the mid-1930s, and the *New China Daily* and the *Liberation Daily* were both published in Yan'an during the anti-Japanese war (1937–1945). In 1948, as the communist forces concluded their victory, the *People's Daily*, probably China's most famous newspaper, was launched in Hebei Province. When Beijing finally fell to the communists in January 1949, the *People's Daily* moved to the capital.

In the early years of the People's Republic, the CCP gave newspapers, alongside radio and film, a crucial role in the dissemination of news, information, and propaganda throughout the country. From the early 1950s onward, private ownership of newspapers was no longer allowed, and all publishing came under the supervision of Party propaganda committees. The *People's Daily* became *the* voice of the government, with its editorials being used to announce new policies and new campaigns to the people—a heritage that to this day makes political observers attentive to its content. Speeches and writings by Chairman Mao were first published in the paper and then read out over the radio and distributed among Party and government offices as well as work units and collective farms throughout the country for discussion at compulsory political meetings (see Cell 1983). Other newspapers were, and occasionally still are, also required to reprint key *People's Daily* editorials.

Literacy started to rise in the People's Republic; however, progress was slow, and the government was keen to improve the situation more quickly. In the early 1960s, for instance, nearly 40 percent of the population was still either illiterate or only partially literate. For this reason, the CCP started the process of language simplification that saw the number of brush strokes and the complexity of Chinese characters reduced to make literacy more easily attainable. Work units also implemented policies to improve literacy among the workforce. The motivations for this literacy drive were multiple. On one hand, literacy rates were a measure of modernity and progress and of the success of the Party in transforming China. The CCP was also genuinely interested in improving the educational and cultural level of the population. At the same time, it is easier to communicate with and mobilize a literate population than an illiterate one, so improving literacy was also strongly in the interests of the Party and the government.

Before the days of television and while radio was still taking root throughout the country, newspapers were one of the principal conduits linking the people and lower-ranking Party officials in the regions with the top levels of the Party apparatus in Beijing. Until radio was fully established, illiteracy therefore left large numbers of people dependent upon intermediaries (i.e., local-level Party cadres) and public meetings for the reception of Party information. In the early 1960s, each copy that Chinese newspapers produced was on average shared among ten readers; still, only about 40 percent of the population had direct exposure to newspapers. Once radio broadcasts of newspaper editorials and political meetings are also taken into account, however, that percentage rises sharply.

Newspapers in the 1950s and 1960s were more than just vehicles for government messages, however; they became full-fledged participants in the political movements of the times. In the late 1950s, following encouragement from the Party itself, newspapers became the battlegrounds for confrontations between intellectuals and the CCP. In the Great Leap Forward years of 1958 and 1959, newspapers were used by local Party officials to declare unbelievable production figures that drove the fervor of unsustainable production that ultimately ended in the deaths of millions through famine. In the mid-1960s, just before the Cultural Revolution, newspapers also became both the battlefields and the weapons of competing factions in the Party. Key newspapers of the time, like the intellectuals' paper the *Guangming Daily*, the *Beijing Daily*, *Qianxian* (*Frontline*), the *Liberation Army Daily*, Shanghai's *Wenhuibao*, and of course the *People's Daily*, published direct and indirect critiques of senior Party figures in opposing factions as the Party started to tear itself apart in the lead-up to the Cultural Revolution.

As it did for other media, the Cultural Revolution severely disrupted newspaper production, and newspaper content became increasingly monotonous. At times, newspapers simply reprinted articles from the *People's Daily*. All publications joined the chorus of Cultural Revolution sloganeering; the deification of Mao; the criticism of Liu Shaoqi, one of Mao's main political opponents; and the vilification of intellectuals, capitalist-roaders, counterrevolutionary revisionists, and rightists. This was a dark period for Chinese journalism—a time when professionalism, objectivity, and adherence to the truth were all forgotten in the name of purely political interests. At the end of the 1970s and in the early 1980s, however, Chinese newspapers were to undergo a revolution of their own, a revolution that would play its part in the radical transformation not only of Chinese journalism but of Chinese society and popular culture as a whole.

Newspapers in the Post-Mao Reform Period

The 1980s were important years for the Chinese newspaper industry. China was coming to terms with the combined effects of economic reform and the Open Door Policy that were starting to transform the country. The new Party leadership under Deng Xiaoping was starting to unseat political categories, particularly notions of class and class struggle, as decisive elements of the economy and to introduce elements of free-market thinking to take their place. At the same time, intellectuals found themselves enjoying new freedoms to speak their minds—at least among themselves—to start once again to think outside the rigidly and narrowly defined scope of doctrinaire Maoism or, quite simply, to be left alone to live their lives in relative peace.

In the newspaper industry, this rapidly changing economic, social, and intellectual climate soon led to calls for the political definition of Chinese media as the mouthpiece of the Party to be rethought or even dropped. In the mid-1980s, key Party liberals such as Hu Yaobang and Zhao Ziyang gave indirect support to such movements so that newspapers started reporting in ways previously unimaginable. Newspapers found new freedoms to report on social issues and to touch upon previously politically sensitive topics such as employment, education, and corruption.

One of the best-known cases illustrating this changing political environment is that of the *World Economic Herald* set up and published in Shanghai in the 1980s. The newspaper, which focused on Chinese and international economic news, persuaded the Shanghai Academy of the Social Sciences and the Chinese World Economists Association—two government organizations—to apply for a publishing license, which they then contracted out to the *World Economic Herald*. The paper then ran itself entirely on advertising and subscriptions as an independent commercial enterprise while paying a regular fee to its license holders. Nonetheless, those at the top of the newspaper were close political allies of the liberal factions in the CCP leadership and therefore enjoyed a considerable degree of political patronage and protection. Indeed, the government on occasion even used the newspaper to leak new policy suggestions in order to test public opinion and reaction. The paper therefore gained a reputation for being politically liberal and daring while openly supporting a reformist agenda. This proved commercially lucrative, but in the end it made the paper politically vulnerable. The *World Economic Herald* constantly tested the patience of the Shanghai Party Propaganda Committee, at that time under the leadership of future premier Jiang Zemin, by publishing outspoken articles. In 1989, however, the fate of the newspaper was about to change. The paper became associated with the student-led pro-democracy movement, and after the events of June when the demonstrations in Tiananmen Square were brutally suppressed it became politically nonviable. It also lost key political patronage with the political demise of Party Secretary Zhao Ziyang, who was forced into internal exile following the troubles in Tiananmen Square. The newspaper was subsequently forced to close down, making it clear that the Party was still able to impose limits on political freedom and freedom of the press.

Crucially, however, these moves toward a less-restricted press in the 1980s were accompanied by new economic imperatives that also transformed the newspaper industry. Under reform, many government organizations saw newspaper publishing as a new business opportunity; this contributed to a massive proliferation of newspaper titles in the 1980s and 1990s. For instance, between the late 1970s and the mid-1980s the number of titles grew by nearly 200 per year, from 186 in 1979 to 1,574 in 1986. By 1989 there were 1,618 newspaper titles being printed in China, and by 1996 this had risen to 2,235—twelve times the number back in 1979 (Zhang 1997). During the Mao period and also for some time after, newspapers operated entirely on government subsidies and finance. With this enormous growth in the number of newspapers being published, however, the government could no longer afford to subsidize them all fully. At the same time, Chinese media across the board were becoming more accustomed to relying upon advertising and sales to enhance their income. The result was that a large number of newspapers saw their costs rising, their subsidies falling, and the pressure to find funding for themselves growing ever greater. Newspapers therefore became commercially oriented and started to focus on sales and advertising rather than simply fulfilling their political responsibilities. By the end of the 1980s, many newspapers were not only financially self-supporting for the first time since

1949—some were also managing to bring in handsome profits.

Throughout the reform period, Chinese newspapers found themselves increasingly operating in the narrowly defined area between market forces on one hand and propaganda responsibilities to the Party on the other. Crucially, the two sets of pressures often pushed in quite opposite directions. The bottom line from the point of view of the market was to sell more newspapers—indeed, as many as possible—and to keep the readers satisfied so that they came back to buy another one the next day. From the point of view of government propaganda, however, the main concern was to tell people what the Party felt they needed to know, which was not necessarily the same as what the people themselves thought they wanted to know.

To the present day, these twin pressures have direct effect upon daily newspaper production. For instance, the Party has always attached importance to "meetings news"—the reporting of local, regional, and national Party and government meetings—and requires news organizations to report meetings under the mouthpiece principle of the media. Yet, following the dull predictability and government-centered content of the Cultural Revolution period, many Chinese readers by the 1980s were thoroughly disillusioned with propaganda and the Party's dry, monotonous renditions of political news. Meetings news is among the least lively. Therefore, newspapers face the dilemma of how to fulfill the expectations that the Party has of them while also keeping their readers happy. How precisely they do this varies according to the type of newspaper, but strategies include putting meetings news in a relatively unobtrusive position well inside the newspaper, keeping story length and profile to a minimum, livening up a dull meetings story by linking it to another, more interesting one—such as one with a strong human-interest aspect—and, if they can get away with it, simply not printing the story at all.

This is just one example showing the kind of decisions that newspaper editors have to face every day, but the general principle applies more broadly across their work. Newspapers have certain obligations to the Party that they must fulfill, and they are also restricted by Party and government regulations as to what they report and how they report it. Meanwhile, they have to make their newspapers lively, interesting, informative, useful, entertaining, and fun in order to maintain and improve both sales and advertising income.

The political troubles of 1989 marked a turning point for the newspaper industry in China. Until that point, economic reform and the open-door policy had nurtured these two parallel sets of changes in newspaper production—political and intellectual liberalization on one hand, and commercialization on the other. After 1989, although newspapers still enjoyed much greater political freedom than they had under Mao, the move toward political liberalization was sharply curtailed. When the *World Economic Herald* was closed down, a clear message was sent to newspaper editors: toe the party line.

This did not mean that the industry stopped changing, reforming, and developing in the 1990s. Rather, the energies for reform were turned more in the direction of commercialization rather than political engagement or pursuing ideas of freedom of speech. Similarly, this did not mean that newspapers stopped pushing the limits of what the Party would accept. Indeed, in some ways it encouraged them to push even harder. Throughout the 1990s and early 2000s, newspaper editors continually sought ways to increase circulation, sell more advertising, and run their newspapers as profitable businesses. This has often entailed challenging Party guidelines and experimenting with new kinds of stories, new styles of presentation, and new conceptualizations of journalism, readers, what people want to read, and what makes good news.

In 2003, the newspaper industry was pushed further toward commercialization by government reforms aimed at reducing the number of newspapers receiving indirect government subsidies. Throughout the 1980s and 1990s, newspapers increasingly relied upon sales and advertising as their main sources of income. There were still many newspapers, however, that enjoyed the cushion of compulsory subscriptions from government departments and offices as well as from many state-owned enterprises. This meant that some newspapers were therefore shielded from the full pressures of the market, as they had a guaranteed income from these subscriptions. However, the government became concerned in the early 2000s about the unnecessary financial burden on some government offices in poorer parts of the country because they were forced to subscribe to large numbers of papers that often no one read. The 2003 reform therefore heavily restricted the number of compulsory subscription titles at each level of the Party hierarchy and forced a host of Party newspapers to become commercially viable or else face closure.

This helps us to see that while all kinds of newspapers continue to develop along increasingly commercial lines, different kinds of newspapers have nonetheless had different experiences and developed in different ways. It is therefore important to understand what the distinctions are among them and the particular contributions of different types of newspapers to Chinese newspaper culture.

Types of Newspapers

In order to account for their different positions in China's contemporary popular cultural landscape, there are several distinctions between different kinds of newspapers that have to be understood. For instance, the vast majority of Chinese newspapers are local newspapers of one kind or another. In 2005, of the 1,931 titles published, 220 (or 11.26 percent) were national titles, accounting for 13.34 percent of total newspaper production; 815 (or 42.27 percent) were provincial-level titles, accounting for 55.1 percent; and 836 (46.48 percent) were city-, town-, or county-level publications, accounting for 30.91 percent. These newspapers can then be broken down into a range of different categories, which require distinguishing between daily and evening newspapers, weekend edition newspapers, metropolitan newspapers that emerged in the late 1990s, and specialized newspapers devoted to particular sectors of news or particular audiences or readerships. We will consider these below. However, there is another fundamentally important distinction to be made in China, between "Party organ" newspapers and "non-Party organ" newspapers.

Party Organ and Non-Party Organ Newspapers

All Chinese newspapers must have a license to publish from the government, and licenses are only issued to government and Party organizations. These could be, for example, departments, ministries, or offices of central, provincial, or local government, military, or academic institutions such as the army, the navy, the air force, universities and research associations, or other Party bodies—the Communist Youth League or the Women's Federation for instance. There is an important but sometimes subtle distinction to be drawn, however, between what are called Party organ and non-Party organ newspapers.

Party organ newspapers are titles that come directly under the supervision and direction of one or another Party propaganda committee. Hence, the *Sichuan Daily* is the Party organ newspaper of the Sichuan Province Party Committee under the jurisdiction of the provincial Party propaganda committee. Similarly, the *Nanfang Daily* (*Southern Daily*) is the Party organ newspaper of the Guangdong Province Party Committee, and the *Guangzhou Daily* is the Party organ newspaper of the Guangzhou City Party Committee. The *People's Daily* is the organ of the national-level Central Committee of the CCP. What this means is that the Party propaganda committee is able to take a stronger, more direct role in the daily running of the newspaper, including, most importantly, the editorial content of the paper.

Non-Party organ newspapers are also attached to government organizations but

Chinese Communist Party member Huang Zhaoxiong reads an editorial from the party mouthpiece *People's Daily* in Fujian Province, China, in 2002. (Corbis)

are not considered the direct mouthpiece paper of their Party propaganda committee. Non-Party organ newspapers therefore come under the supervision of the propaganda committees but not under the same kind of immediate direction. Hence, Party organ newspapers have a stronger obligation to publish Party and government propaganda as directed by the Party committee. They may therefore be directed to publish political news such as stories about Party and government meetings, leaders' visits, mass campaigns, and government policies or decrees. Non-Party organ newspapers, by contrast, have greater leeway to avoid such news, place it in less prominent positions within the paper, or report it in ways they think will be more attractive or less off-putting to their readers. They cannot deviate from the party line, but they can sometimes decide to ignore it or treat it more lightly.

Nonetheless, non-Party organ newspapers cannot avoid Party directives on major events or policy issues. For instance, in the late 1990s when the Party was very concerned about the quasi-Buddhist spiritual movement called the Falun Gong, which it saw as a threat to its authority, all general newspapers and many special-interest titles were also required to include articles, editorials, and features condemning the cult. Similarly, the Party occasionally directs all newspapers to print major speeches from party leaders or to report on national party congresses or major new policy directions. In such cases, non-Party organ newspapers are not usually exempt. High-profile issues such as Tibetan or Taiwanese independence, the events of 1989, or the achievements of past leaders also leave non-Party organ newspapers no flexibility or independence in reporting.

In terms of popular readership of newspapers, the distinction between Party organ and non-Party organ newspapers is therefore important. Readers are well aware of which newspapers are more closely linked to the Party and the government and read them accordingly. They may skip the first pages of Party organ newspapers to avoid the political news and go directly to the social, sports, entertainment, or local news on the inside pages. Alternatively, they may choose to avoid such newspapers altogether and buy more lively, non-Party organ titles. On the other hand, if readers particularly want to read political news they would probably turn first to the Party organ titles.

Categories of Newspapers

Classifications of Chinese newspapers generally identify eight categories of publications in addition to the distinction between Party organ newspapers and non-Party organ newspapers.

1. National newspapers (such as the *People's Daily*, the *Guangming Daily*, and the *Liberation Daily*). These are papers that are distributed nationally but which are also linked to national-level government or Party institutions such as ministries or central government offices.
2. Specialized professional newspapers (such as for lawyers, engineers, or doctors). Although these generally have specialized content aimed at narrowly targeted readerships, in recent years some such newspapers have found new commercial success with a broader general readership. For instance, some legal newspapers, which report court cases, criminal investigations, and of course crimes, have proven popular with the general public.

3. Industry newspapers devoted to a particular sector of the productive economy such as the electronics industry, the textile industry, the leather industry, forestry, or fishing. These are often produced by ministries or government departments to cover their particular area of competence and help workers, enterprises, and administrators keep up-to-date with the latest news, legal or regulatory issues, technologies, and international developments in their sector.
4. Evening newspapers. The Party launched several titles, such as Guangzhou's *Yangcheng Evening News* and the *Beijing Evening News*, in the late 1950s tasked with providing readers with a broader range of news than the strictly politically oriented daily papers. Evening newspapers still had political and propaganda responsibilities like their daily counterparts; however, they also offered softer news dealing with more cultural and social issues aimed at an urban readership. Evening newspapers have continued to the present day with generally similar associations. They include both long-standing titles launched in the 1950s and 1960s and news publications launched much more recently.
5. Digest newspapers. These are newspapers that collate stories, often on a weekly basis, from other sources. Some of the most popular of these have been digests of translated foreign news stories that were once restricted viewing, available only to Party members of a certain rank. In the reform era, these papers became widely available on the streets in the large cities or by postal subscription.
6. Interest-group newspapers. Some newspapers, often produced under the auspices of special-interest organizations such as the Communist Youth League or the Women's Federation, aim at a particular group in society such as workers, consumers, youth, women, or the elderly. Some of these, such as the *Beijing Youth News*, have become nationally popular general readership newspapers even though nominally retaining their special focus. The *Beijing Youth News* is one of the most successful newspapers in the country and has also been closely associated with journalistic innovation and professional reform.
7. Lifestyle papers. These are themed newspapers focusing on different lifestyle issues such as television and entertainment; music, sports, and other pastimes; food and cookery; fashion; consumption; travel; or the arts.
8. Military newspapers. The armed services produce their own newspapers aiming particularly at soldiers, sailors, airmen, and other military personnel.

To these categorizations we should also add another couple of categories of newspapers that have emerged since the late 1980s. These are weekend editions and so-called metropolitan dailies (*dushi bao*).

In the late 1980s, the *Nanfang Daily* newspaper—the Party organ of the Guangdong provincial Party committee—launched a special weekly newspaper called the *Nanfang Weekend* (*nanfang zhoumo*). As a Party organ paper, the *Nanfang Daily* was obliged to report relatively dull political news and had heavy propaganda responsibilities to the Party committee. In the increasingly competitive and commercially oriented Guangdong newspaper market, this was a disadvantage in terms of business. The newspaper formulated an ingenious strategy to deal with the problem, however. The *Nanfang Weekend* was not a Party organ newspaper and as a weekly newspaper also had fewer propaganda responsibilities imposed upon it. It was therefore able to concentrate on often more intriguing and attractive social news and human-interest stories and feature articles dealing with issues such as crime, corruption, employment, education, health, and consumerism as well as emerging social differences in Chinese society. The paper did not criticize Party policy, but by discussing some of the negative social consequences of economic reform it moved into territory that at one time would have been entirely out-of-bounds to newspapers of any kind.

This "division of labor" between the politically oriented *Nanfang Daily* and the commercially and socially oriented *Nanfang Weekend* was an enormous success. The *Nanfang Weekend* rapidly became a national bestseller and was emulated by other newspaper groups across the country. As a result, the number of weekend edition titles nationally rose from less than 20 in 1990 to more than 400 in 1994 (Zhao 1998: 134).

Later in the 1990s, often in a similarly commercially motivated move, many newspaper groups launched tabloid-style "metropolitan" newspapers that have also become some of the best-selling titles throughout the country although generally remaining locally focused in content. These are once again non-Party organ newspapers, and they have often taken a more sensationalist and populist approach to the news. They are strongly driven by commercial motives and as a result have often also stretched the limits of Party control as far as possible in order to boost sales.

Newspaper Differences

In order to understand the culture of Chinese newspapers, it is important to understand the differences between them in terms of content, their relationship to the Party, their relationship to the market, their sources of income, and the nature of their readership. The common classification of newspapers outlined above, combined with the distinction between Party organ and non-Party organ newspapers, covers a lot of these issues. However, it is also possible to identify some general rules of thumb that indicate how different kinds of newspapers are positioned in the market and in relation to media consumption in general. These can be considered under the following headings:

- Size
- Nature of content
- Local or national focus
- Methods of distribution
- Nature, size, and importance of the parent organization
- Nature of license holding
- Degree of financial independence
- Commercial or political orientation

The **size** of a newspaper can be measured in various ways. These could include total circulation of the paper, advertising revenue or turnover, number of subscriptions, number of employees, or degree of public visibility and awareness. These different criteria do not produce identical rankings, but there is clearly some interrelation between them—a newspaper with a large circulation is likely to attract advertisers, require more staff, and have a higher public visibility. Whatever criterion is used to measure the size of the newspaper, however, size matters.

Larger newspapers, whether Party organ or non-Party organ papers, are likely to be more closely supervised by the Party to ensure political correctness because of their greater readership. Smaller newspapers, by contrast, particularly those with small circulation, can often stretch the rules a little further and be more adventurous with style, presentation, and even content than can their larger counterparts. Chinese consumers often buy according to brand awareness, however, which means that larger, well-established titles often still have an advantage over smaller newcomers.

Bearing in mind that size directly affects the degree of political supervision of a newspaper, it clearly also indirectly affects its **content**. It is a two-way relationship between size and content, however, as special-interest newspapers often have relatively small circulation, for instance. The nature of a newspaper's content is ultimately also related to all the other criteria listed in this section.

General-news newspapers are usually considered more politically sensitive because they are the most popular newspapers in the country and they carry news on local and national government, current affairs, international news, economic news, political news, and cultural and social news. Many of them, including some of the largest like the *Guangzhou Daily*, are not surprisingly therefore Party organ newspapers. Meanwhile, sports, entertainment, and other lifestyle papers rarely deal with politically sensitive issues and have free rein in terms of content. Even economic, business, and financial newspapers are considered relatively apolitical and experience less Party attention than general newspapers.

The relationship between size and **local or national focus** of a newspaper is not as straightforward as it might seem. One might expect local newspapers to be considerably smaller than national newspapers. However, the large majority of China's more than 2,000 newspaper titles are actually local newspapers, and the majority of newspapers bought and read by Chinese people are also local newspapers. At the same time, some of the more successful "local" newspapers of different kinds like the *Beijing Youth News*, the *Guangzhou Daily*, the *Yangcheng Evening News*, *Nanfang Weekend* (*Southern Weekend*), or Shanghai's *Wenhui Bao* are also distributed and recognized nationally. As a result, they also have circulation figures and advertising revenues to challenge and indeed to beat some of the top national newspapers.

Due to the hybrid nature of the Chinese newspaper industry finding itself somewhere between government propaganda and commercial principles, circulation figures do not necessarily give a clear indication of the popularity of a newspaper, and one has to consider the **methods of distribution** of a newspaper in order to understand this better. Government departments and offices, state-owned companies, and other Party and government organizations are obliged to subscribe to lists of Party organ, industry, and specialized professional newspapers. Such newspapers therefore enjoy a cushion of guaranteed income from obligatory subscriptions that can make them less market-sensitive and less commercially oriented. They may therefore enjoy quite a large circulation but not be particularly popular newspapers. By contrast, metropolitan daily tabloids, weekend editions, and evening papers as well as lifestyle and consumer-oriented special-interest newspapers generally rely to a large degree on newsstand sales and advertising for their revenue. This makes them far more responsive and attentive to readers' demands.

The **nature, size, and importance of the parent organization** also affects newspaper content and the relationship between the newspaper, its content, and the Party. Newspapers run by large, important government departments are likely to be obliged to play a stronger propaganda role than those with less prominent links to the Party. Similarly, newspapers run by less political areas of the Party or government (e.g., the Chinese Academy of Science or the Ministry of Railways) may have much less cause to be troubled by propaganda issues. However, another related issue is the **nature of license holding** of the newspaper.

The key issue of license holding relates once again to the link with government. It also relates to the **degree of financial independence** that a newspaper has from its parent government organization. In the 1980s and increasingly in the 1990s, many newspapers were set up with contracted-out publishing licenses—rather like that of the *World Economic Herald*—so that although the newspaper is officially registered to a particular government organization, it is editorially, practically, and financially independent. The newspaper effectively rents permission from the license holder to use the license but remains responsible for editorial content, printing, and distribution as well as all taxes and other expenses. Through such a system, China has developed a semi-independent press that is relatively free to experiment with news content and presentational style as well as general business and organizational practices. This semi-independent press has to be distinguished from Party organ and other newspapers more closely related—either editorially or financially—to government departments, offices, and organizations (see Huang 2000).

China's semi-independent press has emerged effectively because Chinese Party and government organizations, as well as newspaper groups themselves, have come to consider newspaper production in two distinct ways following the general development of newspapers in the reform period. On one hand, there is clearly still the conceptualization of newspapers as propaganda tools for the government. On the other hand, there is also the idea that newspapers are businesses. They offer a service to paying consumers, with the intention of making a profit. For some newspapers it is this latter conceptualization that is paramount, and they are principally **commercially oriented** as opposed to Party organ newspapers, which are far more **politically oriented**.

All of these criteria ultimately combine to form the character of any particular newspaper.

Newspapers, Government Control, and Censorship

Many of the differences between newspapers outlined above center around the question of commercial versus political orientation, and we have seen how the conflicting pressures coming from the market and the Party have shaped a range of new kinds of newspapers such as weekend editions, evening newspapers, and metropolitan

The People's Daily: *The People's Paper?*

China's most famous newspaper is the *People's Daily,* the Party organ newspaper of the CCP's Central Committee. In combination with China Central Television (CCTV) and China People's Radio, the *People's Daily* is one of the principal voices of the Party and the government. It was founded in June 1948, just before the final victory of the CCP in the civil war and the setting up of the People's Republic, and it soon became nationally and internationally recognized as *the* Chinese national newspaper. In the 1950s and 1960s, the *People's Daily* was often the launching ground for new policies and new mass-mobilization campaigns which first came to public attention through the paper's editorials or through Mao's speeches published in the paper. In the Cultural Revolution period, the paper became a weather vane for subtle changes in political direction as well as one of the main vehicles for the national idolization of Chairman Mao.

In the post-Mao era, the *People's Daily* once again heralded the changes about to take place in the country with the introduction of economic reform and the open-door policy, and it has continued to be the voice of the Chinese leadership. Yet, in the reform era, the *People's Daily* and its position in China's popular cultural landscape have experienced a significant change. Whereas once the *People's Daily* was read by almost everyone who was literate, in contemporary China relatively few people read it on a daily basis. This does not diminish the political significance of the paper for understanding government policy; however, it does mean that it has a much lesser importance for understanding everyday newspaper culture in China.

The *People's Daily* is still one of the best-selling newspapers in China, with a circulation in the early 2000s of around 4 million. It relies very heavily on compulsory subscriptions for its circulation, however. In fact, in the late 1990s and early 2000s it could be impossible to find a copy for sale on the streets of even Beijing. With the massive proliferation of newspaper titles in the 1980s and the vastly increased choice of reading, most Chinese newspaper readers now prefer other titles. As other newspapers in the competitive market environment find new ways of attracting readers with social news stories, entertainment news and gossip, human-interest stories, and so on, the *People's Daily* becomes daily more stolid by comparison.

Occasionally, major speeches or editorials are still reproduced in other daily newspapers, particularly Party organ newspapers, but in general the vast majority of the Chinese population in the early 2000s would be unlikely to know, or to have seen, the contents of the day's *People's Daily.* The paper's readership is now largely concentrated among government and Party officials, scholars, and politically inclined intellectuals. It is no longer the daily paper of the majority of the Chinese people.

tabloids. They have also reconfigured the fortunes of the *People's Daily.* We have also seen how many newspapers tread a careful line between these two sets of pressures. Yet this begs questions of how government control and censorship actually work. How, for example, have newspapers been able to push the limits laid down by the Party? How have these innovative changes in Chinese newspapers been allowed to come about in a country where all the media has to be state-owned and is not, strictly speaking, allowed to publish anything critical of the CCP?

At the national level, the State Administration for Press and Publications (SAPP, also known as the General Administration for Press and Publications), which comes under the direct control of the State Council, oversees newspaper production throughout the country and is responsible for formulating, publishing, and implementing regulations relating to the industry. National-level newspapers such as the *People's Daily* (see sidebar) will also come under the supervision of their appropriate government or Party organization. In the case of the *People's Daily* this is the Central Committee of the CCP. Most of the country's more than 2,000 newspaper titles, however, are supervised on a daily basis not by national-level but by local-level Party cadres and committees.

The foundations of Party control of the media therefore rely on two key locally situated practices: self-censorship and post hoc accountability for what has been published. The CCP's various propaganda committees could not realistically censor every newspaper in the country before publication. It would be too time-consuming as well as unfeasible practically if newspapers are to operate in a commercially competitive market. This means that the responsibility for deciding what goes into a newspaper on a daily basis lies with the newspaper's chief editor and its editorial board.

Most daily newspapers will have a daily editorial meeting at which all the senior editorial staff and desk editors will be present. In the case of Party organ newspapers, this editorial board could also include members of the relevant Party committee to which the newspaper is attached. These meetings discuss public or Party reactions to the previous day's publication as well as the plan, layout, and priorities of that day's issue. All senior editorial staff will be Party members and therefore have an obligation, though not necessarily any particularly strong personal allegiance, to the CCP. They are therefore responsible for ensuring that government guidelines on news reporting and content are adhered to.

All editors are also very aware of the potential consequences of not keeping to these rules. In serious cases, they could personally lose their jobs and Party membership as well as their entitlements to housing and other benefits. In very serious cases, they might even face legal proceedings or imprisonment, and the newspaper could be shut down or have its license suspended. To publish anything wildly out of line with government or Party thinking could therefore have grave repercussions, and this is the main incentive for effective self-censorship.

As newspapers operate in a highly competitive market, however, the same editors are also under pressure to meet market demands, to sell more newspapers and more advertising, and to generate more income. Hence, importantly the dual pressures of government control and commercialism come to bear upon the same key figures within newspapers as organizations. If political censorship and commercial editorial decision-making were separate, China's newspapers would look quite different from the way they do now. In this way, commercially motivated editorial boards, particularly of non-Party organ newspapers, try to lead with the more sensational and enticing news stories even if occasionally they know that they may be stretching or even breaching Party guidelines. It is at this point that post hoc accountability comes to bear. In such cases, if the Party propaganda committee feels a line has been overstepped, but assuming that the breach is relatively minor, they will contact the newspaper's chief editor directly the following day and issue a warning not to make the same mistake again. In this way, the system of Party control works effectively but also incorporates a sufficient degree of leeway that allows newspapers to experiment, and there is a constant game of give-and-take between more adventurous journalists and Party officials. If journalists try something new that crosses a line but proves popular with readers and if Party officials do not complain, then it is likely that it will rapidly become common practice throughout the industry.

Typical Content of a Daily Newspaper

As we have seen, Chinese newspapers vary considerably. It is therefore impossible to summarize the typical content of all Chinese newspapers. However, the best-selling and most popular newspapers in China are general-interest daily or evening newspapers. In order to give an indication of Chinese newspaper content and its contribution to contemporary Chinese popular culture, it is therefore useful to consider the content of a typical Chinese daily such as the *Chengdu Daily*, the *Beijing Daily*, or the *Guangzhou Daily*. First we can identify common features of many such newspapers, but then it is useful to consider the content of a typical edition of a particular newspaper. The newspaper chosen is the *Guangzhou Daily*, which not only is one of the most popular and best-selling newspapers in China but being a highly commercially oriented Party organ newspaper bridges the gap between the two dominant pressures in the Chinese newspaper industry.

General Features of a Daily Newspaper

Chinese dailies vary in size according to their budget, the amount of advertising they carry, and the size and wealth of the area they serve. A large broadsheet layout is still the most common format, although in the early 2000s the smaller, tabloid style became increasingly popular, particularly with metropolitan dailies. Up until the late 1980s, a typical daily newspaper would have as few as eight or sixteen pages, and some had fewer than that. In the early 2000s, however, a typical daily newspaper in a fairly large city would have somewhere between twenty-four and fifty to sixty pages including advertising and the various supplements. Most daily general-interest newspapers would be printed in at least two but possibly as many as four sections, generally labeled using the roman alphabet plus the page number of the section. Hence, a typical paper might have pages A1 to A16 plus B1 to B8 and so on, depending on the number and size of the sections.

Chinese newspapers are predominantly focused on domestic news, with only around 10 to 15 percent of an average daily newspaper being devoted to foreign news, even though Chinese readers have a great interest in foreign affairs. Bearing in mind that most daily newspapers read in China are local newspapers, most carry a good proportion of local news stories. Daily general-interest newspapers are usually divided into sections for main news, national news, international news, and local news. Depending on the particular newspaper, they will then often have sections covering financial and economic news, sports, leisure, and entertainment. Many will then have regular sections—possibly daily or perhaps weekly—on topics such as food, motoring, property, health, technology, shopping, and fashion. These may also take the form of pull-out supplements. Some of the larger dailies that cover fairly large geographical areas may also publish either different editions for different areas or a core newspaper with special supplements covering local news for different areas. The *Guangzhou Daily* publishes a Guangzhou edition and also a Pearl River Delta edition, which has an extra supplement covering news from the Pearl River Delta region in southern Guangdong Province.

An average daily newspaper, like Western newspapers, will generally have what are considered the stories of most consequence, or the most attractive to readers, on the front page. These may be local, national, or international stories. Party organ newspapers invariably have relatively large proportions of domestic political news in their first few pages if not throughout the main section of the newspaper. Non-Party organ newspapers may prefer to lead with a particularly eye-catching local news story such as new plans for city development, crime stories, or stories relating to issues of high immediate interest to readers, such as on transport, education, health care, employment, crime, or migration.

Until the mid-1990s, it was generally uncommon to find color photography in daily newspapers, and the photos used were often fairly modest in size. However, as technology improved and became more affordable, color printing became more and more viable so that soon many newspapers could include one or more color photos even if they were restricted to the front page and back page. By the late 1990s, various newspapers throughout the country attempted to attract readers through high color visibility, using large, bright color pictures alongside very large-print color headlines, particularly for the front page and the sports pages but in some cases also other pages throughout the paper. In this respect, there was some emulation of Hong Kong newspaper style.

Example: The Guangzhou Daily

The *Guangzhou Daily* is one of China's largest and most successful newspapers. In the early 2000s, it sold around 3 to 4 million copies a day and made more money from advertising sales than probably any other Chinese newspaper. The *Guangzhou Daily* is distributed nationally, but its main sales are in the city of Guangzhou itself and throughout Guangdong Province, particularly in the wealthier Pearl River Delta region spreading down from Guangzhou toward Hong Kong and Macao.

The October 18, 2006, edition of the newspaper was fairly typical in terms of daily content and layout. In all, there were fifty pages for the Guangzhou edition of the newspaper, which was divided into three main sections (A, B, and C) of thirty, eight, and twelve pages respectively. There were also two additional supplements, for the cities of Dongguan (Section DG, eight pages) and Foshan (Section FS, eight pages), aimed at those local markets.

The paper had six pages of main news stories (A1–A6). The front page had two leading political stories that were both "meetings" news. Both stories, one on the left side of the page and the other under the banner, reported on city and provincial authorities discussing strategies to promote commerce in the city, with a focus on enhancing export trade through cultivating strong brand names for Guangdong products. These stories reflected the Party organ role of the *Guangzhou Daily.* The eye-catching story on the page is not either of these lead stories, however, but the one in the middle of the page with a large, full-color action photograph of two policemen on a motorcycle. The accompanying story reported the setting up of a new special police motorcycle flying squad in action on their first mission. Together with military police and other special services, they were in pursuit of smuggled motorcycles. On the inside pages were a series of reports on other local issues, including education and a special report on the hopes and prospects of a group of teenagers turning eighteen. Page A6 carried a full-page special report and obituary on the death on October 14, 2006, of Wang Guangmei, the widow of former premier Liu Shaoqi, who had been ousted from power by Mao in the Cultural Revolution and died shortly afterward (see Chapter 1). It did not go unnoticed in China that it took four days for this news to be publicly reported, an indication of the kind of control that is still occasionally imposed on what are considered sensitive political issues.

Other special reports included one on counterfeit antique ceramics uncovered in the city and another full-page report on a new full national and international roaming mobile-phone package being offered by China Mobile. There were three pages of international news, led by a story of events surrounding a key vote at the United Nations. There were then five stories—some of the most interesting reading for local people—of city news items from Guangzhou; these included stories on financial problems facing the unemployed, local transport, education, and health care issues. The later pages of section A included columns for property, motoring, finance and investments including stock market news, Pearl River Delta news, sports, comment, and serialized fiction.

The second section of the paper, pages B1 to B8, covered leisure and entertainment news as well as lifestyle, consumer, and health issues. Section C was dedicated to technology, IT, and consumer electronics reports, including stories on computers and computer makers, the mobile-phone industry, and air-conditioning. There were also three pages on looking for study places at schools and universities in China and overseas and another three pages of employment advertisements and articles. Finally in this section were three more pages of small ads for local goods and services.

In fact, the popularity of the *Guangzhou Daily* does not come particularly from its leading news stories, which can be rather dull and formulaic and are generally considered less interesting than the reporting in rival titles such as the *Nanfang Metropolitan News* (*nanfang dushi bao*). The strengths and attractions of the *Guangzhou Daily*, for many, are to be found in the internal pages and supplements. Local news is popular, as are the softer news sections (sports, entertainment, health, finance, property, and lifestyle). The *Guangzhou Daily* has another key asset, however: its advertisements. Many readers are attracted to the paper not so much for its news as its consumer-oriented information and small ads pages for goods and services of all different kinds. This reminds us that newspapers are not just vehicles for news—they also serve other important social functions.

Newspaper Reading as Changing Cultural Practice

Newspaper reading is not just a matter of buying a newspaper and reading it; rather, it is a range of social and cultural practices and an important feature of contemporary Chinese popular culture. To start with, one has to ask, why do people read newspapers? What are their motives? What do they hope to find out from their newspaper? We might also ask how people choose their newspaper in the first place. This then leads one to ask *how* people read their newspapers.

To answer these questions, we have to extrapolate from the content of newspapers to how people interact with them in socially, culturally, and historically constituted contexts—that is to say, newspaper reading has to be understood as embedded in a range of experiences, expectations, hopes, and understandings. The news stories and information found in a newspaper are not neutral but are produced according to cultural and social norms and are read in ways that draw upon readers' experiences and understanding of the world around them to which that news refers.

The earlier sections of this chapter have explained how newspapers themselves have changed in China over the last twenty to thirty years. It therefore follows that the way people read and use newspapers has also undergone a substantial transition over this period. In the Mao period, newspapers were highly politicized objects and they played a fundamental role in political practices that were fundamental to the operation of Chinese society at the time. Newspaper reading was also in many ways a collective experience. Even if only a single individual read a newspaper, he or she would know that hundreds of millions of others were reading the same thing all over the country. People would also be involved in public or work unit meetings to discuss what they read in their newspapers and to be told by Party cadres what its significance was, how they should understand it, and how, subsequently, they should act upon it.

In the post-Mao period, by contrast, although the political element of newspaper production and reading has not disappeared, people's reasons for reading newspapers have diversified and the functions that newspapers serve have multiplied. At the same time, the notion of community that many of them support is likely to be local and fragmentary, similar to television, as much as national. Newspaper reading has become a far more individual practice as well as a more selective practice. The larger, more successful, and popular newspapers like the *Guangzhou Daily* often aim at as broad a readership as possible by trying to include something for everyone. This is partly why the thickness of some leading newspapers has increased considerably since the late 1980s.

Chinese people's lives in the post-Mao period have become much more individual-centered, and people have far more personal decisions to make than they did in the past. Newspapers now serve much more practical functions than they did in the Mao period in helping people to make these decisions. For instance, they offer advice and information on issues relating to consumption and consumerism (see below), health care, education, or employment, while they also guide people through the range of entertainment available to them in television, music, cinema, and theatre. Newspapers now offer much broader and more informative international news than was ever available under Mao so that newspaper reading has become much more a matter of following what is going in other parts of the world, learning about foreign countries and people, and situating China in an international political scene. All of these issues are new to the reform period.

This is not to say that all of the old reading habits have disappeared. For instance, under Mao, Chinese newspaper readers became very skilled interpreters of political news. Everyone knew that what they read in their newspapers was highly selective in terms of being what the Party wanted people to read. Hence, it was important to be able to understand subtle word choice that indicated possible changes of policy direction, leadership rivalry, or new targets of mass-mobilization campaigns or political struggle, since this could mean the difference between life and death.

In the post-Mao era, these skills are put to different use. Chinese people are still very aware of the political nature of newspapers and other media. They are also very aware of what is political news and propaganda and what is not. One of the differences between the Mao era and the present is that in the past, virtually all reporting was politicized and seen as propaganda. As more and more aspects of daily life have become depoliticized over the last couple of decades, some areas of news reporting, such as business, sports, transport, health, and social news, have become much less politically sensitive. Other areas of news, such as entertainment and consumer affairs, have only really emerged as news topics in the reform era, yet the sports, entertainment, lifestyle, and social news pages have become some of the most important and popularly read pages in today's newspapers. Hence, readers are now faced with a range of political, less political, and nonpolitical news and features that simply did not exist in the past.

The close interpretive reading skills developed in the Mao era can nonetheless still be used today to follow and identify political changes. The difference is that the importance or relevance of doing so has been greatly reduced. The same kinds of skills are also put to use to identify political and nonpolitical news, to realize which are propaganda stories and which are not, to understand the significance of that propaganda—remembering that the term "propaganda" is not always seen as negative in China—and to identify what may be propagandistic elements of an otherwise more interesting news story. These skills therefore serve to sort out what is rhetoric from what is not.

In these various ways, newspaper reading has therefore become a far more selective practice. Some people may want to follow political events and deliberately select a Party organ newspaper and read the political pages. Others may feel tired of government propaganda and either select a less political paper or skip over the propaganda stories of a Party organ newspaper. Others may buy newspapers for the advertisements they carry. Some people will choose specialized newspapers according to their personal interests—a sports paper to follow their favorite soccer team (whether it be Beijing,

Shanghai, Manchester United, or Real Madrid), a financial paper to check their stock prices, a television newspaper to plan their viewing, or an entertainment newspaper to follow the gossip on the stars. None of these choices were an aspect of newspaper reading in the Mao era.

Newspaper reading is also now more than ever one media practice among others, and this affects the way people engage with newspapers. In the Mao era, apart from reading newspapers, most people could listen to the radio, and they would discuss news, politics, and media content at political meetings. With the exception of reading large-print posters of political slogans that lined the streets and watching the occasional film, however, for most people this was the sum of their media experiences. In the 2000s, in addition to radio, newspapers, and political posters—which are still widely used—Chinese people now regularly watch television, go to the movies, watch DVDs and videos at home, read magazines, call friends and relatives throughout China and overseas, surf the Internet at home or in Internet cafés, send and receive text and multimedia SMS messages on their mobile phones, and listen to all kinds of music on cassette, CD, or MP3. The Chinese media landscape has completely changed.

This does not mean that newspaper reading has diminished in importance, however. Indeed, one could argue that newspapers have become all the more relevant to people's everyday lives as a result of this diversifying media landscape. Newspapers are now securely positioned among these other media practices, and newspaper reading does not so much compete with them as interact with and enhance them.

In terms of news, for instance, many people watch the television or listen to the radio for the latest, up-to-the-minute news or for a broad idea of what has been happening locally, nationally, and internationally. They will hear what has happened from these sources, yet they still buy newspapers. This is because as well as report those same news stories, newspapers offer a complementary and supplementary news service. There is more space in a newspaper for more shorter or less consequential news stories, and newspapers are also turned to for more detail, in-depth analysis, or commentary—things there is often little time for in a broadcast news bulletin. Many newspaper stories also find themselves recirculating on the Web, creating another cross-media relationship between print journalism and the Internet (also see below).

Apart from news, newspapers also feed upon, inform, and stimulate other media practices. Newspapers tell people what is on the television or radio and offer information, recommendations, criticisms, and commentary on programs, actors, and other stars. Similarly, they offer information and commentary on cinema, theatre, literature, and other arts. Newspapers often also recommend Web sites, DVDs, books, and music, and they promote magazines and other newspapers. All of these contribute to newspaper sales and constitute a prominent feature of Chinese newspaper culture.

Newspapers and Consumer Culture

The relationship between newspapers and consumer culture is multifaceted. In a straightforward sense, as items of consumption, newspapers feature directly in Chinese consumerism. This is important because newspaper editors operating in a largely competitive market environment have therefore come to treat their readers as consumers. They are trying to sell a product which they hope people will find useful and interesting and will hopefully buy again in the future.

There are other ways in which Chinese consumer culture features in the production of newspapers, too. For instance, the conceptualization of newspaper readers as consumers relates to readers not only as people who buy newspapers but as consumers of other goods and services. In a similar way to that in which newspapers guide, encourage, and relate with other media practices, so also Chinese newspapers guide, encourage, and relate with consumerism, particularly in the large cities. Indeed, a large proportion of daily newspaper content is directly or indirectly related to consumption (Latham 2006).

Lifestyle and entertainment sections of newspapers—which might be four-or-more-page pullouts—are almost entirely oriented on consumption, with articles on shopping, food, restaurants, entertainment, television, books, music, and other media, motoring, property, home improvements, information technology products, sports, hobbies, travel and tourism, and fashion. Newspapers guide consumers to bargains; they offer advice on different products; they introduce emerging markets and latest fashions; and they tell people what to look out for when shopping or buying services. At the same time, these sections carry a large number of advertisements. Hence, in many ways newspapers give a running commentary on contemporary Chinese consumer society and tell people how to shop—how to be consumers within it.

This aspect of newspaper consumption also fits well with the increasingly competitive, commercial nature of the newspaper industry. As newspapers have come to rely increasingly on sales, subscriptions, and advertising for their income, promoting and advising on a lively consumer culture brings its own paybacks in terms of increased sales and more advertising. This produces a symbiotic relationship between newspapers and consumer culture that reveals the key role played by the former in maintaining and promoting the latter.

Chinese journalists are very proud of their high professional standards, and both individually and institutionally they work hard to maintain the high level of objective reporting that is common throughout the industry. In the competitive and commercially oriented reform period, however, some journalists and newspapers have turned to different forms of "paid journalism," which creates another link between newspapers and consumer culture, albeit one that many journalists regret.

Paid journalism involves receiving some kind of payment or recompense from companies to write articles or features that present their products or services in a positive way. This mild form of bribery is similar to public relations in the United States—only in China the company is in a stronger position because it deals directly with the journalist. Paid journalism may relate not only to consumer goods and services but to other business journalism in general. Newspapers that regularly write product review articles and comment upon and guide readers toward the latest fashions are in a strong position to influence consumer habits.

Newspapers and the Internet

At the end of the 1990s, Chinese newspapers faced a new set of challenges and opportunities with the increasing popularity of the Internet, particularly in large urban centers where Internet use was higher. The Internet had started to change the way that Chinese people looked for and obtained news and information. Newspapers had to adapt to this changing situation and find their own place in an emerging Internet culture.

At first, some of the larger newspapers experimented with electronic versions of their newspapers, effectively trying to reproduce the print version on the Internet and using the new technology as a new mode of delivery. Two problems arose. One, the print format was not ideal for the Internet and proved cumbersome or difficult to read. Two, as online newspapers were effectively free, they did not bring in much revenue and rarely paid for the work required to publish and maintain them.

As a result, in the early 2000s, as the Internet became more widely used, newspapers changed their online presence. First, they generally adopted more standard portal-style formats, with headline links leading to the news stories and subsections or channels relating to particular types of news—sports, international news, national news, culture, and so on. Second, many newspapers started collaborating in order to provide a more comprehensive service at a lower operating cost. Hence, large news portal Web sites emerged as cooperative projects—possibly between several newspapers and television and radio stations. For example, Beijing's *Dragon News Network* was set up in the late 1990s and run jointly by six Beijing newspapers as well as radio and television stations in the capital. The larger, wealthier newspapers set up and maintained their own news Web sites but ran them separately not as online versions of the newspaper so much as semi-independent sources of news in themselves. So these news Web sites, as well as republishing articles from the print versions, would also have their own dedicated journalists and editors writing their own versions of news stories specifically for the Internet.

The Internet has also completely changed people's access to newspaper articles in two ways. First, it has made newspaper articles available from a whole range of newspapers including general, local, and specialized titles that would never have been accessible in the past. Before the Internet, it would be very difficult for ordinary Chinese people to read articles not published either in a national newspaper or in one of their local newspapers. Readers in Wuhan would have had little access to articles in Chengdu, Guangzhou, or, for that matter, even Beijing newspapers. The Internet has changed that. Not only can readers go online and go directly to newspaper Web sites, but by searching using any of the main portals or search engines they can find a whole range of articles reproduced from all kinds of publications.

Second, the Internet has created a new news archive that makes past newspaper articles available to readers in a way never previously imaginable. Some newspapers have online archives of their own past issues that may be searchable by topic or keywords, and then once again the main portals and search engines will find articles from all kinds of newspapers going back several years. In the past, such a possibility simply did not exist, and to find the same information would at best have taken weeks, if not months, of searching through multiple library newspaper archives scattered around the country; at worst it would have simply been impossible.

The Future of Newspapers in China

Over the last twenty years, Chinese newspapers have proven to be one of the most adaptable and forward-looking media in the country. Newspapers have led the way in changing journalism, in stretching the limits of Party control of the media, in experimenting with new kinds of stories, and in transforming themselves into successful commercial enterprises. Indeed, in the early 2000s television was only starting to be able to do things with social news reporting that newspapers had initiated nearly a decade and a half earlier. In recent years, newspapers have also proven adaptable to the new technological possibilities brought by the Internet and telecommunications. In July 2004, the country's first cellphone newspaper—that is, an edited-down version of a newspaper or combined editorial content from different newspapers delivered electronically to a mobile phone—was launched by the *China Women's News* (*zhongguo funü bao*). Just a year later there were dozens of cellphone newspapers around the country. Consequently, although print newspapers represent what are now called the "old media"—that is, the kind of media that were common before the technological revolutions of the 1980s and 1990s—in China, at least, they have nonetheless been at the forefront of change and open to experimentation with new technologies. This is likely to continue to be the case.

In the early 2000s, the proliferation of newspaper titles was starting to slow down, and if anything the number of titles was starting to decline. This trend is also likely to continue as the newspapers that remain heavily dependent on state subsidies have been forced to become commercially viable or else close down. The government has been keen to tidy up the newspaper industry by reducing the number of publications and has also shown a preference for fewer, larger, and stronger media organizations over many smaller ones. As there is clearly money to be made in newspapers, however, new titles will continue to be launched.

In terms of Chinese popular culture, therefore, as newspapers become increasingly commercially aware they will become ever more sensitive to the demands of their readership. The future is likely to lie in more specialized newspapers and trying to offer more personalized newspaper consumption. This will include ever-broadening interests covered in daily general-interest newspapers as well as greater use of new technologies like the Internet, broadband, e-mail, and SMS or MMS messaging to offer readers new kinds of selective news services. Newspapers will also continue to adapt to new technologies and changing Chinese society. To date, this has proven to be their strength. Newspapers will therefore continue to find new functions for themselves in China's consumer society; they will follow broad social and cultural trends and help their readers themselves adapt to these changes.

However, until there is a radical change in government attitudes to the media—and that does not seem ready to happen anytime soon—the area of politics and political news reporting will only change very gradually. The innovative energies of the newspaper industry will for the time being continue to push in commercial directions, not political ones. Nonetheless, as the commercial development of newspapers and the culture of newspaper reading since the early 1990s have shown, the multifaceted contribution of newspapers to contemporary Chinese popular culture has, in some instances, been enhanced and developed by political control, not necessarily restricted by it.

A to Z

Advertising. With the commercialization of Chinese newspapers from the 1980s onward, advertising, along with newspaper sales, has become one of the two pillars of financial success or stability in the industry. Some of China's top-rated newspapers, such as the *Guangzhou Daily*, owe their rating to their success in raising advertising revenue more than their journalism.

Beijing Youth News (Beijing qingnian bao). One of China's leading newspaper innovators carefully negotiating a line between its Party organ duties and popular journalism. The *Beijing Youth News* is one of the most popular papers in China. In 2005, the Beijing Youth News Group also became the first mainland Chinese newspaper group to float a subsidiary company on the Hong Kong Stock Exchange.

China Daily. The main English-language daily newspaper in China, produced by the central government principally as an information and propaganda title aimed at foreigners, both those living and working in China and those overseas.

Dushi bao. Often known as "metropolitan newspapers," these are generally tabloid-format local newspapers aiming at the popular market. They include titles like the *Nanfang Metropolitan News* that have been at the forefront of pushing Party and government restrictions on journalism.

Editorials. Have played a key role in the political history of the PRC. *People's Daily* editorials were often the first place that new policy statements would be made public in the Mao era and are still used for conveying important central political messages or statements of position by the Party and the government. Meanwhile, the editorial comment has also become a popular feature of many commercially oriented newspapers, although they clearly stick to politically acceptable issues and positions.

Evening newspapers (wanbao). Noted for their less political content and a focus on "social news" emphasizing human-interest stories and issues close to people's everyday lives. In the late 1950s, the Party launched several evening newspapers including thenationally recognized *Yangcheng Evening News* and the *Beijing Evening News*, tasked with providing readers with a broader range of news than the strictly politically oriented daily papers. Evening newspapers offered lighter, "softer" news for an urban readership, although they still retained their political and propaganda responsibilities. With the popularity of this kind of reporting, many evening newspapers have flourished in the post-Mao reform period.

Guangming Daily (guangming ribao* or *the "Enlightenment" Daily). Known in China as the main national newspaper for intellectuals. Launched in June 1949, the paper was originally the paper of the China Democratic League. In 1957, the newspaper reported widely on forums critical of the Communist Party, earning itself a critical reputation as well as some severe criticism in return from the leadership. In the 1980s, the paper became a mouthpiece for the interests of intellectuals, focusing editorials on their political status and working and living conditions. Facing severe financial difficulties in recent years, the paper relies heavily upon institutional subscriptions from Party and state work units such as schools, universities, and publishing and cultural organizations.

Guangzhou Daily. One of China's largest-circulation newspapers and the wealthiest in terms of advertising revenue. The paper is the Party organ newspaper for the Guangzhou City Party Propaganda Committee (see above).

Internet. The Internet is already one of the most important developments in the contemporary Chinese newspaper industry. Many newspapers have established an online presence in one form or another, such as a news portal or a full electronic version of their printed newspaper. The Internet will continue to play an increasingly important role in the daily operation of newspapers in China.

Liberation Daily. One of the first Chinese communist newspapers, set up in Yan'an in the late 1930s.

Literacy. Has clearly been a key issue affecting the role of newspapers in Chinese society. The CCP has always placed high value on improving literacy rates among Chinese people, at least in part so that they would be able to read government messages in newspapers. In the Mao period, key newspaper articles and editorials were often read out and explained at public political meetings.

Metropolitan newspapers. See *Dushi bao.*

Nanfang Weekend (nanfang zhoumo* or *Southern Weekend). One of China's groundbreaking newspapers, launched in the late 1980s by the *Nanfang* (*Southern*) *Daily* newspaper group. The paper avoided political news and focused on human-interest stories and topical social issues such as education, employment, health care, and transport. Started as a local newspaper in southern Guangdong Province, it soon enjoyed a large national circulation.

New China Daily. One of the first Chinese communist newspapers, set up in Yan'an in the late 1930s.

Party organ newspaper. A newspaper that comes directly under the supervision and direction of one or another Party propaganda committee and which consequently has a higher level of political propaganda responsibilities than non-Party organ newspapers.

People's Daily. The most famous and prestigious national daily newspaper in China. The *People's Daily* is the official organ newspaper of the Chinese Communist Party's Central Committee and one of the principal mouthpieces of the CCP. In the Mao period, through its editorials the paper was often used as the vehicle for launching new political campaigns. Newspapers throughout the country were required to republish these pieces, which were often the focus of political study meetings. In the post-Mao period, the symbolic significance and mouthpiece function of the paper remain unchanged. In a commercialized and highly competitive market, however, the character of its readership has narrowed.

Red China Daily. One of the first Chinese communist newspapers, set up in Shanghai in the late 1920s.

Red Flag Daily. One of the first Chinese communist newspapers, set up in Shanghai in the late 1920s.

State Administration for Press and Publications (SAPP, aka General Administration for Press and Publications). The government body that oversees all newspaper and magazine publishing in China. It is structured along the usual Chinese government lines of a central, national-level office and then branch offices at the different regional levels: provincial, city, and county. SAPP is responsible for formulating and implementing regulations relating to all kinds of publishing as well as monitoring industry output and developments.

Weekend editions. Starting with the *Nanfang Weekend* launched in the late 1980s, in the post-Mao period, weekend editions have exploited their relative freedom from politics to great commercial advantage and set new agendas for the Chinese press. Weekend editions do not carry the same burden of political propaganda reporting that other newspapers, including evening papers, usually bear. They generally focus on longer feature articles about social issues—crime and corruption, education, health, consumerism, and so on—and have proved enormously popular with readers throughout the country.

Wenhuibao. One of China's oldest newspaper titles, based in Shanghai and dating back to the early twentieth century. In 1948, a Hong Kong branch of the paper was set up, which, with political developments, subsequently became a separate newspaper and known as one of the left-wing, generally communist-supporting papers in Hong Kong. The Shanghai *Wenhuibao* is still one of the most popular daily newspapers in the city.

World Economic Herald. An influential and popular newspaper operating in the 1980s. The paper was closely associated with top reformist leaders including Zhao Ziyang and generally supported a pro-economic reform and open policy agenda. In 1989, it was closely associated with the student democracy movement, and losing political favor it was soon forced to close down by the Chinese authorities.

Xinhua News Agency ("New China" News Agency). The official state and Party news agency in China, charged with collecting and supplying news, information, and analysis to news organizations throughout the country and overseas. It officially exists as a department of the State Council, but it is also answerable to the Central Propaganda Committee of the Chinese Communist Party (CCP), and its primary function is the promulgation of propaganda for the CCP and the government. It therefore plays a crucial role in the daily operation of newspapers in the country, being their primary source of all agency-supplied news and information. In the 1990s, considerable investment in the agency from central government has seen it grow and develop to offer a professional and commercial, as well as politically motivated, news service with 106 overseas bureaus in addition to its 36 domestic bureaus and numerous sub-bureaus throughout the country.

Yangcheng Evening News (Ram City Evening News). One of China's best-known local evening newspapers that is distributed nationwide. Established in 1956 and produced in Guangzhou (locally known as "Ram City" because of a local legend), the paper has a long-standing reputation for being a relatively critical and independently minded newspaper offering lively news coverage of issues close to people's everyday lives. The *Yangcheng Evening News* has been a commercial success in the post-Mao reform period and expanded its operations to set up the Yangcheng Evening News Group, home to five other daily and weekly titles; its own book-publishing house; and a number of other business interests.

References and Further Reading

Anderson, B. 1983. *Imagined communities: Reflections on the origins and spread of nationalism.* London: Verso.

Cell, C. P. 1983. "Communication in China's mass mobilization campaigns." In G. C. Chu & F. Hsu (eds.) *China's new social fabric.* London: Kegan Paul International.

Huang, C. 2000. "The development of a semi-independent press in post-Mao China: An overview and a case study of Chengdu Business News." *Journalism Studies,* Vol. 1, No. 4, 649–664.

Latham, K. 2000. "Nothing but the truth: News media, power and hegemony in South China." *China Quarterly,* No. 163 (September 2000), 633–654.

———2006. "Powers of imagination: The role of the consumer in China's silent media revolution." In K. Latham, S. Thompson, & J. Klein (eds.) 2006. *Consuming China: Approaches to cultural change in contemporary China.* London: RoutledgeCurzon.

Lee, C. C. (ed.) 2000. *Power, money, and media: Communication patterns and bureaucratic control in cultural China.* Evanston, IL: Northwestern University Press.

Lee, L. O. & Nathan, A. J. 1985. "The beginnings of mass culture: Journalism and fiction in the late Ch'ing and beyond." In D. Johnson, A. J. Nathan, & E. S. Rawski (eds.) *Popular culture in Late Imperial China.* Berkeley, CA: University of California Press.

MacKinnon, S. R. 1997. "Toward a history of the Chinese press in the Republican period." *Modern China,* Vol. 23, No. 1.

Zha, J. 1995. *China pop: How soap operas, tabloids and bestsellers are tranforming a culture.* New York: New Press.

Zhang, X. 1997. "China's newspaper industry: Continuing down the road of corporatization." In J. M. Weng, X. Zhang, Z. Zhang, & K. M. Qu (eds.) *China's development situation and trends 1996–7.* Beijing: China Society Publishing House.

Zhao Y. 1998. *Media, market, and democracy in China: Between the party line and the bottom line.* Urbana and Chicago, IL: University of Illinois Press.

6

Magazines

Magazines are one of the most publicly visible components of Chinese popular culture. Alongside newspapers, they adorn the millions of newsstands scattered around China's cities, towns, and villages, and with their bright colors and glossy photographs they are an eye-catching feature of Chinese public space. Cover girls—sometimes having little to do with the contents of the magazine—entice passersby from kiosks, street-side stalls, and shop windows all over the country. They also parade up and down trains, buses, ferries, airplanes, airports, railway and bus stations, and jetties from the heart of Beijing to the remotest parts of China's transport infrastructure. In this way, although magazines have less political significance than other media, they have a public presence that rivals all others, and an average Chinese newsstand in a metropolitan center like Beijing, Shanghai, or Guangzhou can sell up to 150 magazines a day.

Magazines are popular with Chinese people from all across the social spectrum. Whether it be a glossy business magazine aiming at China's new middle classes, a literary digest aimed at intellectuals, or a collection of sensational real-life stories targeting the general populace, there is a magazine for just about everyone, covering all popular interests as well as professional, industry, and occupational demands. In 2001, there were more than 8,800 different magazine titles, covering IT and computers, sports, video games, music, hi-fi, literature, art and calligraphy, economics, business, television, cinema and other entertainment, martial arts, theatre, performance, automobiles, fashion, home furnishing, health, agriculture, philosophy, and much more. By 2005, this had increased further to more than 9,400 titles.

Clearly, there are links and similarities between newspapers and magazines in Chinese popular culture. Many newspaper publishers, for instance, also publish magazines, and many topical newspapers, such as entertainment, professional, and niche-interest papers, are

A construction worker looks at magazine posters while eating his lunch next to a newsstand in Beijing, China. As publishing regulations have relaxed in China hundreds of magazines have emerged, many of them focusing on beauty, fashion, and the lifestyles of television, movie, and pop stars. (AP/Wide World Photos)

competing with magazines for similar kinds of readers. Furthermore, many of the administrative and regulatory principles covering newspapers—regarding ownership, content restrictions, and politics, for instance—also apply to magazines. However, there are also notable differences between the position of newspapers and the position of magazines in China's popular cultural landscape.

Although, as we have discussed in the last chapter, newspapers serve a range of functions across the popular cultural spectrum, one of their key functions is clearly the provision of news, and current affairs of different kinds has a prominent position in newspaper content. Unlike other major international markets, where newsmagazines are often among the national best-sellers, until recently there were relatively few news and current affairs–oriented magazines in China. The early 2000s brought a small flurry of news and current affairs titles—although usually slanted toward the less sensitive areas of business and economic news—but most Chinese readers do not turn to magazines for their news and current affairs coverage.

Some of the fastest-growing magazine categories in recent years have been science, technology and IT, fashion, health and beauty, and automobile magazines.

Consequently, just a few years later in 2005, the Chinese magazine market was already looking slightly different. Of the 9,468 titles printed in that year, 49.9 percent (4,713) were science and technology magazines, including IT, computing, and telecommunications magazines; 24.7 percent (2,339) were philosophy or social science magazines; 12.4 percent were cultural or educational magazines; 6.5 percent were literature and art magazines; and 5 percent were general-interest magazines. The other 1.5 percent were children's magazines and pictorials (SAPP 2006).

Semi-detachment from news and politics has been key to the development of a broad magazine sector over the last couple of decades and is also important for understanding how magazines in the 2000s are closely collaborating with China's intensifying urban consumer culture.

Historical Overview

The history and development of magazines in China is closely intertwined with that of newspapers, and the issues relating to the development of mass readerships discussed in the previous chapter relate also to the development of magazines. From the beginning of the twentieth century and through the Republican period, there developed a healthy culture of journal publication catering principally to two urban readerships. On one hand, there were academic and intellectual journals. These published critical essays, short stories, poetry, and other literature. *New Youth* (*xin qingnian*) was probably the most famous such periodical and the most closely associated with the May 4th literary movement. The readership of these journals comprised students, political activists, revolutionaries, and urban intellectuals. On the other hand, there were urban-based popular journals covering a range of general-interest news, film, entertainment, fashion, science, and fiction, often with a relatively high pictorial content. These too were generally read by urban elites of different kinds, as general literacy levels were still relatively low among the less privileged sections of the population. Despite the incorporation of news and current affairs into magazines of the time, however, their content was often more commercially rather than politically motivated.

Magazine publication, like other media production, was also heavily affected by the war against the Japanese in the 1930s and 1940s as well as the continuing battles between communists and nationalists. Many journals were forced to close down or move around the country as a result of fighting and political and social instability. The content of many magazines that managed to continue publishing in the unoccupied areas of the country was also strongly affected by anti-Japanese sentiment and political propaganda of different kinds. However, the culture of magazine publishing and reading became well established in this period, particularly among urban intellectuals.

In the newly founded People's Republic of the 1950s, magazine publishing continued to thrive, although as with other media production it came fully under CCP control and was heavily politically motivated. The political, news, and educational orientation of China's magazine publishing in the 1950s is clear from the list of leading publications for 1955: *Current Affairs Pocket Magazine* (*shishi shouce*), *Learning* (*xuexi*), *Political*

Study (*zhengzhi xuexi*), *The New Observer* (*xin guancha*), *World Affairs* (*shijie zhishi*), *The People's Pictorial* (*renmin huabao*), and *The Popular Illustrated* (*lianhuan huabao*) (Chang 1989: 33). One quarter of all magazine circulation was accounted for by two youth publications: *Chinese Youth* (*zhongguo qingnian*) and *The High School Student* (*zhongxuesheng*) (Chang 1989: 33).

In 1957, there were 600 periodicals published in China. Of these, 130 were social science titles, 230 were natural science titles, 110 related to literature and the arts, and 130 were devoted to minority and foreign languages (Chang 1989: 32). Official figures reported magazine circulation peaking in 1958 at nearly 530 million copies, dropping back to around 230 million by the end of 1961 in the aftermath of the economically, socially, and humanly disastrous Great Leap Forward. At the height of the disruption caused by the Cultural Revolution in 1968, by contrast, there were just 22 titles being published nationally, with a circulation of less than 28 million copies.

The 1970s saw a rapid recovery in magazine publication as the political turmoil calmed down, with 476 titles published in 1975 and total circulation approaching 440 million once again. In 1978, this was up still further to 930 titles and 760 million printed copies. This was followed in the 1980s with a further proliferation of titles comparable with the expansion of other media such as newspapers and television at the time. By 1985, for instance, the number of titles published had reached 4,705, with 2.56 billion copies printed. In 2001, there were 8,889 magazine titles published in China, with a total of 2.89 billion copies printed throughout the year, and by 2005 there were 9,468 titles with a total of 2.76 billion copies printed (SAPP 2006). From this, one can see that although since 1985 there has been a large increase in the number of magazine titles, there has been only a relatively modest overall increase in the number of copies printed and a slight decline since 2001. This reflects the diversification and specialization of Chinese magazines in recent years.

The 1980s also saw the reintroduction of more commercially oriented thinking into magazine production as publishers started to become more aware of the notion of pleasing, attracting, and enticing readers as much as informing, educating, and instructing them, as had generally been the case in the past. In the 1990s, this commercial spirit was more thoroughly developed as an increasingly competitive magazine market emerged and Chinese readers nurtured ever broader interests, demands, and expectations and enjoyed greater leisure time and disposable income. Against this backdrop, magazine publishing also became an ever more attractive investment for government departments and media organizations looking for new sources of income.

Kinds of Magazines

Glossy fashion, entertainment, and automobile magazines, including Chinese versions of international bestsellers such as *Cosmopolitan* and *Elle*, are among the most eye-catching publications on Chinese streets.

They sit on streetside newsstands along with dozens of other titles competing for readers' attention. They are playing an important role in transforming Chinese print culture; however, it is important to

An advertisement on a newstand for the Chinese edition of *Cosmopolitan* magazine in 2005. (Corbis)

remember that there are also literally hundreds of millions of copies of other, less visible magazines sold every year. These include titles with some of the top circulations in the country such as *China Comment* (*banyuetan*), the CCP political affairs magazine; *Reader* (*duzhe*); and *Story Club* (*gushihui*)—these magazines may have a less immediately obvious public presence on Chinese streets, but they sell millions of copies of each issue.

Difference in visibility is partly due to the different major modes of distribution used by different magazines. Most of the popular Party magazines, although they may be found on newsstands, mail most of their copies to paid subscribers. For Party organ magazines (see Chapter 5 for discussion of Party organ newspapers), these also include large numbers of compulsory subscriptions by Party and government offices (although these were reduced in 2004).

This complex mixture of market-driven street sales, commercial magazines, Party magazines with propaganda responsibilities, compulsory subscriptions, and direct distribution methods means that it has become difficult properly to assess the relative popularity of different magazines. As with newspapers, the most highly subscribed-to might not in the end be the most popular. There are also regionally focused markets for small magazines that may be locally very popular but do not have the resources for large-scale national distribution.

In considering the different kinds of magazines in China we therefore need to include Party magazines, commercial magazines, professional or occupational magazines, intellectual magazines, and other special-interest magazines. As the number of foreign magazine titles in China increases, it is also worth considering their place in China's magazine culture, and it is important to include illegal magazines that are sometimes both popular and readily available on Chinese streets.

Party Magazines

Party magazines are those that have a similar institutional role and function to Party organ newspapers (see Chapter 5). They are magazines produced by the propaganda committees of the Party which have strongly educational and politically defined responsibilities. For example, *China Comment* is the political affairs magazine produced by the Xinhua News Agency under the direct supervision of the CCP Central Ministry of Propaganda (*zhonggong zhongyang xuanchuanbu*), which also produces the Party's best-known and long-standing political theory magazine *Seeking Truth* (*qiushi*).

Like Party organ newspapers, many Party magazines used to rely on compulsory subscriptions which were cut back by government reforms in 2004. Many titles lost either or both direct and indirect subsidies and faced the full force of open market competition. As a result, many had to shut down.

Party magazines have an ambiguous position in contemporary Chinese popular culture. On one hand, they include some of the best-selling and largest-distribution magazines in the country. In terms of Chinese politics, titles such as *Seeking Truth*—launched in 1958 under the name *Red Flag* (*hongqi*)—have long histories of high-profile political importance and influence dating to the Cultural Revolution and earlier. On the other hand, Party magazines in the 2000s are not widely read by the general population. Those most likely to read magazines such as *Seeking Truth* (which had more than 1 million subscribers in 2000) are Party cadres, government officials, students, and academics—that is to say, those who *have* to read them for some reason, professional or educational, rather than those who would do so for leisure or out of casual interest.

Some leading Party magazines such as *China Comment* also made efforts in the early 2000s to enliven their presentational style, including launching bold, attractive Web sites. However, they cannot be detached from their politically defined content. In this way, Party magazines to some degree represent the past in the present. While China's consumer society and magazine markets have moved on to much more lively and glossy activities, Party magazines still embody the Party mouthpiece principle of media production.

Commercial Magazines

Starting in the 1980s, as many new magazine titles came into production, a new kind of Chinese magazine started to emerge, one that was no longer simply politically and ideologically oriented but also commercially oriented. This became a much stronger trend in the 1990s. Some of these were new titles; others were old magazines that underwent transformations and revamped their editorial content and presentational style. As with other media, this move fundamentally changed the nature of magazine content, which started to become much more conscious of what readers were interested in rather than what the Party thought they ought to know.

For instance, *Family* (*jiating*) magazine (launched in the early 1980s) and *Family Doctor* (*jiating yisheng*) magazine, both printed in Guangdong Province, became popular best sellers first in Guangdong and then nationally as their reputation grew. These, and other magazines like them, took what was a politically and organizationally defined set of responsibilities (e.g., family welfare or family medicine) to write articles that attracted the average reader—particularly women—by touching on issues such as sex and sexuality, aging, beauty, mental health, and other similar issues. Written in light, accessible style and dealing openly with issues rarely if ever discussed in other sectors of the media, these magazines were able to carve out new niches for themselves.

Some of the most successful were those aiming at urban female readers. In addition to *Family*, other regional women's titles, such as *Lady Friends* (*nüyou*) from Shaanxi

Province and *Bosom Friends* (*zhiyin*) from Hubei Province, have become national best sellers through content that is a light mixture of health and beauty, consumer affairs, popular psychology, and emotional and personal issues as well as real-life human-interest stories presented in easily digestible and novel formats.

The late 1990s saw another boom in commercial magazine publication as new kinds of titles hit the Chinese streets with great success. In particular, there was a wave of fashion and entertainment magazines that proved very popular, including the Chinese versions of *Elle*, *Madame Figaro*, and *Cosmopolitan* but also homegrown Chinese fashion titles that to some degree emulated the high production values of their internationally recognized rivals. Shanghai became the hub of Chinese fashion publishing, being home to leading titles such as *Healthy Girl* (*jiankang nühai*), *International Clothes Trends* (*guoji fuzhuang dongtai*), *Modern Family* (*xiandai jiating*), and *Young Generation* (*qingnian yidai*).

Chinese fashion magazines, including the Chinese versions of international titles, are not entirely unlike fashion magazines elsewhere, with a strong mix of advertising, clothing fashion, famous models, perfumes, jewelry, and cosmetics as well as light lifestyle stories on issues such as friendship, relationships, work, and health. However, the degree of nudity, sexual content, and discussion of sexually liberal lifestyles is considerably less than in some well-known European and U.S. fashion titles such as the English-language editions of *Cosmopolitan*.

In the early 2000s, as the women's fashion magazine market became established and increasingly crowded, commercial magazine publishers started looking for new niches including men's health and fashion, automobiles, travel and tourism, home furnishing, and cultural themes.

Professional or Occupational Magazines

With the large increase in the number of magazine titles in the 1980s, the breadth of magazine coverage also expanded. Government offices of all kinds, if they were not already doing so, looked toward publishing a magazine or newspaper for their particular area of responsibility or expertise. This ensured that every profession and economic, agricultural, or industrial sector soon had its own magazine or even range of magazines to choose from.

Hence, China has magazines for forestry, fishing, fish farming, all kinds of agriculture, horticulture, light and heavy manufacturing, electronics manufacturing and research, telecommunications, information technologies, mining, different areas of medicine from neurology to acupuncture and moxibustion, the travel industry, and the legal profession. These are the magazines that inform workers in these various sectors of important professional issues such as national and international industry trends, new products and technologies, regulatory changes and developments, employment opportunities, and contract tenders.

It is possible to see these kinds of magazines as, being closely linked to work and the economy, less immediately part of Chinese popular culture that tends to conjure up notions of entertainment, music, the arts, performance, and media in particular. For many Chinese people, though, professional magazines may actually be the only magazines they read on a regular basis.

Intellectual Magazines

China has a long history of influential intellectual magazines and journals. In the early twentieth century, intellectuals and revolutionaries published short stories, essays, and political commentaries voluminously in the various and often short-lived literary and political journals of the time. The political circumstances in the early twenty-first century are rather different, but the importance of magazines and journals for Chinese intellectuals has persisted.

There are still countless literary, film, arts, and cultural magazines aimed not at the general consuming public but at intellectual readers including academics, writers, artists, journalists, students, Party officials, and increasingly China's professional middle classes. In the 1980s, intellectual journals played a key role in what became known as the "Cultural Fever" movement in which Chinese cultural roots were subjected to wide-ranging forms of challenge and interrogation through literature and popular novels, film, television, music, and other forms of artistic production (Wang 1996). Some journals, such as the Guangzhou-based *Nanfeng Chuang* (*Window on Southern Winds*), were even closed down in the mid-1980s as the authorities became concerned about the extent to and speed with which some of the new ideas and debates were spreading.

Film magazines and journals played an important part in the redefinition of Chinese cinema as the so-called Fifth Generation of filmmakers emerged with innovative and challenging new works. Intellectual magazines also became one of the forums of debate surrounding the controversial television program *River Elegy* (*Heshang*—see Chapter 3). In the 1990s, following the Tiananmen Square incident of 1989, this critical role of intellectual magazines was at least temporarily stifled as the Party became ultrasensitive to any kind of potential challenge to its authority. Nonetheless, magazines and journals have continued to play a key role in the development of intellectual debates of all kinds to the present day.

Other Special-Interest Magazines

Professional, occupational, and intellectual magazines as well as many commercial titles are all special-interest magazines of sorts, and this is a good example of how these categorizations of magazines are interrelated and overlapping. However, there are also other special-interest magazines that cater to interest groups of different kinds. These are principally magazines aiming at relatively small groups with particular hobbies or leisure interests that are likely to be much less commercially profitable than fashion, automotive, home furnishings, or women's magazines.

There are magazines for interests such as calligraphy, stamp-collecting (a very popular pastime in China), traditional forms of theatre, *qigong* and martial arts, and much more. Such magazines play key facilitative roles in supporting popular leisure activities and pastimes and hence in enhancing China's popular cultural scene.

Foreign Magazines

China's entry to the World Trade Organization (WTO) in December 2002 is generally seen as the turning point for many Chinese industries and markets—including those of the media—for opening up to greater international involvement. Following WTO entry, China did indeed start to open up certain sectors of the media to foreign involvement that had previously been closed, and the magazine industry did start to open up further; however, the magazine sector was in fact already partly open to foreign involvement some twenty years earlier.

In 1980, the U.S. company International Data Group (IDG) set up a Sino-U.S. joint venture with a 49 percent share in the China Computer World Publishing Company—the first Sino-foreign media joint venture of the post-Mao era. By 2004, IDG was involved in the publication of thirty-two different magazines in China, many of them communications technologies titles including *Computer World*, *Microcomputer World*, *Network World*, *IT Management World*, and *Home Computer World*, with a total readership of around 30 million.

IDG was by far the earliest foreign company to enter the Chinese magazine industry, but twenty years after its initial joint venture was launched it was joined by a number of other leading international publishers who similarly managed to sidestep the legal barriers. These included another U.S. IT publisher, Ziff Davis (ZD), with titles such as *Personal Computer*, *Weekly Computer News*, *Electronics and Computing*, and *Electronic Commerce* (*EC*); and Taiwanese publishing group BNI, with mainland titles including *eLife*, *PC Shopper*, *DragonMD.com*, *Digitimes*, and *Eg@mer*. McGraw-Hill has also licensed its *Business Week* title and content to the China Foreign Economic Relations & Trade Publishing House since 1986.

As we have seen, fashion publishing also gave foreign companies opportunities to play their part in contemporary Chinese popular cultural production. In 2004, more than fifty foreign magazines were publishing Chinese-language editions for mainland China. The best-known titles getting into China relatively early were *Elle*, *Cosmopolitan*, and *Madame Figaro*. Hachette Filipacchi Presse, the publishers of *Elle*, also became involved in a range of other titles, covering fashion, sports, health, and motoring, with investments of millions of dollars.

Foreign companies entering the Chinese magazine market have found that they have had to adapt to the local situation in various ways. Clearly, there are legal and regulatory issues to be dealt with, and at least in theory all editorial content has to be in Chinese hands. How, precisely, magazines decide to approach and fit themselves to the Chinese market has immediate consequences for their content. For instance, the three fashion magazines mentioned above adopted three different strategies, with quite different consequences for their magazine content. At least early on, *Elle* basically translated the international edition of its magazine with appropriate editing to satisfy Chinese tastes or restrictions. *Madame Figaro*, on the other hand, collaborated with the Chinese magazine *Zhuiqiu* (*Search*) in a more cooperative joint venture. Meanwhile, *Cosmopolitan*, which was available in different editions in Hong Kong and Taiwan long before the Chinese mainland, adopted a more conscious localization strategy attempting to cater more specifically to the Chinese market.

Hence, at the end of the day what has been effectively imported has often not been the magazines, as such, but the brand that their name carries, attached to China-focused content. Nonetheless, Chinese magazines have been quick to copy what is seen as successful international experience, and the layouts, styles, formats, and gloss of foreign magazines have often influenced their Chinese rivals.

Illegal Magazines

In addition to officially recognized and openly marketed magazines, there are various kinds of illegal publications that feature in China's popular cultural landscape and should not be ignored. Pornography is perhaps an obvious example, but there are also religious and spiritual publications as well as what the government would call superstitious and unscientific publications such as almanacs.

It is impossible to tell the full extent of pornography in China, but "soft porn" titles—some printed in China and some illegally imported from Hong Kong or Taiwan—have at times over the last two decades been openly available from vendors in the large metropolises. However, the authorities run regular clean-up campaigns to clamp down on such publications, which undoubtedly mostly circulate out of sight.

Religious magazines and booklets are often smuggled into China by foreign missionary groups and are distributed by followers—both Chinese and foreign—on university campuses and through religious meetings. There are also numerous illegal Chinese "house churches" that sometimes produce newsletters for their members, although the penalties for doing so can be severe. In the early 2000s, the banned Buddhist spiritual movement known as the Falun Gong produced a wealth of books, magazines, and other literature that circulated widely before the group was outlawed. Subsequently, the authorities ran concerted crackdowns on Falun Gong followers and destroyed millions of pieces of literature. Folk almanacs giving astronomical predictions and folk remedies are also often illegally published and sold on the streets, often by poor people from the countryside.

Magazine Reading and Popular Culture

One of the key differences between magazines and other media contributions to China's popular cultural landscape relates to the nature and length of a magazine's social life. Newspapers are transient—news goes out of date fast, and newspapers have too many other uses, such as for packaging and as kindling. Television and radio programs come and go all the more quickly, and few people record them for later viewing, even if they have the equipment to do so. The Internet requires special locations or relatively expensive equipment and, despite the existence of the technology, for most Chinese people remains something inflexible and nonportable or even something they have heard of but never used.

Magazines, by contrast, are much less time-sensitive, particularly considering the relative paucity of newsmagazines. They are incredibly portable and very shareable and, being generally more durable than newspapers, lend themselves kindly to multiple readings. All this means that magazines participate in Chinese popular culture in quite different ways from other media.

Magazine reading is a more leisurely activity than other media consumption and is often associated with filling long stretches of time such as train journeys and other travel or with passing time at a job that is dull or inactive or involves long periods of waiting, such as gatekeeper, night watchman, or some kinds of office or retail work. Given such contexts as these, as well as simply reading while relaxing at home, magazines are often involved in more meditative contemplation of cultural production than other, more directly informative media.

Fashion, automobile, travel, and home furnishing magazines, for instance, stimulate aspirations, dreaming, fantasy, inquisitiveness, and curiosity as well as offer practical advice and information. Short story and fiction magazines as well as true-story magazines—which are very popular with travelers—carry readers off into the imagined worlds and lives of others. Of course, other media, particularly television programs and films, can do some similar things, but the nature and context of magazine reading often makes it unique among media practices and gives it a special role in the nurturing of different kinds of popular cultural imagining.

Magazine reading also has a broader significance in Chinese popular culture because of its relationship to other media and other popular cultural activities. Magazine reading, like newspaper reading, is not an isolated cultural practice but often one that interacts with others. For instance, reading fashion, automobile, home furnishing, or food magazines supports, motivates, and promotes these different areas of consumption. Reading sports magazines is part of being a fan of a particular sport or being actively involved in sports of different kinds. Similarly, magazine reading is closely related to other media activities such as watching films, listening to music, watching television, and reading books.

There are dozens of film magazines alone in China, not to mention the national and locally distributed television and entertainment magazines. These are often published by television stations as a combination of a television listings guide and general entertainment news, information, gossip, and interviews. Such magazines, particularly if produced by a television station, nudge readers toward particular programs and particular actors, stars, and television personalities. Research is limited on how far people's viewing habits are swayed by recommendations and promotions in newspapers or magazines such as these, but there is clearly a link between the two. Similarly, people's choice of films—whether Chinese or foreign, at the movie theater or at home—music, and books are all affected by reviews, criticisms, and promotions in magazines. In this way, magazines play an important part in the general inter-media relationships that pertain to Chinese popular cultural practices.

Commercialism, Advertising, and China's New Social Classes

For various reasons, largely related to the logistics and structure of the magazine publishing industry, in the early 2000s Chinese magazines contributed to and started to thrive upon the new social divisions that have emerged in Chinese society in the reform period.

First, the trend toward commercial magazine publishing tended to highlight special-interest magazines of different kinds as a means of targeting new niche readerships. This was enhanced by the fact that magazine publishing was seen as a relatively low-investment media industry in which private businesspeople could start to get involved in relatively small projects such as locally distributed special-interest magazines. Hence, magazines have often identified and targeted particular social groups.

Second, problems with distribution in particular meant that much of the country's magazine consumption was weighted toward the cities. Consequently, the urban magazine markets—those for fashion and automobile magazines, for instance—started to become saturated, with numerous similar titles competing for an ultimately limited number of consumers. Publishers therefore started looking toward new, faster, and more efficient modes of distribution to smaller towns and rural areas—such as postal subscriptions—in order to help them break out of increasingly cramped urban markets. As a result, magazine publishers also started thinking about more rural-focused magazine content.

Third, as a result of the history of state control, management, and subsidy of the magazine industry, even in the early 2000s, the majority of leading magazines relied upon newsstand sales and subscriptions, as opposed to advertising revenue, for their main income. With the heightening commercial spirit of the times, however, this started to change; particularly, new commercial titles started targeting advertisers as a key source of income over and above sales. Later, the large, established magazines also started paying greater attention to advertising. This had a further effect of focusing content on particular social groups in order to sell more advertising.

In the 1980s and early 1990s, the frequency of most Chinese magazines was monthly, bimonthly, or quarterly. There were very few weekly or biweekly publications, and these tended to be newspapers. As the commercial market for magazines heated up in the late 1990s and early 2000s, however, more and more magazines started shortening their production cycle to become weekly or semimonthly titles. This not only enabled them to sell more copies of their magazines, it enabled them to sell more advertising and compete more effectively with rival publications.

These various commercially driven trends in the magazine industry substantially affected magazine content. In particular, magazines started targeting the emerging middle classes, who not only had increasing disposable income but occupied positions of influence in both government and private circles.

For example, in the early 2000s, *Sanlian Life Weekly* was considered to be one of China's most successful magazines even though it had a distribution of only around 200,000 in 2004. The magazine was launched in 1995 and later became partly owned by the Hong Kong–based media conglomerate and operators of the popular Chinese Internet portal Tom.com (www.tom.com), the Tom Group. The magazine built up a reputation for being relatively hard-hitting and one of the few news and current affairs titles on the market. The key to its success, however, has been its popularity with advertisers because it is associated with a wealthy and influential readership of businesspeople, officials, intellectuals, and company executives.

Another example of the relationship between advertising, magazine culture, and social classes can be seen with the case of automobile magazines, which started becoming very popular in the large cities from around 2003. China has for decades been thought of as the country of the bicycle; however, as Chinese people have become wealthier, as the middle classes have become larger, as the cost of automobiles has become cheaper, and as government controls on automobile ownership have been relaxed, more and more private individuals and families in China bought or started thinking about buying their own automobile. Indeed, in the early 2000s, China's automobile industry and automobile market were among the fastest growing in the world.

This change in consumer habits therefore created a whole new magazine market. Automobile magazines are popular throughout the world where there is an automobile culture, but even in a country the size of China, while private car ownership was effectively impossible, there was no market for automobile magazines. Once automobiles started becoming obtainable, this all started to change. Since autos were still only realistically available to the relatively wealthy, however, automobile magazines have been targeted once again at the wealthy middle classes. Furthermore, the emergence of automobile magazines was driven in part by the automobile industry, which was eager for new and effective forms of targeted advertising. Automobile magazines therefore filled not only a market demand from consumers but a demand from manufacturers and advertisers.

Automobile magazines do more than simply advertise or picture cars, however. They depict certain lifestyles and write for particular audiences with a whole range of assumptions about houses, tastes, children, families, social values, attitudes, and personal aspirations. In this way, automobile magazines identify and demarcate a particular social group as envisaged by the editors. This in turn feeds back into readers' conceptualizations of themselves and others. Hence, through their imagery, depicted lifestyles, and glossy, aspirational advertisements, automobile magazines have come to play a role in the social imagination and self-definition of China's new middle classes.

Conclusion: Magazines and Popular Culture

Magazines occupy an important position in China's popular cultural landscape, for at least five reasons. First, magazines have a long-standing historical tradition in China of serving both the urban masses and intellectuals. In the last few decades, magazines have again come to fulfill both of these roles.

Second, although as mass media products magazines are subject to the same kind of political definition as other media, they have carved out distinct nonpolitical niches for themselves. This has enabled them to get closer to their readers and to interact with them in the more personal areas of their lives—friends and personal relationships, home furnishing, clothing, food, music, entertainment, and so on. Magazines have also enabled China's popular cultural consumers to feel closer to entertainment stars through personal interviews, special reports, and photographs.

Third, the nature of magazines and magazine reading also lend themselves to the more imaginative and contemplative aspects of what media theorist John Hartley has called "popular reality"—that is, the communication of ideas and sharing of more or less stable cultural meanings through encounters with journalism: the creation, maintenance, and transformation of a popular cultural "semiosphere" (Hartley 1996). One of Hartley's key points of emphasis, in fact, is that aspects of popular reality that do not relate to news are just as important as those that do. Chinese magazines are increasingly playing a role in this kind of popular cultural production.

Fourth, magazines play important articulatory roles linking readers to other media, different forms of consumption, and the formation, definition, and transformation of China's new social divisions, both in terms of different interest groups and in terms of emerging social classes.

Finally, magazine consumption is on the increase. It has become more and more part of Chinese urban popular culture and is fanning out to the countryside. The durability and portability of magazines also makes them ideal vehicles for the spread of urban popular cultural ideas and ideals into rural areas. As the magazine industry improves its distribution infrastructure, there is every possibility that in coming years, magazines will also become increasingly part of rural popular culture, helping to define a rural popular reality as much as they have to date nurtured an urban one.

A to Z

BNI. A large Taiwanese publishing company that has developed a range of largely IT-related magazine titles in China including *eLife*, *PC Shopper*, *DragonMD.com*, *Digitimes*, and *Eg@mer*.

Bosom Friends. See *Zhiyin*.

Cosmopolitan. This international women's fashion magazine has been published in China since the late 1990s. Although the content is different from its versions in other languages, the glossy presentation and style is similar and has acted as a model to be emulated by other Chinese fashion titles.

Duzhe (The Reader). One of China's most popular magazines for young people, with short stories and serialized fiction.

Elle. This international women's fashion magazine from Hachette Filipacchi Presse has been published in China since the late 1990s. Like its rivals *Cosmopolitan* and *Madame Figaro*, the magazine's glossy presentation and style has strongly influenced Chinese fashion publishing.

Family. See *Jiating*.

Family Doctor. See *Jiating Yisheng*.

Healthy Girl. See *Jiankang Nühai*.

Hongqi (Red Flag). The original name of the magazine launched in 1958 that later became *Qiushi* or *Seeking Truth*, one of the country's leading political magazines.

IDG. The International Data Group was the first foreign company to set up a Sino-foreign joint venture in the media sector in post–Cultural Revolution China. The company started with a 49 percent share in the China Computer World Publishing Company in 1980, long before others were able to follow suit, and has developed a range of media and other Chinese business interests since then. By 2004, the company was involved with thirty-two different magazines in China, largely related to information technologies.

Jiankang Nühai (Healthy Girl). Another of China's popular fashion magazines in the style of *Cosmopolitan*, *Elle*, and other international fashion titles.

Jiating (Family). Launched in the 1980s as one of several innovative new kinds of Party magazine that had one eye on public education and the other on commercial sales. The magazine carried a wide range of articles on health, relationships, and women's and welfare issues that were not often publicly discussed elsewhere. Subsequently, the magazine became very popular with readers throughout the country, women in particular.

Jiating Yisheng (Family Doctor). Like *Jiating*, this magazine, which attracted a wide popular readership in the 1980s, was published in Guangdong Province and carried a range of articles on health, beauty, and relationships. The magazine was particularly popular with women readers.

Lady Friends. See *Nüyou*.

Madame Figaro. Like *Cosmopolitan* and *Elle*, this international fashion title has been published in China since the late 1990s. Unlike its rivals, however, it has been published in close collaboration with a Chinese magazine, *Zhuiqiu* or *Search*.

Nanfeng Chuang (Window on Southern Winds). A popular intellectual magazine of the 1980s, often investigating cultural issues with a political edge. The magazine was closed down in the mid-1980s as the Chinese authorities became concerned about the political implications of some of its intellectually radical content.

New Youth. See *Xin Qingnian*.

Nüyou (Lady Friends). One of a clutch of women's magazines that attracted a large urban readership in the 1990s. The magazine, published in Shaanxi Province, became a national best-selling title with its mix of articles on consumer affairs, health issues, cosmetics and beauty, and popular psychology and other human-interest stories.

Pornography. Commonly available in China, even if it is illegal and strictly controlled by the Chinese authorities. Much pornography is now Internet-based, but there are still many magazines in circulation. Some are produced illegally in China, but many are illegally imported.

Qingnian Yidai (Young Generation). One of China's home-grown popular fashion magazines in the style of *Cosmopolitan*, *Elle*, and other international fashion titles.

Qiushi (Seeking Truth). One of China's best-known political party magazines, launched in 1958 as *Red Flag* (*hongqi*). The magazine played a prominent role in the politics of the Mao period in particular and in the Cultural Revolution. More recently, as politics has retreated from the forefront of Chinese social life, the magazine has lost its former prominence; however, it is still considered an important political title.

Reader. See *Duzhe*.

Red Flag. See *Hongqi*.

Seeking Truth. See *Qiushi*.

Subscriptions. Although there are hundreds of magazine titles available on the streets of China, many magazines either are subscription-only or distribute most of their copies through subscriptions. This applies to Party magazines in particular (see above). Traditionally, magazine subscription has been arranged through the post office, but more recently some magazines have moved toward direct distribution methods.

Window on Southern Winds. See *Nanfeng Chuang.*

Xin Qingnian (New Youth). One of China's historically most important and influential intellectual journals, published around the time of the May 4th Movement in 1919. Edited by Hu Shi, a leading intellectual reformer of the time, the journal provided a forum for radical cultural debate and a place for young writers of radical vernacular literature, including Lü Xun, Yu Dafu, Zhou Zuoren, Mao Dun, and many others.

Young Generation. See *Qingnian Yidai.*

Zhiyin (Bosom Friends). Another popular magazine along with *Nüyou*, *Jiating*, and others reaching a large national readership, predominantly women, with a light, journalistic mix of writing on health issues, emotional issues, relationships, consumer topics, and human-interest stories.

References and Further Reading

Chang, W. H. 1989. *Mass media in China: The history and the future.* Ames, IA: Iowa State University.

Hartley, J. 1996. *Popular reality: Journalism, modernity and popular culture.* London: Arnold.

Lee, C. C. (ed.) 2000. *Power, money, and media: Communication patterns and bureaucratic control in cultural China.* Evanston, IL: Northwestern University Press.

Lee, L. O. & Nathan, A. J. 1985. "The beginnings of mass culture: Journalism and fiction in the late Ch'ing and beyond." In D. Johnson, A. J. Nathan, & E. S. Rawski (eds.) *Popular culture in Late Imperial China.* Berkeley, CA: California University Press.

Li, Z. 1998. "Popular journalism with Chinese characteristics: From revolutionary modernity to popular modernity." *International Journal of Cultural Studies*, Vol. 1, No. 3, 307–328.

MacKinnon, S. R. 1997. "Toward a history of the Chinese press in the Republican period." *Modern China*, Vol. 23, No. 1, 3–32.

SAPP. 2006. "The basic situation of the national news and publishing industries in 2005." At SAPP website (www.gapp.gov.cn), downloaded September 2006. Article reference: http://www.gapp.gov.cn/GalaxyPortal/inner/zsww/zongsu3.jsp?articleid=6375&boardpid=145&boardid1=1150101011150f

Wang, J. 1996. *High culture fever: Politics, aesthetics, and ideology in Deng's China.* Berkeley, CA: University of California Press.

Zhao,Y. 1998. *Media, market, and democracy in China: Between the party line and the bottom line.* Urbana and Chicago, IL: University of Illinois Press.

7

Cinema, Film, and Video

In recent years, Chinese cinema has become one of the most internationally visible areas of contemporary Chinese popular culture. Since the mid-1980s, when young filmmakers of the so-called Fifth Generation (see below) started making films that hit cinema screens throughout the world, Chinese cinema has established for itself a recognized position on the international cinema circuit of film festivals, competitions, and art-house distribution. Some of those young filmmakers twenty years later were internationally recognized names—directors Zhang Yimou and Chen Kaige and actress Gong Li in particular.

However, it is not only in the last twenty years that cinema has become an important feature of Chinese popular culture. Since the 1930s, cinema has had a crucial role to play in formulating and embodying ideas of Chinese modernity; in the development of revolutionary Chinese intellectual and political movements; in entertaining, educating, and informing ordinary Chinese citizens; in promoting the policies of the Chinese Communist Party; and in raising the profile of Chinese artistic production on the international stage. Chinese cinematic production is a fundamental component of China's recent historical and contemporary artistic, entertainment, and political heritage.

When considering the role of cinema in contemporary Chinese popular culture, in addition to trying to understand Chinese films past and present one must look at a much broader range of influences. First, it is crucial to take into account that apart from much of the People's Republic period under Mao, Chinese people in the twentieth and twenty-first centuries have been watching many films that were not made in mainland China or even that were not made in China at all. Unsurprisingly, the Hollywood film industry has had a key role to play at different times in the history of both Chinese filmmaking and film viewing. At different times, so too have European and other foreign film industries. Hong Kong cinema in particular has enjoyed a special relationship with mainland Chinese film watching during the post-Mao reform era. Hence, our understanding of cinema

Chinese film director Chen Kaige (left) poses with Chinese movie star Gong Li (right) at the Festival Palace in Cannes on May 14, 1996. Kaige's film *Temptress Moon* was presented to the jury of the 49th International Cannes Film Festival. (AP/Wide World Photos)

in Chinese popular culture has to include film production in China and also the viewing of both Chinese films and foreign or Hong Kong films in China.

A second issue that must be taken into account in understanding film in contemporary China is that film is not an isolated medium. It is easy to associate film principally, or even solely, with going to the movie theater. However, films are of course also shown on television—there are specialized film channels to choose from as well as films shown on mainstream entertainment channels—and there has for years been a lively legal and illegal market for videocassettes, video compact discs (VCDs), and more recently DVDs. This means that film viewing consists of a far more dispersed and varied set of social practices than straightforward movie-theater attendance and also ranges across different media. Indeed, film consumption also includes reading newspapers, magazines, and Web sites.

A third issue to consider is the different kinds of film and cinema that feature in the Chinese popular cultural landscape. This includes different genres of films—martial arts films, historical films, thrillers, comedies, documentaries, educational films, and propaganda films—as well as films of different national origin. There is also another important distinction that needs to be taken into account, however: the contrast between popular commercial cinema and so-called art-house or intellectually oriented cinema. In the often politically motivated accounts of Chinese film or cinema history as well as intellectually motivated discussions of contemporary Chinese cinema, the latter is regularly emphasized at the expense of the former. Intellectuals and politicians alike both often prefer thinking about films considered more sophisticated, culturally aware, or socially and politically critical to thinking about films considered to be straightforward, undemanding commercial entertainment. There are often good reasons for this preference, but in understanding the diverse manifestations of and contributions to Chinese popular culture that film makes, both are equally important.

The fourth issue to remember is that cinema, like other media in China that we have discussed, is considered to be part of the state and Party propaganda machine, but also like other areas of Chinese media, it is undergoing reform that aims in part at least at greater commercialization and international competitiveness. Once again, in this respect the issue of censorship comes into play, and it is important to know roughly how Chinese film censorship works. In fact it is at first sight slightly paradoxical that when dealing with a country where all domestic films have been made by state-owned, state-run, state-financed, and state-controlled film studios under the supervision of senior Party cadres, we hear so often of exported films having been "banned by the authorities in China." Why, one might ask, should the authorities either want or need to ban something they have ultimately been responsible for producing? The answer lies in understanding how the censorship mechanism works.

The ways in which film content is directly censored include the compulsory approval of screenplays prior to production. Yet it has often been easy for filmmakers, in the post-Mao era at least, to stray from the original (approved) script without being stopped in the process. This may be due to lax implementation of supervisory procedures, broadly sympathetic studio managers, or other contingent factors. This means that films either explicitly or tacitly approved at the local level may contravene the principles laid down and imposed by the central authorities. That is how films subsequently considered sensitive can still be made.

However, there is a fail-safe mechanism in the system that has prevented such films from being seen by Chinese audiences if the central authorities disapprove of them. Until 2004, the state barred any person, group, or organization other than those designated by the Party at the central level to be involved in film distribution. This has meant that movie theaters have been solely dependent upon the central authorities for the films that they have been able to show,

Illegal sale of pirated DVDs in Beijing. (Corbis)

and those authorities have ultimately had the ability to ban any film simply by refusing to distribute it.

This leaves one other important issue to consider: piracy. The illegal copying of videocassettes and later VCDs and DVDs has been rife in China since the 1980s. In the early 2000s, literally millions and millions of illegally copied, or pirated, audio and video products were in general circulation in China and were accepted as part of everyday life by the vast majority of the population. This has two immediately significant implications. First, it completely undermines the system of centralized state film censorship through distribution. The authorities restrict the number of foreign films allowed into China each year (since 2004 the limit has been twenty), yet on the streets of any town in China there are many more pirated foreign films readily available. What is more, they generally cost a fraction of the price of a movie ticket. Second, this means that pirated video products have a significant economic impact. The industry as a whole, from filmmaking to projection, is ultimately affected by piracy. Reduced box office sales clearly affect theater owners, but it also means that the filmmakers receive less money for investment in future films. Piracy is therefore an important feature of the Chinese cinema, film, and video scene.

Chinese Cinema to 1949: An Overview

The first moving picture film equipment in China arrived in Shanghai in 1896, although

Undated photograph of a Mongolian showman turning the crank of his portable movie house. Young viewers paid a small fee to see a short film. (Corbis)

the first public projection of a film came in Beijing in 1902. Within a year of that, foreign newsreels were being shown regularly in Shanghai (Howkins 1982: 66). The first locally made film for Chinese audiences was made by the proprietors of the Fengtai Photoshop in the Liulichang area of central Beijing near Tiananmen Square. The photoshop moved to Shanghai in 1909, and over the next couple of decades that city established itself as the center of the Chinese film industry. To this day, Shanghai is home to China's largest film studios and is one of the most important centers of film production in the country.

Other cities also developed their own cinema industries, with movie theaters and production companies taking their place in the urban landscape, particularly in cities with a strong foreign presence or influence such as the treaty ports of Tianjin and Guangzhou. At this time, cinema was still a new technology and, in China at least, an unproven form of business. Hence, movie theaters spread first in the treaty ports, where at least a foreign audience could usually be ensured for films imported principally from Hollywood.

Cinema was welcomed with a great deal of enthusiasm in these cities, and many entrepreneurs saw the potential of the new medium; however, there was a large turnover of production companies in the early years, many of which made no films. Of around 160 companies set up in the 1920s, less than a third made any films, and by 1930 less than a dozen of these were still active (Clark 1987: 7). This was a time of technical, artistic, and entrepreneurial experimentation, and clearly many of those involved ultimately fell by the wayside. By the end of the 1920s, however, Chinese companies were producing nearly fifty films a year.

In terms of understanding the emerging Chinese popular cultural landscape at this time, there are two important points to note. First, China's developing cinema culture was very limited in geographical and demographic scope. It was heavily concentrated in the more cosmopolitan urban centers of Beijing and the treaty ports. Second, although a Chinese film industry was starting to find its feet, by far the majority of films viewed in China were foreign. In 1929, compared to approximately 50 Chinese films made, there were 450 foreign films projected in China. About 90 percent of these were from the United States, which was already establishing itself as a leading global film exporter. The imbalance between the number of domestically produced films and the number of imported films continued through the 1930s. In 1933, there were 67 Chinese films made as opposed to 600 foreign imports including 500 from the United States. In 1936, 88 percent of all films shown in China were foreign (Clark 1987: 7).

At this time, Chinese movie theater audiences were predominantly urban, were relatively sophisticated or Westernized, and lived in a largely Westernized cosmopolitan environment. Chinese movie theaters and their audiences were not homogeneous, however. In many ways, different theaters were showing different films for different kinds of audiences. In particular, there were theaters that specialized in foreign films and others that specialized principally in Chinese films, clearly aiming at different audiences. Of course, some foreigners went to Chinese films, many Chinese went to foreign ones, and some theaters put on both kinds of films. The distinction between theaters showing different kinds of films, however, also produced a broad division in audiences according to preference and taste (see below and Zhang 2004: 15–16).

An important issue in these cross-cultural situations, particularly once movies with sound became popular, was language. This was handled in different ways by different theaters at different times. One of the most common ways of overcoming language issues—usually with imported films for Chinese audiences—was to use narrators or translators who would stand by the screen and give a running commentary. Later, some theaters also started distributing printed plot summaries to the audience, while others eventually adopted the practice of projected subtitles or sidetitles. Whichever of these methods was adopted, there was clearly some degree of cultural negotiation going on in the translation process.

The 1930s are seen by many as the heyday of Shanghai cinema, and some of the classics of Chinese cinema were made in the city at this time, including *Street Angel* (dir. Yuan Muzhi, 1937), *Goddess* (dir. Wu Yonggang, 1934), *Song of the Fishermen* (dir. Cai Chusheng, 1934), and *Twin Sisters* (dir. Zheng Zhengqiu, 1933). It is important to be aware of the relationship between politically or socially motivated films and straight commercial entertainment films. Sometimes this distinction was clear-cut; however, much of the time it was not, as nearly all films were ultimately made for commercial distribution and relied on drawing audiences and revenue for their success. Hence, even the politically or socially motivated films that sought to heighten awareness of social and political issues were often made to be entertaining, following classic melodramatic narrative formats and cinematic styles (Ma 2002). The distinction between these two kinds of film is important not only for considering left-wing cinema of the period, as film historians tend to do, but for remembering the large number of purely commercial films also in circulation at the time.

The emphasis in Chinese film histories on the classic social realist films of this period is understandable. In light of subsequent historical events—the victory of the CCP in the civil war and the establishment of the People's Republic—the earlier social realist films retrospectively have a greater importance for the later development of the industry than their commercial entertainment counterparts. However, it is important when trying to understand Chinese popular cultural consumption of cinema in the 1930s to remember that many filmgoers, if not the majority of them, liked watching both foreign films and the commercial entertainment love stories and sentimental melodramas that made up much of Chinese film production. Intellectuals may have sought to appropriate film for political motives, but that does not mean that audiences necessarily complied with their wishes.

In this respect, Chinese cinema of this period also has to be seen against a broader popular cultural backdrop of the time. In Shanghai and other large metropolitan centers or cosmopolitan treaty ports, reading fiction and magazines were also popular pastimes (cf. Lee 1999). Some of the best-selling and most popular books of the time were what are commonly known as the "Mandarin Ducks and Butterflies" literature, referring to traditional sentimental fiction centered around melodramatic love stories. The name comes from the clichéd metaphors in such literature of mandarin ducks and butterflies to refer to young lovers and courtship, one of its common themes. The popular taste for this kind of literature—which was also commonly found in serialized form in popular magazines—clearly influenced film production of the time, and film producers and studios had considerable success in making commercial entertainment films in much the same vein.

Nonetheless, the 1930s were turbulent times in China, and Shanghai was a hive of political and intellectual activity. The city was the birthplace of the CCP, which was established in 1921, and left-wing activists worked hard to promote revolutionary consciousness among the city's large proletariat. At the same time, Shanghai was home to some of China's most important writers, like Ba Jin, who sought refuge in the city's foreign concessions to evade political persecution in other parts of China, and Mao Dun, the famous Communist novelist and intellectual.

In the early 1930s, a group of such intellectuals formed the League of Left-Wing Writers, an organization with links to the CCP that provided a forum for political and artistic discussion as well as some direction of ideological and propaganda work through artistic and cultural production. In 1932, the League set up a subsidiary Film Group made up of scriptwriters—who had particularly prestigious positions in Chinese filmmaking—directors, producers, and other filmmaking professionals. The group did not make films itself, but several of its members were prominent filmmakers at some of Shanghai's top film studios. In particular, Mingxing Studios employed key members of the group, including its leader, Xia Yan. Subsequently, films became distinctly more politically oriented and left-wing. In fact, many of those who emerged as a new generation of filmmakers in the first decades of the People's Republic had come from Mingxing Studios in the 1930s.

Left-wing filmmaking was closely associated with the movement toward social realism in cinema reflecting also the political and cultural agenda of the May 4th literary writers. Social realist film emerged from a fundamental discontent with the nature of society, in particular the injustices inflicted upon its poorer and disenfranchised members. Hence, social realist filmmakers, partly influenced by Soviet political and cinematic theory, chose provocative themes intended to heighten awareness of social inequalities and injustices, such as the plight of prostitutes, the suffering of the poor, the cruelty and selfishness of greedy landlords, and the excesses of KMT (nationalist) troops and leaders. The broad point of social realism was to portray realistically the misery and difficulty of China's underclass in order to advocate their cause and raise awareness among audiences.

For example, the 1937 *Street Angel* tells the story of Xiao Hong, a young woman who sings in a restaurant to entertain the customers. The film picks up on the theme of prostitution and the mistreatment of women in a commoditized capitalist society, also famously dealt with in director Wu Yonggang's 1934 silent classic *Goddess*, starring one of 1930s Shanghai cinema's most famous stars, Ruan Lingyu (see sidebar). In *Street Angel*, Xiao Hong and her elder sister live in a room above the restaurant, where they are mistreated and bullied by the restaurant owner and his wife—their adoptive parents. Xiao Hong's sister has been forced into prostitution by the couple, and they plan to sell Xiao Hong to a local hoodlum as his concubine. Xiao Hong discovers

Ruan Lingyu

In her short and tragic life, Ruan Lingyu (1910–1935), also known as Lily Yue, became one of the most famous stars of early Shanghai films. Following her much publicized suicide in March 1935 her name was engraved in Chinese cinema history. Director Stanley Kwan tells her story in his acclaimed 1992 Hong Kong film *Ruan Lingyu* (also known as *Centre Stage* or simply *Actress*), starring Maggie Cheung.

Born Ruan Fenggeng, Ruan Lingyu came from a poor family. Her parents were of Cantonese origin, but her father, a factory worker, died when Ruan was just six years old. With the family facing severe financial hardship, Ruan's mother went to work as a maid in a wealthy household in Shanghai and managed to pay for her daughter's education up to the age of sixteen. In 1925, however, Ruan met Zhang Damin, the sixth son of one of Shanghai's wealthiest and most influential families, and went to live with him, effectively becoming his wife.

This was Ruan Lingyu's break into the film industry. In 1926, her brother-in-law Zhang Huicong, who was acquainted with people in cinema, persuaded her to go for an audition despite having no formal training as an actor. The film director Bu Wanceng signed her up immediately at Mingxing Studios, where she made her first five films before moving to the Da Zhonghua Baihe Film Company in 1929. In her short time at Da Zhonghua (Great China), Ruan made another six films, showing the intensity of production in the industry at that time, before leaving in 1930 to join the Lianhua (United China) Film Company. It was there that she became acquainted with leading left-wing filmmakers and made the films for which she has subsequently become best known in Chinese film history. These were early experiments in social realism and left-wing-oriented films dealing with tough social issues.

Ruan's most famous role was probably the lead in *Goddess* (1934), which tells the dramatic story of a poor prostitute who nonetheless did everything in her power to fulfill her duty as a virtuous mother in getting her son through

their plan, and with the aid of street musician Xiao Cheng—who is in love with her—and his friends who live in the neighboring tenement block, she and her sister manage to escape to a hideaway in another part of town. The restaurant owner eventually tracks them down and communicates their whereabouts to the hoodlum to whom Xiao Hong was to be sold. He in turn goes to their hideaway and in the ensuing struggle kills the sister. The film ends with Xiao Hong and her friends vowing revenge in what should be seen as loosely symbolic presaging of the Communist Revolution to come more than fifteen years later.

Street Angel is not only a social realist film, however. Like other films of its time, it was also strongly oriented toward commercial success and is a good example of the kind of political-commercial hybrid mentioned earlier. It opens with a series of slapstick gags skillfully executed by famous and popular left-wing actor Zhou Dan (Xiao Cheng), initially setting a lighthearted scene before the more serious messages are dealt with. The film also contains a number of songs performed by the leading actors, and the tragic story of the elder sister is given a distinctly melodramatic treatment. Hence, although the school. The film highlights the evils of prostitution and the plight of women who might have impeccable moral souls despite the immoral lifestyle that a male-dominated and commoditized society imposes upon them. Its tragic ending, which sees Ruan's character in jail—separated from her son—can be read in two opposite ways. On one hand, it can be viewed as a further condemnation of the injustices of contemporary society and the impossibility of a good woman's virtue being acknowledged and allowed to flourish. On the other hand, however, it can serve to reaffirm the public moral stance on prostitution and prostitutes which would depict prostitutes as an evil threat to social stability and public morality.

Another of Ruan's acclaimed film roles, also her last, was as Wei Ming in *New Woman.* The film, directed by Cai Chusheng, one of Shanghai's leading left-wing filmmakers, tells the equally tragic story of a woman schoolteacher and writer, Wei Ming, who is almost forced into prostitution in order to pay for medical treatment for her daughter and ultimately commits suicide in despair. Once again, the film focuses on the injustices of a society that does not allow a woman in straitened circumstances to find a moral route to survival.

Ruan's life off-screen somehow mirrored the moral ambiguity and dilemmas of her on-screen roles, and it is impossible not to draw a parallel between her own suicide in 1935 and that of Wei Ming in *New Woman.* Ruan's relationship with Zhang Damin deteriorated over the years. He became a heavy gambler and lost much of their money. Meanwhile, Ruan became involved with another wealthy Cantonese businessman, Tang Jishan. A complicated series of accusations and counter-accusations led to a series of lawsuits and legal confrontations that culminated in an impoverished Zhang accusing Ruan and Tang of forging documents in order to illegally acquire his property. To avoid being publicly labeled an immoral woman, Ruan killed herself by means of a drug overdose two days before the case came to court, as press interest in her private life, her sometimes turbulent relationships with these two unfaithful men, and the impending court case intensified.

social message of the film is clear from its subject matter, main characters, and plot, it also contains a range of entertainment features to make the film watchable and appealing to everyday audiences.

The late 1930s brought massive disruption to the Shanghai film industry, with the outbreak of the war with Japan and the occupation of the city by invading forces. Most film production in Shanghai closed down as many of the personnel from the industry fled to other parts of China. Most notably, people fled to Hong Kong, which was a British colony but would be occupied by the Japanese from 1941 to 1944; Chongqing in western China, where the nationalist government relocated after the fall of Nanjing (the Chinese capital at that time); or Yan'an, the remote northwestern hideout of Mao Zedong and the CCP following the Long March of 1934–1935.

From 1937 to 1945, there was relatively little filmmaking going on because of the disruption and lack of resources and materials caused by the war. Anti-Japanese propaganda films featured prominently in Chinese film output, particularly in Hong Kong prior to 1941. After 1945, the Japanese occupation was brought to an end, but the

Crows and Sparrows

Crows and Sparrows (dir. Zheng Junli) is one of the most acclaimed films of the 1940s and 1950s, if not the entire postwar period, and it is a classic of Chinese social realist cinema. The film was made and set in Shanghai in 1949, the result of collaboration between a dedicated group of left-wing filmmakers at the Kunlun Studio watching the collapse of the KMT establishment all around them as the Communist forces approached the city.

The film tells the story of a group of poor tenants in a Shanghai house exploited by their KMT landlord. The landlord, an officer in the Nationalist army, is preparing to leave Shanghai in the light of the communist advance. He therefore sells the house and orders all the tenants to leave on very short notice. The film then plays sensitively with the different characters of the tenants and their reactions to the crisis. The happy ending of the film, in which cooperation among the tenants sees the downfall of the landlord and their reappropriation of the house, is not entirely unexpected, and the film replays standard social realist themes concerning the plight of the downtrodden poor, the injustices of contemporary society, the immorality of property-owners, and KMT corruption. However, it does so in a less predictable way than its less sophisticated predecessors. Characterization is not all black and white, and the tenants of the block along with other ultimately positive characters in the story variously show cowardice, cunning, bravery, selfishness, leadership, indecisiveness, and other ambiguous personality traits. It is a far more complex story of human interaction and social relationships than a straightforward affirmation of poor equals good, rich equals bad.

The story of the film's making is also worth telling. Before production, the filmmakers presented to the KMT government censors an edited version of the script depicting the film as a light-hearted comedy. It was not long, however, before the authorities found out that the film being made was not the same one as presented in the script. They ordered a stop to its filming and demanded the immediate handover of the reels already shot. Yet the filmmakers managed to finish the film, often on the run from the authorities, smuggling the reels from one safe house to another and keeping the constantly changing script out of reach. The film was finally completed in the first few months after the communist liberation of Shanghai and was soon lauded as the best film of the year; in 1956 it was awarded the honor of the best film for the entire 1949–1955 period.

civil war between the communists and the nationalists flared up into all-out conflict as the two sides fought for the control of the country. In these years, some filmmakers returned to Shanghai and, even in sometimes extremely difficult circumstances, made some classics of Chinese cinema such as *Crows and Sparrows* (dir. Zheng Junli, 1949—see sidebar), *Spring River Flows East* (dir. Cai Chusheng, 1947), and *Spring in a Small Town* (dir. Fei Mu, 1948).

There was no actual filmmaking in Yan'an between 1937 and 1945 because of equipment shortages; nonetheless what happened there in that period was to prove significant for the future development of the Chinese film industry in two key ways. First, the left-wing filmmakers who fled Shanghai and ended up in Yan'an became more closely linked to the CCP and more integrated into its structures and modes of operation. This included organization into theatre troupes, film units, and other training and educational groups organized along the lines of the Party's military-style discipline. This was significant for the future of Chinese cinema, as many of these filmmakers after 1949 became prominent figures in the new film industry of the People's Republic. At the same time, the kinds of party and administrative structures that were developed in Yan'an were the basis upon which party and government organization in the postwar period were to be modeled (Clark 1987).

Second, the ideological basis of artistic production that was to be adopted under the People's Republic was outlined, developed, and executed under Mao during the Yan'an years. Most notably, Chairman Mao made a series of speeches in Yan'an in 1942 known as the Talks to the Yan'an Forum on Literature and Art. These were sophisticated speeches outlining Mao's fundamental aesthetic theory, which was based on two principles. First, literature and art should serve political purposes—that is, the purposes of the CCP. In short, art was to have a political motivation and not to be thought of as simply for "beauty" or "art's sake." Second, artistic production should aim to widen its audiences as far as possible—it should be inclusive, not elitist or exclusive—and it should aim to raise the political awareness and "quality" of members of those audiences.

The Talks to the Yan'an Forum on Literature and Art did not specifically address filmmaking, being more concerned with drama, novels, short stories, poetry, visual arts, and music; however, the principles applied to these other art forms in the Yan'an period were also applied to thinking about film. Furthermore, Mao's Yan'an theories were to become the founding principles of the film industry in the postwar period.

PRC Cinema under Mao: Socialist Realism and Propaganda Films

The birth of the People's Republic of China in 1949 was to have long-lasting and far-reaching effects on the Chinese film industry. The film industry changed in terms of its structure, organization, and mode of operation as well as in terms of the content of films. Film was appropriated by the CCP as a fundamental propaganda and educational tool; the film studios were nationalized and incorporated into the political and administrative structures of the Party and the state.

The CCP saw many advantages in using film as a means of communicating with the Chinese people. It could be easily controlled from the center in terms of funding, censorship, and distribution. Unlike theatre, films could not improvise or alter their message in their live encounters with audiences. With the setting up of mobile film projection units that traveled deep into the countryside to show films to peasants in even the remotest areas, in the days before television and with high levels of illiteracy, film offered an effective way of reaching a very wide audience.

Consequently, the Chinese authorities put considerable investment into the film industry, which saw enormous growth over the period from 1950 to 1960. Over this ten-year period, viewings of films rose from 150 million to 5.4 billion; the number of movie theaters in China increased from 522 to 1,800; the number of mobile projection units went from 500 to 9,000; the number of workers in the film industry grew from 3,000 to 90,000; and the number of major studios quadrupled, from three to twelve (Pickowicz 1974: 340–341).

Film output also grew sharply over this period, categorized into feature films, newsreels, documentaries, educational and scientific films, and artistic and animated films. In 1951, a low year, output was 1 feature film, 36 documentaries and newsreels, 3 educational and scientific films, and 0 artistic films; meanwhile, 58 foreign films were dubbed into Chinese. In 1958, output reached a high of 103 feature films, 255 newsreels and documentaries, 154 scientific and educational films, 54 artistic and animated films, and 151 dubbed imports (mainly from the Soviet Union) (Pickowicz 1974: 343).

This much larger, nationalized film industry was also more centralized and controlled by the Party, whose propaganda committees now took up a key supervisory role in film production. Experienced film workers in the early 1950s were in short supply, and the industry relied largely upon the skills of those who had worked in Shanghai in the 1920s, 1930s, and 1940s. At this time, however, a new political wind started to blow through the industry, influencing decisions about who could take what roles and what kind of films could be made. Many of the key personnel in the old Shanghai film industry who had worked with the KMT or been associated with the CCP's political opponents fled to Hong Kong and Taiwan, where they played a crucial role in the revitalization of the film industries in those territories. Those who remained in China may have found work in the film industry but were excluded from influential positions. Meanwhile, the left-wing filmmakers from Shanghai and Yan'an found themselves at the heart of the newly expanding mainland film industry.

These left-wing filmmakers, however, who were used to a fair degree of autonomy in how they formulated their political messages in film, now found themselves subject to increasingly rigid and rigorous political formulations of what films should be about, how they should convey their messages, and how they should portray characters. Following strong Party criticism of a number of films that followed the established Shanghai social realist style for being too politically ambiguous, filmmakers were made brutally aware of the changing climate of film production. As a result, they became far more cautious about plot, characterization, and representation of landlords, capitalists, and so on, being careful not to upset the new political power-holders (see sidebar, *The Life of Wu Xun*).

This trend marked the move from social realism to socialist realism. The terms are clearly similar, and they also refer to closely related forms of cinema; however, there are important differences between the two in the Chinese case. In the PRC, the broadly left-wing political motivation that had driven the social realist filmmakers of the 1930s and 1940s to portray and speak out for the poor, the downtrodden, and the unprivileged became a far more rigid and dogmatic adherence to the party line. At the same time, what had also been generally a commercially driven cinema became a politically driven project, with a far more narrowly and strictly defined role to play in supporting, promoting, and explaining Party policy. This meant that the balance in the left-wing films of the old Shanghai between political messages and commercial entertainment tipped heavily in favor of the former. With the new, nationalized cinema no

The Life of Wu Xun

The Life of Wu Xun (dir. Sun Yu, 1950) was a watershed film made at the dawn of the new era following the communist victory in 1949. The film was made along the lines of other social realist films of the late 1940s; however, severe criticism of the film by the CCP was to enhance the transition from a relatively unregulated social realism to the more dogmatic style of socialist realism. *The Life of Wu Xun* tells the story of a member of the rural gentry who sought to alleviate the suffering of local villagers, indicating the hardship and injustices suffered by the poorer members of traditional Chinese society. Although the film was fairly well received by audiences, it was subsequently condemned by Party critics in 1951 for its ambiguous characterization and plot. The criticism centered around the character of Wu Xun, who was "ambiguously" a member of the landlord class but also helping the peasants. This did not fit neatly with the party line at the time, which categorized people as good or bad purely on their class background. The representation of Wu Xun in the film was therefore considered to reproduce and perpetuate attitudes and thinking representative of China's feudal society.

Following this case, many filmmakers became very wary of Party censure and erred on the side of caution in their subsequent work. Consequently, film characterization and narratives were simplified and adhered more closely to Party dogma.

longer dependent on box office revenues to survive, the commercial imperative to please audiences was therefore diluted.

As a result, the socialist realist films of the 1950s and 1960s offered far more clear-cut, stereotypical representations of good and bad characters. Storylines became more predictable and politically defined. In fact, the whole industry was absorbed into the Yan'an ideology that had been cultivated in the 1930s and 1940s. Not only did this mean following the philosophy laid down by Mao in his speeches from Yan'an, it meant a greater Soviet influence on Chinese filmmaking, at least in the 1950s—before the political rift with Moscow—when Soviet influences were strong in many areas of Chinese society.

This does not mean that good films were not made during this period. Despite some heavy political messages at times, the film industry now had better, more reliable funding than it had had for nearly two decades. The top directors and producers were also experienced, conscientious, and proud filmmakers who never ceased striving for high quality. Indeed, there were many high-quality, enjoyable, and popular films made in the 1950s and early 1960s.

The relative political liberalization in the early 1960s, following the disastrous years of the Great Leap Forward and its aftermath, also gave filmmakers a little more breathing space. Although films still had to meet the Party's expectations in terms of propaganda function and permissible content, there was a little more flexibility at this time in terms of plots and characterization, giving audiences the chance to watch some slightly less predictable films.

However, the film industry came under attack from the Party leadership in both 1964 and 1965, presaging the devastation of the Cultural Revolution, and filmmaking was once again forced into a political straitjacket. Slightly more liberal-minded films that could be seen as indirectly criticizing the Party, such as Xie Jin's *Stage Sisters*, were banned from full public distribution. Indeed, *Stage Sisters* only reached the general public in 1979, fourteen years after being made.

With the arrival of the Cultural Revolution in 1966, the film industry faced the same upheavals that tore the whole country apart. Feature film production ceased completely from 1967 to 1969, and many of the 1930s and 1940s filmmakers who had become key figures also in the postwar industry were subjected to public and private criticism, suspended from their posts, arrested, and imprisoned, as were many intellectuals at that time. Many did not survive. At this time, cultural production came under the general supervision of Mao Zedong's wife, Jiang Qing, herself a former film actress. With few films being made and many existing films now considered politically unacceptable, Chinese film audiences suddenly found themselves watching the same few films over and over again. For some of this period, the only films that could be watched were the eight revolutionary operas—films of the uniquely Chinese revolutionary hybrid of Western-style ballet and traditional Chinese performing arts such as Beijing opera.

Mao Zedong with his wife Jiang Qing. Jiang, an ardent supporter of Mao but also a strong political mover in her own right, was a powerful force during the Cultural Revolution in China. (Library of Congress)

Filmmaking started to return to some kind of normality in the 1970s following the excesses of the early Cultural Revolution years; however, political control of film production and content remained strict. In 1973, Jiang Qing's ban on showing films made between 1949 and the start of the Cultural Revolution was lifted, and gradually film production increased again, although the number of films made was still lower than in the late 1950s. Chinese studios made four feature films in 1973, seventeen in 1974, and thirty-nine in 1976, the year of Mao's death (Zhang 2004: 222).

Post-Mao Cinema and the "Fifth Generation"

In the post-Mao period, the recovery in the film industry strengthened and film production started to blossom once again. There were twenty-eight feature films made in 1977, forty in 1978, and sixty-five in 1979. Films also started being imported again, with seventy films, principally from Japan, the United States, and the United Kingdom, imported in 1979 (Howkins 1982: 67–68).

Generations in Chinese Cinema

The history of Chinese cinema has often been told in relation to "generations" of filmmakers. To summarize: Up until the 1980s there were four generations. The First Generation consisted of the very early pioneers of film in China, like those at the Fengtai Photoshop in Beijing and the early experimental filmmakers of the 1910s and early 1920s in Shanghai. The Second Generation refers to the filmmakers of the late 1920s and 1930s in Shanghai who brought Chinese cinema to maturity, particularly the left-wing filmmakers such as Xia Yan, Zhao Dan, Yuan Muzhi, and Sun Yu. The Third Generation refers to the early post-1949 filmmakers in the People's Republic. As we have seen, many of the Second Generation filmmakers also found places for themselves in the new PRC film industry, but there was also an expansion and cultivation of new talent. One of the most important and famous of these filmmakers is Xie Jin, who started his career in the 1950s, made a string of successful and well-recognized films in the late 1950s and early 1960s, and returned to filmmaking after the Cultural Revolution to make national blockbusters well into the 1990s.

The Fourth Generation filmmakers truly formed a bridge between the Third and Fifth generations in that they overlapped and worked alongside both. This is the generation that started learning filmmaking in the 1960s, although they made few if any recognized films until after the Cultural Revolution. Some came to prominence in the later 1970s as the industry recovered and some in the early 1980s. Probably the most important Fourth Generation filmmaker to influence the future of Chinese cinema was Wu Tianming; others include Zhang Nuanxin, Xie Fei, and Zheng Dongtian. Wu had worked as an actor in the early 1960s and then as an assistant producer with top filmmakers in the 1970s before making his directing debut at the end of the decade. The impression he has left on China's film industry is not only for his own films but for the role he played as the head of Xi'an Film Studios from 1983 onward in the support and cultivation of the Fifth Generation filmmakers, many of whom made their early films at the Xi'an studios.

The term Fifth Generation refers broadly to the new generation of filmmakers that emerged after the Cultural Revolution. They were the first group of students to graduate from the Beijing Film Academy following its reopening in the late 1970s, and they made a cluster of nationally and internationally recognized films from the early 1980s onward. Most notably, the term Fifth Generation is associated with the work of cameraman-turned-director Zhang Yimou as well as Chen Kaige and Tian Zhuangzhuang. The less internationally well-known members of the Fifth Generation include Wu Ziniu, Zhang Junzhao, Huang Jianxin, and Hu Mei.

The late 1970s and early 1980s saw a new flourishing of the Chinese film industry in many different ways. More films were being made; moviegoing audiences were booming, reaching an all-time peak in the mid-1980s; and the Beijing Film Academy reopened its doors to students for the first time since the Cultural Revolution. At the same time, many of the formerly criticized film workers who survived the Cultural Revolution were rehabilitated, and established film directors started experimenting once again with the limits of Party control. Furthermore, film became embroiled in a much broader intellectual debate about the nature and importance—past, present, and

Chinese director Xie Jin on the set of *The Last Aristocrats* in New York. The film was the first official Chinese film to be produced in the United States. (AFP/Getty Images)

future—of Chinese culture and cultural production that became known as the "culture fever" (*wenhuare*) of the 1980s.

This was also the time that has been uniquely associated with the new, Fifth Generation filmmakers (see sidebar). These directors have made diverse contributions to Chinese cinema, and although they are often spoken of collectively and some of them did work together at different times on different films, particularly in the early years, it is important also to realize that they each had their own ideas, styles, and interests. Zhang Yimou often dealt with issues of Chinese culture and women's traditional roles in society—for instance in *Red Sorghum* (1987), *Judou* (1989), and *Raise the Red Lantern* (1991). Tian Zhuangzhuang was particularly noted for his focus on ethnic minority cultures, with films set in Tibet and Inner Mongolia—*On the Hunting Ground* (1985) and *Horse Thief* (1986). In stark contrast, Huang Jianxin focused on more contemporary themes including Party bureaucracy and political subjectivity in films such as *The Black Cannon Incident* (1985). In this sense, the Fifth Generation is not a "school" of filmmaking as such, nor is it a rigidly defined group of filmmakers with anything like a formulated manifesto. Rather, it is the loosely constituted group of filmmakers working in the early 1980s with certain common interests, ideas about filmmaking, objectives, and backgrounds.

The commonalities start with their training as filmmakers and the historical, political, and cultural context of the early post-Mao era. All of the Fifth Generation filmmakers had lived through the Cultural Revolution, many of them had been sent "down to the countryside" during those years to work with and learn from the peasants in the fields, and some of them also spent time in the army. All of them were of the generation that missed out on educational and employment opportunities because of the disruption in the country during the Cultural Revolution period. They had also experienced the excesses and extremes of the political violence, the cultural and political censorship, and the dogmatic approach to artistic production that had engulfed the country in the late 1960s and early 1970s, and with all this fresh in their minds they embarked on their studies to become filmmakers.

At the Beijing Film Academy, they were all steeped in the traditions of Chinese filmmaking, including the social realism of the 1930s and 1940s and the socialist realism of the 1950s and 1960s. They were also given the chance to see many foreign films from all over the world including the United States, Europe, Japan, and the Soviet Union. They had access to works by international film theorists such as Andre Bazin and Christian Metz, whose theories were translated and interpreted in ways particularly suited to the new context of Chinese filmmaking (see Zhang 1997).

It was also at this time that Chinese intellectuals, including filmmakers and film theorists, started questioning the nature of Chinese film and where it should go in the future. Key debates emerged over questions like: What constitutes "national" cinema? What is the relationship or balance between technology and culture in film production? Is film a medium for the presentation of theatrical and literary forms (as it had generally been understood in China since at least the 1930s), or does the nature and character of film itself create its own art form? (see Semsel & Chen 1990). These are questions that have long been discussed by film theorists around the world; however, at this point in China's cultural, artistic, and political history they were put to use in the development of a broad project of transformation.

One of the key starting points for the Fifth Generation filmmakers in their thinking about Chinese cinema and how to transform it was the monotonous predictability of socialist realism. Although they each developed their own ways of dealing with this issue, they nonetheless shared various ideas, styles, and methods that can be discussed together. To react to the predictability of socialist realism, the new generation of directors wanted to make films that would make their audiences think, make them engage with the films they watched, and make them ask questions of those films and their subject matter. They sought to do this by using different cinematographic methods from those commonly used in the past. They therefore used long, single-take shots instead of short, highly edited ones. They commonly had minimalist soundtracks, which accentuated silence or the sounds of nature and skillfully focused attention on the equally minimalist dialogue. These methods also helped generate a contemplative atmosphere in films that encouraged audiences to ask themselves what was going on. The idea was to create a new, challenging, unpredictable aesthetic space that compelled audiences to engage with films in new ways (Zhang X. 1997; Zhang Y. 2004).

The films were also experimental with their subject matter. The first Fifth Generation film, *The One and Eight* (dir. Zhang Junzhao, 1983), for instance, dared to tell the story of a wronged army officer accused of desertion in the anti-Japanese war. The imprisoned officer, along with convicted criminals, argues for the right to be set free in order to be able to fight. When this happens, what was for some of the convicts a purely self-centered cause becomes one of impassioned patriotism as they take to fighting the Japanese. In presentation, the film was shocking for Chinese audiences in 1983, who were still accustomed to the neat political packaging of socialist realism. The war films of the past, which told of of heroic exploits by men in spotless uniforms, were replaced with the gritty realities of captivity, deprivation, and war accompanied by the imperatives of survival and the violence of military culture.

Yellow Earth, released the following year, was less startling but no less innovative. It was also the first film to draw concerted international attention to the Fifth Generation filmmakers. With unforgettable camerawork by cinematographer Zhang Yimou depicting stunning panoramas of northwestern China's unrelenting loess landscape, the film portrays a Communist army officer sent out to collect folk songs from peasants in some of the remotest parts of the country. With minimal dialogue but an intense focus on human relationships, *Yellow Earth* tells the story of the soldier's encounter with a family of poor peasants in an unliberated area of Shaanxi Province. The film depicts the weight of tradition in such areas, with the young daughter of the family betrothed to a middle-aged peasant in the village against her will. She asks the soldier to take her away to join the army; he refuses, although promising to return. When he does, he finds the village stricken by drought and the young girl having drowned in the Yellow River in an attempt to run away and join the communists. The film is slow and in places ambiguous. It defies many of the conventions of narrative cinema and forces the viewer to ponder the significance or relevance of how the ultimately simple story unfolds. There are no ready answers in the film, which nonetheless plays with some clichéd elements of socialist realist films: the soldier converting feudal peasants to the revolutionary cause and the dignity of the peasantry faced with a bitter life, to name just two. The predictability of these narratives, however, is undermined at every turn by the unexpected, in terms of both plot (the girl dies; the peasants continue to suffer; the soldier is impotent in the face of nature and tradition) and cinematic presentation (camera angles and framing, reluctance to exploit moments of melodrama, and long, contemplative shots of inactivity).

The new group of filmmakers soon drew national and international attention. At home, their films were controversial, and some were withheld from Chinese audiences. Overseas, this only enhanced their fast-growing reputation for being rebellious critics of the long-standing communist government; however, such an understanding of their work fails to appreciate the complexity and subtlety of what they were doing. It is true that they were personally often critical of the heavy political control of artistic production in China and they aimed to destabilize the propagandistic certainties of the past. Yet it also has to be remembered that they worked with government funding, in state-owned-and-run film studios. These were not straightforward independent dissidents but

Gong Li

Actress Gong Li, at least for foreign audiences, became the face of Fifth Generation Chinese cinema. She appeared in many of Zhang Yimou's internationally renowned films and had a much-publicized off-screen relationship with Zhang, the best known of the Fifth Generation directors. Gong Li was catapulted to domestic and international fame for her leading role in *Red Sorghum,* in which she portrayed a young woman sold into marriage to an aging leper but who subsequently becomes the strong-spirited head of the family distillery following her new husband's untimely death. *Red Sorghum* is also seen as a film exploring the realms of sexuality and gender and, as such, placed Gong Li in the international public gaze as an object of desire. She was to find later success in similarly defined roles in Zhang Yimou's *Raise the Red Lantern, Judou,* and to a lesser degree *Shanghai Triad.*

However, Gong Li also acted in quite different roles—in Zhang's *The Story of Qiu Ju,* for instance, she played an unglamorous peasant woman seeking justice for her husband, injured in a dispute with the village leader. In Chen Kaige's epic *Farewell My Concubine* she played Juxian, the lover of opera star Duan Xiaolou and consequently the rival of Duan's stage partner, Dieyi (Leslie Cheung), who is obsessed with artistic perfection and also homosexually attracted to Duan.

Gong Li's popularity at home was probably less than that overseas, but she has nonetheless become a nationally and internationally recognized film actress working in Hong Kong. One of her most unlikely roles was in Stephen Chiau's knockabout comedy *The Flirting Scholar* (1992) offering an irreverent version of Chinese history and tradition. Nonetheless, Gong Li will always be particularly associated with the role of the often sullen, mysterious Chinese beauty depicted in those late 1980s and early 1990s Fifth Generation films. As one Western commentator once put it, "What is remarkable about Gong is not so much her poise or versatility, but her ability to signify Chineseness, femininity and mystery outside her own culture" (Reynaud 1993: 15).

intellectually motivated filmmakers who sought to ask cultural, artistic, philosophical, and moral questions that touched upon but also went far beyond issues of politics.

The late 1980s saw a transition from an initial experimental phase of development for Fifth Generation film that had been largely motivated by domestic intellectual and artistic debates to a new phase of larger budget film production with substantial international funding and transnational audiences and critics. In 1988, *Red Sorghum* became the first Fifth Generation film to win a major prize at a Western film festival when Zhang Yimou walked away with the Golden Bear Award at the Berlin International Film Festival. This has for many film critics become the marker of the turning point in Chinese film history that saw the new cinema become increasingly market-sensitive and transnationally oriented (Lu 1997).

By this time, Western art-house film audiences had started to become more aware of the changes taking place in China and saw films like Chen Kaige's *Yellow Earth* and later *King of the Children* (1987) as well as Tian Zhuangzhuang's *Horse Thief* and Zhang's *Red Sorghum* become increasingly regular features at international film festivals and on the art-house film circuit. This trend also drew the attention of international funding for Chinese filmmakers, and over the next few years Chen, Zhang, and others of the Fifth Generation enjoyed international recognition and support for their work. Films made in the late 1980s and early 1990s with considerable international funding included Zhang Yimou's highly acclaimed *Judou* and *Raise the Red Lantern*, both dealing with the injustices of young women forced to marry into wealthy families. Zhang also had international success with *To Live*, an epic tracing the turbulent history of China's twentieth century through the eyes of one family, and *The Story of Qiu Ju*, about a young peasant woman who doggedly seeks justice in the Chinese legal system for her wronged husband. Meanwhile, Chen Kaige's *Farewell My Concubine* and Tian Zhuangzhuang's *Blue Kite* were also well received abroad.

Chinese director and cinematographer Zhang Yimou poses at the AFI Film Festival premiere of *Curse of the Golden Flower* in Hollywood, California, in 2006. (Corbis)

This new phase in the development of post-Mao Chinese cinema also created controversy in China, however. On one hand, the authorities and many Chinese people were pleased to see Chinese cinema finally being recognized at an international level, but on the other hand, many critics accused the Fifth Generation filmmakers of "auto-orientalism." In other words, they considered many of the internationally successful films to offer distorted, partial, and unnecessarily negative representations of China, Chinese people, and Chinese culture that catered to foreign stereotypical expectations more than they dealt with the contemporary realities of a rapidly changing Chinese society. The critics argued that representations of women's inequality, the poverty of rural and western China, and the oppressive weight of tradition (as in *Red Sorghum*, *Judou*, *Raise the Red Lantern*, *Horse Thief*, and *Yellow Earth*) or the political excesses of the Cultural Revolution (as in *Farewell My Concubine*, *Blue Kite*, and *To Live*) played to foreigners' prejudices and misunderstandings about China while dwelling excessively in the past and neglecting the transformations that China had undergone since the times and events depicted in the films.

Hence, these films were surrounded by contradictions. They were made in China by filmmakers often still connected with state film studios, yet their distribution was often limited, censored, or even banned within China. They gave Chinese cinema an unprecedented international presence and were received by overseas critics and audiences with great acclaim. Yet they were considered by many Chinese to offer a misleading representation of the important features of Chinese culture and society in the late twentieth century. Foreign audiences enjoyed them for the insights they gave into enduring features of Chinese culture, while Chinese decried such representations as distorted, out of date, and Eurocentric.

The filmmakers denied the charges of auto-orientalism and defended their right to make films about what they wanted to. They insisted their films were the product of their own artistic interests and attitudes and were not influenced by the expectations of foreign funding bodies, festival organizers, or audiences. It is worth noting, however, that after this spate of historical dramas exploring the nature of enduring Chinese values, culture, and tradition, both Zhang Yimou and Chen Kaige went on in the 1990s and early 2000s to make films more solidly oriented on domestic Chinese audiences. Some (Chen's *Together*, 2003, and Zhang's *Keep Cool*, 1997, and *Not One Less*, 1999) were set in contemporary China, and others were historical epics dealing with major events in ancient Chinese history such as the unification of China in the second century BC under the first emperor, Qin Shi Huangdi (as in Zhang's *Hero* and Chen's *The Emperor and the Assassin*, both 2002). Indeed, both *Hero* and *The Emperor and the Assassin* were given high-profile launches in Beijing's Great Hall of the People with the clear suggestion that the director was not looking to confront the Chinese authorities and was placing an emphasis on commercial entertainment, as opposed to art-house filmmaking (Zhang 2004: 292–293). Tian Zhuangzhuang was banned from filmmaking in 1989 after entering *Blue Kite* into the Tokyo Film Festival without prior permission from the Chinese authorities, but in 2002 he returned to filmmaking with a politically safe remake of the 1940s classic *Springtime in a Small Town*.

As the Fifth Generation became more internationalized from the late 1980s on, there is also a sense in which international success reduced the group to just three key directors—Zhang Yimou, Chen Kaige, and Tian Zhuangzhuang—and as noted, after 1989, Tian was prohibited from making films. Zhang Junzhao had some international success with *Ermo*, a film about a peasant woman's burning desire to buy a television set (see also Chapter 3). Other directors such as Huang Jianxin and Hu Mei, although continuing to make films, remained more domestically focused and outside of academic circles attracted relatively little international attention. It is therefore often said that the real intellectual, artistic, and innovative force of the Fifth Generation filmmakers has to be sought in the early films, from 1983 to about 1987 and the turning point marked by *Red Sorghum*. At this time, a unique configuration of Chinese social, intellectual, and political history following the Cultural Revolution combined with unprecedented social and artistic liberalization enabled the Fifth Generation to break the mold of decades of socialist realist filmmaking in China.

The Sixth Generation and Beyond

In the early to mid-1990s, what became known as the Sixth Generation of Chinese filmmakers emerged; however, there is no clear handover or transition from the Fifth to the Sixth Generation in the way the terms might seem to suggest. As we have seen, some would argue that the Fifth Generation as an artistic and intellectual movement effectively came to an end in the second half of the 1980s. Yet it was after that that the leading Fifth Generation directors enjoyed their greatest fame and successes both domestically and internationally. Meanwhile, this was also the time that several Fifth Generation filmmakers such as Zhang Jianya, the director of *Mr. Wang: Flames of Desire* (1993), and Xia Gang, director of comedies such as *After Separation* (1992), saw their careers mature and develop.

Even more than Fifth Generation, the term Sixth Generation requires qualification. In some cases, the term is used to apply to almost any young director coming to the fore after the Fifth Generation. Yet the Sixth Generation does not have the same kind of common film background or life experiences to link them together that the Fifth Generation filmmakers had. It is therefore a category of some dubious utility. Nonetheless, it is widely used, and we can identify some common interests and themes in Sixth Generation films.

In the 1990s, Zhang Yimou and Chen Kaige were forging ahead with production of their transnationally funded epics. At the same time, critics and commentators were starting to reflect upon the Fifth Generation phenomenon. One of the critiques of the Fifth Generation has been that by concentrating excessively on remote rural locations and stories set in a clearly separate past featuring issues of tradition and cultural oppression, the Fifth Generation (Zhang and Chen in particular) failed to engage with the pressing social and cultural issues of contemporary China (see, e.g., Zhang 1997). In this critique we can identify the opening that the Fifth Generation left for the new filmmakers of the 1990s.

Zhang Yuan's *Beijing Bastards* (1993), generally taken to be the first main Sixth Generation film, dealt with the hard-hitting subjects of youth alienation, extramarital pregnancy, and the emergence of new youth cultures centered around rock music and alternative lifestyles. The film features recordings of music by 1980s rock star Cui Jian, who fell rapidly from favor with the Chinese authorities after supporting the 1989 pro-democracy demonstrations, and it was shot without permission from the authorities, giving it a strong claim to being an "underground" film production—something that was bound to please overseas critics and audiences.

It is this "underground" status, along with the attention to social issues and problems, particularly among young people in a rapidly changing society, that started to distinguish the new generation of filmmakers from the prevailing Fifth Generation trend. Zhang Yuan went on to make films dealing with equally hard-hitting subject matter: alcoholism in *Sons* (1996) and homosexuality in *East Palace, West Palace* (1997). Zhang was not alone, and there were others who started in a similar way, making unauthorized films dealing with gritty social issues.

Wang Xiaoshuai started his Sixth Generation career with another internationally recognized film, *The Days* (1993), which dealt with similar issues of alienation and despair in the new China. In *Frozen* (1996), he followed the story of extreme performance artists in Beijing who put themselves through exceptional pain in the name of radical protest art. Another budding Sixth

Director Zhang Yuan in front of the statues in Tiananmen Square. Considered a controversial underground Sixth Generation filmmaker, Zhang Yuan's films have often dealt with alternative lifestyles and sensitive social issues. (Corbis)

Generation director, He Jianjun (also known as He Yi), dealt with similar issues of desperation and personal crisis in post-socialist China in another 1993 film, *Red Beads*.

Jia Zhangke has also attracted worldwide attention for his heavy social critiques of post-socialist China in a series of films set in the traditional Fifth Generation territory of poverty-stricken northwest China. In contrast to the Fifth Generation's use of remote peoples and places as a means of aesthetic distancing, Jia uses a heavy documentary style to emphasize the negative side of economic reform and the real experiential distance between those in the wealthy, rapidly developing eastern coastal provinces and those struggling to make a living in the poorer, less developed areas of the country.

In *Xiao Wu* (1998) (aka *Pickpocket*), Jia tells the story of a petty criminal on the margins of society who sees the basic principles of loyalty and fidelity that he holds dear in his relationships gradually undermined by the new, apparently unprincipled ethic of China's emerging free-market society. His later film *Platform* (2000), which can almost be seen as a prequel to *Xiao Wu*, offers an equally depressing characterization of the breakdown and dysfunctionality of human relationships in post-Mao China. The film follows a state-run theatre troupe in Shaanxi Province that undergoes privatization in the post-Mao period. Rather than being liberated by the change, the members of the troupe find themselves touring dead-end towns with a dead-end show and no realistic prospect of escaping the squalid drudgery that comes to characterize their lives.

Jia Zhangke's films are a particularly good example of a documentary style that characterizes much of the work of the so-called Sixth Generation filmmakers and that raises complex questions about truth, objectivity, and representation. Although not documentaries, films like *Xiao Wu* and *Platform* (as well as *Beijing Bastards*, *The Days*, *Frozen*, and *Red Beads*), by dealing with the gritty "realities" of everyday life in post-Mao China have a strong sense of presenting the viewer with the "real" China or "the truth" compared to more glamorous official propaganda representations or the geographically and temporally distanced ethnographic realities of many Fifth Generation films. In 2006, Jia also won the top Golden Lion Award at the Venice Film Festival for his film *Still Life* (*sanxia haoren*) telling the story of how the giant Three Gorges Dam project in central China affected ordinary people forced to leave their homes for the flooding.

The Sixth Generation emerged at a similar time as what has become known as the Chinese New Documentary Movement—another loose grouping from the early 1990s of journalists, filmmakers, and intellectuals who started making unauthorized documentary films using small, lightweight, and relatively inconspicuous digital video cameras. Although making different kinds of films, these two groups of filmmakers have had similar interests and shared ideas. Many of the documentary

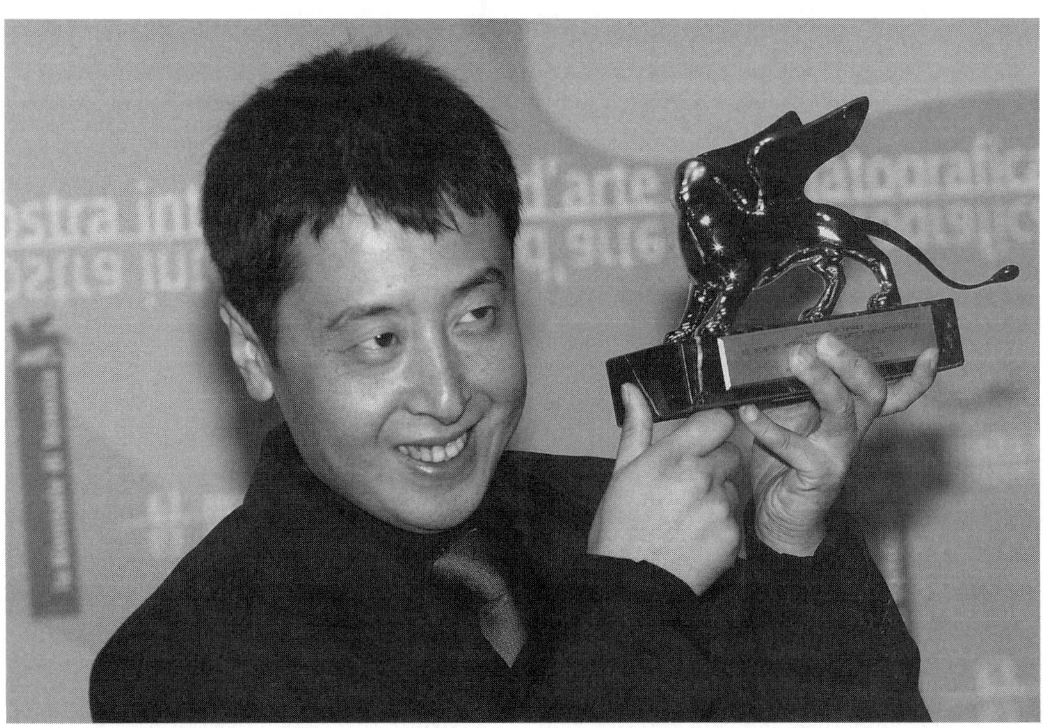

Chinese director Jia Zhangke receives a Golden Lion Award for his film *Still Life* at the 63rd Venice Film Festival in 2006 in Venice, Italy. (AFP/Getty Images)

films, like the Sixth Generation films, sought to "uncover" the less palatable realities of worker exploitation, poverty, social inequality, and environmental decay.

Chinese film historian Zhang Yingjin identifies another group of filmmakers, one within the Sixth Generation, emerging from the periphery of the state studio system (Zhang 2004: 289–291). The similarity between these directors and the other Sixth Generation filmmakers was principally in their choice of subject matter. Like their counterparts, they focused on questions of youth alienation and discontent voiced through popular music (e.g., *Dirt*, dir. Guan Hu, 1994; *Weekend Lovers*, dir. Lou Ye, 1995) and lived out in alternative lifestyles (*Rainclouds over Wushan*, dir. Zhang Ming, 1995; *Steel Making*, dir. Lu Xuechang, 1997). Once again, with these filmmakers there was a strong sense of documentary realism that distinguished them from their predecessors. As Zhang Yingjin (2004: 290) has put it:

> Whereas the [Fifth Generation directors] are associated with rural landscape, traditional culture, ethnic spectacle, grand epic, historical reflection, allegorical framework, communal focus, and depths of emotion, the [Sixth Generation directors] are sided with an urban milieu, modern sensitivity, a narcissistic tendency, initiation tales, documentary effects, uncertain situation, individualistic perception, and precarious moods.

Sixth Generation films, however, have to be seen in the broader context of late 1990s and early 2000s Chinese cinema. The first thing to note is that like their Fifth Generation predecessors, the Sixth Generation directors have enjoyed greater fame and success overseas than they have in China itself. This is in no small part due to the fact that their films have not been officially distributed in China. Although some have circulated on pirated VCDs and DVDs, the lack of official endorsement severely restricts the degree of publicity and debate that can accompany them.

The second thing to note is the increasingly competitive commercial climate that took over the Chinese film industry in this period. With cinema attendance in sharp decline from the second half of the 1980s, the priority of the beleaguered Chinese film industry became popular commercial successes. The leading Fifth Generation filmmakers enjoyed commercial success overseas in the early 1990s, but their films were generally not box office hits at home. The Sixth Generation directors enjoyed even less domestic success, for obvious reasons.

In the mid-1990s, the Chinese authorities relaxed their opposition to Chinese-foreign cooperation, nurturing the production of films like Ye Daying's *Red Cherry*, a Sino–Russian–Hong Kong collaboration that broke box office records in 1995, and Zhou Xiaowen's *The Emperor's Shadow*, a Hong Kong–China co-production and the second best selling film of 1996. In the later 1990s and early 2000s, the leading Fourth and Fifth Generation directors were caught up in the race for commercial success with films like *The Opium Wars* (dir. Xie Jin, 1997) and Zhang Yimou's *Hero*, which broke all Chinese box office records, as well as Chen Kaige's *Together*, ranked second in the domestic charts, and his popular *The Emperor and the Assassin*, in 2002.

At the same time, another transnational collaboration, working under the name of Yima, started producing low-budget but popular urban youth movies such as Zhang

Chinese actors Jet Li (left) and Zhang Ziyi, stars of the film *Hero*, pose at the film's United States premiere in Hollywood. The film tells different versions of the same story of attempts to assassinate the soon-to-be first emperor of China who unified the country for the first time during the Qin dynasty (221–207 BC). (Corbis)

Yang's *Shower* (1999). Yima was set up by an American working with the Xi'an Film Studio and with funding from Taiwan and in many ways has targeted the same urban youth market niche as the Sixth Generation filmmakers. The fundamental difference, however, is that their productions have been authorized and they have chosen to take a lighter-hearted, optimistic approach to the subject matter rather than the Sixth Generation's angst-ridden, alienated perspective. For example, *Shower* deals with issues of a rapidly changing society through the story of an eldest son who returns home to Beijing to care for his mentally disabled brother. The film traces how the son sees the old Beijing he grew up with disappearing behind the facades of modernity; it does so, however, in the fashion of a bittersweet comedy, not a heavy meditation on deteriorating human relationships.

In 2001, another transnational film, Feng Xiaogang's *Big Shot's Funeral*, broke box office records once again, although this was an entirely different kind of project from Yima's low-cost productions. The film had a budget of US$3.5 million and was partly funded by Columbia Asia, marking a tentative step by Hollywood to enter the Chinese film market. The film brought Hong Kong and Chinese stars together and set new box office records in 2002 before being overtaken by *Hero* later in the year. Feng followed up his success with other popular commercial hits including *Cellphone* (2003) and *World without Thieves* (2004). In 2006, he won the Future Film Festival Digital Award for his film *The Banquet*, an extravagant historical court epic dubbed by some as a Chinese-style *Hamlet*.

It is important to pay attention to the commercialism of this emerging era for several reasons. First, it reminds us that although much of the international critical interest in recent Chinese cinema has revolved around the radical filmmakers of whatever generation, the box office interest in China has usually been elsewhere. Second, as with early Chinese cinema in the 1930s, some of the toughest competition over the years has come from overseas with films like *Titanic*, the Harry Potter movies, and the *Lord of the Rings* trilogy and Hong Kong blockbusters like *Infernal Affairs I–II*. Indeed, it is important not to overlook the popularity of Hong Kong films in China from the 1980s onward both in theaters and on television and video. In terms of the role that film plays in contemporary Chinese popular culture as experienced by ordinary people in China, Hollywood and Hong Kong films and stars are at least as important, if not more so, than Sixth Generation filmmakers, for instance. Third, in the long run, commercialism proved to be one of the strongest forces in Chinese cinema in the late 1990s and early 2000s, ultimately overcoming strong political and artistic sentiments that had previously led directors in quite different directions.

That is not to say that political films were no longer made. Indeed, following the events of 1989, the government put renewed effort into communicating its message to the people, and film was given a definite role to play. In the 1990s, the government subsidized a succession of historical war films and political biographies of early CCP leaders like Mao Zedong, Zhou Enlai, Liu Shaoqi, and Deng Xiaoping. These were intended to nurture a stronger sense of attachment to the Party among members of the younger generation in particular, whose lives had become increasingly detached from the revolutionary ethos, culture, and mythology that had so strongly shaped previous generations. Nonetheless, these political films often enjoyed poor box office revenues and were more important as a semilucrative mode of subsistence for state film studios than as a strong ideological force among Chinese youth.

Moviegoing Audiences Past and Present

To understand cinema as a part of Chinese popular culture, it is important to consider not only the films themselves but the range of social practices that constitute film as a social phenomenon. Clearly, the activities of filmmakers, administrative bodies, government, financiers, and so on are all important, as we have seen. Just as important, though, is the social context of watching films. Where, how, and with whom one watches a film can fundamentally change the way the film is enjoyed, disliked, understood, or interpreted. In fact, a fundamental shift since the 1980s has seen more Chinese people watching films at home on videocassette, VCD, or DVD than going to the movie theater, and moviegoing itself has also changed enormously over the years.

Moviegoing in prewar Shanghai was characterized by a differentiated range of experiences. First, early 1930s ticket prices ranged from 0.2 yuan (approximately US$0.04) up to 2 yuan (about 40–50 cents in the early 1930s) (Zhang 2004: 15–16, 74–75), depending upon the kind of film and movie theater. Some theaters specialized in the latest releases, and these charged the most for tickets. Others usually presented only second-, third-, or fourth-run films, for which the price was considerably less. Then there were at one end of the spectrum highly fashionable and prestige venues with impressive design and expensive interior decoration and at the other end low-cost, very basic theaters with little in the way of comfort. More recent releases cost more, and once movies with sound arrived, they were also more expensive. In this way alone, movie audiences were to some degree self-differentiating according to wealth and taste.

The movie theater also was a key embodiment of modernity, with its basis in new technology, the exoticism of film's strong foreign associations, and the taste of luxury often offered either in the space itself or on the screen. In particular, the top-end, expensive first-run theaters, with grand architecture, air-conditioning, luxurious seating, and stylish refinements

Newly installed cinema seating at Beijing's Daguanlou movie theater, which has been open for business for all of the 100 years Chinese cinema has been in existence. (AFP/Getty Images)

carried with them connotations of high social status, fashionability, and modern living. For upwardly mobile socialites, these would be the places to be and to be seen. In this case, moviegoing was not just about watching films but socializing and participating in a lifestyle.

There were also other ways in which social position related to moviegoing and tastes for different films. On the whole, the wealthier, social-climbing, or fashion-conscious Chinese favored Hollywood films, compared to the mainly "students, shopkeepers, office clerks and other petty bourgeois" (Zhang 2004: 75) who were the principal consumers of Chinese films. In all of these various ways, we therefore have to consider the range of experiences that people had when "going to the movies."

The war years severely disrupted cinema production but also clearly affected moviegoing both in terms of film content and viewing contexts. Moviegoing could become a nationalistic, anti-Japanese, or otherwise politically motivated experience in the unoccupied parts of China. It could alternatively constitute a form of escapism from the difficulties of everyday life. Nonetheless, many theaters closed down, and the hard times meant for many that moviegoing was a luxury of days gone by.

After the war, there were two key areas of change: the political definition of film and the expansion of China's film audiences throughout the country. The newly enhanced political role and function of film in society was to change moviegoing from being a relatively independent, individual act of consumer choice to one of political engagement and subjectivity. Going to watch a film was no longer an escape into fantasy so much as a participation in

A worker hangs a movie poster inside a Shanghai subway station in 1999. (Getty Images)

Maoist notions of political education, nationalism, and the formation of citizens. This may have had some appeal and popularity in the early, more euphoric days of the People's Republic; however, after a short while urban audiences started losing interest in films that became increasingly predictable, monotonous, and simplified in terms of characters and plot.

Later on, in the 1960s and 1970s, watching films also became an organized experience of mass political participation. Work units organized trips to the movies for their workers or showed films in dining halls or theaters at their workplace. Watching films could also be accompanied before or after by discussion in political meetings. In these ways, watching films entailed entirely different forms of social interaction from in the prewar years. It was far less an entertainment of choice than it had been in the past, and at times of high ideological dogmatism many questioned whether it was actually entertaining at all.

The second key change involves the way that the medium of film spread out from the large metropolitan centers, where it had always been heavily concentrated in its prewar commercial heyday, to other cities and smaller towns as well as the countryside. This change was closely associated with the political transformation of film in that it was precisely because the government and the Party saw new educational and propagandistic possibilities for film that they were keen for as many people as possible to watch it. Work units were equipped with projection facilities; new projection teams were set up to travel around showing films where there were no movie theaters, including many rural teams that brought cinema to peasants in the countryside who otherwise might never have seen a film.

In this way, China for the first time had something approaching a national cinema audience. In the past, Chinese cinema audiences had always been very localized, restricted to a small proportion of the population, and had also been watching different films—some Chinese, some foreign, some politically motivated, and some simply entertainment. In the PRC after 1949, by contrast, film watching became for the first time something familiar to a large proportion of the population, and for the first time they were also all largely watching the same films or at least the same kinds of film.

In the late 1970s and early 1980s, once the political turmoil of the Cultural Revolution period had died down, moviegoing peaked once again, with record audience levels attracted by more interesting films, a more relaxed political environment, and, importantly, a relative lack of other forms of entertainment. As the 1980s progressed, it also became easier to go to the movies of one's own volition even if organized mass film-viewings were still arranged (and continued into the early 2000s in universities and some other state work units). This peak of moviegoing was to be gradually undermined, however—to a large degree by technological developments in home entertainment, although the rising standard of living and level of disposable income clearly also played a part (see Chapter 3).

First, television burst onto the Chinese popular cultural scene. Television offered novelty, variety, and convenient news and entertainment in the comfort of one's own home. Second, toward the end of the 1980s, families now increasingly equipped with televisions started also to acquire videocassette recorders. This further enhanced home-viewing options and particularly negated the need to go to the theater in order to watch films. Third, in the 1990s VCDs started to take over from videocassettes, and the video piracy that had already developed became more widespread. By the second half of the 1990s, it was easy to buy pirated VCDs of the latest Hollywood films as well as Hong Kong and Chinese films, often even before they hit the theaters either in China or in other parts of the world. The quality of pirated video was highly variable, but with prices a fraction of the cost of a movie ticket, the effect on the film industry—and theaters in particular—has been enormous. In the 2000s, VCDs have been replaced by DVDs, the quality of pirated copies has improved, and the cost of legal copies of films has also come down.

At the same time, from the 1980s onward, there has gradually developed a whole range of other entertainment possibilities—music, dancing, discos, sports, theatre, dining, bowling, and all the many other activities discussed in other chapters of this volume. Consequently, film watching for many in China has gradually become separated from the notions of moviegoing and large public audiences. By contrast, film watching is an increasingly flexible, personal, domestic experience.

Cinema Reform, the Market, and the Future of Chinese Cinema

In the early 2000s, as mentioned, film piracy became a major problem for the Chinese film industry. This and other developments in China's film sector produced a sense of crisis, leading to proposals for far-reaching reforms in the sector. In the early 2000s, many Chinese film studios were losing money, many movie theaters were also in trouble, and there was a heightened sense of foreign competition.

Foreign competition came in several forms. Since the 1990s, China had agreed to allow a small quota of foreign films to be imported into China, but under the agreement conditions for China's entry into the World Trade Organization (WTO) in 2001, China also agreed to increase this quota to twenty per year. This may not seem like a large number, but it doubled the existing quota at a time when foreign films were already dominating Chinese box office receipts. It could also be argued that with video piracy making virtually all foreign films—and certainly all international blockbusters—available in China regardless of import quotas, the increase was irrelevant; that was partly true. The Chinese film industry relied almost entirely on box office receipts to fund new films, however. It was therefore very sensitive to a doubling of the number of the most competitive films in the market, which were distributed on a revenue-sharing basis (i.e., half of the revenues went overseas).

Under the WTO agreement, China also started opening up its cinema sector to foreign involvement, and in the early 2000s large international distributors like Warner Brothers started opening chains of joint-venture movie theaters in the large cities like Shanghai, Guangzhou, and Beijing. This too was seen as a challenge to the domestic film industry, which had always had a close relationship with cinema distribution in China. Hence, with falling revenues for cinemas and studios, the increasing popularity of home entertainment (including the arrival of broadband Internet and digital television video-on-demand), an increasing challenge from video piracy, and both legally and illegally imported films, the Chinese film industry was feeling besieged.

The late 1990s had already seen the emerging strength of commercial imperatives, which became all the stronger in the early 2000s. To some degree, the domestic film industry was already fighting back as, with films like Feng Xiaogang's *Big Shot's Funeral* or *Cellphone* and Zhang Yimou's *Hero*, it started producing its own real blockbusters to challenge Hollywood on a more equal footing. In 2004, there was still a strongly perceived need for substantial reform, however, and the authorities were considering a range of initiatives with the specific aims of making the Chinese film industry more commercially viable and more competitive when confronted with foreign films and piracy generally.

In particular, there were proposals to introduce a classification system for films, to partly decentralize regulatory supervision, and to open up the film distribution sectors to private and foreign capital. The introduction of rating certificates classifying films as for children, teenagers, or adults was seen by many as a means of enhancing the competitivity of domestic films by allowing filmmakers to deal with more adult issues, to be slightly more adventurous with content, and to be liberated from the obligation to produce only films that were suitable for all the family.

The future of China's film industry therefore hinges on a number of key issues. In 2004, there were already signs that the film industry was starting to work with other media sectors such as television stations and broadband providers to adapt to the changing technological environment. The arrival of 24-hour movie channels, video-on-demand, and digital cinema technologies are all likely to be turned to the advantage of the industry.

The problem of piracy—which is not exclusively a Chinese one—will not be resolved easily, if at all. The key issue will therefore be how well China's film industry manages to develop strategies for living with and providing alternatives to home entertainment or at least making sure that they are getting paid for their contributions. In the early 2000s, the cinema sector, partly through foreign joint ventures, was in fact already starting to look at the whole cinema experience to make it more attractive to audiences. New, stylish multiplexes offering a broader range of foodstuffs and entertainment services were starting to attract people back into theaters that had for a long time been badly decorated relics in need of refurbishment.

Meanwhile, the content of films is likely to become increasingly entertainment-oriented and feature more stunts, comedy, and action, avoiding sensitive or unpopular political issues. It is also likely to become more transnational in the sense that on one hand, Chinese films will increasingly be looking for additional recognition and revenues overseas, and, on the other hand, the commercial imperative will encourage Chinese filmmakers to look ever more closely at emulating, adapting, or bettering features and characteristics of successful international films.

A to Z

Anti-Japanese film. Films with a strong anti-Japanese propaganda sentiment made during the anti-Japanese war (1937–1945) predominantly in Hong Kong up until 1941 and in Chongqing, the seat of the exiled nationalist government.

Beijing Bastards. The first so-called Sixth Generation film, directed by Zhang Yuan in 1993 and telling the story of a group of alienated Beijing youths whose life centers around their rock group.

Big Shot's Funeral. An urban comedy set in Beijing, directed by new-generation commercial director Feng Xiaogang in 2001 with some international funding from Columbia Asia. A major box office success in 2002, bettered only by Zhang Yimou's *Hero*. The film is often seen as representative of the new commercial entertainment-oriented era in Chinese cinema.

Black Cannon Incident. One of the lesser known but highly acclaimed Fifth Generation films, directed by Huang Jianxin in 1985. The film is a political satire on the absurd machinations of political bureaucracy.

Centre Stage (aka Ruan Lingyu or Actress). A Hong Kong docudrama directed by Stanley Kwan in 1992 and starring Maggie Cheung. The film tells the tragic story of 1930s Shanghai film star Ruan Lingyu, who committed suicide in 1935 at the age of twenty-four.

Chen Kaige. Along with Zhang Yimou, one of the most successful and internationally recognized Fifth Generation filmmakers. Director of among others *Yellow Earth*, *Farewell My Concubine*, *King of the Children*, *Together*, and *The Emperor and the Assassin*.

Crows and Sparrows. A classic social realist film, directed by Zheng Junli, made in Shanghai on the eve of the Communist takeover and telling the story of a group of tenants facing eviction by their Kuomintang landlord preparing to flee to Taiwan.

Dai Jinhua. A renowned Chinese intellectual in the area of Chinese cultural studies. A well-respected commentator on contemporary Chinese cinema and media.

Ermo. A late Fifth Generation period film directed by Zhou Xiaowen in 1994 and starring Gong Li as a young peasant woman determined to buy the largest television set in the nearby town in a case of one-upmanship with her neighbor.

Farewell My Concubine. A later Fifth Generation classic, directed by Chen Kaige in 1993, this is an epic film telling the story of two Beijing opera performers from childhood in the early twentieth century up until the early reform period. The film is much acclaimed for its treatment of issues of sexuality and human relationships.

Fifth Generation. The first class of film directors to graduate from the Beijing Film Institute after the Cultural Revolution. They were renowned for their innovative cinematic styles and daring treatment of both familiar and unfamiliar subject matter.

Goddess. A classic tragedy of 1930s left-wing Shanghai cinema, starring Ruan Lingyu and directed by Wu Yonggang in 1934. The film tells the story of a young woman forced into prostitution in order to pay for her son's education.

Hero. Zhang Yimou's most successful film in terms of box office revenues, topping the domestic charts in China in 2002 before also earning good box office receipts and critical acclaim overseas.

Hibiscus Town. A very popular and much renowned film made in 1986 by the Fourth Generation film director Xie Jin. This political melodrama tells the story of the injustices inflicted upon peasants in a small town during the Cultural Revolution.

Hu Die. One of the most popular female Shanghai movie stars of the 1930s alongside Ruan Lingyu. One of her most famous films was *Twin Sisters*, directed by Zheng Zhengqiu.

Infernal Affairs. A Hong Kong film directed by Andrew Lau and Alan Mak that topped mainland Chinese movie charts in December 2002 and later became the inspiration for Martin Scorcese's Oscar-winning film *The Departed.*

Jia Zhangke. A respected director associated with the so-called Sixth Generation. He is particularly renowned for his uncompromising representation of the negative aspects of economic reform in Chinese society in films such as *Xiao Wu* (aka *Pickpocket*) (1998) and *Platform* (2000). In 2006, Jia won the Golden Lion Award at the Venice Film Festival for his film *Still Life* (*sanxia haoren*) dealing with the effect of the giant Three Gorges Dam project in central China on people forced to leave their homes by the flooding.

Judou. A Fifth Generation film directed by Zhang Yimou in 1989 telling the story of a young woman, Judou, forced to marry the cruel, impotent patriarch of a wealthy family but who develops a relationship with the old man's adopted nephew. The film is often discussed for its treatment of suppressed male desire and oppressed women in traditional society.

King of the Children. Loosely based on a short story by author Ah Cheng, this 1987 film directed by Chen Kaige tells a story of a young schoolteacher in a remote mountain village. The film was not particularly well received either critically or by audiences.

League of Left-Wing Writers. A group of intellectuals associated with and linked to the Communist Party. In the 1930s, they set up a film group which was to become closely involved in the development of Shanghai's left-wing and social realist cinema.

Lianhua Film Company. One of the main film companies in 1930s Shanghai, formed as a conglomeration of existing studios at a time of fierce commercial competition and financial hardship for the film industry. The company was the result of efforts by Luo Mingyu, a Shanghai businessman who saw the need for a drastic restructuring of the industry. The company operated on a revenue-sharing basis with its member studios and sought to revive the domestic film industry through the reinvigoration of "national cinema."

Life of Wu Xun. A controversial film which started production in the late 1940s under Nationalist control in Shanghai but finished under the CCP regime in 1950. Directed by Sun Yu, the film was well received by audiences in 1951, although it was to mark a watershed in the transition from social realism to socialist realism. Following a bitter *People's Daily* editorial written by Mao Zedong himself severely criticizing the film for its promotion of feudal values, the whole of the film industry was thrown into disarray as filmmakers became uncertain and fearful about what was and what was not politically acceptable in the new era. The result was a shift toward simpler, more dogmatic plots and characterization.

Mingxing Studios. One of the leading Shanghai film studios in the 1930s, particularly associated with many of the left-wing filmmakers including Xia Yan, whom the proprietor invited to the studio to help it out of financial difficulties. The studio produced some of the classics of 1930s cinema, including *Twin Sisters*, *Street Angel*, and *Spring Silkworms*.

New Documentary Movement. A loose grouping of "underground" documentary filmmakers, such as Wu Wenguang, often working with small portable digital video cameras. The movement is also associated with the Sixth Generation filmmakers for its similar interest in exposing the less positive aspects of post-Mao Chinese society.

Old Well. An internationally recognized film directed by Wu Tianming in 1987 and starring Zhang Yimou. The film tells the moving story of efforts to dig a new well in a remote village in western China where there has been a shortage of water for generations.

The One and Eight. The first Fifth Generation film, directed by Zhang Junzhao in 1983 with cinematography by Zhang Yimou. The film marked a radical break with the tradition of socialist realism and political melodrama that was the norm. The film tells the story of a Communist Party officer mistakenly accused of desertion and thrown in with common criminal prisoners in the anti-Japanese war.

The Opium Wars. The official film made to commemorate the return of Hong Kong to Chinese sovereignty in 1997. Directed by veteran filmmaker Xie Jin, it celebrates the actions of Qing imperial official Lin Zexu, who fought the British in the nineteenth-century battles over the rights to import opium into China and which ended in the "unequal treaties" ceding Hong Kong to British control.

Platform. A film by Sixth Generation filmmaker Jia Zhangke in 2000 telling the story of a theatre troupe being privatized in the post-Mao era. Set in small-town northwestern China, the film dwells on the poverty of human relationships in the new China.

Ruan Lingyu. One of the top 1930s film stars in Shanghai, noted for her performances in left-wing films such as *Goddess* and *New Woman* dealing with the downtrodden fate of women in contemporary urban China. She committed suicide in 1935 to escape scandal associated with a series of court cases brought by her estranged husband.

Sixth Generation. The general term used for a loose grouping of young filmmakers emerging in 1990s China after the Fifth Generation heyday. They are particularly noted for their gritty, urban realism and "underground" filmmaking without official permission.

Street Angel. A classic of 1930s Shanghai cinema that mixes commercial entertainment with hard-hitting social realism in the melodramatic story of two sisters being forced into prostitution and concubinage by their employer-landlord.

Tian Zhuangzhuang. A Fifth Generation director known for ethnographic-style films dealing with ethnic minorities. He had early international success with the film *Horse Thief*, set in Tibet.

Twin Sisters. A classic of 1930s social realist cinema, directed by Zheng Zhengqiu in 1933. The film tells the story of the contrasting fortunes of twin sisters separated in childhood and both played by top 1930s star Hu Die.

The White-Haired Girl. A classic film of socialist realist cinema, directed by Wang Bin and Shui Hua in 1950. An adaptation of a political opera, the film tells the story of suffering of a young girl at the hands of traditional feudal society who is saved by a young Communist soldier.

Wu Tianming. An acclaimed Fourth Generation director who was also responsible for nurturing many of the early Fifth Generation filmmakers in his role as head of the Xian Film Studios.

Xia Yan. A renowned filmmaker, scriptwriter, intellectual, and leader of the League of Left-Wing Writers film group in 1930s Shanghai. Xia Yan was one of the key inspirational leaders of left-wing Shanghai filmmaking.

Xie Jin. One of the most important and respected postwar Chinese film directors, with a career stretching from the 1950s into the 1990s. He is generally associated with political melodramas; his acclaimed films include *Stage Sisters* (1965), *The Legend of Tianyun Mountain* (1980), *Hibiscus Town* (1986), and *The Opium Wars* (1997).

Yellow Earth. The first Fifth Generation film to achieve international recognition. Directed in 1984 by Chen Kaige with camerawork by Zhang Yimou, it is a classic of Fifth Generation cinema telling the story of the relationship between a Communist soldier collecting folk songs in the remote northwest and a family in a highly traditional and feudal society.

Zhang Junzhao. Although one of the less internationally known Fifth Generation directors, Zhang was director of the first acclaimed Fifth Generation film, *The One and Eight* (1983), telling the story of military prisoners in the anti-Japanese war period with cinematography by Zhang Yimou.

Zhang Yimou. The most internationally recognized and successful of the Fifth Generation directors, having started out as a cinematographer on *The One and Eight* (1983) and *Yellow Earth* (1984). His famous directing successes include *Red Sorghum* (1987), *Judou* (1989), *Raise the Red Lantern* (1981), and more recently *Hero* (2002).

References and Further Reading

Berry, C. (ed.) 1991. *Perspectives on Chinese cinema.* London: BFI.

Browne, N., Pickowicz, P. G., Sobchack, V., & Yau, E. (eds.) 1994. *New Chinese cinema: Forms, identities, politics.* Cambridge: Cambridge University Press.

Chow, R. 1995. *Primitive passions: Visuality, sexuality, ethnography, and contemporary*

Chinese cinema. New York: Columbia University Press.

Clark, P. 1987. *Chinese cinema: Culture and politics since 1949*. Cambridge: Cambridge University Press.

Howkins, J. 1982. *Mass communication in China*. New York: Longman.

Kuoshu, H. H. (ed.) 2002. *Celluloid China: Cinematic encounters with culture and society*. Carbondale and Edwardsville, IL: Southern Illinois University Press.

Lee, L. O-F. 1999. *Shanghai modern: The flowering of a new urban culture in China 1930–1945*. Cambridge, MA: Harvard University Press.

Lu, S. H. 1997. *Transnational Chinese cinemas: Identity, nationhood, gender*. Honolulu: Hawaii University Press.

Ma, N. 2002. "An outline for viewing *Street Angel*—the textual and critical difference of being radical: Reconstructing Chinese leftist films of the 1930s." In H. H. Kuoshu (ed.) 2002. *Celluloid China: Cinematic encounters with culture and society*. Carbondale and Edwardsville, IL: Southern Illinois University Press.

Pickowicz, P. 1974. "Cinema and revolution in China." *American Behavioral Scientist*, Vol. 17, No. 3, 328–359.

Reynaud, B. 1993. "Gong Li and the glamour of the Chinese star." *Sight and Sound*, Vol. 3, No. 8: 12–15.

Semsel, G.S. & Chen, X. (eds.) 1990. *Chinese film theory: A guide to the new era*. New York: Praeger.

Zhang, X. 1997. *Chinese modernism in the era of reforms: Cultural fever, avant-garde fiction and the new Chinese cinema*. Durham/London: Duke University Press.

Zhang, Y. (ed.) 1999. *Cinema and urban culture in Shanghai, 1922–1943*. Stanford, CA: Stanford University Press.

——— 2004. *Chinese national cinema*. London: Routledge.

8

The Internet and Telecommunications

The Internet and telecommunications have had a fundamental impact on contemporary Chinese popular culture since the end of the 1980s (in the case of telecommunications) and the mid-1990s (in the case of the Internet). They have changed the ways in which people interact and communicate with each other as well as offered a wide range of new forms of leisure and entertainment. Perhaps the first time that the potential of telecommunications technologies became clear was in 1989 at the time of the Tiananmen Square demonstrations. In April and May of that year, but particularly in the two weeks after martial law was imposed and television and radio were strictly controlled in the lead-up to June 4, telephones and fax machines came into their own as sources of news and information. In particular, people in Hong Kong started faxing into China newspaper articles, letters, and other information on what was going on in China and Hong Kong and how the rest of the world was reporting the events. The crux was that whereas television and radio could be turned off or tightly controlled, fax machines could not. This example gives an indication of the kind of boundary-crossing effects that telecommunications technologies, including later the Internet, have had in China.

With the Internet, Chinese people—particularly young people—have started communicating with e-mail and instant messaging services, in chat rooms, on bulletin boards, and through short messaging services (SMS) to mobile phones. They now enjoy access to endless sources of information that could not have been imagined even twenty years ago. Online gaming has become a popular leisure activity among young people, particularly in the cities; e-commerce is starting to offer alternative ways of shopping; and broadband is offering new ways of enjoying films, music, and television. These are changes that have affected many parts of the world in recent years; however, the impact in China is all the greater for the fact that up until the 1980s the country was largely closed to the outside world, people had limited leisure time, disposable income, and entertainment opportunities, and their government closely guarded information of all kinds.

Although the Internet is a very visible marker of the kinds of cultural and communicative changes that have been taking place in China, it is important not to neglect the less noticeable impact that telecommunications have had on Chinese people's lives. It could even be argued that telephones, pagers, fax machines, and cellphones have in some ways had a more fundamental and far-reaching effect than the Internet on Chinese social interaction in the last two decades. For one thing, the telephone revolution predates the Internet revolution by nearly a decade. Furthermore, whereas there is now nearly one phone for every two people in the country, Internet users constituted only around 10 percent of the population in 2006, and they are mainly concentrated in the large metropolitan areas. In other words, Chinese people generally are far more likely to have had their lives changed by telephones than by the Internet. At the same time, the kind of interpersonal communication that telephones, particularly cellphones, facilitate has opened up new, informal sources of information transfer that offer a fundamental alternative to centralized mass media.

In the future, the Internet and telecommunications will also play a crucial part in the development of Chinese popular cultural practices. In 2004, China already saw its first SMS novels published and distributed to mobile phones. In 2005, the country's first mobile-phone television drama went into production, and third-generation mobile-phone services will become available in 2007 offering people new ways to play games, search the Internet, receive news, watch television, and engage in individual social interaction. In 2005, Internet television was already starting to challenge the established boundaries between broadcasting and telecommunications, and with broadband Internet connection becoming more widely available, network convergence between television, computer, and telecommunications networks will be an important feature of future entertainment platforms in China.

A Chinese girl talks on a cell phone. Even though the Internet has been credited with major advances in the telecommunications revolution in China, earlier devices such as mobile phones, faxes, and pagers predate the Internet by as much as a decade or more and have had equally far-reaching effects on Chinese social and cultural practices. (iStockPhoto.com)

A man uses a mobile phone as actor Luo Ji takes a break (left) during the filming of an episode of the mobile-phone drama *Appointment* in Shanghai, China, in 2005. *Appointment* is a super-modern love story squeezed into five-minute episodes made to be shown on mobile phone screens half the size of a credit card. Its makers hope the 25-minute series will capture attention in China's crowded mobile phone market, where entrepreneurs are competing furiously to come up with the latest gimmick. (AP/Wide World Photos)

The Growth and Organization of the Internet in China

In July 2006, official statistics put the number of Internet users in China at 123 million, with 54.5 million computers online having grown from 33.7 million in January 2002 (CNNIC 2005). This still represented less than 10 percent of the country's population, but it shows the extent of the growth in Internet use since the mid-1990s. In 1994, for instance, there were only 1,600 users in the whole country. However, it is also important to note that Internet users are very unevenly distributed throughout the country: In large cities like Beijing, Shanghai, and Guangzhou, as much as 25 to 30 percent of the local population uses the Internet but in more remote, rural, or less economically developed regions of China—such as Tibet, Guizhou, Henan, and Hunan—only 2 or 3 percent are Internet users.

The Internet in China is made up of various different networks, set up for different educational, research, military, trade, and commercial reasons. Over the years, these have changed names, merged, and come under different supervisory bodies so that by 2005 there were nine main interconnecting

Tibetan monks surf the Internet at an Internet cafe in 2006 in Lhasa, the capital city of the Tibet Autonomous Region, China. There has been an increase in Chinese tourists going to Lhasa using the recently completed Qinghai-Tibet railway, bringing an extra 3,000 people a day into Tibet. Critics say that it could threaten the cultural and even the physical landscape of the fragile Tibetan plateau while others argue that it will aid the modernization and economic development of the city and the region. (AFP/Getty Images)

networks (see Table 8.1). Although these national computer networks date back to 1987, when the first educational and research-oriented networks were set up, the official birthday of the Internet in China is usually considered to be April 20, 1994, when the Chinese computer networks were internationally linked to the global Internet.

From 1994, a key issue that dictated the development of the structure and functioning of the Internet was that of funding and ownership combined with commercial and inter-ministerial rivalry. Much of the early infrastructural development of the Internet was funded by the central government, with the lines predominantly owned by the dominant state telecommunications operator, China Telecom. China Telecom, in turn, leased the lines to the various new network operators. As the Internet developed, however, different ministries and telecommunications operators all came to own their own networks, leading to rivalry and competition between them. In the early days, this was particularly so between the then Ministry of Electronic Industries (MEI) and the Ministry of Posts and Telecommunications (MPT), though these were later merged in 1996 to form the Ministry of

Table 8.1

Main Chinese Internet Networks in July 2006 with International Bandwidth Allocation (Mbps)

Network	Established	Operator and/ or ministerial interest	International bandwidth (Mbps), July 2006 (source: CNNIC)	Percentage of total, July 2006
CSTNET	1987 (CANET and IHEP Network) 1990 (CRNET) combined in 1996 as CSTNET	CAS	17,465	8.15
CHINANET	1993 as CHINAPAC renamed in 1995	Initially MPT then MII through China Telecom	122,587	57.24
CERNET	1994	SEC	4,796	2.24
UNINET	1999/2000	MEI then MII through China Unicom	3,652	1.7
CHINA169	2004 incorporating CNCNET (launched 1999) and CHINAGBN (launched 1996)	MR, SARFT, CAS, Shanghai Municipality through China Netcom	60,888	28.04
CIETNET	1999/2000	MOFTEC	2	Negligible
CMNET	1999/2000	MII through China Mobile	4,785	2.23
CGWNET	—	Military	—	
CSNET	—	MII, China Satcom	—	

Abbreviations used:

CSTNET—China Science and Technology Network
CAS—Chinese Academy of Social Sciences
CANET—China Academic Network
IHEP—Institute of High Energy Physics
CRNET—China Research Network
MPT—Ministry of Posts and Telecommunications
MII—Ministry of Information Industries
CERNET—China Education and Research Network
SEC—State Education Commission
CNCNET—China Network Communications Network
CHINAGBN—China Golden Bridge Network
MR—Ministry of Railways
SARFT—State Administration for Radio, Film, and Television
CIETNET—China International Economics and Trade Network
MOFTEC—Ministry of Foreign Trade and Economic Cooperation
CMNET—China Mobile Network
CGWNET—China Great Wall Network
CSNET—China Satellite Network

Information Industries (MII). In 2000, however, other ministries were involved with rival networks, including the Ministry of Railways and the State Administration for Radio, Film, and Television (SARFT) in CNCNET and CHINAGBN (now under CHINA169) and the Ministry of Foreign Trade and Economic Cooperation (MOFTEC) in CIETNET—the China International Economics and Trade Network.

There is also a clear division in China between the ownership and control of the infrastructure and Internet service provision on one hand and Internet content provision on the other. The first Internet service providers (ISPs) offering Internet access to businesses and the general public were launched in 1995. These were predominantly owned and run by regional branches of China Telecom because of the high line-leasing costs which heavily burdened the small number of independent operators. Internet content provision, on the other hand, has always had one foot firmly in each of the private and state sectors. There was a dot-com boom in the late 1990s that saw the establishment and rapid growth of different kinds of Internet content providers (ICPs) in China. These included the country's leading commercial Internet portals (see below). However, there was also a corresponding slump in 2000–2001, following the global downturn in the fate of dot-com enterprises and investment, and it was not really until 2003—when more diverse and innovative forms of revenue such as SMS, ringtone downloads, and online gaming were found—that some ICPs started to become truly profitable.

The early 2000s also saw the diversification of ways of accessing the Internet—in particular, increasing availability of broadband and increasing use of mobile Internet devices, including WAP (wireless application protocol) phones, laptops, and palmheld organizers. According to CNNIC, in July 2006 more than 62 percent of China's Internet users (77 million) were using broadband connections at least some of the time. Although the use of mobile devices is still relatively small as an overall proportion of Internet users, in January 2005 this nonetheless constituted the fastest area of growth in Internet access and was a sign of what the future holds, particularly with the arrival of third-generation (3G) mobile technologies.

A Chinese woman calls from a public China Telecom telephone in Shanghai, 2002. (Corbis)

Who Uses the Internet?

Since the late 1990s, there has been a marked change in the profile of the average

Internet user in China. In the early days, there was a predominance of IT specialists and enthusiasts with a relatively specialized knowledge and interest in the Internet. They were almost entirely male, fairly young, and well-educated. For instance, in 1998, one of the first CNNIC official surveys found that 92.8 percent of China's then 1,175,000 Internet users were male, 79.2 percent were between the ages of twenty and thirty-five, and nearly 60 percent were educated to bachelor's degree level or higher. More than 25 percent of them lived in Beijing, and 18.8 percent of them worked in the computer industry.

By the early to mid-2000s, Internet users had become more broadly representative of the general population. In July 2006, the ratio of male to female users was, as it had been for several years, around 6:4; the proportion of technology experts had dropped to just over 12 percent; around 28 percent had attained a bachelor's degree or higher; and only 3.9 percent lived in Beijing. Internet users were still relatively young, however—if anything, getting younger: Just over 82 percent were under the age of thirty-five, including 14.9 percent under the age of eighteen (compare this with less than 12 percent of users in 1998 being under the age of twenty).

In fact, Internet users' age is a good reminder that although Internet users have become more representative of the general population over the years, they are still predominantly young, with a large proportion of students (more than 32 percent), and mainly in the large cities and more developed eastern coastal provinces. Indeed, in January 2005, nearly 55 percent of Internet users lived in the eleven eastern coastal provinces and metropolitan areas—Guangdong Province alone accounted for 12.6 percent.

Over the years, Chinese Internet users have also gradually shifted from using the Internet predominantly at work to predominantly at home and increasingly in Internet cafés. In the late 1990s, only a minimal number—3 to 4 percent—of users accessed the Internet from Internet cafés, with the majority accessing from work. In 2006, by contrast, more than 72 percent of users used the Internet at home, 35.1 percent used it at work, and 29.5 percent used it in Internet cafés. This reflected the increasing number of households with a personal computer in the home, the increasing use of the Internet for leisure, and the large number of young people in particular going to Internet cafés.

What Is the Internet Used For?

In its short history in China, use of the Internet has changed along with the changes in its users. In the early days of the mid- to late 1990s, it was largely used for finding information about computers and information technologies (including software downloads) and looking for hardware, components, and accessories. As Internet users became more diverse and general in their interests, so people's uses of the Internet became more diverse. Importantly, this was accompanied and facilitated by the development of Chinese-language Internet content of different kinds.

In the early 2000s, although the Internet was used for communication—with e-mail, chat rooms, bulletin boards, and so on—it was seen primarily as a source of information, and news in particular (see below). People used the Internet to find all sorts of information that had previously often been hard to get hold of. For instance, government offices set up Web sites and published news, official announcements, statistics, analytical articles, and other information related to their sector of operation. In the past, much of this information would not have been available at all, would have been available only to certain groups of people, or else would have been very difficult to get hold of. With the Internet, many bureaucratic, gatekeeping, and other obstructive procedures that had previously kept official information away from the general public suddenly disappeared. Of course, sensitive information is still not available to the general public, and there are still restrictions in place on access to many kinds of official information. Yet the Internet has brought about a fundamental change in the accessibility of official information and thereby also helped change people's relationships to the government.

Probably more important for the average Internet user, however, were other kinds of information, relating to leisure or work interests of different kinds—IT and computers, cinema, television, music and other entertainment, science and education, sports, or financial information, for instance. This information is available either through the main Internet portals (see below) or through specialist sites run by individuals, organizations, or commercial businesses much as in other parts of the world.

The early 2000s also saw a gradual shift in uses of the Internet away from simply searching for information to using the Internet for various leisure and entertainment purposes. As an indication of this, in January 2000 nearly 60 percent of users said that their main reason for using the Internet was looking for information of different kinds, compared to less than 10 percent using it for leisure and entertainment purposes. By January 2005, the proportion of information-seekers had slipped to less than 40 percent, and the proportion of leisure users was up to nearly 36 percent. Importantly, this change has accompanied the continuing transformation of online content. In January 2000, most Web sites were principally offering information of one kind or another, but by January 2005, a much broader range of online services had become available. These included entertainment offerings such as online gaming, on-demand films and television programs for broadband users, music downloads and file-sharing, online books and literature, animation, images, ringtones and other downloads for cellphones. Consequently, use of the Internet was starting to become much broader than simply looking for information, even though that clearly remained a key characteristic of Internet use.

It is almost impossible to tell the story of the Internet without mentioning pornography, and, as in most other parts of the world, pornography also features in China's Internet culture. It is illegal in China to post sexually explicit materials on the Internet, and the authorities implement various measures to control access also to foreign porn sites (see below). Inevitably, though, Chinese Internet users still manage to access sexually explicit sites.

Chinese "netizens," as Internet users are known in China, also increasingly use the Internet for a range of other services, including shopping, banking, share-trading, job-hunting, and distance learning. E-commerce was slow to take off in China because of concerns about online security and the quality or state of goods bought online—indeed, whether goods would even turn up—and problems with making payments. Gradually, these problems have been addressed, and throughout the early 2000s, more and more people were buying things online, particularly books, music, and DVDs. Early on, most people buying goods online preferred to pay for them by mail or on delivery. As more and more Chinese people obtained credit cards, however, online payment has become an increasingly popular option, greatly facilitating online purchases. In 2003, U.S. online auction giant eBay bought one of its Chinese counterparts called Eachnet, and late in 2004 the two sites were made interconnectable, though in 2006 the Chinese market was still dominated by rival auction site Taobao.com.

Government Control

The Internet in general has often been considered as a vehicle for global democratization and open access to information. Such arguments have their flaws, not least because there are various ways in which people's everyday Internet use can be and is "directed" in certain ways following commercial and political interests. Search engines and portals, for instance, operate using various techniques that filter, rank, or prioritize search results in a way that favors certain sites. Nonetheless, the Internet does, for many people around the world, provide access to many different kinds of information, opinions, and social interactions that would not otherwise be available to them. As we have seen, this is also true of China.

The fact that Chinese Internet users have access to a wealth of previously unimaginable sources of information does not mean that the Internet is a "free" area of uncontrolled and unrestricted interaction, however. There is a range of ways in which the Chinese authorities in particular, but also others, control Chinese Internet access and content. These include site blocking, the use of commercial pressures, requirements for self-censorship and regulation, restrictions on online news production or reporting, and the arrest of online dissidents. Indeed, deterrence is a key feature of Internet control in China.

One of the most conspicuous and widely noticed forms of government control of the Internet in China is through site blocking. The Chinese authorities regularly block access to foreign sites, particularly prominent news sites like CNN and the BBC and sites expressing views unacceptable to the Chinese government, such as Taiwanese or Tibetan independence or human rights Web sites. This means that surfers simply cannot view such pages on their screens. At the same time, the authorities have introduced a number of filtering devices that screen sites for particular words and phrases to help them block the ones they do not like.

Although this site blocking can be fairly effective, it is not by any means comprehensive. For one thing, the degree and nature of such blocking has tended to change over time. One year, a site may be fully accessible; the next, it might be blocked; six months later, it could be available again. There is also a degree of randomness to the blocking. CNN and the BBC might be blocked, but ABC or NBC might not. Similarly, lesser-known news media Web sites with very similar, or even more critical, content—such as the United Kingdom's Channel 4 News—might remain untouched. There are also ways in which blocked sites can be accessed, usually through other Web sites specifically set up for the purpose. Finally, there is the matter of language. Considering that the language of many of the blocked foreign sites is English, they are not readily accessible to many Chinese Internet users in the first place. Most Chinese people using the Internet use Chinese-language Web sites and services, and although many users will also have some basic working knowledge of English and other languages, the majority of Internet users are not suitably proficient in English to be able to use the English-language Internet as a matter of routine.

Just as important as site blocking, if not more so, is the use of other forms of regulation and self-censorship in shaping Chinese Internet content. For instance, in the late 1990s, there were regulatory gray areas in relation to the Internet and news reporting because the existing regulations referred to traditional media such as newspapers, television, and radio. There were few regulations dictating what Web sites could and could not do. Consequently, some of China's leading Internet portals started writing their own news stories for a short while before being stopped by the authorities. Subsequently, the Ministry of Culture issued new regulations banning any site from carrying news stories that did not come from an officially recognized news agency or source, such as the Xinhua News Agency, the *People's Daily*, or CCTV but also including other regional and specialized newspapers and broadcasters.

At the same time, regulations were introduced requiring Web site operators to keep copies of all pages on their site for several months, in case the authorities should wish to inspect them. This also included records of chat room and bulletin board activity, which had become freely used for posting content sometimes quite critical of the Chinese authorities. In this way, Web site operators were made responsible for what appeared on their sites, under the threat of losing their licenses and being closed down. Subsequently, webmasters became far more attentive to what was posted on their sites, both their own content and any users' postings. In this way, the kind of self-censorship regime that operates in other media sectors was fairly successfully introduced to some areas of the Internet.

Interestingly, however, this kind of self-censorship has not only applied to Chinese Web sites. In late 2004, human rights organizations accused some of the best-known international search engines, which were making concerted efforts to establish themselves in the Chinese market, of doctoring their search results to exclude sites sensitive to the Chinese government. Over the next couple of years, this became openly accepted and standard practice for major international sites such as Google and Yahoo!, even if they occasionally received criticism in the West for doing it.

Open online political dissidence is rare in China, largely because of its likely consequences. Nonetheless, there are regular reports of cases before the courts of people accused, and usually found guilty, of posting unacceptable materials online. The government developed a particular sensitivity to Internet activity following the mobilization of the Buddhism-inspired Falun Gong religious group in the late 1990s when a silent protest—organized through the Internet—of tens of thousands of Falun Gong supporters materialized outside the residential compound of the nation's top leaders, taking them completely by surprise.

Online dissidents, like any others, are often sentenced to years in prison for the publication of articles critical of the Chinese leadership or otherwise unacceptable to the authorities; however, it is important to point out that although most international attention is drawn to suppression of political freedom, for the Chinese authorities and many Chinese citizens a greater concern is suppression of pornographic or violent content. Indeed, the Chinese authorities actually find themselves more regularly challenged by tackling problems of sexual rather than political content, and, in recent years, Chinese public attention has been more focused on the potential dangers of online gaming (see below) than political dissidence.

Concerns over violence, online gaming, and sexual content on the Internet have found another forum of expression in relation to Internet cafés, or "netbars" as they are known in China. Netbars became very popular, particularly with young people, in the early 2000s. They became places where young people went to play online and offline games and socialize with their friends and make new ones as well as surf the Internet more generally. In this way, netbars have a particular significance in terms of contemporary Chinese youth culture as places for social interaction as well as accessing Internet services.

A combination of factors led to the transformation of the netbar sector and the introduction of tougher regulations controlling the operation of Internet cafés, however. In the early 2000s, as netbars became more popular, parents, teachers, and government officials became concerned about the amount of time that young people spent in netbars and in front of computers, particularly the amount of time spent playing online games. One of the factors helping to transform the sector was the development of better, more sophisticated and playable games designed to employ the faster data-transfer capability of increasingly available broadband connections. When, in June 2002, a fire in a Beijing Internet café killed twenty-four people, most of them young students, it provoked further dismay in the general public and prompted the authorities to clamp down on Internet café operation.

The fire actually coincided with the issuing of new regulations covering netbars that responded to government and parental concerns; however, the fire added poignancy to

Firefighters stand in front the 24-hour Lanjisu Cyber Café in Beijing, China on June 16, 2002, after a fire on the second floor of the concrete two-story building broke out around 2:45 a.m. and killed twenty-four customers trapped by iron bars over the windows. (AP/Wide World Photos)

their implementation and led to thousands of netbars being closed down, either temporarily or permanently, following government inspections. New regulations subsequently addressed two issues: the safety of netbar users and the negatively perceived effects of spending time in netbars. Public concerns expressed in the media focused on the amount of time students spent playing games, the disruptive effects it had on their studies, and the negative influences of violent games as well as the possibility that young people went to netbars to access porn sites. Netbars were therefore barred from locating within 200 meters of schools and were not allowed to admit people under the age of eighteen.

The combination of concerns about safety and content following the Beijing netbar fire also indirectly led to a shift from small, privately owned, independent Internet cafés to large regional or national chains of netbars. The new regulations stipulated a minimum size for netbars—at least sixty computers, with at least two square meters of floorspace for each computer—that made it more difficult for smaller businesses to comply. At the same time, the government was happy with the development of large chains because chains would likely be more concerned with complying with rules and regulations and thus be easier to direct and control, particularly considering that several of the largest chains were run by the large state-owned telecommunications operators: China Unicom, China Netcom, and later China Telecom.

News and the Internet

The kind of information most commonly sought by China's Internet users in recent years has always been news. Furthermore, various surveys in the early 2000s found that for many of China's netizens, the Internet had become their principal source of news, taking over even from television. In terms of contemporary Chinese popular culture, Internet news therefore has a growing importance as a new way in which Chinese people come to make sense of the world around them.

Internet news in China may be characterized as subject to forces pulling in opposite directions. On one hand, since news Web sites are either (a) sites run by official news agencies and sources or (b) portals drawing upon other officially recognized sources, there is a sense in which the Internet is just another source of officially sanctioned news. On the other hand, there are various ways in which the Internet can function to undermine the authority of such sources. For instance, there have been various news stories in recent years where the Internet has made it difficult for the Chinese authorities to be economical with the truth. With the Internet, local reporters, eyewitnesses, or people close to events can make their accounts available to national audiences in a short space of time. Famous examples would include an explosion at a rural school that killed more than forty people, many of them schoolchildren, in March 2001. The fact that the school had, to make up for a shortage of funds, housed an illegal fireworks factory was made known on the Internet, and once in the public domain it was impossible to ignore. The authorities were therefore forced to acknowledge what had happened and take action accordingly.

A similar case involved thousands of rural villagers in Hunan and Henan provinces becoming HIV infected through contaminated needles used in commercial blood-donation drives in the 1990s. By the early 2000s, as many as 80 percent of the population of some villages were HIV positive and hundreds of people were dying of AIDS. Although the scandal eventually drew national and international attention, initially there were efforts by the authorities to downplay the tragedy while the Internet again played a crucial role in publicizing the story. There is a similar story to tell with China's SARS outbreak in 2003. Initially, the Beijing authorities tried to mask the seriousness of the situation, but they were later forced to acknowledge the full extent of the outbreak, at least in part due to stories and information circulated on the Internet.

The Internet also makes a much wider range of sources available to readers online than would conventionally be available. Hence, on the Internet it is possible to read articles from local and specialized newspapers that would otherwise be very difficult or even impossible for many Chinese people to get hold of. In this way, the number of different critical perspectives on events that are accessible to people has been multiplied dramatically and it would be too simplistic to dismiss them all as just propaganda. Different kinds of newspapers and newspaper reports can offer quite different perspectives on many stories, with some having greater critical leeway than others (see Chapter 5).

At the same time, the Internet has given official news sources new opportunities to break out from some of their traditional limitations. For example, the newspaper the *People's Daily*, the official organ of the Central Committee of the Chinese Communist Party, is, although internationally recognized for its importance as an indicator of Chinese government policy, for the average Chinese reader a rather dull, dry, and dreary "official" (or propaganda) newspaper. In fact, in contemporary China a relatively small amount of the population reads it regularly. The *People's Daily* Web site, however—*People's Net*—is far more than simply an online version of the newspaper; it covers a much wider range of news topics in far more detail than the print paper ever could, enabling it to report in a more relaxed and less rigidly propagandistic fashion on topics like entertainment, lifestyle, and fashion that traditionally the paper would not have covered in great detail. In this sense, the Internet has made some of the major news organizations, such as the *People's Daily* or CCTV, more like news agencies rivaling the official Xinhua News Agency.

The Internet has seen the formation of collaborative alliances among news organizations. In the late 1990s and early 2000s, news organizations were starting to see the potential of the Internet as well as feeling the obligation to establish an online presence in an increasingly competitive news environment. Many newspapers, radio stations, and television stations set up their own Web sites, often largely based on what they produced in their other media formats. This strategy soon ran into problems, however—two in particular stood out. First, even if a relatively small office could do the work of publishing to a Web site news stories produced for other media, it was nonetheless costly because the Internet provided no real sources of income at that time. Readers did not pay for the service and advertisers were few and low-paying, the Web site therefore effectively became little more than a marketing vehicle. Second, it was not clear, apart from a free service, what the news Web sites actually offered over and above their traditional media counterparts.

Consequently, the online news sector underwent a transformation. While news organizations were putting up their Web sites, the main Internet portals were also establishing themselves as quick, efficient, and more comprehensive sources of news, in part at least because of the very fact that they did not produce their own news but offered ways of accessing a broad swathe of different news sources. This therefore set the trend for the Internet sector as a whole. Within a couple of years, individual news organizations started joining forces and resources to set up news portals of their own, with the advantage that in addition to functioning as portals they had the authority to report news for themselves. Examples are Beijing's Dragon News Network, run jointly by six Beijing newspapers as well as radio and television stations in the capital; and Guangdong's Southern Network (*nanfangwang*), which draws together resources from the province's famous *Nanfang Daily* newspaper group, Guangzhou's Yangcheng Evening News Group, the Guangdong Provincial Administration for Radio, Film, and Television, the Guangdong Provincial Administration for Press and Publications, and other regional media organizations.

Portals and Online Gaming

Internet portals occupy a central position on the Chinese Internet landscape. This centrality is related to their role in offering Internet users easy access to diverse sources of news and information. In recent years, however, the commercial success of China's leading portals has come about through diversification from this traditional role, and portals now offer far more than simply information.

Chinese Internet portals are lively, colorful sites that have a powerful visual impact. There is a Chinese term, *renao*, which means "hot and noisy": It is used to describe the atmosphere you might find at a busy fairground, a packed shopping mall, a Chinese temple festival, a birthday party, or another lively social gathering. It is generally used as a positive term, to convey excitement, noisiness, brightness, movement, clamor, and stimulation. We might say that Chinese Internet portals are metaphorically *renao*. They are spattered with eye-catching animated Flash advertisements. They are packed with links to different channels and sections covering everything from dating to technology. They sometimes have sound effects or music, and they use bright, almost psychedelic, colors. Most English-language portals, by contrast, seem dull, dry, static, and lifeless. Importantly, in this regard, most Chinese portals target a young audience for whom a sense of *renao* is attractive. Portals offer e-mail accounts; chat rooms; mobile-phone short messaging services; ringtones, wallpapers, and other mobile-phone downloads; newsgroups; bulletin board services; instant messaging; online shopping; gaming; job recruitment services; and more—all in addition to the standard news, information, and search engine facilities.

The most well known and popularly used national portals are Sina.com, Sohu.com, and Netease (www.163.com), all of which are listed on New York's NASDAQ stock exchange. Other favorites include Hong Kong–based Tom.com, instant messaging portal qq.com (see

Journalists from China's official news agency Xinhua report directly to their Web site from the National People's Congress in 2001. (AFP/Getty Images)

below), the Chinese version of Yahoo!, the large news portals discussed above, and dozens of other, smaller portals, particularly aiming at local or regionally specific audiences. Although there are government-owned portals such as the news portals of Xinhua, CCTV, and *People's Net*, the leading commercial portals such as Sina, Sohu, and Netease are privately owned or cooperative companies. Indeed, China's portals have produced some of the country's wealthiest dot-com millionaires in recent years.

The diversity of services offered by China's portals reflects the diversity found elsewhere on the Internet, and for this reason portals offer a useful way of understanding some of the Chinese popular cultural forms that have emerged in recent years, particularly related to news, information, and entertainment. Portals also reflect the strong youth orientation of much of China's Internet culture. The diversity of services arose principally as a result of commercial pressures in the wake of the 2000 global hi-tech slump, but it is also a result of following popular cultural demands. In the early years, portals relied upon advertising revenues for their main—and in many cases only—income. As national and international advertisers suddenly lost faith in the over-hyped Internet future, though, this source of revenue shrank drastically. Advertisers preferred other media, and prices dropped sharply. Consequently, China's leading portals all started looking for alternative sources of revenue.

Netease

Netease (www.netease.com) is one of China's top three Internet portals. It was set up by twenty-six-year-old businessman Ding Lei, who subsequently became a multimillionaire, as a software company in Guangzhou in 1997. The company made its name through and founded its subsequent success upon its bilingual English-Chinese e-mail software that was adopted by many other sites around the country. In addition to offering e-mail, however, the company's Web site gradually offered more and more comprehensive news channels covering the main national and international news as well as sports, the economy, entertainment, leisure, science and technology, IT, fashion, motoring, and much more.

Like the other Chinese portals, however, the company rode the hi-tech frenzy of the late 1990s only to suffer the slump of the early 2000s. Up until that time, again like its rivals, much of the portal's revenue came from advertising, but with the collapse of confidence in Internet companies, the advertising market fell through the floor. Netease was forced to lay off workers and rebuild its business strategy. Along with the other portals, Netease gradually developed alternative sources of revenue, particularly through SMS text messaging services, other value-added mobile-phone services such as ringtone and image downloads, and paid e-mail accounts. It was the first of the three rival portals to turn a profit in 2002 and developed its revenue base by extending into online gaming and other services. In 2004, its online gaming service had become one if its main sources of revenue, accounting for about 60 percent of total income. In particular, the site's in-house online role-playing games *Westward Journey Online* and *Fantasy Westward Journey Online* proved particularly popular.

In the early 2000s, the simultaneous expansion of China's mobile-phone services and the popularity of SMS text messaging saved portals from difficult times. Portals started offering news and information SMS as well as the capability to send personal SMS messages from their Web sites to mobile phones. As the SMS bandwagon gained momentum, it also led to other mobile phone–related services like ringtone downloads, cartoon images, jokes, and photographs. By 2005, the SMS market was well established and worth around US$2.7 billion. Nonetheless, growth in SMS had started to slow, and portals were once again looking carefully at other sources of revenue.

One of these new sources of revenue, which has also become a major feature of youth Internet culture, is online gaming. Online gaming is a market estimated to be worth around US$540 million in 2005, drawn from an estimated 26 million online gamers. The two most popular kinds of online games in China are role-playing games (i.e., generally, games in which players assume the roles of fictional characters on various kinds of fantastic adventures) and oppositional games, including forms of chess, combat, and quizzes. However in the early 2000s, the majority of the most popular online games played by Chinese netizens were of South Korean design.

One of the most popular gaming Web sites is 17173.com, which was launched by NetDragon, one of China's pioneering game developers, in 2000 as China's first

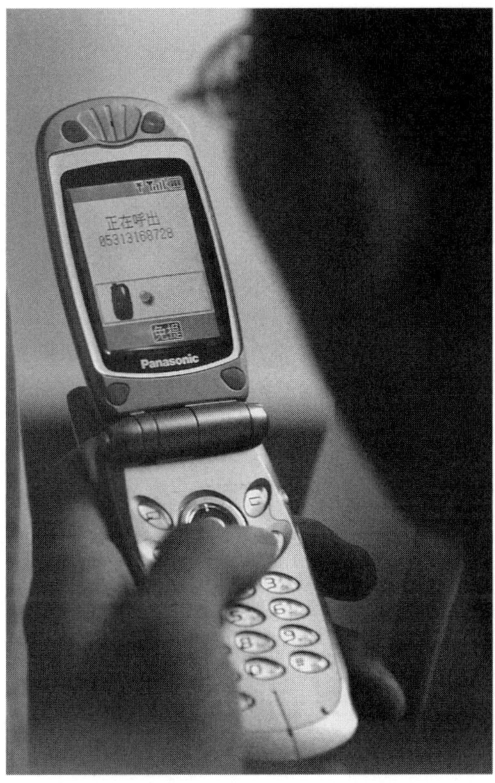

A man sends a text message on a mobile phone in China. Chinese people sent nearly 430 billion text messages in 2006 with annual growth in text messaging standing at around 40 percent. (AFP/Getty Images)

online gaming portal. The site has more than 100 game zones and in 2004 claimed more than 4.5 million registered users, making it the country's largest gaming information and community Web site. Net-Dragon employed about 100 professional game writers, making it one of the largest game developers in China. The company was bought out by Sohu.com in late 2003 as part of the portal's strategy to challenge rival Netease's dominance as an online gaming portal.

The most successful Chinese game developer, however, is Shanda Interactive Entertainment, a Shanghai-based company that developed some of its leading games in collaboration with South Korean companies and which floated on the NASDAQ stock exchange in 2004. In 2006, the company claimed to have more than 1 million simultaneous players at peak times and more than 200 million registered users of its games. Shanda's market-leading MMORPG (massively multiplayer online role-playing game) *Legend of Mir II*, launched in 2002, has been the basis for its success, although the company has since developed a whole range of new games.

Online gamers are mainly young people in their teens, twenties, or early thirties, and a large amount of online gaming goes on in Internet cafés. Indeed, a visit to a Chinese netbar in one of the large metropolitan centers in the early 2000s would usually find the majority of the terminals occupied by young people, mainly male, engrossed in a computer game of one kind or another with a can of Coke for company. The culture of online gaming is not an entirely solitary experience, however. Groups of friends will often meet up in Internet cafés and play games together, compare scores, offer tips and advice, try new games together, and generally socialize around online gaming as a group activity. At the same time, online gaming forms a common basis for social interaction among young people, from schoolyards to university campuses and beyond. There are popular magazines devoted to online gaming and a host of Web sites, chat rooms, and bulletin boards devoted to individual games as well. It is in this sense that online gaming has to be seen as more than simply a leisure activity or a source of revenue for portals and others. For some, online gaming has become a major feature of contemporary Chinese youth culture and social interaction.

E-mail, Instant Messaging, and Popular Culture

There are other ways in which the Internet plays a key role in youth culture and social interaction, particularly through the possibilities that it offers for new kinds of communicative practices. In addition to SMS, the Internet offers new forms of communication, including above all e-mail and instant messaging. Unlike other parts of the world, e-mail is relatively little used in China. Nonetheless, its importance should not be underestimated, and even though people do not send a lot of e-mails, in the 2000s more than 90 percent of Internet users had on average two e-mail accounts each.

Official surveys consistently found in the early 2000s that the average Internet user sent less than ten e-mails per week and received even fewer. In fact, in 2005, most Internet users received more junk e-mail than they did legitimate e-mail. One reason that e-mail is relatively lightly used is because of the popularity and accessibility of mobile phones, and in recent years text messaging in particular has offered an easier, more flexible alternative to e-mail. The fact that more people own cellphones than computers, combined with the portability of cellphones, it is not surprising that SMS and speaking to people on the phone are often preferred over computer e-mail.

E-mail does, however, have advantages over SMS and mobile phones Clearly, for work purposes—sending documents and other files, for instance—e-mail is useful. For students or people working away from home, e-mail has real attraction as a low-cost or free alternative to long-distance calling. With ever more Chinese people traveling or looking to work or study overseas—and thus with ever greater need for the ability to communicate with companies, schools, or friends and relatives abroad—e-mail plays a relatively discrete but important role in long-distance contact and communication.

Instant messaging, by contrast, combines the functionality of e-mail with the "renao" of portals and gaming, contributing a sense of fun to communication. The most popular and successful instant messaging service in China is called QQ (at www.qq.com), offered by a company called Tencent. At the same time, other portals have not neglected the commercial opportunity that instant messaging clearly offers. Netease, for instance, has its own subscription instant messaging service, PoPo, competing with QQ.

QQ works like other instant messaging services in that once a user is logged on, other users are informed that he or she is online and they can communicate one-to-one or in group discussions. However, the distinctiveness of QQ is in its presentation. The service is famous for its cute cartoon character images that users choose to represent themselves online (such representations are called "avatars"). When a user registers, that person chooses a nickname and an image that becomes his or her screen presence. Japanese cartoons are very popular with young Chinese people—the main users of instant messaging services—and in this way using QQ can also become a way of living out a fantasy, cartoon role. Users register their age, gender, and other details, but until 2005 at least such information was easily falsified. Like many chat rooms, bulletin boards, and other instant messaging services, until recently QQ therefore offered relatively easy anonymity. From 2005, following pressure from the authorities, QQ introduced a new registration system requiring proof of identification to participate in chat rooms or groups (though even this system could be circumvented).

QQ was China's first instant messaging service and by 2006 was used by about 75 percent of China's instant messagers. However, Tencent also started to move the site in the direction of a more diversified, but heavily youth-oriented, portal service. The QQ home page offers a range of news services including general national, international, and economic news, but the emphasis of the site is quite heavily on gaming, music, sports, entertainment, and leisure. QQ also offers SMS and in 2004 turned to promoting its own online gaming zone in an effort to consolidate its position as one of China's leading youth culture Web sites.

However, QQ's unique contribution to popular youth culture has been in getting young people chatting with each other online, offering forums for discussion of gaming, sports, entertainment, dating, education, and much more. Other Web sites and other portals offer the same services and opportunities, but QQ has established itself as the primary site for online social interaction among young people.

Chinese Culture Online

The Internet has opened up a whole range of new opportunities for cultural production and participation ranging from leisure and entertainment to poetry and literature. Online gaming is a good example of a new form of popular cultural activity that has emerged with the expanding use and popularity of the Internet. The Internet has also spawned a plethora of new consumer opportunities, particularly targeting young users. For instance, youth mobile-phone culture, centered around SMS, multimedia messaging services (MMS), the exchange of ringtones, photos, cartoon character images, jokes, and other gadgets and gimmicks that can be downloaded is all interrelated with the Internet. The Internet is where many of these services are located and is the vehicle that makes them feasible.

In terms of popular culture, as we have seen, the Internet is also increasingly becoming a facilitator of leisure and entertainment consumption. In this regard, the increasing availability of broadband is important. Broadband Internet use for entertainment is still only enjoyed by a minority of the Chinese population as a whole, yet, in the large cities in particular, it is becoming increasingly available and popular. Many new housing estates and apartment blocks, for instance, particularly those aiming at China's expanding middle classes, are now built with broadband connections in place. Broadband is important because it facilitates use of the Internet for streaming video, fast music and movie downloads, and again online gaming, for which fast connection speeds are often very important. The most popular use of broadband in China—apart from generally surfing the Internet and gaming—is for video-on-demand. There is a growing number of dedicated broadband sites offering movies, music, and television programs in return for a monthly subscription fee.

It is not only popular consumer culture and entertainment that has found new possibilities on the Internet. The world of Chinese literature has also reconstituted itself online, but in doing so it has also found new forms of literary expression. Literature-related Web sites take various forms and affect literary production and consumption in different ways. At one level, for instance, there are various online book clubs and booksellers who have made it easier for people, particularly people in poorer or more remote parts of the country or those in smaller towns without large bookstores, to obtain books of different kinds. The large portals also have their own "culture" channels or pages, which mainly cover literature, visual arts, and history, although these are often blended with a spattering of cartoon youth culture, pop music, environmental issues, personal psychology, and rather nationalistic and propagandist coverage of important historical events and personalities.

At another level, the Internet has opened up the world of literature to many writers who would previously have found it difficult to publish their work. For instance, there is a range of literature-centered Web sites that offer people the chance to have short stories, or even novels, published online. Perhaps the most famous of these in China is Rongshuxia.com ("Under the Banyan Tree"), which in December 1997 was one of the first literary Web sites to be launched. The site drew a lot of national and international attention in 2000 when it published the diary, with entries right up to his death, of Lu Huanqing, a man dying of cancer. The site is aimed at young people but is also popular with older Internet users with literary interests, including university professors, teachers, and other intellectuals. The site, which in 2005 claimed as many as 5 million page views a day, offers users the chance to publish short stories or novels, critical essays, and poetry as well as a range of reviews and a literature discussion forum. There are also books for sale and the chance to befriend and chat with other visitors to the site. Having published more than 2 million original pieces of literature since its launch, "Under the Banyan Tree" has changed the face of Chinese literary publishing.

The online diary format, some would say inspired by Lu Huanqing's account on "Under the Banyan Tree," has also inspired other controversial forms of writing. One case that drew particular attention in the Chinese media was the weblog ("blog") of a journalist from the southern city of Shenzhen. The journalist, named Li Li but writing under the name of Muzimei, started detailing her regular one-night stands with different men in June 2003. She drew particular public attention only after several months when she revealed details of an affair she had had with one of China's most popular rock stars. Li Li's diaries were read by hundreds of thousands of netizens but also caused outrage, with her section of the blogging site being closed down several times due to thousands of insults being posted by angry readers. In a society that is generally reserved about its sexuality and tolerates very little nudity or public reference to sex, such a diary posed a real challenge to social and cultural norms and expectations as well as raising questions about publishing, literature, journalism, and artistic production.

Another publishing scandal arose at around the same time, when another woman writer known as Bella (Beila in Chinese) had three novels composing her "September 11 Trilogy" published online by her agent (at www.beila.net). The novels were subsequently published in book form and her agent started rumors, subsequently challenged, that a Hollywood film studio had bought the film rights for US$1 million. The agent also managed to get prestigious intellectuals to write positive critiques of the books, which were also published online. The real controversy, however, arose when another Chinese intellectual, Cao Changqing, questioned the veracity of the film claims and other claims that had been made about the books. The case therefore raised a host of new questions about book marketing; use of the Internet as a new way of promoting literature; the relationship between commercialism, publishing, and the Internet; and of course marketing ethics and the reliability of the Internet.

On another level, the Internet has enabled writers to experiment with new literary forms. One example is interactive poems, which, exploiting the possibilities of hypertext, can change according to words chosen by the reader. For instance, the last character in the line of a poem might have to be selected by the reader, and depending on which character is chosen, perhaps from a list of options, the rest of the poem changes. In these ways, the Internet is not simply a vehicle or a medium but is stimulating cultural creativity and innovation.

The Future of the Internet and Popular Culture in China

One thing is certain about the Internet in China: It is going to become increasingly important as a feature of popular cultural production and consumption. The number of Internet users in China is still relatively small as a proportion of the population, even if the level is quite high in large metropolitan centers. This means that there is still a lot of room for expansion of the Internet in the country as a whole. Given more time, it is also likely that the population of "netizens" will continue to become more representative of the population as a whole, with more older people, a more representative balance among different professions, and more equal distribution between smaller and larger towns and urban and rural areas.

Many of these changes will take years if not decades to be clearly seen, but the broadening of the Internet user base will nonetheless lead to greater use of the Internet in more diverse ways for a wider range of purposes. To some degree, the future will be dictated by technology, and with the pace of technological development in recent years it is impossible to forecast much beyond a few years. That said, we can see that the convergence of the Internet with other broadcasting networks such as cable television is likely to come about along with the greater use of broadband connections. Broadband will make the Internet an increasingly viable alternative to conventional mass media, particularly once broadband-enabled television sets become widely available so that people can watch movies, MTV, and other television programming as easily as, as comfortably as, and with equal picture quality to their cable or satellite television.

The Internet will continue to be a major feature of commercial popular youth culture. Online gaming will become increasingly sophisticated and probably increasingly popular for some time to come, although it will also always have its critics, particularly those worried about negative effects on young people. With the arrival of third-generation mobile phones, the interrelationship with mobile-phone culture is also deepening. SMS will continue to be popular, and no doubt new kinds of SMS will be developed. The Internet will become increasingly accessible from cellphones while also enabling the further development of new cultural forms such as mobile-phone television, photography, animation, music, and literature.

China's Telecommunications Revolution and the "Digital Divide"

China's telecommunications revolution has been a relatively recent, rapid, and far-reaching phenomenon that has changed many aspects of Chinese social interaction. At the beginning of the 1980s, it was not even possible to apply for a phone. At the end of the 1980s, it was still very rare for an average Chinese family to have their own fixed-line telephone in their home, even in the most developed cities, and waiting-list times were measured in years. Yet by the end of the 1990s almost everyone in the large cities had their own cellphone as well as a fixed-line phone at home.

The trajectory of this ongoing telecommunications revolution has seen people gradually find themselves within reaching distance of increasingly sophisticated technologies. First, people had limited access to public fixed-line phones, which subsequently became more widely available, usually operated by attendants in kiosks on almost every street corner or in tobacconists and small family stores. At the end of the 1980s, people increasingly had pagers, which worked effectively alongside this comprehensive network of public phones, and in the mid-1990s, more and more people started getting their first mobile phones. At this time it also became easier and quicker to get a fixed-line domestic phone, which could be particularly important in more rural areas to which cellular networks did not necessarily extend. In the late 1990s, mobile phones were ubiquitous in the large cities and became increasingly sophisticated into the early 2000s. By 2004, so-called 2.5G ("second-and-a-halfth generation") GPRS and CDMA1x cellphones became available in the larger cities, facilitating limited Internet access and MMS and anticipating the arrival of third-generation (3G) phones in 2007.

By June 2006, there were 791 million phone users in China, including approximately 365 million fixed-line subscribers and 426 million cellular subscribers, which means an average of more than one phone for every three people in the country. China's telecommunications revolution has, however, not only been about the spread of telecommunications technologies around the country. It is also important to see the expansion of telecommunications in China as closely related to affordability. Not only have telecommunications technologies become available, they have been affordable to the average Chinese citizen. In this respect, other telecommunications technologies have also worked to keep prices down and have extended the benefits of the telecommunications revolution to broader sections of society. These technologies include Internet protocol—or IP—telephony, particularly for long-distance calls and so-called Little Smart (*xiaolingtong*) or personal handy system (PHS) cellphones.

IP telephony took off at the end of the 1990s and started to boom in the early 2000s, with all of the main telecommunications companies offering prepaid phone cards with which one could call long-distance—both nationally and internationally—at

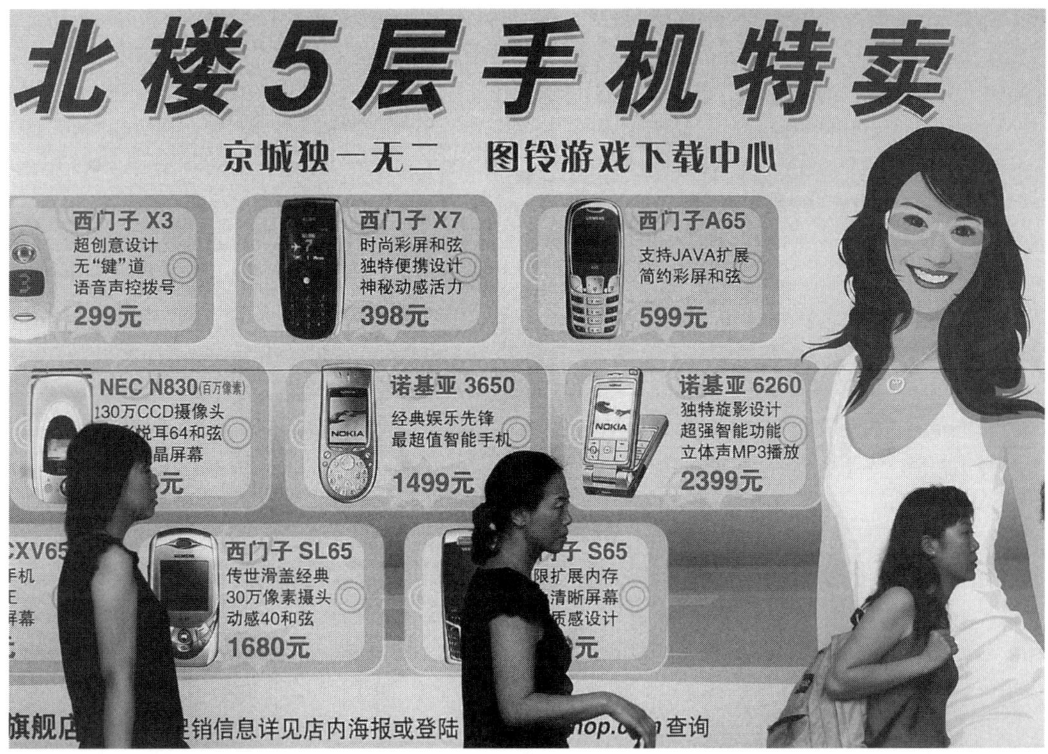

Three young women walk past a poster for mobile phones at Xidan Commercial District of Beijing, China. The number of mobile phone subscribers in China grew to more than 450 million in 2006, with more than 35 handsets per 100 Chinese citizens. (Corbis)

rates considerably lower than from a standard phone. The technology works using Internet "packet" technologies rather than standard telephone technologies at very low cost to the service provider, which means that they can offer cut-rate calls without losing money.

PHS phones are a kind of mobile phone that has a limited roaming range because it actually works by linking via a local base station into the fixed-line telephone network. Strictly speaking, it is therefore not a cellphone, although it looks like one and appears to work like one. The key difference is that whereas a cellphone bought in Shanghai will work in Tianjin, Wuhan, or another Chinese city, a PHS phone will not.

There are two features of PHS phones that have made them significant in China's emerging telecommunications landscape. First, they are considerably cheaper than standard cellphones, not least because they utilize one-way charging (caller pays), whereas with standard GSM (global system for mobile communications) or CDMA (code division multiple access) cellphones both callers and receivers pay. Second, when PHS was new to China—imported from Japan—it was treated with some suspicion by the authorities, who were wary of threatening the business of China Mobile and China Unicom. Consequently, PHS phones were first launched in, indeed restricted to, some of the poorer, more rural areas of the country. In this respect, PHS is one of the few technologies that does not contribute to the "digital divide" in China between rural and urban areas and between the wealthier, more economically and technologically developed eastern coastal provinces and the central and western hinterland provinces.

China's telecommunications revolution has always had a strong urban bias. The new technologies generally have been introduced in the large cities and have filtered down to poorer and more remote regions of the country. Some rural areas, such as the Pearl River Delta in Guangdong, then soon caught up with the cities. The situation in most parts of rural China is, however, very different from the cities. While young middle-class executives in Shanghai may be surfing the Internet on their cellphones, many more remote villagers in China still have only basic landline service. In the early 2000s, fixed-line phone penetration to villages was around 90 percent nationwide; however, in the poorer and more remote areas this may have meant only a handful of phone lines—in some cases even only one—to a village of several hundred or several thousand people. With this in mind, it is clear how far China's telecommunications revolution has also been responsible for the growing digital divide.

The Cultural Significance of Telephones and Telecommunications

The growing digital divide in China gives an indication of the kinds of differences that telecommunications can make in people's lives. Any visitor to China's large metropolitan centers in the mid- to late 2000s will be struck by the range, diversity, and ubiquitousness of telecommunications, particularly the highly visible mobile phone. It is hard to turn around in any part of Shanghai, Guangzhou, or Beijing, for instance, without seeing someone talking, listening, texting, or reading something on his or her mobile phone.

Mobile and fixed-line phones have become such a common feature of everyday life in the towns and cities that they have transformed many ways in which people interact socially. For example, as recently as the early 1990s, even in the largest cities, it was fairly common to visit the houses of friends or relatives unannounced simply because it could be practically difficult to give any advance notice. By the end of the decade, however, not only were unannounced visits becoming more rare, they were being supplemented by other ways of meeting people. So, for instance, instead of arriving at a friend's house, sitting and chatting a while, watching the television a bit, and then moving on, friends became increasingly likely to call and say that they were going to a restaurant, a bowling alley, a movie theater, or some other entertainment venue and suggest that their friends meet them there. In this way, the telephone, especially the cellphone, has helped to change the nature of social interaction with friends and relatives at home and to shift the social setting away from the domestic sphere to more public, commercial venues. Hence, at the same time, telecommunications have supported and facilitated China's burgeoning urban-based consumer culture (see Chapters 9 and 10).

The affordability of telecommunications services in China has also played a key role in helping the technology change forms of social interaction. For instance, we can consider long-distance communication. From the mid-1980s onward, the Chinese population became increasingly mobile as a result of economic reforms. It became more practicable and affordable for individuals to travel; millions of people migrated from the countryside either to local small towns or to large cities possibly on the other side of the country looking for more lucrative work in China's new factories and businesses. Young graduates increasingly found work outside of their local area, and middle-class professionals were increasingly recruited from and looked for jobs in other cities. From the mid-1990s at least, telecommunications in many ways facilitated this mobility and certainly made it easier to handle. Even low-paid workers and students could afford some calls home.

In the relatively recent past, going away for work meant long periods of time away from family and friends, at best depending for communication on a postal service that was efficient but at times slow, at worst having very little contact with one's closest family members for months on end. With telephones, faxes, cellphones, and pagers it not only became easier to keep in touch with friends and family, it became the norm for many. It also became easier to make arrangements in advance with employers, relatives, hotels, hostels, and friends. In these ways, although telecommunications have in some ways contributed to social division with the digital divide, they have played a crucial role in overcoming previously existing national and international barriers of distance.

Indeed, though international attention has often been paid to whether or not Chinese people have been able to receive foreign media broadcasts or publications as an indication of how far the country and its people have been "opened up" to the outside world and the Internet is often discussed in relation to democratization, the role of telecommunications is often neglected. This is partly because telephones are not, strictly speaking, mass media. Yet with 791 million phone users in China, one should not underestimate the significance of the telephone as a medium of communication *among the masses*. Hence, as hundreds of thousands, if not millions, of Chinese go abroad to study, to visit relatives overseas, on vacation, or to work, the telephone has come to play a crucial role in keeping these Chinese connected to home but also in letting people in China find out more about other parts of the world. In the past, Chinese overseas relied on local Chinese communities and postal links to home, and often in the end became at least partly rooted in their new environments. In the contemporary world of increasing Chinese migration, it is that much easier for the diaspora to feel more closely linked to home.

Telephones, cellphones in particular, have also found themselves at what some would call the cutting edge of cultural production. For instance, there are novels written and distributed via SMS to cellular subscribers. There have also been SMS poems, and in 2005 the country's first television drama written specifically for mobile-phone distribution went into production. In these cases the phone is not simply one possible medium among others for transmitting a novel or a television drama. Rather, they come to shape and form the cultural product itself due to the limitations of the technology: the number of characters available in a message, the size of a video screen, download speeds, and so on.

China's first text-message novel, for instance, was written by Qian Fuzhang, a businessman, in September 2004. Called *Out of the Fortress*, the 4,200-word novel (the length of some short stories) was "published" by being sent to tens of thousands of paying cellular subscribers, seventy characters at a time in twice-daily installments. In return, Qian was paid around US$20,000 by the text-message distribution company. This therefore also opens up a new dynamic in the relation between cultural production, distribution, and commercialism. It is not new for people to pay to see cultural products, but the mode of distribution and payment in this case broke new ground. The language of the novel has been hailed by some critics as a new form of literary writing because of its terse, poetic style reminiscent in some ways of classical Chinese. However, at the same time, the novel was conceptualized as a way of distributing a new form of literature to a mass mobile audience—for commercial reasons. Indeed, Qian subsequently auctioned the rights to *Out of the Fortress* in Shenzhen in 2005.

China's first mobile-phone television drama, called *The Appointment*, was similarly constrained by the format of the medium to be used to distribute it. *The Appointment* was shot in five-minute episodes, five minutes having been established as the limit for comfortable viewing of such a small screen. The program, which is a romantic love story about the meeting of a beautiful girl and two motorcyclists, was also specifically written with a young audience in mind, as they were considered to be those most likely to watch it, given the distribution format.

These examples show the close relation between China's consumer culture, cultural production, and commercialism. However, there is another sense in which cellphones feature in contemporary Chinese consumer culture: as fashion items and markers of status, prestige, or contemporariness. Chinese mobile-phone manufacturers in the early 2000s, in fact, considered the shelf life of mobile phones—that is, the length of time that a new model was seen as new and fashionable—to be somewhere between three and six months. This gives an indication of the kind of turnover of mobile phones in China. Of course, it does not mean that people buy new phones every three to six months, but it does show the speed at which mobile-phone fashion operated.

SMS, MMS, and 3G

In this chapter we have already seen the importance of SMS text messaging. Apart from offering a new, cheap, convenient, and sometimes fun form of communication, SMS played a key role in helping China's leading portals become profitable and indirectly affected the popularity of e-mail. There are other ways also in which SMS has come to transform even some of the most traditional contexts of communication.

For example, how SMS has changed modes of social interaction can be seen by considering Chinese New Year celebrations. It is traditional in the days after Chinese New Year for people to visit relatives and friends at their homes, where they sit for a while, possibly take gifts, and eat traditional foods. This practice still occurs; however, SMS has created a new form of

New Year's salutation that in some cases even comes to substitute for visits to friends. With friends who are geographically distant, SMS has also offered a way of greeting them that did not exist in the past.

Over the one-week-long Chinese New Year holiday in 2005, more than 11 billion SMS text messages were sent in China, generating revenues of around US$134 million. These included different kinds of messages—pre-written messages, jokes, stories, and traditional Chinese rhyming couplets downloaded from the Internet as well as personally written messages. In the previous year, around 10 billion SMS messages were sent over the same period, constituting nearly 5 percent of the total number of 217 million text messages sent that year.

SMS has also changed people's relationship to mass media. In some ways, SMS works like a mass medium—when people subscribe to news headlines or information services, for instance. A more radical transformation of media consumption, however, has occurred through the interactivity that SMS has enabled. In recent years, it has become increasingly common for television programs, radio programs, newspapers, and Web sites all to have SMS hotlines that people can use to submit their ideas or opinions on different issues. SMS has also enabled home participation in quiz shows and variety and other entertainment programs as well as competitions organized around large national occasions or sporting events like the Olympic Games. Similar practices have developed in other parts of the world, but such media interactivity has a particularly strong resonance in China, where for decades people have been used to the notion of passively accepting what the media told them. The use of SMS in these ways does not amount to democracy or radical freedom of speech, as messages can always be controlled and selected; however, this kind of media interactivity has started to change people's perceptions of the media, making it seem more approachable, closer to the everyday lives of ordinary people, and less rigidly instructive or propagandistic.

In 2003, multimedia messaging services (MMS) started to become available in China, opening the way for people to send photos and other images as mobile-phone messages. At the same time, some limited mobile-phone television services also became available, although picture quality was not particularly good. MMS messaging is relatively expensive compared to SMS, however, and many people do not have MMS-capable cellphones, which are at the more costly end of the spectrum. MMS, although widely available in 2004 and 2005, did not immediately sweep the market as SMS did a few years earlier. One reason for that may be that many Chinese people were eagerly anticipating the arrival of 3G services, which would upgrade the quality and nature of the service once again. At the time of writing this book, it is still too early in 2007 to see how quickly and in what ways 3G will change Chinese popular culture, but considering the fascination that people exhibit for mobile phones and other hi-tech devices, it will certainly have far-reaching effects. Most likely, mobile phones will be increasingly used for accessing the Internet, playing games, and watching short movie clips or television programs. An important occasion in the development of 3G will be the Beijing 2008 Olympics, when it must be expected that people will be eagerly watching clips of sporting events, the opening and closing ceremonies, and related news on their cellphones.

3G Technologies and Chinese Telecommunications Markets

In the early 2000s, the Chinese authorities were faced with some difficult decisions about which 3G technologies to adopt in the country and to whom they should issue operating licenses. The Chinese authorities' decision about issuing 3G licenses to the country's leading operators was not just a matter of administrative bureaucracy. It was also a matter of deciding between different technologies and also the organization of the entire Chinese telecommunications sector.

There are two main global 3G technologies. One is called WCDMA (wideband code division multiple access), which was developed principally by European companies to succeed and be compatible with the second-generation GSM (global system for mobile communications) platform used in Europe and other parts of the world. The other technology is called CDMA2000 (code division multiple access 2000) and has been developed principally with the U.S. market in mind to succeed the second-generation CDMA platform used in North America. China is predominantly a GSM market. The Chinese authorities publicly backed the launch of the country's CDMA service by China Unicom, the only CDMA telecommunications operator, in 2003. Yet in 2005, of 340 million cellular subscribers only around 25 million were CDMA users—the rest were GSM.

China therefore had to make a decision about which technology to adopt and how without jeopardizing compatibility with either the European-centered WCDMA or the North American CDMA2000 markets. To complicate things, the Chinese also developed their own 3G technology, called TD-SCDMA (time division synchronous code division multiple access), with some collaboration early on from German technology company Siemens. TD-SCDMA was developed, in fact, to be compatible with both of the other platforms.

The other issue involved with 3G decisions related to the organization of the Chinese telecommunications market. In the early 2000s, there were four main telecommunications operators: fixed-line and broadband operators China Telecom and China Netcom, the leading cellphone operator China Mobile, and the only company with a license to operate both fixed-line and cellular services, China Unicom. China Tiecom (or Railcom) was a smaller fixed-line operator that operated the telecommunications system that used to belong to China's railway network, and China Satcom was responsible for the specialized satellite telephony sector. The market was dominated by the four main operators, however.

For years, China Telecom and China Netcom wanted to be allowed to enter the more lucrative cellular sector but were not allowed by the Ministry of Information Industries. However, it was widely agreed that they should be given 3G licenses allowing them to compete directly with China Mobile and China Unicom for the first time. Nonetheless, concerns about the cost of four separate companies all investing in setting up rival networks at great expense led some people to argue that the telecommunications operators should be paired off and work collaboratively on just two competing networks. Hence the decision about 3G licenses ultimately stood to reconfigure the entire competitive environment of the Chinese telecommunications market. At the time of writing this book, this decision has still not been made public, although it appears that TD-SCDMA will be given a privileged position in the market.

A to Z

Alibaba.com. One of China' leading business-to-business e-commerce Web sites. Alibaba.com also owns auction site Taobao.com.

Baidu. China's leading search engine, which also floated on the NASDAQ stock exchange in 2005.

Bertelsmann. German media corporation and owner of Chinese literary Web site Rongshuxia.com ("Under the Banyan Tree") since 2003. Bertelsmann also owns and operates China Books Online, one of the country's leading Internet book retailers.

CDMA2000. One of the third-generation mobile-phone technologies to be deployed in China from 2007. The technology is the third-generation successor to the North American CDMA cellular platform.

China Mobile. The larger of China's two mobile phone operators, with the country's largest GSM network.

China Netcom. China's second-largest fixed-line telecommunications operator, based in ten northern Chinese provinces (including the capital Beijing). China Netcom was formed from the division of the old China Telecom in February 2002.

China Telecom. Originally China's only telecommunications operator, before rival operators China Mobile and China Unicom were set up in the mid-1990s. In February 2002, China Telecom was divided into two, with the company's operations in the ten northern provinces handed over to the new China Netcom and the remainder forming the new China Telecom.

China Unicom. The smallest of the four main telecommunications operators, China Unicom was set up in the 1990s specifically to promote and increase competition in the telecommunications sector. Although the company is the only telecommunications operator allowed to run both fixed-line and mobile-phone operators, it is predominantly known for its cellular operations and in particular its CDMA service launched in 2003.

CNNIC. The China Internet Network Information Center, known as CNNIC, is the government body charged with the everyday administration and monitoring of the Internet in China. CNNIC overseas the allocation of domain names and other administrative tasks but is also known for its semi-yearly surveys of Chinese Internet use.

Dangdang.com. China's leading online book and music retailer.

Ding Lei. The founder of Netease, one of China's largest and most popular Internet portals.

EachNet. China's leading auction Web site. The company was bought up by U.S. and global Internet auction giant eBay in 2003, and the two sites were linked in 2004.

GSM (global system for mobile communications). The European mobile phone technology standard and also the dominant second-generation mobile platform in China.

Heike. The Chinese term for hackers. Hacking is a problem in China, as in other parts of the world. In China, however, hackers feature regularly in minor nationalistic reciprocal tussles with political opponents. Hackers have a attacked Taiwanese military and political Web sites, Japanese Web sites claiming sovereignty over the disputed Diaoyutai Islands, and U.S. Web sites at times of heightened tension such as the spy-plane dispute of 2001. In all these cases, Chinese sites have also been attacked by hackers from the other sides.

IPv6. The new Internet protocol being developed through international collaboration and starting to be deployed in the mid-2000s. China has worked closely with Japan and South Korea to promote the technology, which would make thousands more Web addresses available.

Joyo.com. One of China's leading e-commerce Web sites, established in 2000. The site is particularly known for its books, music, and video retailing. The site was bought by international online bookseller Amazon in September 2004.

Kingsoft. One of China's largest and leading software developers, awarded state funds to work on developing indigenous Chinese online gaming software in the early 2000s.

Li Li. A Shenzhen-based journalist also known as Muzimei who became famous for her online sex diaries in 2003.

Ministry of Information Industries. The MII is the main government body overseeing the telecommunications and Internet sectors. However, many aspects of Internet content regulation—including the control and monitoring of the Internet café sector—come under the jurisdiction of the Ministry of Culture.

Netease. One of China's three NASDAQ-listed Internet portals that became profitable in 2003. The portal (www.netease.com) has recently established itself as the main portal among the top three for online gaming. Along with Sina.com, it is also one of China's most popular and most visited Web sites.

Numbers. Many of China's leading Web sites adopt numbers for their Web addresses, particularly choosing lucky numbers such as 8, 3, and 1, which in Chinese sound like words meaning economic success, life, ease, and so on. So for instance, 8848.com is a leading e-commerce site, Netease's Web address is www.163.net, 3721 is China's second-largest search engine (after Baidu), and 17173.com is one of the country's leading online gaming portals.

Out of the Fortress. Reputedly China's first SMS text message novel, written by Qian Fuzhang in 2004. The 4,200-word novel was "published" by being sent to paying mobile-phone subscribers, seventy characters at a time in twice-daily installments.

People.com.cn. The Web site of the *People's Daily* newspaper. This is far more than just an online version of the newspaper. It is a fully comprehensive news portal and news agency covering all areas of Chinese news production, with specialized channels covering IT, culture, entertainment, film and television, and leisure activities.

PHS (personal handy system). A limited-roaming mobile-phone technology that actually operates by a wireless link to the local fixed-line phone network. Also known as "personal access system" and locally known as *xiaolingtong* ("little smart") in China.

PoPo. The name of Netease's instant messaging service set up to compete with the market leader QQ.

Qian Fuzhang. A businessman and author of China's first mobile-phone SMS text message novel, *Out of the Fortress*, published in September 2004.

QQ. By far China's most popular instant messaging service, famously recognizable by its cute penguin logo. The service is operated by Tencent (*tengxun*). In recent years, the QQ Web site has also broadened its ambitions to become a leading entertainment and leisure portal aiming at young people. The site carries general news as well as sports, entertainment, and leisure news in addition to a popular online gaming channel.

Rongshuxia.com ("Under the Banyan Tree"). China's best-known literary Web site that gives registered users the chance to publish short stories, novels, and critical essays on the site. The site became particularly well known in 2000 for publishing the diary of Lu Huanqing, a man dying of cancer.

Shanda Interactive Entertainment. China's foremost online game developer, based in Shanghai and launched in the NASDAQ stock exchange in 2004.

Sina.com. With Netease and Sohu.com, one of China's leading portals and search engines, covering news and various kinds of entertainment and offering the usual SMS, MMS, and other value-added telecommunications services.

Sohu.com ("search fox"). Marginally the smallest of the three main portals, known particularly for its search engine facility. In 2004, the site launched an updated and improved search engine technology called *sougou* ("search dog").

Taobao.com. China's largest auction Web site, owned by Alibaba.com.

TD-SCDMA (time division synchronous code division multiple access). China's home-grown 3G technology developed by various Chinese telecommunications equipment suppliers originally in collaboration with German technology company Siemens.

Tencent (tengxun). The parent company of the QQ instant messaging Web site and service.

Tom.com. One of China's most popular portals, Tom.com is actually Hong Kong–based and owned by Hong Kong tycoon Li Ka-shing.

WCDMA (wideband code division multiple access). The European 3G technology replacing GSM second-generation mobile phones.

Xiaolingtong. The Chinese name for PHS phones, meaning "Little Smart" or "Little Clever."

Xinhuanet.com. The news portal of the state news agency Xinhua. A thoroughly comprehensive Web site covering every area of Chinese news production.

Yahoo! China. The Chinese subsidiary of the global Internet giant. In the early 2000s, Yahoo! was keen to develop its presence in the Chinese Internet market through various collaborations and acquisitions. Most notably, Yahoo! linked up with search engine 3721.com and developed an online auction service in collaboration with Sina.com.

Zhonghua Net. Another of China's popular but slightly less well-known search engines after Baidu, 3721, and Google.

Zhongsou (zhongguo sousuo). One of China's popular but slightly less well-known search engines after Baidu, 3721, and Google.

References and Further Reading

Bu, W. 2006. "Internet use among Chinese youth." In X. Jieying, S. Yunxiao, & J. Jianxiao (eds.) 2006. *Chinese youth in transition.* Aldershot, UK: Ashgate Publishing Ltd.

CNNIC. 2005. *Statistical report of the development of the Internet in China (2005/1).* Beijing: China Internet Network Information Center (CNNIC).

Hartford, K. 2003. "West Lake wired: Shaping Hangzhou's information age." In L. Chin-Chuan (ed.) 2003. *Chinese media, global contexts.* London: RoutledgeCurzon.

Harwit, E. & Clark, D. 2001. "Shaping the Internet in China: Evolution of political control over network infrastructure and content." *Asian Survey,* Vol. 41, No. 3, 377–408.

Hu, X. 2002. "The surfer-in-chief and the would-be kings of content: A short study of Sina.com and Netease.com." In D. S. Hemelryk, M. Keane, & H. Liu (eds.) 2002. *Media in China: Consumption, content and crisis.* London: RoutledgeCurzon.

Hughes, C. & Wacker, G. 2003. *China and the Internet: Politics of the digital leap forward.* London: RoutledgeCurzon.

Latham, K. 2007. "SMS, communication and citizenship in China's information society." *Journal of Critical Asian Studies,* June 2007. Vol. 39, No. 2, 296–314.

McCormick, B. L. & Liu, Q. 2003. "Globalization and the Chinese media: Technologies, content, commerce and the prospects for the public sphere." In L. Chin-Chuan (ed.) 2003. *Chinese media, global contexts.* London: RoutledgeCurzon.

9

Consumption in China

A large part of what we think of as popular culture is related to things people do for pleasure and in their leisure time. This includes using the various media discussed in other chapters. There are also popular cultural practices involving leisure activities unrelated to the media. At the same time, in recent decades, the notion of popular culture has become inseparable from discussions of consumption and consumerism because of the associations of contemporary societies around the world with commercialism, advertising, shopping, and economic activity. China, where consumption and consumerism have been dominant features of the post-Mao era, is no exception. The combination of market reforms implemented from the early 1980s onward, together with the relaxation of the political climate and the reduction of political intervention in people's everyday lives, means that Chinese people have increasingly found themselves with greater disposable income and more leisure time and opportunity to spend it. The chapters in this part of the book consider the importance of leisure activities and practices of consumption for understanding contemporary Chinese popular culture.

Consumption and consumerism in China are often particularly associated with the urban areas and large metropolises like Beijing, Shanghai, and Guangzhou. Although much of what we will discuss in these chapters will relate to urban-focused leisure and consumption in particular, it is important not to forget rural consumption. Indeed, we should remember that economic reform was actually first implemented in the countryside with the introduction of the household responsibility system that reallocated communal land to individual families and delegated responsibility to the household unit for agricultural production. Peasants throughout the country benefited from the greater economic and lifestyle flexibility that reforms gave them and found new opportunities for earning money through sideline production or nonagricultural employment. Consequently, between 1978 and 1985, both rural income and rural consumption more than doubled, outstripping similar growth in urban areas in the early years of reform (Chao & Myers 1998: 353–354), even if the rise in urban consumption subsequently soared ahead of the countryside in the 1990s.

To fully understand the impact of economic reform in post-Mao China, it is important to try to imagine living in China in the early 1980s. In a society where thirty years of revolution had been founded upon the definitive importance of production and the values of asceticism, the new opportunities for consumption and the availability and accessibility of consumer goods represented a fundamental change in people's lives. Up until that time, many of people's basic needs—such as for oil and for rice and other grains—were met by a system of state allocation through vouchers acquired through one's work unit, and the little money that people had was spent on meeting other basic needs. State-owned department stores were the main source of consumer goods such as radios, bicycles, clothing, bedding, and furniture; however, they were often poorly stocked, and purchasing such items required years of saving and waiting.

In the 1980s, the economic reforms offered entrepreneurs the chance to start buying and selling goods as traders for the first time in decades. So-called free markets (*ziyou shichang*) cropped up all over the country. These were often designated streets that were closed to traffic in the evenings so that small traders could set up tables selling products for cash—mainly clothing, leather goods such as belts and bags, or foods. At first, these markets had a very improvised character; however, they were revolutionary in China's social and popular cultural space of the time. They soon became places where people went for a casual stroll in the evening, to meet friends and relatives, and to socialize and peruse the goods on display. Within the space of a few years, the more successful traders moved into small shops, often first those lining the market streets. From then on, consumer activity and opportunities snowballed. More and more goods became available, and old barriers to consumption started to come down. For instance, in the mid-1980s some of the best-stocked stores in the country—the so-called friendship stores aimed primarily at foreign visitors—and the country's growing number of luxurious five-star hotels were all off-limits to Chinese not working in them. Until the end of the 1980s, China also had two forms of currency (as mentioned in Chapter 1): foreign exchange certificates (FEC) and renminbi ("people's money," abbreviated Rmb). FEC were issued to foreign workers, students, and tourists and were for years the only currency legal for foreigners to use. Not accepted in most shops and restaurants, FEC also worked to control foreigners' consumption. As FEC were the only currency legal in large hotels and friendship stores, however, there was a thriving black market in FEC-Rmb exchange for local people who wanted to buy high-class consumer goods or obtain foreign currency (only FEC could be exchanged) and for foreigners who wanted to buy things with renminbi. In the late 1980s, the hotels and friendship stores were gradually opened up to local people and renminbi became increasingly accepted across society; FEC were eventually scrapped in the early 1990s. At the same time, rationing systems were dismantled and the open market became better supplied. These breathtakingly rapid changes constituted a complete transformation of many of the basic principles upon which people's everyday economic activities and understandings had been based.

At this time, popular cultural attitudes also started to change from being necessarily oriented toward society and the common good to being more individualistic, materialistic, and self- or family-oriented. In the 1980s, Chinese people found themselves suddenly in the position of being able to buy, or aspire to buying, the so-called four-goods: color television sets, washing machines, refrigerators, and stereo cassette players. In the 1990s, these were eclipsed by motorcycles, videocassette recorders, VCD players, pagers, faxes, and mobile phones. In the 2000s, the high-level goods in demand became cars, DVD players, desktop and notebook computers, multimedia mobile phones, and digital televisions. Yet China's consumer society is not only about coveting, buying, and owning material goods. Consumption in China is also about consuming food, entertainment, art, drama, music, sports, and the full panoply of media services discussed in earlier chapters. Consumption has also come to play a key role in new forms of social interaction. All of this is what is sometimes called China's "consumer revolution" (see, e.g., Davis 2000; Chao & Myers 1998; Wu 1999).

However, these changes have not come about through economic changes alone. One of the most important and far-reaching transformations in people's lives in the reform period that has made the emergence of consumption and consumer society possible is that relating to people's leisure time. The post-Mao era has brought fundamental changes in the quantity and quality of people's leisure time (Wang 1995). On one hand, people work less. In the Mao era, it was common to work six or seven days a week, whereas by the 1990s the workweek for many people was reduced to five days (as mentioned in Chapter 3). The length of time off for national holidays, such as for Chinese New Year and National Day (October 1), has also been increased. Other important factors come into play, however. In the Mao era, time off from work was also considered important for the maintenance of a healthy, enthusiastic workforce; however, the Party's strong emphasis on political education meant that many workers, peasants, and soldiers spent a lot of time in political meetings and education of one kind or another. This reduced the amount of personal leisure time that they could enjoy. In addition, the lack of electricity in some areas, the high price or scarcity of gas or other fuels, and the lack of refrigerators, washing machines, and other labor-saving devices meant that people also spent far more of their non-working time cooking, shopping, washing clothes, cleaning, and doing other everyday chores. All of these factors contributed to reducing the amount of leisure time that people enjoyed.

The quality or nature of leisure time has also changed. Not only have the political meetings and compulsory education sessions largely disappeared, the range of leisure opportunities available to people has changed dramatically. In the Mao era, life was far more strongly oriented toward the collective, usually represented by the work unit—for instance, the factory, the government office, the hospital, the school, or, in rural areas, the village. Even under Mao there was some degree of popular entertainment in both cities and the country-side, including in urban areas cinema, theatre, radio, and music and in rural areas radio, traveling film units, and folk music.

Yet going to watch a film or listen to a concert was a very different experience in the Mao period compared to the post-Mao period. Tickets were rarely, if ever, available for individual purchase, and most people's experiences of going to the cinema or theatre would have been collective. Every once in a while, work units would be allocated blocks of movie tickets, for example, and arrange for large groups of workers to go together on trips—so that even the choice of film was usually made by other people. Similarly, tourism on an individual basis was virtually non-existent, and long-distance travel was virtually impossible outside of work trips for meetings or as rewards for model workers. This collective use of leisure time and the collective enjoyment or experience of leisure activities was greatly reduced in the post-Mao period and increasingly supplemented or replaced by individual consumption. Consequently, leisure time also became more individually organized and domestically focused. These changes coincided with the rise of television (discussed in Chapter 3), and as people watched more and more television, leisure time became far more family- and television-centered.

These changes in leisure time were crucially accompanied not only by increasing disposable income but by increasing opportunities for spending time and money in different settings and contexts from the past. Through the 1980s, cinema, theatre, and concert tickets became increasingly available in the cities, and by the 1990s they were generally open for purchase to anyone who wanted them. At the same time, China saw the emergence of imported and indigenous leisure, sports,

A girl sings karaoke in China. Karaoke became increasingly popular with Chinese people of all ages, but especially young people, from the 1980s onward. (iStockPhoto.com)

and entertainment activities like dancing—disco to ballroom—ten-pin bowling, karaoke, golf, tennis, traditional opera singing, photography, tourism, and martial arts. All of this was in addition to the expansion of television, cinema, newspapers, magazines, books, VCDs, and DVDs.

In the late 1990s and early 2000s, China's "consumer revolution" was still undergoing constant transformation. By the 2000s, the notion of free market consumption—being able to buy anything so long as you have the money, being able to choose among different makes, models, and suppliers of consumer goods, and being able to buy for the pleasure of buying or owning something—has become a regular principle of everyday life for a large proportion of the Chinese population. The ideas of the market, private ownership, and entrepreneurialism are broadly accepted and understood, and even those people who can not afford many consumer goods are nonetheless used to the idea that if or when they become richer those opportunities would also become available for them.

The gradual maturation of China's consumer society has also contributed to the increasing social divisions in the country between rich, poor, and middle classes; between young and old; between rural and urban areas; and between the more economically developed eastern coastal provinces and the poorer central and western hinterland. This occurs in various ways. Clearly, wealth is a key factor affecting leisure time and the ability to consume. Furthermore, people reveal their tastes, preferences, likes, dislikes, attitudes, and values through their consumer choices, even if it is not necessarily a deliberate or even conscious process. In China, such defining information can be evinced in small things, like the brand of cigarettes smoked, or large things, like buying an expensive foreign car or a luxury villa. Consumption is potentially a constant indicator of social standing, family background, and personal identity.

The difference between rural and urban areas also shows how consumption contributes to and reveals social divisions. On one hand, the opportunities for consumption are clearly different in the countryside than they are in the cities, regardless of wealth. Often one of the first things peasants will do when they find themselves with more money is spend it on better and more food for themselves and their families. Rich peasants are likely to show their wealth through the purchase of cars or motorcycles, through building or adding on to houses, or through wedding, funeral, or other festival expenditures. Indeed, expenditures on popular religious practices, including temple renovations, contributions to temple celebrations, consultations with deities, or hiring geomantic ("geomancy" refers to the way that positive and negative energies flow through the landscape, as in principles of feng shui) or other religious specialists, could be considered among China's emerging consumer practices. Less conspicuously, peasants are also likely to spend their money on education for their children and grandchildren, on farming technologies, on machinery, or on land.

By contrast, in the cities, there is rarely the opportunity to build a house or buy land, and tractors serve little purpose. The practical difficulties of parking can even make cars less feasible consumer items for those wealthy enough to afford them. At the same time, the opportunities for consumer spending in cities are far more numerous. There are hundreds, even thousands of restaurants to choose from, there are multiplex movie theaters, concert halls, theaters, bowling alleys, discos, bars, pubs, driving ranges, and much more. The choice of leisure, entertainment, and sporting activities, often at relatively affordable prices, especially for the emerging middle classes, is enormous in the large cities and often abundant in even the more modest-sized towns.

The division between rich and poor also largely informs the east-west, or coastal-hinterland, divide in China. For many in the large metropolitan centers of the east, typified by Shanghai, Beijing, Guangzhou, and Tianjin, the consumer-oriented lifestyle has become precisely that—a way of life. The novelty of consumption comes not in consumption itself, but in what one consumes—which of the latest mobile phones to upgrade to, which of the new ethnic restaurants to go to this week, and so on. In the poorer and less economically developed parts of the country, consumption and consumerism are also accepted as features of everyday life. Poorer peasants and town-dwellers are well aware of what is available in the shops—of new consumer goods, their prices, and how to get them; however, restricted spending power means restricted participation in consumer society. This means that people's relation to consumption is more likely to be aspirational and involve saving, anticipation, and desire rather than regular and immediate fulfillment or satisfaction of perceived needs or desires.

Age is also an important issue in understanding consumer habits. Younger people are more likely to spend their money freely on goods, entertainment, and leisure activities. They are more likely than their parents or grandparents to be fashion conscious, to be fascinated and excited by technologically innovative goods, to eat out in restaurants, and to go to bars, discos, and sporting events. The older generations, particularly those that lived through the tougher, more ascetic years of the Mao period, often have quite different attitudes toward spending, saving, and satisfaction. They will spend more money on better food if they have the opportunity but will be quite likely to cook at home, not eat in restaurants. They are more likely to save money for their own or their children's futures and have a more pragmatic attitude toward home furnishings, interior design, and other forms of presentational consumption.

In different ways, China's consumer society has accentuated and in some cases transformed notions of gender. Some consumer items are often associated with gender stereotypes—washing machines are for women and cars or computers are for men, for instance—and the ways in which they are purchased, used, and deployed often means that such items serve to reproduce and reinforce the stereotypes in society. At the same time, China's social, visual, and physical space has been transformed by advertising over the last two decades. The advertising that permeates urban social space in China drives a perceived need for women to be more "feminine." Bikini-clad—often Western—women promote products and services of all kinds in magazines, on television, on billboards, on the Internet, and elsewhere. Although this is a familiar situation in many parts of the world, in China it takes on a particular significance because of the history of gendered representations in the country, where gender differences were always downplayed and de-emphasized under Mao, with uniform clothes, no use of cosmetics, and the social emphasis on comradely or heroic collective behavior rather than sexual attraction, fashionability, and femininity.

Consumption in China has increasingly become a marker of differences, a way of identifying differences and making them visible, and a way of generating diverse desires and aspirations as well as offering diversity of opportunity. Particularly in the cities, but also in other ways in the countryside, consumption and consumerism have become key features in contemporary Chinese cultural and social experiences. Indeed, many China scholars attribute a key role to consumption and the availability of consumer goods in maintaining social and political stability in contemporary China (see, e.g., Tang 1996; Ci 1994). This argument arises from the question of how Chinese people, who had spent decades following their political leaders and making enormous personal sacrifices down the road to a class-free utopia, could suddenly cope with being told that the political basis of that quest was not important after all. Capitalism was suddenly welcomed into a country where just a few years before, some people had been even been "struggled" to death for their past associations with capitalists. The answer to this question, according to some scholars, is through consumption and consumerism. They argue that people's political disorientation emerging from the ideological void left by the collapse of strict Maoism is compensated for by the immediate gratification of material desires and by the satisfaction that people have taken from their ability to consume, the improved standard of living it has brought them, and the notions of individual freedom that this entails (see, e.g., Ci 1994; cf. also Latham 2002).

Consumption has also come to figure in the reconceptualization of the Chinese populace. Under Mao, Chinese citizens were defined, represented, and discussed in Marxist terms through their relation to the mode of production (i.e., their class background), as participants in the socialist transformation of the nation, as members of the collectively valued "masses," and as "children" of the caring father figure of the nation (Mao himself). In the post-Mao period, by contrast, not only has the importance and prevalence of all of these definitions either disappeared or been greatly diminished, but new conceptualizations have come to take their place. One of these conceptualizations, to be found in the media, in policy formulation, and in everyday social interactions, is of Chinese people as consumers—as people who buy things, who support the economy through purchasing power rather than production, and who make an economic or even political difference through their exercise of consumer choice.

The figure of "the consumer" has become an important feature of media production, for instance. Newspapers, television stations, magazines, radio stations, and Web sites all target their output to a greater or lesser degree at "consumers" (Latham 2006). They are aware of their readers, viewers, or listeners as not only consumers of their output but consumers of many other things also. Hence, media content is often geared toward informing consumer choice, advising on potential consumer pitfalls, and promoting further consumption through advertising. Related to this notion of the consumer, Chinese people now also have "consumer rights." Legislation in the 1980s and 1990s laid down the legal status of the consumer as someone able to expect certain standards of service and quality (Palmer 2006). All of these are new and constantly evolving conceptualizations of Chinese people that constitute a radical transformation of those from the past.

Contemporary Chinese popular culture has to be understood in relation to these changes in leisure time and this constantly evolving consumer society. Many popular cultural practices are themselves consumer or consumption-related practices, whether they are related to entertainment, media and advertising, shopping, eating, or playing sports. The following chapters therefore devote special attention to several important consumer issues.

Chapter 10 looks more closely at how people spend their leisure time, how that leisure time has become more private, and how it has changed over the last couple of decades. Considering the changing spaces of Chinese leisure and consumption, an important feature of the discussion will be how consumption is often not only an economic practice but a very social practice with important implications for understanding social interaction through popular cultural practices. One of the most obvious examples of this is the consumption of food, whether that is in the family home, at a traditional Chinese teahouse, in a Western fast-food restaurant, or at a wedding celebration. Chinese culture is inextricable from and unimaginable without its food. The contexts of Chinese food consumption are changing, however, and with them also the significance of eating in contemporary Chinese popular culture.

Chapter 11 looks more specifically at two key areas of contemporary Chinese popular culture: sports and martial arts. The area of sports, in particular, has come to play an important role in popular cultural practices and consumption. Mediated sports is big business, from coverage of North American basketball to European soccer, the Olympics, and beyond. It occupies a highly visible position in media space and constitutes a key area of popular interest. With increasing brand awareness and merchandising, the role of Chinese consumption of international sports paraphernalia—replica jerseys, photographs, books, magazines, and so on—is also likely to play a key role in future market valuations of international sports businesses such as the United Kingdom's Manchester United or Spain's Real Madrid soccer clubs or the Chicago Bulls basketball team in the United States. Sports are not just for spectators, however; increasingly in China sports have also become something for people to participate in. Chinese boys have long kicked around soccer balls in schoolyards, and certain key sports, such as table tennis, martial arts, and volleyball, are issues of national and cultural pride; recent years have also seen a proliferation of other sporting activities available to people in their leisure time, Chinese athletes have started to claim more prominent positions on international sporting stages, and sports of many different kinds increasingly have to be taken seriously as a constituent of contemporary Chinese popular culture. What is more, the significance of sports in China has been greatly magnified by the international attention focused on the Beijing 2008 Olympic Games.

References and Further Reading

Chao, L. & Myers, R. H. 1998. "China's consumer revolution: The 1990s and beyond." *Journal of Contemporary China*, Vol. 7, No. 18, 351–368.

Ci, J. 1994. *Dialectic of the Chinese revolution: From utopianism to hedonism.* Stanford, CA: Stanford University Press.

Davis, D. S. (ed.) 2000. *The consumer revolution in urban China.* Berkeley: University of California Press.

Latham, K. 2002. "Rethinking Chinese consumption: Social palliatives and the rhetorics of transition in postsocialist China." In C. M. Hann (ed.) *Postsocialism: Ideals, ideologies and practices in Eurasia.* London: Routledge.

———2006. "Powers of imagination: The role of the consumer in China's silent media revolution." In K. Latham, S. Thompson, & J. Klein (eds.) *Consuming China: Approaches to cultural change in contemporary China.* London: RoutledgeCurzon.

Palmer, M. 2006. "The emergence of consumer rights: Legal protection of the consumer in the PRC." In K. Latham, S. Thompson, & J. Klein (eds.) *Consuming China: Approaches to cultural change in contemporary China.* London: RoutledgeCurzon.

Tang, X. 1996. "New urban culture and everyday-life anxiety in China." In X. Tang, & S. Snyder (eds.) *In pursuit of contemporary East Asian culture.* Boulder, CO: Westview Press.

Wang, S. 1995. "The politics of private time: Changing leisure patters in urban China." In D. S. Davis, R. Kraus, B. Naughton, & E. J. Perry (eds.) *Urban spaces in contemporary China: The potential for autonomy and community in post-Mao China.* Woodrow Wilson Center Series. Cambridge: Cambridge University Press.

Wu, Y. 1999. *China's consumer revolution: The emerging patterns of wealth and expenditure.* Cheltenham: Edward Elgar Publishing Ltd.

10

Leisure Time, Space, and Consumption

Understanding contemporary Chinese popular culture requires understanding what people do in their leisure time. Leisure time is a crucial setting of popular cultural activity. Simply considering the media-related activities discussed in earlier chapters is enough to show the importance of leisure time for popular cultural practices. Although some people may read the newspaper or use the Internet at and for work, the vast majority of people watching television, listening to the radio, reading a newspaper or magazine, surfing the Internet, watching a DVD, or going to the movies are doing it in their own leisure time. If we then add shopping, eating, playing, watching and following different games or sports, and consumption and consumerism more generally, the point is made all the more emphatically.

Understanding people's leisure activities requires attention to both the quantity and the quality of leisure time. We are also talking about the way that leisure time is experienced—the way it is conceptualized, appropriated, and controlled. This is something that has undergone a massive transformation since the Mao era, as discussed in the last chapter. People's experiences of leisure time have shifted from being fairly heavily controlled in terms of both the amount of time and how it could be spent to being minimally controlled with an increasing wealth of hobbies, pastimes, sports, and entertainment opportunities now available to them. Leisure time was depoliticized in the 1980s, became increasingly embroiled with China's consumer society in the 1990s, and is an unquestioned part of everyday life in the 2000s. This transformation has also seen leisure time shift from being collectively oriented to being individual and family-oriented. To follow many of these changes, it is useful to think through not only the changes in leisure time that people have enjoyed but the changing experiences of leisure space.

Leisure time has a close relationship to issues of space, both physical and social. We will therefore start the discussion by considering some of the fundamental changes that have occurred in the experience of space from the Mao to the post-Mao era and how physical and social space have undergone continual transformation through the 1980s and 1990s. Space subsequently reappears as a theme in several of the following sections. For instance, we will see how the new array of leisure activities that people now engage in has also contributed to changing experiences of space. Leisure and consumption have moved in two directions in the post-Mao era. On one hand, leisure time has been increasingly spent outside of the semi-public space of the work unit and has moved into more commercialized public domains. On the other hand, there has been a retreat from the work unit into the more private realm of the domestic environment.

It will also be important to consider the crucial ways in which leisure activities entail new forms of social interaction, sometimes in quite new contexts, and how these can be closely linked to the changing experiences of leisure time and space. How these issues all come together will be clearly exemplified in the section on food, where, among other things, we find that the formal spaces of more traditional Chinese restaurants as sites of consumption have been supplemented by the more informal spaces of international fast-food outlets.

Leisure, Consumption, and Social Space

Changes in the nature of leisure practices have been accompanied by shifting spatial configurations of leisure time. In the Mao era, one's spare time would still often have been spent within the physical and social environment in which one worked. Many urban Chinese lived in dormitories or apartments owned and provided by their factories or work units, and in the majority of cases a large proportion of this accommodation would be found actually on the site of the work unit or nearby. Political education and meetings in off hours would be conducted at the work unit—in communal halls, on sports fields, or in factory yards, for instance. At the same time, many of the nonpolitical leisure opportunities that were available to workers were also within the space of the work unit, which might have provided table tennis halls, badminton, basketball, volleyball, or other sports facilities as well as show occasional films, host visiting theatre troupes or musicians, and organize occasional collective trips to movie theaters, exhibitions, stage theatres, or other artistic venues. In this way, leisure time was largely spent within the social and physical space of the work unit itself or in the company of one's colleagues.

The idea of social space—that is, the experience of space through social relationships—in understanding leisure time is important because it helps focus attention on the kinds of social interactions that accompany leisure activities. There is a significant difference between the social experience of watching or participating in a work unit table tennis competition and going to a commercial bowling alley in another part of town, for instance. The former involves a familiar and personalized physical space filled with familiar faces and established social relationships with all their complexities. The people present are also largely involved in a communal social activity. Going to a commercial bowling alley, by contrast, involves an unfamiliar physical space populated by small groups of complete strangers all engaging in their own relative bubbles of social interaction.

The social space of leisure time in the Mao era was therefore largely collective but in some ways not straightforwardly public. Leisure time was often spent in the presence of others—that is, with people not from one's own family—but these other people would have included relatively high proportions of friends, neighbors, and colleagues and relatively few complete strangers. In the post-Mao era, there were three major transformations of the social space of leisure time. First, there was an increasing focus on the domestic space as a primary setting of leisure activity. Second, there was an extension of public space to include more non–work unit areas and greater interaction with a general public beyond the work unit. Third, there was greater commercialization and commodification of leisure time and space. Let us consider these in turn.

The increasing importance of domestic space in post-Mao leisure time and consumption is closely related to the emergence of television as one of China's primary leisure activities. Although there are some public aspects of television viewing in China (see Chapter 3), the vast majority of television is watched at home. Hence, through the 1980s and 1990s, Chinese people found themselves spending more of their time in the domestic setting with the television set turned on. Television is not the only leisure activity pursued at home, however; several other forms of media and leisure activity are also wholly or partly

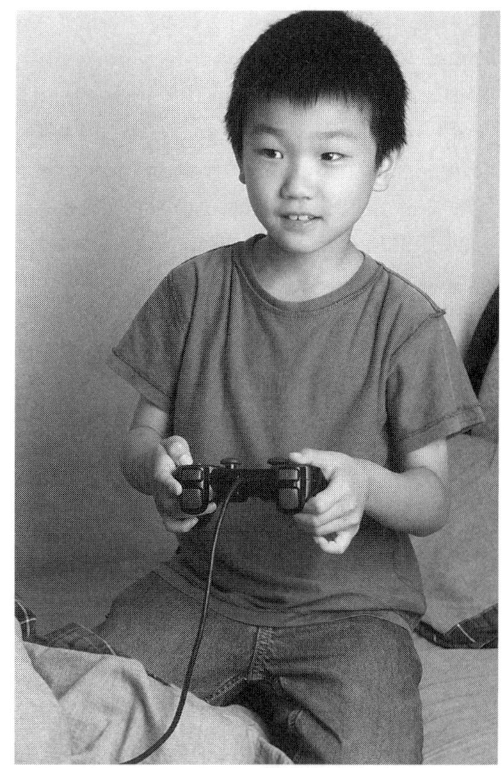

A Chinese boy playing a video game. (iStockPhoto.com)

located in the domestic sphere. These include some that carry over from the Mao period, such as listening to the radio and reading, but also include new activities such as surfing the Internet, playing video games, listening to music CDs, watching films on videocassette, VCD, or DVD, and chatting with friends or family on the phone.

The space of people's homes has itself also become an important site of consumption and social transformation in the post-Mao era. Under Mao, most urban homes shared cooking and bathroom facilities with their neighbors, internal decoration was minimal, and the domestic space was largely utilitarian. In the 1980s, the domestic domain underwent a transformation through consumption, accompanied by the general trend from the late 1980s onward for people to buy and own their own homes rather than rely on the work unit. By the 2000s, virtually all homes were privately owned. Domestic space found itself being transformed by the acquisition of newly available and affordable goods: It was filled with refrigerators, television sets, washing machines, radios, sewing machines, glossy photo calendars, and new furniture. In the 1990s, this transformation entered a second phase, in which couples paid more attention to features of interior design such as lighting, coving, hung ceilings, curtains, shelving, built-in cupboards, and parquet floors. There was a new fascination with do-it-yourself home improvements, interior design magazines and Web sites, and transforming the home into a display of personal taste and an arena of domestic comfort (Davis 2002: 237–238). With these home improvements, many families installed their own bathrooms and kitchens if possible, and new apartment blocks were no longer built with shared facilities. This in itself marked a substantial transformation of the physical and social space of the home, making it less "public," offering fewer opportunities for neighborly tensions, and secluding it as a more personalized, family space.

A trend accompanying this retreat from the work unit into domestic space has been the extension of public space beyond the work unit. The reform era gave people

A sharp contrast from the Mao era, from the 1990s Chinese living spaces were transformed by more attention to domestic comforts and interior design. (iStockPhoto.com)

ever more reasons to spend time away from the work unit, in other parts of their towns and cities. Among the first attractions were the "free markets" discussed in Chapter 9. By the end of the 1980s and into the 1990s, there were more and more street stalls, shops, restaurants, movie theaters, exhibition halls, and other sporting and cultural venues to visit, and as families started to feel the financial benefits of reform they also found themselves more able to take advantage of what their cities started to offer. In this way, the social space of leisure and consumption expanded into new areas. In the Mao era, people were not confined solely to their work units—there were shops and restaurants to visit, but people's relative poverty and limited spending opportunities, combined with the limitations on leisure time discussed earlier, afforded them little reason or opportunity to venture beyond the general social arena of the work unit. By the late 1990s and 2000s, however, the visible and invisible boundaries that defined the limits of the work unit had a much reduced significance in people's lives. Consumption and leisure had become very public practices, with eating out and going to any of the range of sporting, entertainment, and leisure venues with friends or family now featuring as normal, everyday practices.

The third transformation of the post-Mao period relates to the increasing commercialization and commodification of leisure time and space. This has occurred as people's leisure pastimes have themselves been commercialized and commodified. In the Mao era, entertainment and leisure were provided by the work unit, at no cost to the worker. In the post-Mao era, everyone has become accustomed to paying for a large proportion of their leisure-time activities. They pay for meals out, movie tickets, soccer games, tee times, or time spent pursuing whatever their particular interest is. This has not only changed the relation between consumer and goods or services, it has transformed the space of consumption. Related to the emerging notion of "the consumer" discussed in the last chapter, Chinese people now experience the spaces of restaurants, shops, and other popular cultural venues as a customer or consumer. They are paying for a service and receive different treatment than they did in the past. Indeed, state-owned shops and restaurants in the Mao and early post-Mao period were notorious for the brusque, disinterested, and unconcerned service that they provided; by the mid- to late 1990s, however, the culture of customer service had spread out from the expensive hotels and other private commercial institutions to become a taken-for-granted feature of the social space of consumption. In the post-Mao era, one now paid for the right to occupy space as a consumer, but in return one could expect a certain level of service and enjoy certain consumer rights.

Leisure Activities

The range of leisure activities that Chinese people can enjoy, particularly in the large and wealthier cities, is enormous. The choice and nature of leisure activities has also been transformed over recent decades, and it is useful to consider the kinds of leisure activities that became popular at different times in broadly chronological order.

The 1980s

The 1980s were very particular years in China. The changes in popular cultural practices that became possible in this decade—the first decade of reform—in other contexts would seem relatively modest; coming immediately after the Cultural Revolution period and all its political upheaval, its social severity, and its politicization of everyday life, in Chinese society they were groundbreaking. Setting up a humble market stall to sell belts or T-shirts, going to eat a simple meal at a privately owned roadside food stand or restaurant, or saving for and buying a television set all constituted radical social and indirectly political acts in early reform-period China. Consequently, when we consider the kinds of leisure activities that people enjoyed at this time, it is important to remember this context. Going to a discotheque was for young people a completely novel experience.

The most notable new leisure activities of the 1980s—most of which were particularly popular with young people—would include going to discos and dances, singing karaoke, eating at newly set-up restaurants and food stands, going to fun parks, and watching television and films on videocassette. There was a strong sense of experimentalism and discovery about this period. For instance, even by the late 1980s, in some of the larger cities like Guangzhou, Shanghai, and Beijing, many discos and dances that young people went to were unsophisticated affairs using portable equipment—colored lights with a simple music and PA system—in rented rooms, in college halls, or sometimes on commercial premises such as in restaurants or shops. By the end of the decade, some restaurants and a few permanent venues were established as places people could go for dancing or karaoke, but they were still relatively few.

It was not just the equipment and venues that were somehow experimental, however. Young people were also busy developing their own understandings of what going to a disco actually entailed. They would be uncertain about what or how to dance—there were few, if any, established styles of dance, there was little recognition of different types of pop music apart from music imported from Hong Kong and Taiwan, and there was a general air of personal and social discovery about young people's dance-going. Against this background, it was not uncommon to find college students mixing improvised disco dancing (often emulating what they had seen in films) with ballroom dancing in the same context. Although discos soon became places for boys and girls to meet each other, they were also generally desexualized settings. Young people often went in their everyday clothes and not dressed particularly with the other sex in mind, and there was, in fact, often a general shyness about interaction between the sexes. Hence, while boys and girls might feel too reserved to dance touching each other, it was common to see young people of the same sex dancing with each other arm-in-arm with no sexual implications whatsoever.

It is important to acknowledge that popular leisure activities in the 1980s also included some from the pre-reform period. For instance, a common weekend activity was going to a local park with the family, hiring a small rowing or paddle-boat on the boating lake, walking, playing, or visiting monuments. As we have discussed, there were also movie theaters, theatrical performances, concerts, and sporting events in the Mao period, which were all part of 1980s popular culture as well. There was a difference between the two periods, however. First, accessibility and availability were greatly increased in the post-Mao period, and theatre, movie, and concert tickets became available for individual purchase. Second, as the amount of free time that people enjoyed increased, they could spend more time involved in leisure activities that even if available in the Mao period they may not have had the time to pursue.

The 1990s

There were several important developments in the 1990s that affected the nature of leisure practices in China. To start with, by the second decade of reform, many Chinese consumers had matured considerably in the sense that they were more fully aware of what consumer choice entailed, they had greater knowledge and experience of different leisure activities, and they were more selective in what they did. In this way, much of the sense of discovery and experimentation disappeared in the 1990s, particularly in the large cities. This consumer maturity was also related to the expansion of Chinese media, the increasing access to information of different kinds—including exposure to international tastes, fashions, and leisure activities—and China's opening up to the outside world through travel, study, and the media and through meeting foreign students, businesspeople, and tourists. Leisure service providers matured also. Restaurants, pubs, and clubs became far more aware of the

Young Chinese golf players practice at Chaoyang Kosaido Golf Club in Beijing. With courses springing up all over the country, golf in mainland China is booming. There are now in excess of 250 golf courses scattered over the country with more being carved out of the landscape each month. (Corbis)

Ten-Pin Bowling

Ten-pin bowling was one of the major fads that swept across urban China in the 1990s. First in the major cities and then later in towns, bowling alleys started springing up using imported equipment often from the United States. Although bowling has only been around for a relatively short time in China, it has already gone through a series of social changes. When the first bowling alleys appeared in the major cities in the early 1990s, they were fairly expensive and enjoyed a high social standing compared to other forms of entertainment. They were new, fun, clean, and smart, but above all they were prestigious. Young businesspeople used bowling alleys as their new playgrounds, and they became useful venues for nurturing friendships and business relationships (see Wang 2000).

As alleys became more and more numerous and the competition for custom became more intense, inevitably prices came down, and more and more people went bowling. The sport then went through a second wave of popularity: mass urban popularity. It enjoyed a new lease on life as its greater availability made what was considered a relatively elite pastime accessible to ordinary people. By the end of the 1990s, however, bowling had become commonplace and, for some, even "old hat." The older bowling alleys started to lose their appeal as their age began to show. In this new market environment, a new economics came into play. New alleys could still draw in the crowds, but increasingly they relied on marketing ploys such as prizes, special offers, and reduced prices to survive in a tough competitive leisure market.

need to satisfy customers and the importance of marketing, presentation, branding, and reputation. Discos became far more sophisticated and emulated international venues with hi-tech music, décor, and lighting systems.

There were other changes in the 1990s that coincided with this maturation of consumer behavior. One of these was the arrival of more and more foreign companies in China, offering more "global" or international consumer and leisure opportunities to Chinese people. Perhaps the most obvious of these were foreign fast-food chains including McDonald's, Kentucky Fried Chicken, and Pizza Hut as well as several well-known fast-food outlets from Hong Kong such as Café de Coral and Maxim. At the same time, the 1990s also saw considerable overseas investment, particularly from Hong Kong and Taiwanese businessmen in various leisure and entertainment sectors including movie theaters, theme parks, fun parks, bowling alleys, driving ranges, pubs, discos, and restaurants. Many of these investments were on a smaller basis than the large fast-food chains, but they were nonetheless significant as they imported experience and successfully proven business models from other Chinese leisure contexts in Hong Kong and Taiwan.

Technological changes were also important for the way that China's leisure practices developed in the 1990s. In relation to media, we have seen how television moved into a new era with the launch of cable and then satellite television, which greatly increased the number of channels that people watched. The videocassettes of the 1980s were also fairly rapidly replaced by VCDs. In the mid-1990s, the Internet arrived in China, and by the end of the decade it was a significant feature of youth culture in particular (see Chapter 8). The 1990s also saw the arrival and spread of the mobile phone as a feature of popular social and cultural interaction. As people became financially better off, they were able to consider buying motorcycles to replace their bicycles, and taxis became an ever more common and more frequently used feature of city life.

By the 1990s, travel and tourism had also started to become more prominent features of Chinese leisure activities and popular culture. Throughout the 1980s, Chinese people became more accustomed to traveling, in a country where it had been largely impossible for decades. For the average Chinese family, however, traveling was still relatively expensive in the 1980s, and most travel was done for either work or business purposes. The country's migrant population traveled largely from rural to urban areas for work. Companies sent employees on business trips or to meetings in other parts of the country, and businessmen and businesswomen increasingly traveled for buying, selling, and attending trade fairs or meetings. It was not until the 1990s that families found themselves able to start thinking more seriously about traveling beyond their home region for pleasure, which they did, at least within China—traveling individually, in families, or in tour groups. Associated with this tourist boom, which came particularly toward the end of the decade, China also developed a range of adventure activities

City traffic in China. As people in China were becoming more financially comfortable in the 1990s, many turned to motorized transport as an alternative to the commonplace bicycle. (Corel)

such as white-water rafting, bungee jumping, and mountain climbing.

The 2000s

The 2000s saw the changes of the 1990s continue a logical progression. The maturation of consumers and service providers, the unrelenting development of new technologies, and increasing foreign investment have all continued to leave their marks on the Chinese leisure and popular cultural landscapes. Consumption and leisure became unquestioned features of everyday life. Technological change brought multimedia mobile phones, DVD players, broadband Internet, and the launch of digital television. The combination of broadband Internet and the popularity of Internet cafés also made online gaming one of the rising stars of the Chinese leisure scene.

Meanwhile, foreign investment and involvement in the Chinese leisure and entertainment industries intensified and moved up to a higher level. The 2000s saw the Chinese authorities collaborate with major international sporting bodies to put the country on the international sporting map. Shanghai in particular became the host of international tennis and golf tournaments and in 2004 hosted its first Formula 1 racing grand prix to much international acclaim. At the same time, international media companies like Warner Brothers, News Corporation, Sony, and Viacom all stepped up their efforts to secure their various footholds in Chinese media markets. The expansion of foreign restaurant chains into the country—at least into the large cities—also proceeded apace. One of the notable arrivals of the early 2000s was U.S. coffee bar chain Starbucks, which catered partly to a growing expatriate and tourist population but nonetheless revolutionized coffee drinking in China's major cities with the introduction of cappuccinos, lattes, and espresso coffees and spawned a host of look-alike café chains.

A Chinese man relaxes beside a statue of Ronald McDonald in front of a Starbucks coffee shop. (Corbis)

Travel and tourism in the early 2000s also took a crucial step forward as China's burgeoning middle classes increasingly looked at international travel and overseas vacations. At first, vacation destinations were mainly in Southeast Asia, with popular tourist destinations being Indonesia, Thailand, and Malaysia. Within a few years, however, tour operators and China's budding international tourists were increasingly looking farther afield to destinations such as Europe and Australia, with the vast majority of tourists traveling in organized groups and on package tours.

The futuristic skyline of Shanghai, China, the country's largest city and an important commercial and industrial center. (iStockPhoto.com)

In all of these changes over the three decades, we can identify the changing social and physical spaces of Chinese popular culture. From the introduction of new private restaurants and discos in the 1980s to the construction of Shanghai's impressive Formula 1 racing circuit in the 2000s, Chinese people have found themselves spending their leisure time in constantly evolving spaces. Nor should we forget the physical transformation of all of China's cities over the reform period, epitomized by the futuristic high-rise skyline of Shanghai's Pudong business district and the tearing down of Beijing's traditional *hutong* (alley) houses. The transformation of China's leisure space has also taken place at every level of experience. At the local, personal level, people have experienced the transformation of their domestic space. People's relationship to the spaces of their work unit has also been reconfigured. They experience the spaces of their towns and cities in dramatic new ways with underground transport systems, reflective-glass office blocks, traffic jams, pollution, and noise. At the national and international level, Chinese people have seen their horizons expanded by travel and tourism.

Leisure, Sociality, and Popular Culture

Reflecting upon the changes in leisure practices and social space over the last two to three decades, it is possible to identify a common thread running through them that links leisure and popular culture. This thread is the social aspect of leisure activities. For instance, in the changes from the Mao period or early 1980s through to the 1990s and 2000s, we have seen how leisure activities became more individual or family-centered, we discussed the sense of shared discovery that young people had at discos in the 1980s, and we have seen how travel and other leisure activities changed from being things one did with one's colleagues to things one did with one's family or as an individual in either a more domestic or a more public context. These transformations of sociality—the ways in which people are "social" and engage with others—in consumer and leisure activities occupy a position at the heart of understanding the transformations in contemporary Chinese popular culture in recent decades.

We can see the importance of sociality in the popular cultural practices that we have been considering by thinking about how many of them are social activities—dining out; going to discos, pubs, or clubs; playing or watching sports; going bowling; and so on. In China, even using the Internet and playing online games in Internet cafés has a social context as important as the gaming itself for many young people (see Chapter 8). More than in Western societies, but similar to many other Asian countries, having fun in China is also often closely related to being with a group of other people: friends, family, colleagues, or even strangers. Chinese people talk, usually positively, about places and situations being *renao* ("hot and noisy"). This adjective might be applied to a fun fair, a party, a shopping center, a night market, or the crowd at a theatrical performance, for example. The term points to the importance of atmosphere, of bustling activity and the presence of lots of

A crowded street at night in China's capital, Beijing. Places that are bustling with activity, such as night markets, are popular leisure venues in China. (Corel)

people. For many Chinese people, this may not be a prerequisite for having fun, but it may be an important contributory factor. Apart from when two people are on a date, having fun is usually enhanced by having a large group of people involved. Most people would think it much better to go to a restaurant, fun park, disco, karaoke party, or football match as one of a group of five or more friends rather than on their own or in twos or threes. For many Chinese people, having fun and being on one's own do not go together. With this in mind, we can see how the changes in leisure time and space that we have discussed affect these kinds of sociality: whom one spends time with (colleagues, family, neighbors, or friends), where time is spent (in the work unit, at home, in a restaurant, or at another leisure venue), and the nature of the social relationships involved (semi-obligatory, kinship, or personally chosen).

There are ways yet in which socializing has been and still is a leisure activity in itself. Particularly in the Mao period and the 1980s, when there were more communal cooking and bathroom facilities and people often had smaller homes, there would be quite a lot of interaction with one's neighbors. Before television, this would have entailed simply sitting and chatting a lot of the time. Later, it could include watching television together after dinner in the evening or popping in and out of each other's houses for a chat. In the 1990s and 2000s, as people's domestic lives became more family-centered and conducted behind closed doors, there were nonetheless far more opportunities for socializing through other consumer and leisure activities outside of the home at restaurants, clubs, and so on. At that time, consumption therefore came to play a greater part in sociality, and there was an increasingly important interrelationship between consumption and social interaction, in which the two became mutually dependent upon each other. Socializing increasingly involved consumption, and vice versa. One of the most important areas where this has been the case is the consumption of food, which also offers an example of the interrelationship between consumption, popular culture, sociality, and space.

Food and Popular Culture

Nowhere is the importance of the relationship between consumption and sociality more striking than in relation to food in China. In one way or another, food has been at the heart of Chinese culture for millennia. Food has always played a key role in Chinese ritual or religious practices, and different levels of social interaction have traditionally been accompanied by food consumption, whether it be the finalization of a business deal, a wedding celebration, a simple visit to a friend's house, or a state banquet. We can therefore say that Chinese food has always been a key—if not perhaps *the* key—component of Chinese popular culture for thousands of years. Chinese food and eating habits are incredibly diverse, however. There are large regional and ethnic differences, and Chinese food also has a long history of change and transformation. It is therefore impossible to summarize all this complexity in a few pages, and all we can do in this section is offer a brief introduction to some of the key social features of China's culinary landscape before focusing on recent changes in Chinese food consumption

Consumption and Popular Religion

One area in which increased consumption in the post-Mao period has generally been greater in the countryside than in the cities is in relation to popular religion. Under Mao, all religious activities were suppressed, and traditional weddings, funerals, temple festivals, and other popular religious celebrations disappeared. In the post-Mao era, many families, villages, and communities have started staging more elaborate ceremonies and celebrations again, drawing to varying degrees upon people's memories and knowledge of how things were done in the past (see, e.g., Siu 1989). This kind of popular religious renaissance has entailed new forms of individual, family, and community consumption.

Weddings and funerals are conspicuous examples. With weddings, for instance, families provide banquets (the size depending largely on the family's wealth or social status), the purchase and presentation of consumer items as dowry, possibly the construction or purchase of a new home, and the hiring of musicians and other helpers.

Over the last twenty to thirty years, thousands of village temples and ancestral halls have been renovated and some of their role in village affairs reinstated. These temples and halls suffered particularly badly in the Cultural Revolution, when they were used as barracks, schools, offices, and warehouses and for keeping animals in. Their contents—statues, paintings, and other religious paraphernalia—were invariably destroyed, defaced, or otherwise badly damaged because they were seen by Mao's Red Guards as part of China's feudal past. Hence, renovation of temples often involved significant structural work, roof replacement, total redecoration, and the purchase or commission of new figures of deities and other religious items. This could be an expensive business.

Much of the expenditure for renovation has come from private sources, usually with large contributions from wealthy businessmen or peasants and combined smaller contributions from less wealthy families. The renewed position of village temples in village life has also seen renewed expenditure on temple visits, with offerings of incense, food, drink, and paper money to deities or donations in return for divining services and consultations. Temple festivals can also involve considerable expenditure on offerings, theatrical performances, or entertainment and banquets, and although not every village and every temple is involved in such expenditure, many are. In the cities, some renovated temples have become popular tourist attractions for Chinese and foreign tourists alike.

Expenditure on popular religion is not confined to festival, ceremonial, and celebratory consumption. In the post-Mao era, Chinese peasants have increasingly returned to what the government would call feudal, superstitious practices such as fortune-telling and horoscopes, exorcisms, geomantic consultations, healers, and almanacs. This kind of consumption is frowned upon by the authorities, who see such practices as unscientific, but they continue nonetheless and involve payment not only for services rendered but for books, calendars, offerings to deities, and more. Many people also buy and set up shrines in their own homes to kitchen gods, ancestors, or popular deities. Such shrines are often found in business premises, set up by proprietors to protect and bring good fortune to their businesses. Particularly popular in business is the martial deity Guan Di (Emperor Guan), known for his fairness, justice, and loyalty.

Farmers tend to the rice harvest in southern China. (Corel)

habits and their importance in understanding contemporary Chinese popular and consumer culture.

China is generally thought of as a rice-eating country, and certainly rice is a staple food for much of the Chinese population. In some parts of China, however—particularly the north—the traditional staple foods are based on grains other than rice, particularly wheat but also barley, millet, or maize, for instance. In these areas, people are more likely to eat noodles, baked or pan-prepared breads, steamed rolls or buns, and meat and vegetable–filled dumplings such as ravioli-like *jiaozi*. In recent years, greater wealth, better transport, a more mobile population, and greater choice and availability of food have all contributed to making rice more commonly eaten in the north and noodles and breads more commonly eaten in the south, particularly in the cities, but the broad division between a rice-based food culture in the south and a wheat and other grain–based food culture in the north still generally holds.

The regional differences in Chinese food by no means stop at the distinction between rice-eating and non-rice-eating areas. China has a range of rich regional cuisines that vary greatly in their use of ingredients, styles of cooking, and range of preferred tastes and flavors. Among these, the most internationally recognized would include Cantonese and Sichuanese cuisine, but there are many others from other provinces, cities, and regions. Indeed, even within Guangdong (Canton) or Sichuan Province there are notable regional differences. Generally speaking, however, there is a lot of similarity among food habits in the wheat-eating

Harvested wheat in China. Even though China is widely thought of as a rice-eating country, people in much of northern China traditionally eat foods based on other grains such as wheat. (iStockPhoto.com)

northern areas, while the rice-eating south can be divided into three broad regions: east, west, and south (Anderson 1994: 42).

In the north, where noodles, millet, wheat, and breads are the staple foods, although pork and chicken are, as in other parts of China, the most commonly eaten meats, there is also more lamb eaten, which reflects ethnic influences from the Mongolian north and Muslim northwest. Other regional specialties include Mongolian hotpots and barbecues with thinly sliced meats and various sauces as well as Peking duck and the small grilled and fried snacks so popular in the capital.

Where rice is the main staple food, there is a basic notion of *fan* and *cai*, where *fan* is rice and *cai* refers to meat or vegetable dishes eaten with the rice. In other words, rice is rarely cooked together with other foods but is cooked and eaten as a separate staple accompanied by other dishes. The eastern part of China's rice-eating region, broadly defined as the lower Yangtze Valley near Shanghai and its surrounding areas, is known for its dishes using sweet bean paste, vinegar, sugar, rice wine, and oil. Noodles are also fairly common, and specialties include crab, shrimp, water plants, and seaweed. Food in the western rice- eating area, notably including Sichuan and Hunan, is characterized by spicy dishes using a lot of chili, star anise, ginger, brown pepper, and other spices. Sichuan dishes also often reflect the mountainous nature of the province, featuring a lot of foods found in the mountains, such as bamboo shoots, mushrooms, pine nuts, and game. Hunan

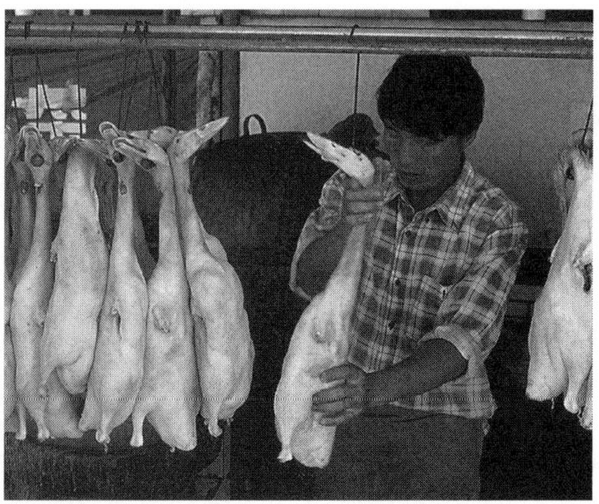

A famous Chinese dish, Peking Duck is a flattened roast duck dish with crispy skin usually eaten with small pancakes, a sweet sauce, and a kind of finely shredded spring onion. (Willem Proos/Travel Pictures)

cuisine is just as spicy as Sichuan but has more bean-based dishes and a large range of its own regional specialties. Food in the southern rice-eating region—best-known in terms of Cantonese cuisine—by contrast is generally more mild in flavor, with a lot of fresh seafood, lightly cooked vegetables, and a wide variety of meats and game. Soups, being a good, easily digestible source of liquid, salt, and other nutrients in a hot and very humid climate, are eaten at almost every meal (see also Anderson 1988: 194–228 on regional food diversity). Although Cantonese cooking is widely acclaimed within China as an important cuisine, other Chinese, particularly in the north, also poke fun at Cantonese people for the range of foods eaten. A popular light-hearted saying has it that Cantonese people will eat anything with legs that is not a table and anything with wings that is not an airplane.

It is also important to distinguish between restaurant food and domestic food. Although both broadly follow the regional characteristics outlined above, there is often a notable difference between food bought when eating out and that cooked at home. In Beijing, for instance, it might be the difference between grilled and fried street snacks, a Mongolian hotpot or barbecue, or Peking duck in a restaurant compared to plainer home cooking with more vegetables, rice, noodles, and breads. In Guangzhou it might be the difference between rich, fairly greasy, and more complicated restaurant dishes—including *dimsum* snacks—compared to less oily, simpler home-prepared dishes with more vegetables and lighter seasoning.

Both restaurant and domestic cuisines are important for understanding contemporary Chinese popular culture, and both are crucial for understanding how people socialize. The time and space of domestic eating, for instance, is an important arena of family communication and discussion, and understanding food and how it is cooked and eaten by Chinese families can reveal a wide range of cultural attitudes and practices. Meanwhile, public eating and dining out offer a wider range of insights into contemporary Chinese consumer culture and how that has become an ever more important arena for social interaction.

Eating and drinking play a crucial role in almost any form of Chinese social interaction. Even on the occasion of a simple visit to friends or relatives, the hosts will usually offer the guest something to drink, at a minimum. In contemporary China, this drink is usually tea and is at least boiled or bottled mineral water. Strangers are given greater hospitality as a demonstration of the host's welcoming attitude and respect for visitors and in order to maintain face. When people visit others' houses they will usually also take a gift, which will often take the form of food or drink. What people

Baozi, a popular kind of filled steam bun found in many parts of China, is usually filled with meat, vegetables, or sweet red-bean paste. (iStockPhoto.com)

give will depend on local customs, tastes, and availability of produce, but one of the standard offerings on such occasions would be fruit. Meanwhile, no Chinese business deal is complete until it has been celebrated with a meal accompanied by some kind of alcoholic drink—usually rice wine or beer. Weddings and other important family occasions are celebrated with feasts and banquets, and specific food items are also associated with different traditional festivals—*jiaozi* dumplings, oranges, and a range of other foods with Chinese New Year, *zongzi* glutinous rice dumplings with the Dragon Boat Festival in the early summer, and mooncakes (*yuebing*) with the mid-autumn festival. Food and drink also accompany many of the other leisure activities discussed earlier.

Food does not just accompany social occasions, however. The way that it is served and consumed can also contribute greatly to the structuring of social occasions and social interaction. For instance, at a banquet or when eating even semi-formally in a restaurant, there will usually be a seating order dictated by a hierarchy of social status and respect. The most important guest or guests should sit next to the main host, who will personally ensure that they are constantly supplied with food and drink. Then, broadly speaking, the further the distance from the host, the lower one's social position in relation to that particular occasion. This kind of spatial hierarchy can also be highly gendered, with men often given priority over women of otherwise equal status on the occasion. The domestic sphere can also be spatially gendered in similar ways, particularly if there are guests present, but also in everyday interaction—even though how exactly this may be the case varies across the country and often from one household to another.

The social aspects of food consumption in mainland China over the last half century have been transformed by pressures from various different directions. In the Mao period, for instance, there were various moves toward communal eating, with the work unit's canteen replacing domestic eating for many meals, particularly in the cities. At the same time, the Communist Party has over the years introduced a whole range of legislation that has sought to equalize the status of men and women. This has not always been successful, and there are more or less subtle ways in which such reforms have reproduced patriarchal practices (see, e.g., Wolf 1985; Stacey 1983), but these changes since 1950 have nonetheless benefited hundreds of millions of Chinese women and they have made many Chinese people—men and women—aware of gender equality issues. At the same time, issues of class, social status, and hierarchy were completely transformed under the communists.

In the post-Mao era, new forms of hierarchy and social stratification have emerged. Class background—one's assigned status that affected jobs, marriage, the allocation of goods and services, education, and many other aspects of life in the Mao period—has become virtually irrelevant in contemporary China. At the same time, greater differentiation between the sexes in terms of employment and social attitudes has also arisen, to some degree reflecting the more traditional values of the past. In relation to eating practices, however, such traditional attitudes have also faced new challenges. With more people eating out more often, in more varied circumstances, and often simply with friends, the formality of restaurant dining has to some degree been reduced.

At the same time, the range of dining venues has grown enormously over the last two or three decades as private entrepreneurs have been allowed to set up their own food stands and restaurants, resulting in a range of dining choices in addition to the state-owned restaurants that survived from the previous decades. These choices also have their own hierarchy. At the top are the large, luxurious restaurants, some associated with top-class hotels, some independent, and some state-owned. These are the often elaborately furnished restaurants with famous chefs of high renown where banquets can cost thousands, even tens of thousands of dollars. There is then a full spectrum of restaurants from these down to small family or individually run eating houses catering to smaller groups, often offering regional specialties and more folk dishes than the haute cuisine found at expensive banquets. The range of restaurants also includes regionally divergent teahouses and ethnic or regional specialty restaurants. Below these, there is an extensive spectrum of street stalls ranging from semi-permanent shed-like structures down to individual street vendors with baskets on a carrying pole.

In the post-Mao era, a range of contemporary alternatives has supplemented this range of Chinese eating options. Most notably, the country has seen the arrival in the large cities—particularly from the 1990s onward—of international foreign

Customers at a Chinese teahouse in Shanghai. (Corbis)

fast-food outlets like McDonald's, Kentucky Fried Chicken, and Pizza Hut. In the early 2000s, there were more than sixty McDonald's restaurants in Shanghai alone. These have proven extremely popular with families and young people and their success can be attributed to a number of factors. On one hand, particularly in the early years there was the novelty factor and the attraction of finding out more about Western food and eating habits. The names of fast-food chains were also often familiar to Chinese people through films, television, and newspapers, which built up a certain kind of curiosity among the Chinese population before the restaurants even arrived in the country. In the longer term, however, explanation for the success of these restaurants has to be found elsewhere. Some reasons are practical—fast-food restaurant chain outlets are usually very clean, bright, hygienic, and spacious, giving them general appeal. At the same time, their food is relatively affordable and attractive to children, even if many older people do not like it.

However, we also have to look for more cultural explanations and consider how Chinese consumers use these restaurants. For instance, fast-food outlets like McDonald's are very popular with young people, at least in part for the opportunity they offer for social gathering. Groups of school or college students or friends after work can find a comfortable place at a fast-food outlet to sit, chat, watch other people, or do homework, all accompanied by a hamburger, a Coke, or an ice cream. Fast-food restaurants also offer cheap, convenient, and anonymous places for young couples to meet. Chinese scholar Yan Yunxiang has argued that the attraction for many young people, and young women in particular, is the informality of the social space in these fast-food restaurants where the formality and hierarchy of the traditional restaurant is removed (Yan 1997; 2000). In relation to gender, Yan argues that McDonald's offers Chinese women the freedom to eat alone, in pairs, or with groups of friends without encountering the social opprobrium that they may well feel when eating alone in a traditional restaurant (2000: 217–218). In this sense, fast-food restaurants can offer a more socially gender-neutral and less hierarchical social space than other eating venues, and it may be not so much the food that is important in consumption but the social space associated with it.

Contemporary Chinese food consumption has also brought about the consumption of ethnicity, particularly in the large cities, through restaurants offering different kinds of ethnic cuisine. These come principally in two forms: Chinese ethnic and foreign ethnic. The latter would have to include the fast-food outlets discussed above, which for Chinese people are very alien and generally associated with the United States. Apart from these, "Western" food also includes various Chinese modifications of French, Italian, German, and other European cuisines, often combined on one menu. Indeed, quite often there is no great effort made at national or regional differentiation in the presentation and consumption of "Western food," which becomes identified by a range of dishes from steaks to sandwiches. Within this spectrum, there is some recognition of usually metonymic stereotype foods associated with some nationalities. For instance, pizza and spaghetti are widely recognized as Italian, although few people would know what Parmesan is. Asian cuisines are also often modified in the Chinese context, just as Chinese food overseas is quite different from Chinese food in China. However, some Asian cuisines are understood better than much Western food. For instance, Japanese, Malaysian, Thai, and Indonesian restaurants are relatively well represented in the major cities. These international cuisines, however unfaithful they may be to their true originals, nonetheless bring the notion of foreign food to life in the Chinese consumer context in ways that simply did not exist in the pre-reform period.

Just as important as the international cuisines are the various Chinese regional cuisines that have become increasingly available in towns and cities. Even in the Mao period, there were some state-owned ethnic restaurants in China, but they were relatively few. In the reform period, people have enjoyed much greater freedoms to move around the country, and some of them have taken their regional home cooking with them. Prestigious, nationally recognized cuisines such as those from Guangdong (Cantonese), Beijing, and Sichuan have long been in demand in other parts of the country. Indeed, cooking was one of the few trades that took people *out* of Guangdong to work in other provinces rather than the other way around, which has been more usual. Particularly from the 1990s onward, other regional cuisines also migrated around the country. To some degree, regional restaurants served migrant populations, but they also serviced increasing consumer demand in places like Guangzhou, Shanghai, and Beijing for culinary tourism—that is, the opportunity to experience other places through eating rather than traveling. Hence, in Guangzhou, for instance, in the 1990s and early 2000s there was a massive array of regional restaurants, covering cuisines from Hunan, Sichuan, Shanghai, Hainan,

Mongolia, Xinjiang, northeastern China, and Chaozhou, to name but a few. Such cuisines also received increased attention in the local culinary press, such as the food pages of local newspapers (see Klein 2006).

Consuming the Foreign

The example of fast-food restaurants raises important questions in relation to Chinese consumption: To what extent are Chinese people consuming "the foreign," in the sense that products have a certain appeal simply because they are foreign, and what are the implications of China's increasing consumption of transnational consumer products such as Coca-Cola, McDonald's, Sony, Nokia, and Volkswagen for contemporary Chinese popular culture? The complex relationship between Chinese society and globalization is beyond the scope of this book; however, these questions are important for understanding contemporary Chinese consumer culture.

Logically, prior to either of these questions we have to ask another one: What does foreign actually mean in the Chinese consumer context? The answer is more complicated than it might seem. "Foreign" is a word that has different uses and significance in different situations. For instance, "foreign" is often used almost synonymously in China with the notion of "Western," particularly when comparing the cultural differences between Chinese and "foreign" ways of doing things—for example, "foreigners" (read Westerners) are individualistic, whereas Chinese are more socially oriented; "foreigners" would split a restaurant bill, whereas Chinese always let one person pay, with the assumption of future reciprocity. At the same time, particularly in relation to consumption, foreign is in actual fact rarely synonymous with Western. Although there are many popular Western (i.e., North American, European, or Australian) products and brands in China, such as Coca-Cola, Starbucks, Dell, Volkswagen, and McDonald's, there are also many other Asian products and brands, particularly Japanese. China's consumer electronics market, for instance, is overflowing with Japanese and Korean brand names—Sony, LG, Panasonic, Samsung, Toshiba, and so on. At the same time, Korean television dramas have become very popular in recent years.

The complicatedness of the "foreign" is brought to the fore when considering Hong Kong and Taiwan: both predominantly culturally Chinese, but politically and historically distinct. Even though Hong Kong sovereignty was returned to China in 1997, it operates under a different political system, has its own economy, and is actually treated by the Chinese themselves as in many ways foreign. Hong Kong journalists, tourists, and businessmen visiting China are often treated more like foreigners, for instance, than like mainland Chinese. Meanwhile, Taiwan is politically still part of China despite its de facto independence for more than half a century. In a similar way, Hong Kong and Taiwanese cultural products fall into a peculiar category of "foreignness"—they are certainly considered to come from "outside" and might often be described as foreign. Yet unlike other Asian or Western products, there is a strong linguistic and cultural affinity felt for Hong Kong and Taiwanese films, television programs, popular music, literature, and lifestyle that make them nonetheless "Chinese" (Gold 1993). In this sense, consuming the foreign has to include products and lifestyles from Hong Kong and Taiwan, but their special appeal and attraction for Chinese consumers has to be acknowledged.

Chinese people certainly have bought many foreign goods—in all senses of the term—over the last couple of decades, and, as we have discussed, there were important ways in which people were experimenting with popular cultural products and practices (going to discos, for example) that were, and were seen to be, predominantly foreign. However, it is much more difficult to say that Chinese people were actually "consuming the foreign"—that is, buying foreign goods simply because they were foreign, although that surely happened on occasion. More often, people bought foreign goods or tried out foreign leisure practices not only because they were foreign but because they had some other appeal, even if that may in some cases have been enhanced by a degree of foreignness.

For instance, with many consumer products we find a popular brand hierarchy that often puts foreign brands at the top, with Chinese brands falling somewhere below. A good example would be television sets. In the 1980s and early 1990s, there was a clear consumer brand hierarchy (as mentioned in Chapter 3) that put the imported Japanese color televisions—Sony, Panasonic, and Toshiba, for instance—at the top, followed by Chinese color sets and then, at least in the 1980s, Chinese black and white sets. The cost of televisions paralleled the hierarchy, with the Japanese sets being the most expensive. The preference for buying foreign was due to a combination of reasons. First among these for many people was quality: The foreign sets were known to be of better quality, to last longer, and to be more reliable. Chinese *guochan* (literally "national product") television sets, by contrast, had the reputation of being more affordable but of poorer quality, likely to break down or wear out more quickly. Only second came the issue of brand status. Hence, although the preference was for foreign sets, this was only in small part due to their being foreign as such. This is confirmed by the fact that by the early 2000s, when Chinese television set production and quality had improved enormously while pricing remained competitive, the preference for foreign sets was greatly corrected. Fashion offers another example. There is a burgeoning Chinese fashion industry that becomes more innovative and successful as the years go by, but leading international brands such as Gucci, Prada, Yves Saint Laurent, and Armani are still generally considered the epitome of fashion consumption.

The case of cellphones is similar. In the 1990s, when mobile phones first started to become popular, there were very few Chinese-made phones. This meant that the foreign brands like Motorola, Nokia, and Ericsson dominated and took a firm grip on the market. Chinese manufacturers soon started producing more models—at first they too were less sophisticated, less stylish, and less reliable, but in the early 2000s the quality of Chinese models improved to become competitive with the foreign brands while remaining cheaper. Once again, the Chinese manufacturers' share of the market grew sharply, even if it was to fall back again a couple of years later, and once again it was shown that the foreignness of the brand was only one part of the consumer equation. Indeed, one also has to note that many of the foreign-brand phones by this time were actually being made in Chinese joint-venture factories, making them less "foreign" than the brand names suggested. As we can see in each of these examples, the importance or relevance of being foreign changes over time. At one time it may carry the sense of novelty or quality, but a few years later that novelty may have worn off and the quality may be little different from other products. In fact, many foreign products have undergone a process of normalization in relation to Chinese popular consumption. Fast-food chains, cola, electronic goods, and mobile phones are good examples. McDonald's hamburgers and Coca-Cola will always be American, yet, at least in the cities, Chinese people are so used to seeing them and to them being a part of their lives that at some level these products cease to be American or foreign—they are just sandwiches and soft drinks. Similarly, mobile phones, DVDs, and MP3 players are essentially "foreign" technologies, but few people would even give it a thought when buying or using them.

By contrast, there are nonetheless instances when such normalization can be suddenly reversed and consumption can also become a highly politicized and nationalistic issue. In the early 2000s, there was a series of diplomatic incidents between the Chinese government and the governments of the United States and Japan. The bombing of the Chinese embassy in Belgrade during the Kosovan-Serbian war and the downing of a U.S. spy plane in 2001 both sparked major diplomatic disputes. Meanwhile, the Japanese claim to the Diaoyutai Islands in the Sea of Japan ensured a constant backdrop of political tension between the countries, occasionally inflamed further by incidents such as the Japanese school history textbook dispute of 2005. At moments of heightened tension such as these, consumer boycotts were used by some ordinary people as a means of nationalistic protest, and U.S. or Japanese businesses could be targeted, along with their embassies, by crowds of stone-throwing protesters, even if the Chinese government has generally done its best to calm such protests.

Conclusion

In this chapter, we have seen how there is a constant interplay between leisure, consumption, and sociality, often mediated by the transformation of social space. Furthermore, we have seen that this interrelationship is constantly evolving and changing. Over the last twenty-five years, China has seen the relative importance of consumption and consumerism in this triangular relationship grow ever greater.

Earlier in this chapter, we saw how thinking about social and physical space is also a useful way of conceptualizing and focusing on the nature of some of these changes in Chinese popular cultural practice. In relation to food, space was an important feature of the discussion throughout—whether talking about the national space, with its geographical distribution of different food habits and ethnic cuisines, or the gendered space of Chinese restaurants. Thinking through the range of different social spaces associated with food—domestic space, restaurants, weddings, markets, temple festivals, shopping malls, and canteens—offers a way of conceptualizing the relationships that characterize Chinese consumption. Thinking about domestic space, for example, requires thinking not only about the physical features of the room but about the kinds of social relationships that populate that space—familial relations, with all their joys, tensions, and rivalries.

The question of social space also highlights the contrasts between public and private in Chinese leisure and consumption. We have seen that Chinese experience has not simply opposed public and private but involved a gradation of different degrees and kinds of public space. In the Mao era, space was largely public—even key areas of the domestic space were shared with others—but the other people one encountered in one's everyday life were largely people familiar from work. In the post-Mao era, the space of leisure time moved away from this public area of the work unit into the more broadly understood commercial spaces of general public consumption—restaurants, discos, bowling alleys, and so on. At the same time, the space of leisure time also relocated more securely into the domestic sphere—a more bounded, limited, and individual family-centered space than that of the past. Expenditure on popular religion in the post-Mao era has seen the transformation and reinvigoration of social spaces centered around temples and ancestral halls.

An old apartment building in urban China. During the Mao era, much of Chinese urban housing was built with shared living spaces, including cooking and bathroom facilities, with minimal interior decoration. (iStockPhoto.com)

All of these spaces have undergone their own transformations over the last couple of decades. As we have seen, the development of private travel and tourism in recent years has seen people's horizons broadened first from the immediately local to a larger local area and then beyond to neighboring towns and cities, to other parts of the province and the country, and for the emerging middle classes now increasingly to other parts of the world.

In all of these examples, we have seen the importance of consumption in people's leisure time and how it plays an important role in Chinese people's social interactions. Consumption is social, and social interaction often entails some kind of consumption. In this way, leisure and consumption have come to occupy central positions in China's popular cultural landscape.

A to Z

Apartments. From the 1980s onward, Chinese people started to have the opportunity to buy their own apartments. This helped drive China's consumer boom as people bought new consumer goods for their homes and spent money on redecoration, interior design, and furnishings.

Baozi. A kind of round, steamed bun with a filling of meat, vegetables, or sweet red-bean paste, eaten for breakfast in many parts of China.

Bowling. One of the new consumer leisure activities imported from the late 1980s onward that became a very popular pastime in Chinese cities.

Brand names. With the rise of China's consumer society, the importance of brand names has increased greatly. While leading international brands from Toshiba to Prada are well-known, there are also many popular and well-recognized Chinese brands.

Café de Coral. A chain of Hong Kong fast-food restaurants offering a mixture of Chinese and Western dishes, often based on a rice-plus-sauce formula. The chain made its first inroads into China in Guangzhou in the early 1990s.

Cantonese food. Although one of China's internationally best-known regional cuisines, the food found in Guangdong Province is quite different and far more varied than the standard international Chinese fare found overseas. It is a mild cuisine that incorporates a lot of seafood as well as an enormous range of meats, including game and vegetables.

Da paidang. The Chinese name for street food stands and small restaurants where one often eats outside on the pavement. These are at the lower end of the restaurant hierarchy and offer basic facilities but often good local specialties. They are particularly popular for late-night eating, as many are open into the small hours or even all night.

Dimsum. The collective term for a wide range of Cantonese snacks ranging from steamed chicken feet to water chestnut jelly cakes. *Dimsum* are the standard Cantonese breakfast eaten with tea or sometimes rice wine. They are often also eaten for lunch, but less so later in the day.

Do-It-Yourself. DIY became very popular in the 1990s as more and more people started to own and redecorate their homes. DIY has been well supported by a range of magazines, Web sites, and television programs.

Ethnicity. With the spread of restaurants offering regional cuisines around the country, Chinese people, particularly in cities, now often have a large choice of regional or ethnic cuisines from around China. This has raised awareness and increased knowledge of different food cultures within China and cultivated a kind of culinary tourism among Chinese consumers.

Fashion. Although leading international fashion brands from Gucci to Yves Saint Laurent are often considered the epitome of fashion consumption, China also has its own burgeoning fashion industry, with adventurous and innovative fashion designers. Fashion shows and fashion programming have also made for popular television viewing in recent years.

Fast food. Largely coming from the major U.S. chains, but also from Hong Kong, fast food has become a part of everyday life for many Chinese. Even if they do not eat the food, city dwellers are familiar with the restaurants, which are also popular meeting places. Chinese fast-food alternatives include so-called rice boxes containing a large serving of steamed rice with two or three ready-cooked Chinese meat, fish, or vegetable dishes.

FEC. Foreign exchange certificates were the only legal currency for foreigners in China up until the early 1990s. In the early years of the reform period, they were also the only legal tender accepted in top hotels, restaurants, and friendship stores principally aimed at a foreign clientele. As the only currency legally exchangeable for foreign currency, there was also a thriving black market that often saw FEC double their face value in *renminbi.*

Gender. Consumption of both food and consumer goods can be strongly gendered in China. Women are often more likely to cook, serve, and wash the dishes in the domestic setting, and pretty, young girls are often preferred as waitstaff in restaurants.

Haier. China's largest manufacturer of electronic consumer goods from televisions to refrigerators and air-conditioners. Haier is a well-respected brand name in China and has an increasing international presence.

Hong Kong. The former British colony is the source of many popular cultural and consumer products, most notably Cantopop pop music, action films, television dramas, and some popular literature.

Jiaozi. Either meat- or vegetable-filled steamed dumplings resembling large ravioli. These constitute a typically northern dish, traditionally eaten at Chinese New Year.

Jiu. The Chinese word for any kind of alcoholic drink (beer is *pijiu*, rice wine *mijiu* or *baijiu*, grape wine *putaojiu*, and so on). Drinking is an important part of Chinese banqueting and hospitality.

Maxim. A Hong Kong–based fast-food chain offering similar fare to Café de Coral but also known for its cakes and pastries.

McDonald's. This U.S. fast-food chain has become very popular with young people and families since the beginning of the 1990s when the first restaurants started opening in China's main cities. However, they are still largely restricted to the large metropolitan centers like Beijing, Shanghai, and Guangzhou. They are popular as much for the relaxed, clean atmosphere as for the food.

National holidays. The Chinese authorities extended key national holidays such as Chinese New Year and National Day (October 1) in the 1990s from one day to one week. These have now become consumer high points in the domestic retail calendar, with manufacturers and shops often looking to cash in on special offers for shoppers.

Ningbo Bird. One of China's top mobile-phone brands, named after the eastern Chinese city where the company is located, near Shanghai.

Peking duck. Also known as Beijing duck, a famous flattened roast duck dish with crispy skin, usually eaten with small pancakes, a sweet sauce, and a kind of finely shredded spring onion.

Pizza Hut. The U.S.-based international pizza restaurant chain established its presence in China in the mid- to late 1990s. The pizzas offered have been adapted to meet Chinese tastes and expectations of Western food: They often use strongly contrasting sweet and savory toppings.

Rationing. In the Mao era, rationing was a normal part of everyday life. Basic foodstuffs such as rice and other grains or oil were obtained in exchange for grain or oil vouchers distributed through one's work unit. Even into the mid-1980s, some state-owned shops and restaurants—selling flour, oil, rice, or noodles, for instance—would only accept vouchers in payment.

Renao. Literally "hot and noisy," *renao* is used to refer to bustling, lively, crowded, noisy, and brightly lit atmospheres. The term can be used to refer to a host of different contexts from restaurants to fun fairs, shopping malls, or artistic performances.

Renminbi. Literally "people's currency." This is the now the only currency in China, but up until the early 1990s there was a thriving black market to exchange *renminbi* for foreign exchange certificates (FEC).

Sichuan food. One of China's best-known regional cuisines, from the western Chinese province of Sichuan. It is known for its hot, spicy dishes with large amounts of chili, star anise, ginger, and brown pepper.

Sports. A range of different sports, from tennis and golf to ten-pin bowling, has attracted China's new consuming masses. However, spectator sports—live, but particularly televised—has become a major form of sports consumption (see Chapter 11).

Starbucks. The U.S. coffee bar chain arrived in China's main cities—Beijing, Shanghai, and Guangzhou—in the early 2000s. Often located within short distances of large international hotels and offices with foreign workers, the success of the chain has been partly based on targeting foreigners and China's burgeoning young middle-class white-collar workers.

Taiwan. Like Hong Kong, Taiwan has become a source of many popular cultural products in mainland China, particularly pop music and television dramas.

Teahouses. Chinese teahouses take a variety of forms. Some of the most popular with Chinese and foreign tourists alike are the traditional-style teahouses with classic Chinese architectural style buildings surrounding courtyards of varying sizes. However, in Guangdong, where *yamcha* (drinking tea) is a local cultural institution and way of life, teahouses are large, multistory modern-style restaurants.

Vegetarian food. Particularly through the influence of Buddhism, China has a long tradition of vegetarian cuisine, often noted for the way vegetarian foods are made to look like well-known meat or fish dishes.

Video. The development of video technologies from VHS to VCD and DVD, combined in particular with rampant video piracy, has ensured that home entertainment has remained a fundamental form of popular Chinese media consumption.

Yuebing ("mooncakes"). Like small pies filled with various very sweet fillings including lotus-seed paste, nuts, and sugar. Some mooncakes considered of the highest quality have an egg yolk in the middle of the filling. Mooncakes are traditionally distributed as gifts and eaten at the mid-autumn festival.

Zongzi. Steamed glutinous rice dumplings wrapped in leaves and containing a mixture of pork, peanuts, and other savory fillings. *Zongzi* are eaten in celebration of the Dragon Boat Festival in the early summer on the fifth day of the fifth lunar month that commemorates the life and death of a classical poet and statesman, Qu Yuan, who reputedly drowned in 295 BC.

References and Further Reading

Anderson, E. N. 1988. *The food of China.* New Haven, CT: Yale University Press.

——— 1994. "Food." In D. Wu & P. D. Murphy (eds.). *Handbook of Chinese popular culture.* Westport, CT/London: Greenwood Press.

Davis, D. S. 2002. "When a house becomes his home." In P. Link, R. P. Madsen, & P. G. Pickowicz (eds.) *Popular China: Unofficial culture in a globalizing society.* Lanham, MD: Rowman & Littlefield Publishers, Inc.

Davis, D. S. (ed.) 2000. *The consumer revolution in urban China.* Berkeley, CA: University of California Press.

Gold, T. 1993. "Go with your feelings: Hong Kong and Taiwan popular culture in Greater China." *China Quarterly*, No. 136 (December 1993), 907–925.

Klein, J. 2006. "Changing tastes in Guangzhou: Restaurant writings in the late 1990s." In K. Latham, S. Thompson, & J. Klein (eds.) *Consuming China: Approaches to cultural change in contemporary China.* London: RoutledgeCurzon.

Latham, K., Thompson, S., & Klein, J. (eds.) 2006. *Consuming China: Approaches to cultural change in contemporary China.* London: RoutledgeCurzon.

Siu, H. F. 1989. "Recycling rituals: Politics and popular culture in contemporary rural China." In P. Link, R. P. Madsen, & P. G. Pickowicz (eds.) *Unofficial China: Popular culture and thought in the People's Republic.* Boulder, CO: Westview Press.

Stacey, J. 1983. *Patriarchy and socialist revolution in China.* Berkeley, CA: University of California Press.

Wang, G. 2000. "Cultivation friendship through bowling in Shenzhen." In D. S. Davis (ed.) *The consumer revolution in urban China.* Berkeley, CA: University of California Press.

Wolf, M. 1985. *Revolution postponed: Women in contemporary China.* Stanford, CA: Stanford University Press.

Yan, Y. 1997. "McDonald's in Beijing: The localization of Americana." In J. Watson (ed.) *Golden arches east: McDonald's in East Asia.* Stanford, CA: Stanford University Press.

——— 2000. "Of hamburger and social space: Consuming McDonald's in Beijing." In D. S. Davis (ed.) *The consumer revolution in urban China.* Berkeley, CA: University of California Press.

11

Sports and Martial Arts

To understand the roles of both sports and martial arts in contemporary Chinese popular culture, it is important to consider two overlapping and interconnected but nonetheless distinct sets of practices: participation and spectatorship. Participation, that is playing sports and practicing martial arts, is fundamental, but mediated spectatorship—through television, film, newspapers, magazines, the Internet, or other contemporary forms of media—is increasingly important in contemporary China, where there is strong interest in both domestic and foreign sports. With martial arts, there is a strong participative interest in traditional martial arts from Shaolin kung fu to tai chi (*taijiquan*) and traditional medicine and healing. At the same time, mediated martial arts in the form of films—often from or influenced by Hong Kong cinema—television series, and books and magazines are also key features of the contemporary Chinese popular cultural landscape.

In contemporary China, in fact, one's first encounter with sports is likely to be in one of its mediated forms—probably on television or in a newspaper. It is important to recognize, though, that mediated sports are not simply a relayed representation of live sports or a form of remote participation—it can be these things, but it is also much more. There are plenty of people interested in mediated sports who never have anything to do with live sports, either through participation or spectatorship, but at the same time there are many ways in which mediated sports draws Chinese people into alternative worlds of national and global sports consumption. This is where sports follow on from the discussion of consumption in the previous chapter, since the importance of sports in contemporary Chinese popular culture is as much about the *consumption* of sports in one form or another as it is about personally participating in it.

These different aspects of sports—spectatorship, participation, and consumption—can also be complexly interrelated and interconnected. A soccer fan may watch his (it is usually men and boys who play soccer in China) favorite team in the local stadium, compare it with the European games he watches on the television, and insist on buying Nike soccer cleats—advertised on the television between games and endorsed by his favorite players—for when he plays with his friends. This example also draws our attention to the global context of sports in China, which cannot be ignored. Modern contemporary competitive sports were largely introduced into China by foreign missionaries in the late nineteenth and early twentieth centuries, even if some of them—such as table tennis and women's volleyball—have subsequently become national sports carrying the pride of the nation. More recently, with economic reform and China's open-door policy, China's sports scene has been opened up to international commercialization and the arrival of foreign players, teams, and sponsors as well as new notions of professionalization, individualism, and competition. At the same time, some Chinese athletes have moved overseas to play a professional role in European soccer or U.S. basketball leagues, for instance.

A useful starting point for considering sports in contemporary China is the historical context of Chinese sports, since there are issues here that have to underpin our understanding of the present. The next section of this chapter therefore is a brief historical contextualization of sports and martial arts in China showing that these topics draw together and juxtapose long-standing cultural practices that date back millennia and far more recent sporting activities that bear strong connotations of modernity, foreignness, global participation, and international recognition. Subsequently, we will consider soccer in contemporary China in more detail as a good example of how practice, participation, consumption, spectatorship, and mediated sports all come together. This is followed by sections on Chinese sports in global context, national favorites, the importance of the 2008 Beijing Olympics, and the role that sports play in everyday society. We will then move on to focus on martial arts under three broad headings: martial arts and sports, martial arts and health, and martial arts and popular culture.

Chinese Sports in Historical Context

It is often noted in literature on Chinese sports that modern competitive sports were introduced through foreign—that is, Western—missionaries, expatriate businesspeople, colonial administrators, and military personnel in the late nineteenth and early twentieth centuries (see, e.g., Brownell 1994; 1995). The Young Men's Christian Association (YMCA) in particular—but other Christian missionary movements also—promoted modern sports including athletics, gymnastics, basketball, rowing, and soccer as important components of a morally, physically, and spiritually healthy modern Christian lifestyle. Missionaries ran schools, colleges, and ultimately also sports clubs to this end and played an important part in introducing the ethos, practice, and appreciation of such sports. Particularly in the foreign concessions of the treaty ports such as Shanghai, Tianjin, and Guangzhou, there were also foreign sports clubs associated with expatriate communities, promoted by both Chinese and foreign trading companies (or *hongs*, as they were known) and the military. These sports were also early reflections of diverging international sports interests. For instance, the British in Shanghai set up a cricket club, a horse-racing track, and rowing clubs, among other things, while Americans introduced basketball, baseball, and track and field athletics.

Nonetheless, the development of Western-style sports in China was not simply a colonial imposition. The Chinese military, led by modernizing reformers, adopted sports and attention to physical fitness as part of the modernization of the armed forces to bring them into line with what was becoming broader international practice. One can also trace a history of military support for sports and martial arts back to the early Imperial period peaking in the Tang dynasty even if it was often opposed by more scholarly officials (Brownell 1995: 35–37). However, in the nineteenth century the series of what were seen in China as almost unthinkable military defeats at the hands of foreign powers (see Chapter 1) forced the imperial regime to look to foreign military techniques, discipline, and technologies as a means of restoring national pride. Sports subsequently became a fundamental part of military discipline. This was even more the case from the 1920s onward when the militaristic nationalist forces of the Kuomintang (KMT) led by Chiang Kai-shek became ever more powerful and the Chinese Communist Party also started to emphasize the importance of military-style physical training and discipline. In the late nineteenth and early twentieth centuries, sports therefore became embroiled in a complex web of political arguments, particularly in relation to nationalism and foreign influence. The communists and nationalistic Chinese often criticized Chinese they saw as subserviently following Western trends and practices in sports, but this did not stop them from simultaneously nationalistically promoting similar—or even the same—sports for their military and physical discipline (Brownell 1995: 43).

However, it is also possible to overstate the role played by foreign influences in Chinese sports. It is true that many of the sports that are popularly followed and in which China excels today were originally Western sports; yet it is important to remember China's own earlier sporting heritage that goes back millennia. There are historical records, through art, literature, and archaeological evidence, that show that Chinese people engaged in wrestling, hunting, forms of soccer, bullfighting, dragon-boat racing, acrobatics, polo, weight-lifting, archery, jumping, skating, running, and swimming back in early imperial history. Clearly, the rules and social, religious, philosophical, and cultural practices associated with each of these sports would have been specific to their times and places and unlike those with which we are familiar today, but we should not forget the substantial historical heritage of Chinese sports that long preceded European and American missionaries.

Indeed, reflecting upon this tradition also helps us to understand how martial arts are intricately connected with China's sporting heritage. Forms of hand-to-hand combat date back to the earliest times in Chinese history. A fundamental cultural distinction in China for thousands of years has been that between *wen* and *wu*. *Wen*—literally "writing"—refers to those aspects of life associated with learning, writing, civility, literacy, high culture, and art, whereas *wu*, "military," refers to fighting, the art of war, physical strength, and martiality. In fact, the contemporary Chinese word for martial arts like kung fu and tai chi is *wushu*, a phrase that has more recently been exported around the world as people take an interest in kung fu fighting and films. Historically, sports have generally been considered as aspects of the *wu* realm of life and since the time of the Song Dynasty (AD 960–1279) there has been a tendency to valorize *wen* over *wu*, particularly among the politically dominant and powerful imperial scholar-officials. This is the reason usually given for why the Western competitive sports imported in the nineteenth century appeared to arrive in a relative sporting void.

The distinction between *wen* and *wu* is not simply a matter of the distinction between civil and military, however. It also maps onto social and conceptual distinctions between intellect and physicality, those areas of life that require refinement of the heart (*xin*—in classical China, thinking was associated with the heart, not the head) and those that require the honing of physical skills. Hence, *wushu* actually entails much more than simply learning punches, kicks, blocks, throws, and so on. Chinese martial arts, like many oriental martial arts, are about understanding, feeling, and cultivating the body and the energies that work in and upon it. They are part of a broader cosmological system centered around notions of harmony related also to notions of feng shui (geomancy, or the way that positive and negative energies flow through the landscape) and Chinese medicine (the understanding of how illnesses of different kinds relate to the imbalance or obstruction of forces and energies within the body).

Despite this long history, the contemporary Chinese sports scene is shaped as much, if not more, by the influences of modern Western sports as by notions of traditional cosmology. In the twentieth century, Chinese society experienced political chaos, revolution and revolutionary rivalries, fighting among different political factions, invasion and occupation by the Japanese, civil war, the founding of the communist PRC, famine, international isolation, the Cultural Revolution, and finally economic reform and liberalization. This was a century in which China was constantly looking to establish and consolidate its own identity in the modern world, and this is reflected in its sporting history.

From the 1920s on, sports were increasingly adopted and appropriated by the Chinese authorities, culminating in the nationalist Nanjing-based government of 1928, which understood how useful sports could be for cultivating national unity and encouraged national games on one hand and participation in international sports on the other (Brownell 1994: 122). Subsequently, China joined the International Olympic Committee in 1931 and sent its first athlete to the 1932 Los Angeles Games. Military sports also crossed political lines in Republican period China, being promoted equally by the Nationalist and Communist forces as a means of maintaining physical fitness, discipline, and morale.

Postwar China saw the official governmental support for sports move up a level. In the Republican period, although the government was keen to promote sports, the social, economic, and political disruption that accompanied years of fighting, occupation, and civil war meant that sports could only ever really be a secondary interest for a minority of people. With the founding of the People's Republic, at least in its first decade, came relative peace, stability, economic growth, and a whole new regime of government-led social discipline.

The communist authorities introduced a system of state sports schools in the mid-1950s, which has more or less survived to the present day, even if the contemporary context and operation of sports in China has changed considerably. The system, modeled on Soviet practice, aimed to institutionalize the identification of national sporting representatives and professionalize their training. The government set up the State Sports Commission to oversee a hierarchical structure of sports colleges, administrative commissions at each level of the government system—the town, county, and city levels, above which came the provincial level and above that the national level with the State Sports Commission itself. Basically, the system was planned to find talented young athletes at the local level and propel them up the ladder as far as they were good enough to go. In terms of national representation, Chinese sports suddenly found top gear, and within a few years Chinese athletes were challenging and breaking world records, even if some were not recognized due to international political squabbles about the recognition of the PRC government by the International Olympic Committee.

In the Cultural Revolution period of the 1960s, China's sports scene was thrown into disarray with the closure of schools, the sending down of urban youths to the countryside, and a strongly egalitarian and anti-imperialist ideology finding its way even into sports. Bearing in mind that many sports schools only reopened in 1971, it is ironic that just a year later a series of diplomatically orchestrated table-tennis matches between the United States and China resulted in the restoration of official relations between the two countries.

China's Liu Xiang celebrates as he crosses the finish line to win the men's 110-meter hurdles final at the Athens Olympic Games on August 27, 2004. Liu won gold by coming in 12.91 seconds ahead of Terrence Trammel of the United States and Cuba's Anier Garcia. (Corbis)

The significance of sports in the post-Mao period has seen further developments of earlier themes. So, for instance, there was a strong nationalistic sentiment generated around the women's volleyball team in the 1980s and 1990s, as well as sports such as table tennis, at which Chinese athletes excelled.

The post-Mao period, in fact, has seen a steady growth in Chinese presence on the international sporting stage, starting with women's volleyball championships in the 1980s and culminating in Chinese representation at the soccer World Cup Finals for the first time in 2002 and a record-breaking medals haul at the Athens 2004 Olympics. The nationalistic importance of sports also persists to the present day, with the hype

Beijing 2008 Olympic emblem. (PRNewsFoto/ Burson-Marsteller Beijing)

surrounding the 2008 Olympic Games to be held in Beijing.

Another key development of the last quarter century, however, has also been the transformation of some areas of Chinese sports into highly commercialized, media-oriented, and spectator-centered practices. In this realm, China's incorporation into international, even global sports, has been far more individualistic. So rather than thinking about Chinese national teams appearing at major sporting occasions, we also find high levels of consumer interest focused on people like Yao Ming, the Chinese basketball hero playing at the highest level in the U.S. National Basketball Association (NBA) championships, or various Chinese soccer players who have found places in top-level European soccer leagues.

Chinese Sports in Global Context

Soccer, in fact, offers a good starting point for thinking about the various different

Yao Ming of the Houston Rockets shoots over Francisco Elson of the San Antonio Spurs during a game at the AT&T Center on December 22, 2006, in San Antonio, Texas. (Getty Images)

aspects of sports in China that we have mentioned above. Soccer is one of the most keenly followed spectator and mediated sports in China, and it is also one of the most commonly played by young people in their spare time. It is also a "foreign" sport but one that in 2002 managed to build a wave of sentiment in the country when the national team qualified for the first time ever, since joining FIFA (Fédération Internationale de Football Association) in the 1930s, for the soccer World Cup Finals in Japan and Korea. Chinese soccer fans are now also increasingly targeted by the leading European clubs as consumers of their various products, from replica jerseys to autographed photos of players and

China's Li Ming (right) fights for the ball with Qatar's Selman Mesbeh during the first half of their first round Asian Cup soccer match in Beijing on July 25, 2004. China won the match 1-0. (Corbis)

tickets for summer friendlies against domestic teams. It is not coincidental that in 2005 the only official alternate-language version of the Web site of "the world's most popular" soccer team, Manchester United, was Chinese (Manchester United 2005)

Despite the fact that China can lay claim to one of the earliest forms of soccer in the world—with a game of kick-ball having been played at least until the Tang dynasty (AD 618–906) (Brownell 1995: 64)—soccer is one of the modern "Western" sports that came to China with missionaries, merchants, and government officials in the nineteenth century. The China Football Association (CFA) was set up in 1924, and China participated in international competitions from the 1930s on. However, the social, political, and military upheavals of the twentieth century in China seem to have made soccer a permanent second or third priority both in plans for national development and participatory involvement (Jones 2004: 56–57). This all changed in the 1990s, when soccer was professionalized, commercialized, and internationalized and took on a form increasingly similar to its organization in other countries around the world.

Prior to that, soccer had been a feature of the national sporting structure set up by the Communist authorities after 1949. It was also one of the sports of the national games, one of the most prestigious—if not also politicized—national sporting events in the country, held once every four years. Yet with little, if any, promotion at the local level in schools or through amateur bodies or soccer associations, unlike in other parts of the world, China has consistently underachieved, relative to its population, in terms of international soccer. The transformation of soccer in the 1990s was therefore a massive step for the game, taking it from a Soviet-style national sports structure to an internationally oriented commercial and professional one.

A fundamental milestone in this transformation was the setting up of the first national professional soccer league in 1994; another, some would say reflecting the provisional success of the moves, was China's qualification for the 2002 World Cup Finals and being ranked seventieth in the world in 2003. The transformation of soccer in the 1990s was not just about organization and payment, however. It was also about the promotion and establishment of soccer as a major spectator sport, as a commercial venture, as a popular cultural leisure activity, and as one of the most widely followed sports in Chinese media. With an average of 18,000 spectators (ranging from 1,000 to 51,000) per home game in the country's top Jia A league in 2001, in a relatively short space of time, China had developed a following for the game comparable with some of the leading European leagues, and soccer became the largest spectator sport in the country (Jones 2004: 60–61).

The sports sections of Chinese newspapers are often dominated by soccer coverage—of both domestic Chinese games and foreign games. In addition to Chinese games, Chinese soccer fans can also watch Italian Serie A, English Premiership, and German Bundes league matches, often live, throughout the European season. In this way, soccer represents an important way in which sports, as a set of popular cultural practices, offers ways for Chinese people to feel involved in the increasingly global world of soccer—and other sports—consumption. This is accentuated by the growing number of opportunities to see major European clubs such as Manchester United and other English Premier League teams playing Chinese teams on their friendly summer Asian tours, tours that are usually motivated in no small part by the commercial potential of developing, maintaining, and catering to Asian—including Chinese—fan bases.

This is also true of other international sports enthusiastically followed by some fans in China. After international soccer, probably the most obvious sport to do this is basketball, particularly through media reporting of the U.S. NBA championships. Indeed, Andrew Morris (2002: 10) has argued that China's heavily NBA-influenced basketball culture has become "an important mode of understanding and negotiating Chinese modernity" and desires because of the way Chinese basketball increasingly "reflects the language of globalisation." Like soccer, Chinese basketball went through major changes in the 1990s with the establishment of new professional leagues and greater access to and interest in U.S. basketball via television, newspapers, and other media.

Prior to the 1990s, basketball as a national and competitive sport enjoyed a higher level of popularity in China than soccer. Basketball was another sport introduced by foreign—principally American—missionaries at the end of the nineteenth century and established itself in the urban centers over subsequent decades, even being voted a "national pastime" in 1935 (Morris 2002: 13). In the early 1950s, both men's and women's national championships were established, and the sport drew the popular attention of all levels of society. In leading Chinese film director Xie Jin's 1957 film *Woman Basketball Player No. 5* the sport was even extolled as a symbol of revolutionary values of hard work, perseverance, and sportsmanship.

In the mid-1990s, the game underwent a new revolution. In 1995, the Chinese Basketball Association (CBA) set up its new professional league, followed the year after by the short-lived China New Basketball Alliance (CNBA), a commercial outfit backed by a Hong Kong company that only survived one season. The CBA, with its twelve-team first division and seventeen-team second division, became the main—and only national—men's Chinese basketball league, followed with varying degrees of enthusiasm around the country. Basketball players, formerly state employees like soccer players, started to be paid for by sponsorship deals arranged with major local or national companies. Subsequently, regional teams all took the names of their sponsors—the South China Hongyuan Tigers, Beijing Vanguard Olympian, Capital Steel Ducks, Zhejiang Wanma Cyclone, and Sichuan Blue Sword

Beer Pandas have all graced the first division of the CBA league.

The commercial success of basketball in China from the 1990s on, however, is not by any means limited to the popularity of the CBA league, which is variable. Perhaps even more than with soccer, Chinese basketball fans have at least one eye on what is happening overseas, and in the United States in particular. The big names for basketball fans in China in the late 1990s included stars like Michael Jordan, Shaquille O'Neal, and Patrick Ewing as much as any Chinese player. This changed in the early 2000s with the success of Chinese national team player, major product sponsor, and cult national hero Yao Ming. However, Yao Ming's success, apart from being an impressive basketball player, was massively enhanced by his being the first Chinese to play in the NBA. In this case, the measure of national Chinese success was being able to join Americans in, if not sometimes beat them at, their own game. In other words, China's basketball scene is totally embroiled with the "global" basketball scene—which effectively means the global marketing of U.S. basketball.

This global aspect to Chinese sports is also found in the way that basketball fans identify themselves with NBA stars. Andrew Morris (2002) argues that it is through the desire for Nike and other U.S. basketball products as well as aspirations to be like not only Yao Ming but Michael Jordan or Patrick Ewing that basketball culture in China is coming to reshape the popular cultural identity of millions of mainly young Chinese. Morris argues that the strongly individualistic elements of contemporary global basketball culture—which include the way that stars are marketed and present themselves—have found their way into Chinese basketball fandom, whether it be through the desire to be a unique hero like Michael Jordan or Dennis Rodman or through the desire to experience the personal exhilaration of scoring a "slam dunk" basket. Yet in understanding this kind of globalization of Chinese basketball culture it is also important to understand that Chinese fans, even when they aspire to being like major NBA stars or owning global brand products, are usually also engaging, in their own ways, with a negotiation of their own very Chinese identities. Indeed, as the case of Yao Ming shows, the point is generally to be successful, as a Chinese, *like* the top American stars, but not become one. Hence, Yao Ming's fame and popularity in China arises not simply from his being an NBA star, but from his being a real *Chinese* NBA star with the potential to pull domestic Chinese basketball up to what is widely recognized to be the highest global level of the sport.

What becomes clear from these discussions of both soccer and basketball is the degree to which the global context of sports in China is closely bound up with consumption and commercialism in recent years. China has also seen new manifestations of the consumption of global sports, particularly with increasingly closely followed spectator sports such as tennis, golf, and motor racing.

In 2004, for instance, Shanghai hosted China's first ever Formula 1 grand prix race at a brand-new purpose-built circuit with impressive facilities of the highest international standard. Motor racing has never been a major Chinese sport, and in 2005 there were no Chinese auto manufacturers or drivers or other participative presence in the sport, and yet tens of thousands of Chinese paid relatively large amounts of

Tiger Woods tees off during an exhibition match at the Mission Hills golf club in the southern Chinese city of Shenzhen on November 10, 2001. Woods was playing in China for the first time, with golf fever sweeping through the more affluent parts of the world's most populous country. (Corbis)

money to attend the races and personally become part of this global sporting consumption. Similarly, in the early 2000s, China started hosting more and more major international sporting events, from WTA tennis tournaments to international golf contests, with leading stars ranging from Roger Federer to Tiger Woods all starting to appear in Chinese competitions.

For once, however, it is possible to say that this is about more than simply commercial interests. The hosting of events like these in China is also about global recognition of China as an economic force, a political force, a contemporary modern nation with state-of-the-art facilities, and generally a major player on the global sporting, political, and economic scenes. As we will see, the epitome of this recognition and frame of mind will be exemplified in the Beijing 2008 Olympics. Nonetheless, although the global aspect of China's sporting landscape is increasingly important, it is also important to understand some international successes in relation to a national as much as a global context.

National Favorites

Perhaps the most obvious sport commonly associated with China is table tennis, which is probably also considered the Chinese national sport above all others. For one thing, it is a sport that the Chinese have dominated internationally for decades, producing countless world champions and Olympic gold medalists, including a clean sweep of five gold medals at the 2005 world championships. In this way, table tennis has long come to stand for Chinese international sporting excellence and to demonstrate the ability of the Chinese to compete and win at the highest international levels, going back before the time that Yao Ming and other contemporary Chinese sporting heroes were even born. It was also through a series of carefully arranged diplomatic table-tennis matches between China and the United States in the early 1970s that political rapprochement between the two ideological enemies was initially achieved, culminating in the restoration of diplomatic relations between the two countries in 1972.

Table tennis, however, offers an interesting counterexample to the commercial consumer culture associated with soccer or basketball. Certainly, China's table-tennis champions are household names. They are now also able to sign up for lucrative advertising deals. At the same time, however, table tennis is closely associated with national pride and success rather than individualistic sporting aspirations, and there is much less association, on the part of spectators, with global sporting corporations than there is with individual table-tennis champions and a history of national success in the sport.

Another sport in this class is volleyball—or, more precisely, women's volleyball. Particularly since the 1980s, when China's women's team won the four-yearly world championships in both 1982 and 1986 plus Olympic gold at Los Angeles in 1984 and a string of five consecutive World Cup titles, women's volleyball, like table tennis, took on the status of a national sport with a huge media and popular following. Winning Olympic gold in Athens in 2004 for the first time since 1984 and after a relatively lackluster period for the women's national team was therefore a hugely popular victory that was treated in China with a sense of enormous pride and satisfaction.

Women's volleyball is one of those sports in China that is able to conjure up strong patriotic feelings, even in times when China's sense of national identity is increasingly being questioned. This ability to arouse national feelings is in no small part due to the particular significance that the women's team's victories in the 1980s had for China as a newly emerging nation after the devastation of the Cultural Revolution period. Significantly, for instance, in the first of their 1980s world-level victories, China beat Japan, which had dominated women's volleyball for some time. The cultural resonances of this victory went far beyond simply beating the reigning champions, however. With China's history of bitter military conflict, suffering, and, as many would see it, humiliation at the hands of the Japanese in the twentieth century, and with Japan's runaway postwar economic success beshadowing China's less economically impressive achievements, this was symbolically a sweet victory indeed. It also resonated with the strong sense of optimism that went with China's open-door policy and nascent economic reforms. This was China declaring its new presence on the global stage before the country's more recent flirtation with commercial sporting globalization.

It is therefore possible to say that table tennis, women's volleyball, soccer, and

China's Lina Wang (left) spikes against Russia's Ekaterina Gamova (11), Irina Tebenikhina (2) and Marina Sheshenina (12) during their women's volleyball gold medal match at the Athens 2004 Olympic Games, August 28, 2004. (Corbis)

basketball are all Chinese national favorite, and enormously popular, sports. Yet they also clearly fall into different categories of significance ranging from the epitome of a globalizing consumer culture with basketball to the height of national, even nationalistic, pride embodied in women's volleyball. Falling somewhere between these two poles is the growing spectrum of Olympic sports at which China is coming to excel. In the early 1990s, Chinese women had some incredible successes in athletics, with six out of nine world championship gold medals in long-distance women's events going to Chinese athletes. Seven Chinese women then all broke world records in the 1,500, 3,000, and 10,000 meters at the Eighth National Games. However, these stunning achievements were soon clouded by accusations of drug use (Brownell 1995: 318–321), and though these were never quite proven, the phenomenal success did not last.

Nonetheless, China has seen its Olympic medals tally steadily rising in recent years, most notably in Sydney and Athens. These successes have produced new Chinese national heroes in a whole range of sports from diving and shooting to badminton. In the Athens 2004 Olympics, for instance,

China won six gold medals in diving, five in weightlifting, four in shooting, three in table tennis, three in badminton, two in athletics, two in tae kwon do, and one each in canoeing, gymnastics, judo, swimming, tennis, volleyball, and wrestling. This shows how particular strengths have developed in diving, weightlifting, and shooting in particular. All of these medalists were treated to a hero's welcome on their return to China, the entire games having been closely followed by the nation's media. They appeared in newspapers, on television chat shows, on radio, and in other media contexts. However, the popular cultural clamor that surrounded them was at least in part motivated by a sense of national anticipation. The Athens 2004 Olympics were the last summer games before the most important Olympic test for China that will come with its hosting of the summer games in Beijing in 2008.

The Beijing 2008 Olympics

The Beijing Olympics bid originally started back in the 1990s with China's attempt to secure the millennium games that ultimately went to Sydney, Australia, in 2000. On a September night in 1993, when the Sydney announcement was made, millions of Chinese dreams and expectations were shattered, but at the same time the seeds were sown for the subsequent clinching of the 2008 games in 2001. This has ensured that the Beijing Olympics will be about much more than the individual sporting competitions. They will once again draw together some of the themes of this chapter in relation to sports—spectatorship, consumption and commercialism, nationalism, and national pride.

The Beijing games will almost certainly draw some of the largest Chinese television audiences ever recorded. Even in the years before the games, they have been drawing widespread official, media, and popular attention. They are therefore expected to become one of the largest spectator events that China has ever seen. At the same time, like any other Olympics in recent times, the Beijing games will also be an enormous commercial spectacle, with hundreds of millions of dollars circulating in sponsorship and marketing deals (Polumbaum 2003). Perhaps the most important popular cultural significance of the games, however, will be as a measure of China's new international standing as a global economic, political, technological, and probably also sporting power.

The awarding of the 2008 Olympics to China was widely seen in the country as a move by the International Olympic Committee (IOC) to put right the error of 1993, which only went to heighten the sense of national pride and anticipation surrounding both the bid and eventually the preparations for the games. The Chinese authorities are keen for the games to demonstrate not only that China is capable of staging one of the largest and most prestigious sporting events in the world but that it can do so with style, in an environmentally friendly way, and with all the technological finesse that the most economically developed countries have come to expect.

As a media event, the Beijing games will be the largest, most complex, and most sophisticated sporting spectacle that the country has ever seen. The development of digital television in China is being planned around the games, the capital and other major cities have been setting up mobile television networks on buses and in taxis so that the games can be watched by people on the move, and third-generation technologies will bring event highlights to people's mobile phones. At the same time, China will be at the center of global media attention for months before, during, and after the games, making this a highly influential period for establishing understandings of China throughout the world—understandings that will remain for years to come.

The global aspects of the Beijing Olympics operate in a two-way street, however. It is not just the world that will be watching China as it takes another step onto the global cultural and sporting stage; Chinese people around the country will be reconceptualizing what it means to be Chinese, the role of China in the world, their relation to their own government, and their pride and nationalistic feelings associated with both the events and sporting success. At the same time, the Beijing Olympics not only will be watched but will be consumed in ways that extend far beyond attendance at sporting events or following them through the media. This could be through eating at fast-food restaurants sponsoring the games, buying products from computers to clothing produced by other sponsors, or simply wandering daily through the forest of advertising and other promotional images that will engulf China's streets at the time. In this sense, the Beijing Olympics will focus a broad range of popular cultural practices dealt with in different chapters of this volume, from media to consumption and sports, all on one concentrated set of sporting events in the summer of 2008.

Sports in Society

So far in this chapter, picking up on the discussion in the previous chapters, we have dealt more with the spectatorship and consumption aspects of sports in China than the participatory aspects. However, participation in sports is equally important, though often less visible and less glamorous, as one of the ways that sports features directly in people's everyday lives and in their social interactions.

The obvious place to start a discussion about sporting participation is with schools and education. As in other countries throughout the world, in China sports are considered an important feature of educational contexts, from primary schools to universities. In fact, pupils and students all across this educational spectrum are expected to participate in daily calisthenics. Sometimes as early as six o'clock in the morning, schools across the country resonate to the often crackly sound of energetic marches and other music to accompany sleepy children's morning exercises. In this sense, China's schools, even today, perpetuate the links between physical and mental fitness and between physical exercise and discipline that date back on one hand to the foreign missionaries of the nineteenth century and on the other hand the more militaristic and nationalistic periods of China's twentieth-century history, not to mention the CCP's notions of keeping the masses healthy and productive.

Sports are a compulsory feature of education in China and, as we have seen, this minimally involves daily physical exercises. It often also involves more, although the kind and nature of other school sports activities depends to a large degree on the financial situation of the school. At a basic level, most schools throughout the country have some kind of schoolyard or open space which doubles as a soccer field, an exercise ground, a basketball court, or

Beijing schoolchildren during morning exercise. Students of all ages are expected to participate in early morning exercises daily. (Corel)

simply a place for children to run around in. A volleyball net and some kind of basketball hoop are also standard features of most schools. Similarly, even modest schoolyards often feature concrete table-tennis tables. Wealthier schools in wealthier parts of the country are then more likely to enjoy better sports facilities for students—possibly a gym, indoor courts, and table-tennis tables.

There are also all levels of sports competitions for schools, with local, provincial, and national games organized as part of the state sporting structures. There are specialized sports schools of various different kinds for children of all ages that specialize in training particularly talented children while also ensuring they receive a basic standard education. The state sports schooling system is complex and bureaucratic, but basically schools fall into one of two categories: part-time or full-time. The former offer extra sports training for students outside their regular school hours, while the latter are boarding schools that offer a full curriculum of both sports training and regular classes, with the emphasis often on the training rather than the classes (for more detail on sports and education in China, see Brownell 1995: 197–208). As mentioned earlier in the chapter, the state sports schooling system was set up in 1955 and established a hierarchy of schools intended to propel the most talented athletes up to the national level where they would receive the highest standard of training and preparation for international competition. Consequently, sports became a matter of not only state discipline but the operation of the state. Top-level sporting performance was acknowledged as being important for the state, and sports training was openly sanctioned by it. All of this means that even in the later reform period, when state-sponsored cultivation of sports in society is being gradually replaced by more commercially motivated practices, there is a strongly established social and national importance attached to both participative and spectator sports.

Unsurprisingly, the emphasis on physical fitness and discipline also features strongly in China's armed forces, where rigorous regimes of physical exercise are a daily feature of soldiers', sailors', and airmen's lives. The military also participates in various national sporting competitions, with People's Liberation Army teams ranging across sports from soccer to basketball to shooting, gymnastics, and so on. Sports are also given an important position in the workplace in China, particularly in state-owned enterprises but also in others.

It is not unusual at any relatively large organization, whether it be a factory, newspaper offices, or a government department, to find some kind of sporting facilities provided for the use of employees. This is in some ways a holdover from the Maoist past when more military-style discipline, partly associated with sports, was a feature of everybody's daily lives. Consequently, the standard and state of repair of such workplace sports facilities varies enormously across the country depending on how recently they have been refurbished. However, in more financially successful enterprises—leading media organizations, successful factories, and government departments being good examples—new sporting facilities, such as a gym, a table-tennis hall, or basketball or badminton courts, can become welcome corporate perks for employees. The use of these facilities then often gives birth to competitive leagues among staff or even between enterprises and organizations. These kinds of sports in the workplace is no longer a feature of everybody's lives, and it is also a matter of personal choice whether employees take advantage of such facilities or not. Nonetheless, this is an indication of the social importance and value still attached to participative sports as a regular and accepted feature of people's working lives.

In addition to organized sports in educational or workplace contexts, participatory sports also include the various informal games played by people using work, school, or college facilities or other commercial facilities. Students are some of the most active informal sports participants in China. Within minutes of arriving at a university or college campus one can find informal games of soccer, basketball, table tennis, badminton, and tennis. On campuses with pools, swimming is also a very popular pastime with students often willing to get up for early morning swimming sessions. Even small and not necessarily wealthy colleges and universities usually also have at least one running track available to students, with basic outdoor gym equipment such as horizontal bars. Similarly, in schools one would usually expect to find children—particularly boys—playing soccer or some other ball game during their breaks.

Outside of schools and campuses, participation in sports inevitably becomes more restricted. Workplace sports facilities are important because they give people the chance to participate in sports with minimal organizational effort. Apart from workplace sports, there are basically two kinds of participatory sporting opportunities open to Chinese people: those that are free and those that are increasingly provided commercially. Both of these tend to be urban-based. Indeed, it is worth noting that China's peasants, apart from those who go into the military or who take up places in sporting schools, are usually too busy making a living and get so much physical exercise in the process that for many, sports are something to be enjoyed on television rather than in person.

Sports in terms of leisure activity outside of places of work or study have become increasingly commercialized in China over the last two decades. In the 1980s, this started on a modest scale with the gradual emergence of commercial table-tennis halls, snooker halls, roller-skating rinks, and other relatively simple sporting facilities—again, often located in parks. In the 1990s, however, the range of sporting activities available mushroomed.

In many of these cases, the boundary between sports and leisure activities starts to blur. For instance, some of these new sports activities, like ten-pin bowling, snooker, roller-skating, and white-water rafting, overlap with leisure activities, and some would say that these are not real sports. However, these have been accompanied by other more clearly recognized sports venues—such as driving ranges and shooting ranges—that have equally been treated as leisure venues. Going out to try one's hand at golf drives could be an alternative to going to a disco or ten-pin bowling for some. For others, it would be part of a serious effort to perfect one's strokes and improve golfing technique. Hence, Chinese commercial sports venues have often thrived as much on popular novelty and fun value as serious sportsmanship.

By the turn of the century, some commercial sports markets were starting to mature—golf presenting a good example. In the wealthier parts of the country such as Guangdong, Shanghai, and the area around Beijing, for instance, the early 2000s saw an explosion not only of driving ranges but full-blown golf courses. This was another sign of the internationalization and transnational development of Chinese sports, picking up on the popularity of the sport in nearby places like Taiwan and Japan and obviously at a greater distance the United States and Europe. Many new golf courses also involved Taiwanese,

A man skates on the frozen lake of the Summer Palace on the outskirts of Beijing. Once the imperial summer retreat, the palace and gardens are now a popular leisure location for local people in both the summer and winter alike. (Corbis)

Hong Kong, or overseas Chinese investment. However, the popularity of golf also reflected the maturing Chinese economy, the emergence of the country's relatively wealthy middle classes with time and disposable income to spare, and the development of China's business culture.

Some golf courses have developed as retreats for the rich, but many have also remained relatively affordable for those on reasonable professional wages. It is not only disposable income that has made the development of golf possible, however. It has also depended upon improvements in transport infrastructure and the availability of space. In the economically developed Pearl River Delta region of Guangdong Province near Hong Kong, for instance, golf courses are often situated in the countryside ten or more kilometers from the center of large cities. In the 1980s, even had people been able to afford it, these ventures could never have survived because few people would have been able to get to them. In the early 2000s, by contrast, the road network was much more highly developed, more people had motorcycles if not access to cars, and public transport was much quicker and more efficient. Hence, in the wealthier areas of the country, China is also seeing its countryside opened up to contemporary commercial consumer culture.

In terms of free sporting opportunities, China's parks are one of the main places that people go to exercise. Many college campus sports facilities such as running tracks or soccer pitches are also often accessible in practice to the general public. In northern China, where the winters are very cold, ice skating is a popular winter activity, with the lake in the park of the Summer Palace in Beijing being a famous and popular location for family skating. Early in the morning, across the country, it is also common to see groups of people—often relatively elderly—practicing tai chi (shadow boxing—see below) or other calisthenic exercises, with or without musical accompaniment. For older people, dancing—usually some variation on ballroom dancing—in parks can also be a popular form of exercise. In all of these cases, groups of friends or acquaintances simply get together, find a convenient location in a park—under a pavilion, for instance, if the weather may be bad—and spend half an hour or more going through various exercises or dances. It is also not uncommon to see younger people practicing martial arts in parks as a form of exercise. However, martial arts, in some ways, present a special case in terms of Chinese sports that deserves particular attention.

Martial Arts and Sports

Chinese martial arts (*wushu*) cover a wide range of activities, from the gentle morning tai chi exercises of old people in parks to various forms of healing and massage to fighting and kung fu films. What links all of these things together are conceptualizations of the body and energy. It is common in Western societies to see oriental martial arts such as judo, karate, and kung fu as forms of sport, on a par with boxing perhaps. However, their classification simply as "sports" in China is more complicated and problematic. The similarities between martial arts and Western conceptualizations of sports relate to the physical training that they entail, how sometimes they can be competitive, and how they are

Morning exercise in Shanghai, China. (Corel)

centered around the cultivation of the body to higher levels of physical attainment. Martial arts are also often practiced specifically as a form of physical exercise and discipline—in the military, for instance. Yet it is important also to acknowledge ways in which martial arts are less easily accommodated within the conventional "sporting" categories.

For instance, many martial arts—tai chi and Buddhist meditation exercises among them—are not competitive. They may involve an imagined, gestural opponent against whom attacks and defenses are imagined to be made, but there is usually no competition involved—no scoring system, no winner, no loser. At the same time, martial arts work upon the notion of enhancing the flow of energy—*qi*—throughout the body, and this controlled energy can then be deployed for a range of possible purposes, from healing massage to meditation to disabling an opponent. Consequently, martial arts have to be seen against a rather different backdrop of practices from those that inform Western sports and that incorporate traditional Chinese medicine, military strategy, artistic elegance, drama, and even forms of nationalism. Indeed, as two Chinese scholars put it, "*Wushu* is not only a kind of sport, but also a unique kind of physical culture" (Zhang & Tan 1994: 155).

Chinese martial arts have a long history stretching back thousands of years into ancient times, and it is beyond the scope of this book to reproduce all the detail and complexity of that long history. There are some key points to note, however. Anyone familiar with Chinese—usually Hong Kong—kung fu films will know that Chinese martial arts are divided into different forms and schools following different techniques or masters, usually ending with the character *quan*, meaning "fist," often translated as "boxing." The principal forms of Chinese martial arts include *Shaolinquan* (Shaolin

Chinese man practicing *taijiquan* in a Shanghai park. (Corel)

boxing), *taijiquan* (shadow boxing), *nanquan* (southern boxing), *changquan* (long boxing), *houquan* (monkey boxing), and *zuiquan* (drunken boxing) (see sidebar). These and other forms of *wushu* typically feature set movements and postures given descriptive and associative names such as "rising straight as a pine tree," "falling like a magpie," or "waiting like a lying cat," all of which are moves in the best-known *Shaolinquan* form. Different forms of martial arts are also based upon the principles of attack and defense against a real or imagined opponent, even if, as with shadow boxing or in theatre, the fighting involved is feigned or imagined.

With the growing popularity of Chinese martial arts around the world, there have been efforts to establish *wushu* as an international sport along the lines of other Asian martial arts, notably judo, karate, and tae kwon do. In 1991, the first World *Wushu* Championships attracted 600 participants to Beijing, and there has been some success, particularly in Asia, in establishing Chinese martial arts alongside other Asian martial arts as recognized sporting events. However, the importance of martial arts in understanding contemporary—and, in this case, also past—Chinese popular culture requires attention to them not simply as sports but as forms of a more broadly understood physical culture.

Martial Arts and Health

One of the main reasons why Chinese people practice martial arts is to maintain and improve their health. To understand this, it is important to acknowledge the close relationships between martial arts and traditional Chinese notions of the body, life, and medicine. These are complex issues that deserve greater attention than can be given here; however, the key principles can be grasped if you consider the core notion of *qi*—the energy of life and the universe—that is seen as flowing not only through and around the body but through the landscape. (The notion of *qi* is also at the heart of Chinese notions of geomancy or feng shui.)

Martial arts then involve the skill of controlling *qi* in the body and using it to enhance physical power and strength. *Qi* is also a key concept and feature of traditional Chinese medicine, where, in a nutshell, good health is seen to result from the appropriate management and balance of yin and yang (the feminine/dark/lunar and the masculine/bright/solar forces of the universe) in the body along with facilitating and maintaining the flow of *qi*. The link that *qi* helps us make between martial arts on one hand and traditional Chinese medicine on the other, therefore, also helps us understand how practicing martial arts might be understood to contribute to good health and curing or reducing the symptoms of illness and generally promote physical well-being.

Taijiquan in particular among martial arts is associated with enhancing health. Its concentration on gentle, steady bodily movement improves blood circulation to increase the supply of oxygen throughout the body and maintains the articulation of joints. At the same time, in Chinese terms, *taijiquan* enhances the flow of *qi* in the body and helps to clear bodily obstructions to this flow that can cause disease. *Taijiquan* is therefore credited with strengthening the heart and arteries, strengthening bones, enhancing the functioning of organs from the brain to the liver, and generally increasing the body's resistance to illness. In fact, *taijiquan* is considered not only a form of *wushu* but also a form of what is known as *qigong*—literally the control or mastery of *qi*. *Qigong* is a difficult notion or practice for some Westerners to understand. Like martial arts, which some would say are all forms of *qigong* anyway, there are many different ways of practicing it, ranging from forms of physically static meditation, in which one concentrates on the body's *qi* located in the *dantian* and then feels it circulate around the body, to more mobile exercise like *taijiquan* itself. Although *qigong* is associated by some with mystical powers, it is also most commonly associated with forms of healing and maintaining good health. *Qigong* therapeutic massage, for instance, puts concentrated *qi* to use for internal healing. It works through the accomplished master emitting *qi* through the hands and thereby enhancing the flow in the body of the ill person. *Qigong* is also potentially dangerous, however. Most practitioners will warn people starting to learn it to study with an established master, warning of the risks of physical or mental illness, even total madness, that can result from not practicing it properly.

Martial Arts and Popular Culture

The notion of *qi* is also important in combative martial arts and as a common feature of martial arts films and television series. When characters in kung fu films have extraordinary powers that enable them to fly through the air, to break rocks or solid objects, or to have mental power over other people through their martial arts, this is through their mastery of *qi*. Of course, the films (which have historically originated

Some of the Principal Forms of Wushu

Shaolinquan. "Shaolin boxing" takes its name from a monastery in the Song Shan mountains of Dengfeng County in Henan Province. Derived from the techniques developed by the monastery's monks from as early as the sixth century AD, it is the most famous and one of the oldest extant forms of Chinese martial arts. Apart from providing the core motif for countless kung fu films over the years, Shaolin boxing is also considered by many as constituting the core of Chinese martial arts techniques. Although it is practiced as a set of movements and postures executed virtually on the spot, the art of *Shaolinquan* is founded upon real fighting skills and can be used in real combat. As a style of martial arts it tends to rely upon quick, precise, fierce attacks but should also combine this vigor with appropriate grace and softness.

Taijiquan. Chinese shadow boxing, as it is sometimes known, or tai chi, is probably the most popular form of regularly practiced Chinese martial arts around the world. Not only popular with millions of Chinese in China and overseas, it has also attracted millions of other practitioners around the world who use it as a form of both physical exercise and meditation. The founder of the *taijiquan* form of martial arts is commonly said to be a former Ming dynasty (1368–1644) general named Chen Wangting, also from Henan Province, who developed it in his retirement. It is noted for its distinctive squatting position, with the legs half bent and used as a base while the body pivots around the waist. However, there are also many different styles of *taijiquan* that have been developed more recently, many of them in the nineteenth century, taking the name of their founding masters, such as the Yang style, the Chen style, and the Wu style. Perhaps the best known of these is the Yang style, named after Yang Luchan, who died in 1872, and his grandson Yang Chengfu, who systematized his grandfather's technique in subsequent decades. Yang-style *taijiquan* is noted for its simple-looking, clean, light, gently flowing movements. It is this style, which emphasizes complete relaxation and concentration of energy in the abdominal area (called *dantian* in Chinese) that is commonly taken up as a form of meditation in the West. The more classic Chen style is by contrast more

more from Hong Kong and Taiwan than the PRC, even if also popular there) have fantasized and exaggerated the powers of *qi* for cinematic effect. There is nonetheless an underlying rationale based upon notions from Chinese medicine and understandings of the body that similarly underpin more familiar practices such as acupuncture and Chinese therapeutic massage.

In martial arts, the control of *qi* is crucial. It is *qi* that enhances power and strength and from which fighting ability arises. In fact, although physical fitness and strength is important, Chinese martial arts concentrate equal if not more attention on the ability to control *qi*. It is for this reason that Chinese martial arts masters—real and fictional—are often not particularly large, muscular characters but slim and of relatively light build. Mastery of martial arts is attained through agility, strategy, and tactics and the control of *qi*, not muscle strength. Hence, understanding martial arts in Chinese popular culture requires understanding the background of how martial arts work.

energetic, with jumps and sudden bursts of energy incorporated into its routine. Some forms of *taijiquan* are also performed using fake swords and spears.

Nanquan. "Southern fist" is a form of martial arts that developed in a range of styles in southern China and also informed southern theatre traditions such as that of older-style Cantonese opera. As with other forms of *wushu, nanquan* has developed in a range of different styles—Mo, Li, Liu, and Hong, to name but a few—yet they share several distinctive features. *Nanquan* is a powerful form of martial arts that makes greater use of the upper torso and arms, with the legs and feet used as firm anchors, although some kicking and jumping is also involved. Southern boxing features quick, powerful strikes with explosions of energy and is said to be characterized by the saying "One shout changes the colour of the wind and clouds, and one strike splits the mountains" (Zhang & Tan 1994: 161).

Houquan. "Monkey boxing" is a form of martial arts based upon imitating the movements of the macaque monkey. Although there is textual evidence to suggest that forms of a monkey dance, combined with fighting movements, dates back to at least the second century BC, the form of martial art known now as *houquan* dates back to the Ming dynasty. It consists of thirty-six movement and posture routines that combine the imitation of a monkey's movements with various fighting stances and tactics from jumping, throwing, and evading to striking and kicking. The art is based around five core principles of physical and spiritual similarity, tactical concentration, lightness of foot, and agility. Practitioners of *houquan* extol its abilities to improve the body's metabolism and increase resistance to disease.

Zuiquan. "Drunken boxing" may be most familiar to fans of Jackie Chan, who popularized the form of martial arts through his *Drunken Master* films. Despite Chan's use of the technique to comic effect on the big screen, there are various established schools of drunken boxing. The art gets its name from its imitation of drunken actions, gestures, and movements, which in part act as a deception, disguising the power and agility of its fighting skills. These make particular use of rolling, somersaulting, falling, pouncing, and pushing movements. *Zuiquan* also deploys a range of evasive movements similar to the swaying and rolling movements of a drunk.

Martial arts feature in contemporary Chinese popular culture in a variety of ways. They are commonly practiced by individuals or groups, from students keen to perfect combative martial arts to retirees who practice *taijiquan* to improve their health. A martial art is usually learned by following the instruction of someone who is already expert in that particular tradition. With combative martial arts, this is often through one-on-one or small group tuition. *Taijiquan*, on the other hand, is often learned by joining one of the many large groups of early morning practitioners. Forms of *qigong* are also popular, and those who become experts start to take on students and, in some cases, if they are able, to offer therapeutic services.

In contemporary Chinese popular culture, however, we also have to deal with the mediated versions of martial arts, ranging from the knock-about comedies of Hong Kong film stars like Jackie Chan (*Drunken Master*, *Rumble in the Bronx*) or Stephen Chiau (*Shaolin Soccer*, *Kung Fu Hustle*) to the cultural nationalism that can be

Production still from *Shaolin Soccer*, 2002. (Miramax/Dimension Films/The Kobal Collection)

associated with Bruce Lee to everyday historical television dramas set in imperial times. Apart from *taijiquan* practitioners in parks, it is these media representations of martial arts that are the most visible, familiar, and commonly known form of popular Chinese martial arts culture.

Historical martial arts television dramas are very popular in China, as are mainland Chinese, Hong Kong, and Taiwanese films (see other chapters). These are often based upon or influenced by the massively popular historical martial arts novels of Hong Kong writer Jin Yong (see Hamm 2005). Since the international success of Taiwan director Ang Lee's *Crouching Tiger, Hidden Dragon* in 2000, there has also been a revival in martial arts films both in Hong Kong and in mainland China. Martial arts have also often found a particular place in films and television programs representing a form of cultural nationalism. In the 1970s, this was true of Hong Kong kung fu film star Bruce Lee, who having studied in the United States and experienced various forms of anti-Chinese racism developed a particular cultural pride in kung fu—a pride that comes through in his films, where often his enemy was the evil foreigner. More recently, martial arts have been used to represent Chinese cultural nationalism in other contexts.

In the early 1990s, the *Once Upon a Time in China* films by Hong Kong director Tsui Hark told the fictionalized story of a real character called Wong Feihong, who has appeared in countless guises in Hong Kong cinema, played by a range of actors from the 1950s through to the present. Wong was a scholar and doctor of traditional Chinese medicine who lived in Guangzhou. He was also an accomplished master of martial arts. In his various filmic representations, he has often been portrayed as a gallant figure protecting the poor and oppressed and fighting against injustice. In *Once Upon a Time in China*, which was a film made in the lead-up to the return of British colony Hong Kong to Chinese rule in 1997, Wong Feihong, played by Jet Li, becomes a figure standing up for the rights of ordinary Chinese people against the cruel acts of foreign colonialists. Although this was a Hong Kong film, and it is predominantly a film intended to entertain—something it does very well—*Once Upon a Time in China* also presents a strong nationalistic image through its martial arts hero. In this film, martial arts comes to stand for something quintessentially Chinese up against foreign modern technology and science.

Martial arts are therefore an important feature of contemporary Chinese popular culture that cut across different areas of interest from media representation to nationalism to physical health and fitness and international sports. They also make a clear link between sports, globalization, and forms of popular cultural media.

Conclusion

In this chapter, we have seen how sports and martial arts in China have a fundamental position in contemporary Chinese popular culture. This position also sits on various different trajectories as both Chinese sports and Chinese popular culture more generally transform themselves and move in new directions. Hence we find that sports, in many ways a relatively late Western import in the long view of Chinese history, has nonetheless established strong roots in Chinese social life. This has been enhanced in the last half a century by the importance attached to sports by the Chinese Communist Party. In the last ten years in particular, some of the most visible aspects of Chinese sports such as soccer, basketball, and Olympic sports have all come to the fore through commercialization, professionalization, and enhanced media exposure.

These sports have also played a key role in the globalization of Chinese sports and popular culture, with a range of complex multidirectional processes changing the face of Chinese sports consumption. On one hand, basketball or soccer in China is no longer simply about Chinese people playing basketball and soccer. It is equally about mediated spectatorship, foreign teams, players, and leagues, and a whole new set of ideals and values that come with them. On the other hand, China has started to supply some of its top athletes to basketball, soccer, and other sports leagues around the world.

Although sports in China increasingly have a global dimension, they also resonate with a set of more nationalistic sentiments. Sports in which China has excelled, such as table tennis, volleyball, and more recently shooting, diving, and weightlifting are still able to evoke a strong sense of national pride among the Chinese populace. Meanwhile, the Beijing 2008 Olympics will feed both the globalization of sports in China and patriotic sentiments. What is more, the Olympics will also ensure a high profile for sports in all national imaginings for some time to come. In fact, what we start to see with these various aspects of sports in China is that there are more and more opportunities for Chinese people to reconceptualize themselves and to re-identify themselves with different local, global, and national discourses, whether that be through the consumption of Nike sportswear, cheering on a Chinese athlete, or reading the Chinese soccer results in the newspaper. Sports are increasingly part of people's lives in one form or another—through participation, spectatorship, or media representation.

There are also good reasons to believe that the visibility and importance of sports within Chinese popular culture will be further enhanced in the future. We have already discussed the Olympics, but leaving that aside, we have only to remember China's changing media landscape. With the digitalization of television and radio, the country has already seen a proliferation of new channels and will see ever more specialized and niche channels in the future (see Chapter 3). With extra airtime to fill, and the popularity of sports both with Chinese consumers and with advertisers and sponsors, the increasing presence of sports on television and to a lesser degree also radio is inevitable. Similarly, in a country where media production is a sensitive political issue, yet there are strong market demands to fill newspapers with popular news, sports offer good copy for the country's increasingly commercial and popular newspapers. At the same time, there is good reason to believe that China's middle classes, with relatively high disposable income and reasonable amounts of leisure time, will continue to grow. This in itself will fuel ever greater interest in sports in terms of both participation and spectatorship, ensuring that more and more commercial sports facilities become available.

In addition to modern sports, we have also seen the equally if not more powerful ability of more traditional physical activities, in the form of martial arts, to mobilize people into participation. Martial arts are also no mere fad or fashion. We have seen how they are not simply a form of exercise or sport but actually relate closely to deeply rooted cultural conceptualizations of the body, life, and even the universe as a whole. This kind of fundamental understanding of life that conceptualizes the body in terms derived from traditional Chinese medicine will not be easily erased. On the contrary, we have seen how these values and understandings now also feature prominently in other areas of popular culture like television series, films, and books. Like sports, martial arts also tie Chinese popular culture into worlds of globalizing commercialism; at the same time, they are able to feed into a range of important national and cultural sentiments more than more modern sports can.

A to Z

Athletics. A core feature of the sports curriculum imported by Western missionaries in the nineteenth century, but until the 1980s not an area of sports at which China has particularly excelled. A series of women's long-distance running world records and world championship medals in the early 1990s put China on the athletics map, and with the Beijing 2008 Olympics approaching, athletics will feature ever more prominently in Chinese sporting priorities.

Basketball. One of China's favorite sports for decades, including in the pre-1949 Republican period. Basketball was also one of China's highest-profile team sports in the Mao period. Since the mid-1990s, basketball has become increasingly commercialized in China and intertwined with growing interest in the U.S. NBA championship, which is keenly watched by millions on television.

Breathing exercises. A common feature of many martial arts and *qigong* exercises. Breath control is used as a common method of meditation and relaxation.

Changquan. A form of martial arts. The term is used in two senses. First, it names a form of martial arts attributed to the Taizu Emperor of the Song dynasty that employs long exercise routines. More recently, the term has come to be used more generally for a range of different forms of martial arts (see Zhang & Tan 1994: 161).

Diving. One of the Olympic sports at which China has started to excel in recent years. At the Athens 2004 Olympics, the Chinese diving team came away with six gold medals, two silver medals, and one bronze medal.

Drugs. Following the phenomenal success of China's women long-distance runners in the early 1990s, there were widespread suspicions and accusations about drug use, particularly surrounding athletes close to coach Ma Junren, who attributed the success to herbal medicine and studying the movements of fast-running animals. The accusations were not proven, but subsequently Chinese women athletes have not on the whole performed at the same level. Na Xinghui did, however, win one of China's two track and field gold medals for the women's 10,000 meters at the Athens 2004 Olympics.

Education. Sports are a compulsory feature of regular Chinese education, but there is also a system of state-sponsored sports schools and institutes mirroring the different administrative levels of government designed to propel talented sportsmen and women to the top of their sport. The system was introduced in the 1950s following Soviet models but exists in a slightly modified form to the present day.

Golf. Golf is a rising sport in China both in terms of playing and in terms of watching, to some degree mirroring the growth of the country's middle classes. In the early 2000s, leading international golfers started coming to China for high-profile competitions, and in the more economically developed parts of the country golf courses started springing up to meet a growing consumer demand to play the game.

Houquan. A form of martial arts based upon imitating the movements, tactics, and agility of the macaque monkey. The form is said to date back to ancient times, when there are records of similar monkey-imitating dances being performed (see sidebar).

Kung fu. A common generic term used to refer to all kinds of Chinese martial arts. Although the term is perhaps more commonly used in the West than in China itself—where the term *wushu* is more common—it is a recognized phrase in China meaning "work," "skill," or "art." The phrase in Chinese has a much broader context of usage than just martial arts, however, and is known as a substitute for *wushu* principally through being reimported from English and its association with kung fu films.

Long-distance running. One of China's stronger areas of track and field athletics.

In the early 1990s in particular, China fielded a very strong team of world record breakers.

Military. The popularity and position of sports in China today, although attributable to a complex range of factors, owes a great deal to the development and modernization of the Chinese military from the late nineteenth century on. On one hand, reformers sought to improve military efficiency and discipline by introducing rigorous physical fitness regimes. On the other hand, society was increasingly encouraged through the twentieth century to adopt the same kinds of military-style sporting discipline as those used in the armed forces.

Nationalism. A recurring and important theme in relation to both Chinese sports and martial arts. For instance, nationalist movements in the late nineteenth and early twentieth centuries promoted sports as a way of improving military discipline and the health of the nation. In communist China, sports were also emphasized as a source of national pride. The Beijing 2008 Olympics are similarly surrounded by a whole of range of nationalist discourses. Martial arts films also raise issues of nationalism and national cultural identity.

Olympics. In 2008 Beijing will host the XXIXth Summer Olympic Games. The games were awarded in 2001 at the second attempt, Beijing having marginally failed in its attempt to secure the 2000 Olympics, which eventually went to Sydney, Australia.

Qigong. The control of *qi*, or "vital energy," in the body through forms of physical exercises and mediation. Martial arts are considered a form of *qigong*, the most commonly associated being *taijiquan*.

Shaolin. A small town in Henan Province, home to an ancient monastery dating back to at least the sixth century AD and where the Shaolin school of martial arts was originally developed. The monastery has consequently been lionized through countless kung fu films from Hong Kong, Taiwan, and mainland China and is still a place where students of martial arts can go to receive instruction.

Soccer. In post-Mao China, one of the most popular spectator sports and pastimes for young men, particularly students. China's participation in the 2002 Seoul-Tokyo World Cup Finals also propelled the popularity of the sport to the highest level. As well as following Chinese soccer, fans also enjoy major European league matches on television, and the world's largest clubs are now increasingly looking to cater to the commercial potential of the Chinese market.

Table tennis. The sport in which China has had the most consistent long-term success, having won countless world championships and Olympic medals over the last half century. Table tennis is the national sport, above others.

Taijiquan. Chinese shadow boxing—a form of martial arts often performed by elderly people as a means of maintaining good health.

Tiyu. The Chinese word most commonly used for "sport." *Ti*, "body," and *yu*, "cultivation," combine to give the sense of enhancing the body through physical exercise.

Volleyball. Women's volleyball is one of China's favorite national sports, particularly since the early 1980s when the Chinese team dominated the sport at an international level, winning a series of world championships, world cups, and Olympic gold medals.

Weightlifting. One of China's more recent Olympic sporting successes. In the Athens 2004 Olympics, the Chinese team came away with five gold and three silver medals.

Wen/Wu. The classical Chinese distinction between cultural and martial skills is referred to using these two terms. *Wen* refers to literature, writing, and written culture and points to the more intellectual and high artistic aspects of traditional scholarly achievement. *Wu*, by contrast, refers to issues related to war and fighting—military strategy and skills.

Wushu. Literally "martial arts." This is the standard Chinese phrase used to refer to the range of different martial arts from *taijiquan* to sword-fighting.

Zuiquan. Literally "drunken fist" or drunken boxing. A martial arts that is based upon poses, stances, tactics, and movements imitating those of someone who is drunk. The style came to recent media fame through the *Drunken Master* films made by Hong Kong kung fu film star Jackie Chan.

References and Further Reading

Brownell, S. E. 1994. "Sport." In D. Wu & P. D. Murphy. *Handbook of Chinese popular culture.* Westport, CT/London: Greenwood Press.

——— 1995. *Training the body for China: Sports in the moral order of the People's Republic.* Chicago: University of Chicago Press.

Dong, J. 2003. *Women, sport and society in modern China: Holding up more than half the sky.* London: Frank Cass.

English-Lueck, J. A. 1994. "Taijiquan and qigong." In D. Wu & P. D. Murphy. *Handbook of Chinese popular culture.* Westport, CT/London: Greenwood Press.

Hamm, J. C. 2005. *Paper swordsmen: Jin Yong and the modern Chinese martial arts novel.* Honolulu: University of Hawai'i Press.

Jones, R. 2004. "Football in the People's Republic of China." In W. Manzenreiter & J. Horne (eds.) *Football goes east: Business, culture and the people's game in China, Japan and South Korea.* London: Routledge.

Knuttgen, H. G., Ma, Q., & Wu, Z. 1990. *Sport in China.* Champaign, IL: Human Kinetics Books.

Manchester United. 2005. *http://www.manutd.com/home* last accessed November 25, 2005. Chinese Web site found at: *http://www.manunited.com.cn/zh_cn/.*

Morris, A. 2002. "'I believe you can fly': Basketball culture in postsocialist China." In P. Link, R. P. Madsen, and P. G. Pickowicz (eds.) *Popular China: Unofficial culture in a globalizing society.* Lanham, MD: Rowman & Littlefield Publishers Inc.

——— 2004. *Marrow of the nation: A history of sport and physical culture in Republican China.* Berkeley, CA: University of California Press.

Polumbaum, J. 2003. "Capturing the flame: Aspirations and representations of Beijing's 2008 Olympics." In C. C. Lee. *Chinese media, global contexts.* London: RoutledgeCurzon.

Riordan, J. & Jones, R. (eds.) 1999. *Sport and physical education in China.* London: E & F Spon.

Tan, H. 2004. "Football 'hooligans' and football supporters' culture in China." In W. Manzenreiter & J. Horne (eds.) *Football goes east: Business, culture and the people's game in China, Japan and South Korea.* London: Routledge.

Wang, G. 2000. "Cultivating friendship through bowling in Shenzhen." In D. S. Davis (ed.) *The consumer revolution in urban China.* Berkeley, CA: University of California Press.

Zhang W. & Tan X. 1994. "Wushu." In D. Wu & P. D. Murphy. *Handbook of Chinese popular culture.* Westport, CT/London: Greenwood Press.

12

Theatre and Music: Setting the Scene

The topics of theatre and music in contemporary Chinese popular culture touch upon many issues that we have already dealt with in other chapters. For instance, Chinese martial arts have played a prominent role in Chinese theatrical performance from traditional theatre to kung fu movies. Similarly, both music and theatre figure prominently in China's contemporary consumer society, leisure, and entertainment scenes—Chinese consumers purchase music CDs and tickets for rock concerts, Beijing opera, or other musical and dramatic performances. Meanwhile, like other arts and popular cultural forms, theatre and music were subject to total politicization in the Mao period but have gradually seen political influence decline and commercial forces take over during the two and a half decades of reform in the country.

Despite these similarities and connections with other areas of contemporary popular culture, theatre and music importantly also have their own particular characteristics and contexts. For instance, unlike cinema, television, radio, or other contemporary media that we have dealt with, theatre has a history that can be traced back centuries. Popular music, meanwhile, covers a range of different forms of performance, from traditional ritual wedding and funeral processions to Hong Kong "Cantopop" and forms of Chinese heavy metal developed with largely Western-derived themes and influences. In these various ways, theatre and music also therefore nicely highlight the juxtaposition of the old and the new—the contemporary and the traditional—in contemporary Chinese popular culture, which also serves to remind us of the importance of understanding historical contexts of and attitudes toward theatre and music in China.

For instance, theatre and music, from the imperial past to the present, have been associated in different ways with immorality, rebellion, and transgression. It is widely known, for example, that theatrical performers in Imperial China were among the few categories of people forbidden from participating in the imperial examinations, which were otherwise open to almost everyone else regardless of wealth, family background, or status. This low assessment of actors' moral standing continued into the Republican period, in the first half of the twentieth century, and is largely explained by the fact that, despite the popularity of their performances, the actors themselves were regarded as being immoral—through associations with prostitution, in some cases homosexuality, and sexual promiscuity with patrons' wives and concubines in particular. Actors have also been involved in important political uprisings, most notably the Taiping Rebellion, led by a well-known Cantonese opera performer in 1850 and whose eventual suppression led to the banning of Cantonese opera performances. In the late Imperial period, theatre performances were increasingly associated with criminality and anti-Confucian attitudes (see, e.g., Mackerras 1975: 92, 96, 106). More recently, the music of one of China's favorite rock stars of the 1980s, Cui Jian, became associated with the 1989 student protests and democracy movement that culminated in the tragedy of June 4. In the 1990s and 2000s, various kinds of rock and pop music have come to offer diversion or distraction to China's urban youth in particular and alternative lifestyles for cliques of socially disaffected youngsters. This was most aptly revealed in Zhang Yuan's early Sixth Generation film *Beijing Bastards* dealing with the lives and troubles of a group of young people centered around a Beijing rock band (see Chapter 7).

However, it is too simplistic to reduce popular music to the cliché of being resistive counterculture. Particularly in China, some of the common Western stereotypes about popular music and subversion take on a rather different character. For instance, China's contemporary rock music has been linked as much to the country's Maoist past as to emulating the West, even if there is also clearly Western inspiration involved (see, e.g., Huot 2000: 154–156). At the same time, some of the most popularly sung karaoke hits are old "revolutionary" favorites from the Mao period such as "The East Is Red" (itself a politically refashioned, originally bawdy folk song). We might also note that China's national anthem was appropriated from the soundtrack of a popular 1940s film. In a bizarre twist of contemporary nostalgia, these "revolutionary" songs that heralded and accompanied the complete transformation of a socioeconomic system have become the new "traditional classics" sung in the now very unrevolutionary context of capitalistic contemporary China. Many scholars of Chinese theatre have noted less the rebellious associations of traditional theatre than its relation to the perpetuation of Chinese cultural attitudes, standards, and values (see, e.g., Ward 1985; Yung 1989). From this array of at times apparently contradictory observations, we can already see that understanding theatre and music in contemporary Chinese popular culture is a relatively complex issue.

Over the next two chapters we will cover three broad areas of music and theatre: what is usually called "traditional" music and theatre, from Beijing opera to ritual processions; revolutionary or Mao period music and theatre; and more modern, often somehow Western-influenced, musical and theatrical forms ranging from pop and rock music to avant-garde theatre. These three areas may seem to map a historical progression from the traditional past to the modern present via a revolutionary interlude; however, as we have already seen, these three eras at times tend to blur into one another and be closely interrelated—traditional Chinese theatrical forms can influence cinema, revolutionary songs can become modern classics, the most valued revolutionary stage operas owed much to traditional theatrical forms as well as Western ballet and opera, and many a pop song is a reworking of either a revolutionary or a traditional folk song. What is more, all of these forms of popular music and theatre still feature in and constitute the contemporary Chinese popular cultural landscape. Traditional music did not disappear with the advent of the People's Republic, nor even with the Cultural Revolution; nor did revolutionary music die with Mao. At the same time, we might also remember that in cities with strong Western influences, such as Shanghai, there is a history of Western popular music, notably jazz for instance, being part of the popular cultural scene going back as far as a century.

Even though the Mao period ended three decades ago, its effects and influences on contemporary Chinese cultural production are still clear and in some ways clearer than ever in relation to music and theatre. Under Mao, as we saw in relation to cinema, all artistic and cultural production was politicized and after 1949 was nationalized. As mentioned in Chapter 7, Mao's 1942 Talks to the Yan'an Forum on Literature and Art outlined the aesthetic principles that were to underpin all artistic production in the following decades. In these talks, Mao repudiated the conception that art could be simply for art's sake and stipulated that all art and literature should serve educational and ideological purposes to unveil social inequalities, exploitation, and the unjust operation of class in society. In terms of music and theatre, this meant that songs, plays, and all kinds of theatrical performance were to carry a political message and support the work of the Communist Party. Mao also outlined how artists of all kinds needed to widen their audiences. Art was not to be elitist or produced for and appreciated by only the rich or educated, but should be for everyone—the "masses." Consequently, the Party devoted considerable attention to collecting folk songs, for instance, so that art could be seen to come from the people and subsequently be produced for the people in terms and forms that they could easily relate to. After 1949, all musical and theatrical groups therefore came under the jurisdiction of the state; musicians, actors, and actresses all became state employees and operated according to politically defined objectives. The politicization of theatrical performance reached its apogee in the Cultural Revolution period. After an initial period in which there was no artistic production at all, in the later Cultural Revolution period a very limited selection of model dramas were approved for theatrical performance. The emphasis at this time was simple, reductionist political messages that portrayed good and evil—defined in terms of class enemies and socialist heroes—in stark terms.

In the post-Mao period, the structures of artistic production were initially affected little by economic reform, even if there was some almost immediate relaxation of political imperatives, pressures, and limitations. Toward the end of the 1980s and into the 1990s, however, troupes of performers were increasingly encouraged to support themselves financially, to form performers' cooperatives, and to generally become less dependent—financially at least—upon the state. Even in the post-Mao period, though, the state system of artistic production left its legacy. Indeed, even though from the 1990s onward, theatre troupes were increasingly dependent upon raising their own revenues commercially, the state system has remained, and performance artists of different kinds have largely remained state employees. Furthermore, even though many people tired of the limited, politicized artistic output of the Cultural Revolution years, increasingly from the 1990s onward there was a certain nostalgia for old songs and plays, particularly among the generations that lived through the Mao period. For these reasons, in order to understand many aspects of the contemporary musical and theatrical scenes, it is still important to consider the influence, perpetuation, and transformation of the past in the present.

Also important to understanding music and theatre in contemporary China is the increasingly transnational and international nature of China's popular cultural landscape. In terms of popular music in particular, there was a strong influence from Hong Kong and Taiwan when, relatively early in the 1980s, pirated tapes of Hong Kong and Taiwanese pop music started circulating widely in mainland China. This music had an immediate cultural advantage over Western and other foreign pop music because it was modern and attractively "foreign" yet understandable and accessible because it was sung in Chinese. At the same time, Chinese bands were starting to experiment with new freedoms and drew inspiration from both Hong Kong and Taiwanese artists as well as foreign bands. Indeed, young Chinese people in particular were also keen to learn more about overseas pop and rock music while discotheques became an ever more popular part of the leisure and entertainment scene (see Chapters 9 and 10). By the 1990s and early 2000s, Chinese artists were themselves recording on international record labels in China, Hong Kong, and Taiwan. As part of China's agreement to join the World Trade Organization (WTO) in the early 2000s, the retail of audio-visual products in China was gradually opened up to foreign participation from 2002 onward, attracting interest from the leading global recording and distribution companies such as Sony and Warner Music.

The following two chapters therefore face a wide spectrum of issues and practices ranging from traditional theatre and music to transnational pop music, even if there are inevitably limitations on what can be covered in such a relatively short space. Chapter 13 will offer an overview of some of the principal theatrical forms in contemporary China. It will introduce traditional Chinese theatre, including its historical background, from imperial times to the People's Republic, and contemporary social, economic, and political contexts. One of the problems when dealing with traditional Chinese theatre, however, is that it actually requires attention to a whole range of different, even if often related, regional theatre traditions. It would be impossible to deal with them all; however, one of these regional forms—Beijing opera—not only is usually thought of as the national traditional theatrical form but offers a useful example of some basic principles and practices such as the use of role types, set theatrical pieces, singing, martial arts, and so on found in many other Chinese theatres. To supplement the account of Beijing opera, we will also look at some of the similarities and differences found in Cantonese opera, which has adapted much more than Beijing opera over the last hundred years to follow other theatrical as well as cinematic trends and fashions. The chapter will also cover modern spoken drama, avant-garde theatre, and other forms of performance art in contemporary China.

Chapter 14 will then focus more specifically on the role that music plays in contemporary Chinese popular culture. Although a significant portion of the chapter will deal with the rise of pop and rock music in China since the beginning of the reform period, it will also cover other forms of "popular" music including traditional ritual music and revolutionary songs. This requires thinking about the various different contexts in which popular music is performed, from discos to wedding and funeral processions to karaoke bars.

References and Further Reading

Huot, C. 2000. *China's new cultural scene: A handbook of changes.* Durham, NC: Duke University Press.

Mackerras, C. P. 1975. *The Chinese theatre in modern times: From 1840 to the present day.* London: Thames & Hudson.

Ward, B. 1985. "Regional operas and their audiences: Evidence from Hong Kong." In D. Johnson, A. J. Nathan, & E. S. Rawski (eds.) *Popular culture in Late Imperial China.* Berkeley, CA: University of California.

Yung, B. 1989. *Cantonese opera: Performance as creative process.* Cambridge: Cambridge University Press.

13

Theatre and Performance

The prominence of theatre and performance in the overall Chinese popular cultural landscape has diminished over the last century. Its importance and significance in understanding that landscape has also been transformed over that time and in some ways has also been diminished. However, theatre is still an important feature of China's popular cultural scene, both in terms of performances themselves of various different kinds and in terms of the influence and relationships that theatre has with other forms of cultural and media production. For instance, the kung fu genres, with which China's television audiences and viewers of Chinese films in China and around the world are very familiar, owe much to traditional Chinese theatre which itself incorporates the choreographed display of martial arts skills and aesthetics into the performance of a narrative. There has also been a long-standing relationship between Chinese cinema and modern spoken drama, which from the first part of the twentieth century was often considered by intellectuals as the primary form of socialist realist performance, of which film was derivative (see also Chapter 7). In this chapter, we will therefore introduce the main forms of theatre and performance that feature and have featured prominently in China's popular cultural landscape.

Theatre and performance are broad categories that incorporate a wide range of different activities. Here we will focus principally on traditional theatre, in all of its regional forms and variations but most notably Beijing opera and then also modern Western-style spoken drama and revolutionary opera. Spoken drama ranges from social realist drama of the first half of the twentieth century through socialist realism in the 1950s, 1960s, and 1970s to avant-garde experimentalist theatre of the post-Mao reform period. Somewhere between socialist realist theatre and Beijing opera, with imported influences from Western-style opera and ballet, we then find the revolutionary model operas of the 1960s—which for a short time in the Cultural Revolution were the only permitted form of theatrical performance in the country.

A member of a Chinese opera troupe. Though interest in the opera has waned in recent times, the art form remains important in Chinese culture. (Corel)

The Chinese binome for modern, Western-style drama is *huaju*, "spoken drama," a term which betrays some of the fundamental differences between spoken drama and classical Chinese drama, which is often referred to in English as "opera"—Beijing opera, Chinese opera, Sichuan opera, and so on. Although there are dangers in using the term "opera" in the Chinese context, where the conventions and practices of music, performance, and acting are so utterly different from their Western namesake, the word "opera" does nonetheless have some advantages in reference to Chinese theatre, compared to alternatives such as "drama." The Chinese term *huaju* highlights one of the fundamental differences between modern Western-style drama and traditional Chinese theatre: It is spoken—and only spoken. There is of course speaking in traditional Chinese theatre also. However, all forms of traditional Chinese theatre also incorporate music—even if only percussion—and singing, usually also in conjunction with some form of choreographed martial arts. The music and the singing are indispensable features of classic Chinese theatre, as in Western opera. Similarly, in Western opera, for an opera aficionado the point of watching a performance is likely to be to enjoy the music and to see how well the production is performed, rather than the story, text, or script of the opera. This is quite different from a conventional Western play, where the story as well as the quality of the acting is usually of fundamental importance. With Chinese "opera," the narrative is secondary and the appreciation of a performance is generally focused not on what happens in the story but on the actors, their singing, acting, and movement or comical skills, and how well they complement each other in performance. The script of the opera is important for how it provides opportunities for performers to demonstrate their skills, not for the significance of the plot—which may be well known to audiences.

Another important contrast between modern spoken drama—which did not exist in China until it was imported at the beginning of the twentieth century—and forms of traditional Chinese theatre is the matter of realism. As we will see below, realism, as with cinema, is a fundamentally important concept in relation to politically motivated stage drama. The fundamental principles of social realist literature and drama and later more dogmatic socialist

Beijing opera is usually regarded as the national theatrical performance genre in China. (Corel)

realist art forms were based upon the idea of making audiences aware of social injustices, exploitation, and class contradictions in society through their realistic presentation in artistic forms. Traditional Chinese theatre, by contrast, relies little, if at all, on realistic representation but is founded upon systems of stylistic movement and gesture, make-up, costumes, voices, and actions. Similarly, historical accuracy or realism is rarely even considered in traditional Chinese theatrical performances.

Traditional Theatre

Historical Background

Chinese traditional theatre performers are often referred to collectively as the children of the Pear Garden, recalling one of the historical heydays of Chinese drama in the Tang Dynasty (AD 618–907). The Tang emperor Ming Huang (AD 712–756) was one of the most enthusiastic imperial patrons of Chinese theatrical performance and supported several theatre schools around the capital Chang An in western China, near the present city of Xi'an. The most famous of these schools was called the Pear Garden, a name which has continued to be associated with drama through the centuries. However, the history of theatrical performance in China goes back further than the Tang Dynasty, with references to acting incorporating music and dance of different kinds appearing in ancient classical Chinese texts going back more than two thousand years.

The roots of contemporary Chinese "traditional" theatre are nonetheless usually traced back to the Yuan dynasty

A Chinese opera performer deploying sylized movements. These are a key feature of Chinese theatrical performance and are used to indicate standard actions or emotions. (Corel)

(AD 1271–1368), from which time there are still existing written scripts or plot outlines of performed dramas. It was also in the Yuan dynasty that two kinds of drama—called *zaju* and *nanxi*—flourished and became popular in northern and southern China, respectively. These were the antecedents of three other regional opera forms—*yiyang qiang*, *bangzi qiang*, and *kunqu*—that developed in the subsequent Ming dynasty (1368–1644) and which along with the *erhuang* and *xipi* forms (often thought of together as *pihuang*) that developed in the early Qing dynasty (1644–1911) constituted the foundation for many contemporary forms of traditional theatre including Beijing opera, which is usually regarded as the national theatrical performance genre. However, it has to be remembered that contemporary genres of traditional theatre are generally hybrid variations of these earlier forms of drama and performances today may be very different from those just 100 years ago, let alone 700 or 800 years ago.

Even this very brief historical overview of Chinese theatre, however, draws our attention to two key issues in understanding traditional Chinese theatre. First, there are different kinds of musical forms upon which different genres of theatre have been based. Second, there are countless regional forms of theatre that may differ from each other in terms of music, language, or dialect and performance traditions. Therefore, when people refer to Beijing opera as "traditional Chinese theatre," they are actually referring to one form of traditional regional theatre among many that has come to represent the country's cultural performance tradition but is not truly "national" in either its origins or its strength of popularity. Even if there are Beijing opera troupes and aficionados situated around the country, it is still most strongly rooted—and popularly appreciated—in the north, around Beijing. In other parts of the country, many traditional theatre fans will like Beijing opera. Many may also regard it as a higher or more superior or refined form of traditional theatre than other regional theatre. However, in various parts of the country one will also a find a strong, if sometimes small, following—particularly among the older generations—for regional theatrical genres such as Shanghai or Zhejiang Yue opera, Cantonese opera, Sichuan opera, Chaozhou opera, and so on.

The Communist Revolution in China was, however, to have an important impact upon traditional theatre troupes and performances. From 1949 onward, traditional theatre production, like all other artistic production, had to serve a new social and political function in line with Mao's views on art outlined in Yan'an in 1942 (see Chapters 7 and 12). However, it is important to note that the coming to power of the communists in China was not in itself detrimental to traditional Chinese theatre. There is a common misunderstanding in the West that communism in China meant the end of all traditional cultural production. This is not the case. As we will see, the Cultural Revolution, in 1966, did seriously challenge traditional theatre and other artistic production. However, the 1950s and early 1960s were not necessarily bad times for Chinese theatre troupes.

For one thing, the Chinese Communist Party actually took a favorable attitude toward theatre—both traditional and spoken drama. For them, there were clearly "feudal" elements of traditional theatre that needed to be expunged, but fundamentally this was a popular—in the sense of coming from and being enjoyed by the ordinary people—form of entertainment and offered important propaganda opportunities. At the same time, the 1950s brought relative peace and social, economic, and political stability to the whole of China in a way that had not been enjoyed for decades. This offered a much more favorable environment for the development of the arts, even with their new political masters, than did the chaos, the poverty, and the social, economic, and political disruption that had characterized the previous decades of war and political strife. Indeed, the 1950s became a period of growth for the arts, including theatre, and the number of theatre troupes rose significantly.

Nonetheless, the communist takeover did mean change. Most directly, it meant the nationalization of China's theatre troupes, even if, as Colin Mackerras points out, this was at first a gradual and cautiously approached process, and total nationalization of theatre troupes was not complete until the mid-1960s (Mackerras 1975: 163–164). Hence, theatre troupes gradually became state work units and the actors employees of the state. Much of this process was complete by the end of 1956, but some private impresarios were allowed to continue operating up until the Cultural Revolution.

The other major change that the Communist Revolution brought to traditional Chinese theatre was in terms of the content of plays. From 1949 onward, the Chinese authorities subjected theatre of all kinds to revision and supervision by a complex array of committees whose fundamental task was ultimately to ensure that all "feudal" elements that could be considered contrary to Party policy or opinion or that might be considered to promote, endorse, or reinstate capitalist or feudal ideologies were removed from opera scripts.

This sounds like a drastic measure, particularly considering that the standard diet of traditional opera stories was entirely focused upon kings, emperors, imperial officials, and Confucian scholars and largely operated around themes of Confucian morality and propriety. Many operas, of course, were blacklisted for what was considered their undesirable ideological content, and from the early 1950s on many operas were no longer performed. However, there was still a good number of traditional operas that were not banned, which were performed up until the early 1960s. In actual fact, the effect on traditional theatre in this period was relatively mild. For one thing, traditional opera stories and characters were not all considered to be bad. There was a host of heroes and heroines who could easily be construed as patriotic and often also stood up for or highlighted the need for justice for the people. At the same time, the traditional theatre was popular with the ordinary working people of China, and consequently there was real political will to both support and exploit it as a form of propaganda art. However, the fact that the Communists chose to concentrate their attention on the *texts* of traditional operas—that is, the ideological content of the stories—meant that most of the fundamentally important features of traditional theatre, such as practices of performance, use of gestures, singing and acting styles, costumes, martial arts, acrobatics, and so on, were left relatively untouched.

Consequently, because the story in much traditional Chinese theatre is often of secondary importance, the effects of censoring opera stories could also often be of secondary importance. The story, in Chinese opera, is important as a means of justifying the action and giving actors the chance to perform what they do best—a tragic story offers an actor the chance to sing a sad aria, a war offers the chance for acrobatics and choreographed martial arts. However, traditional theatre audiences, even if they pay attention to the story, are not likely to judge, appreciate, or enjoy a performance on the basis of the story. Experienced traditional theatre audiences will be looking for how well the actors perform—how good their singing, their martial arts, and their gestures and actions are. They will be looking at actors' stage presence, looking at how well actors perform together, listening to how well the music is performed, and paying attention to the atmosphere created by the performance. These are all fundamental features of traditional opera appreciation, but they can also be relatively little affected by the editing out or alteration of some feature of the story line considered politically incorrect.

The political problems for traditional Chinese theatre really started arising in the years leading up to the start of the Cultural Revolution in 1966. From 1963 on, Mao's wife, Jiang Qing, gradually took ever greater control over the performing arts. The political line taken from Mao's Yan'an speeches became ever more hard-line and ever more focused on propaganda and ideological correctness rather than paying attention to what "the masses" wanted. Consequently, what had previously been tolerated in terms of content now became unacceptable. More and more traditional operas were banned, such that by the time of the outbreak of the Cultural Revolution there were already very few still being performed. Over the chaos of the next few years, only a limited selection of modern revolutionary "model" operas were allowed to be performed, and many actors suffered humiliation, arrest, imprisonment, and beatings at the hands of Mao's youthful Red Guards. After 1968, there were moves to revive some traditional opera performances, but it was not really until later, after Mao's death and the fall of the Gang of Four, that the political pressure on traditional theatre gradually started to ease.

The post-Mao era saw a revival of fortunes for traditional opera troupes. They enjoyed greater artistic freedom and were increasingly able to perform without having to worry excessively about the possible political interpretations of traditional stories and operas. However, this new era also brought traditional Chinese theatre performers a whole new range of challenges. These principally centered around the development of the media and communications technologies on one hand and the commercialization of art, leisure, and entertainment on the other. Hence, by the second decade of reform many troupes were having to try to fund themselves, often through rural festive performances, while also seeing their audiences increasingly distracted by television, cinema, new consumer and leisure activities, and later also the Internet.

Common Features of Traditional Chinese Theatres

Although there are many regional forms of drama and they vary considerably, there are several key features that can be identified in many of them. These include the use of role types, set-piece actions and movement sequences, musical instruments, limited use of props, and scenery and costumes.

Role Types

The use of role types is common in most forms of traditional Chinese theatre and in general distinguishes Chinese theatrical forms from Western ones. Perhaps the nearest that Western theatre gets to Chinese role types is in pantomime or the Italian classical *commedia dell'arte* theatre, where certain kinds of characters (like a pantomime dame) can be identified across different productions. In China, however, role types are fundamental. The number of role types varies from one form of regional theatre to another and also depends upon the number of subcategorizations that one counts. The system of operation of role types may also vary from one form of theatre to another. Below, we will consider the differences between Beijing and Cantonese opera, for instance. However, basically the use of role types involves the categorization of characters in dramas into leading and secondary male role characters, leading and secondary female role characters, old men and women characters, soldiers, officials, and so on. Although actors may eventually become adept at two or more different role types (depending on their skill and also the particular kind of opera involved), they will always first learn and subsequently specialize in performing one principal role type. Hence, a bearded male role character actor will always play bearded male role characters—often imperial officials and advisers, for instance. Each role type also has its own repertoire of ways of singing, actions, set pieces, movements, gestures, and voices.

Actions and Movements

In addition to role types, traditional Chinese drama also features set-piece actions and stylized sequences of movements. These formulaic actions and movements range from simple gestures (such as of welcome, surprise, or shock) to relatively simple events (such as entering or leaving a room or getting on or off an imagined horse) to fairly long and complex series of movements used for commonly recurring actions or events (such as ceremonial entrances and exits, contemplation of a perplexing or worrying issue, or forms of ceremonial meeting, fighting, or journeying). At one time, all traditional Chinese drama was performed without scripts on the basis of no more than a plot outline possibly accompanied by a list of character entrances and exits. All the rest was left to a combination of improvisation and set-piece actions and movements. Using special codes and signs, actors could communicate to each other and the accompanying musicians what it was they were about to do. Historically, therefore, set-piece actions are among the fundamental tools and building blocks that enabled actors to perform. In contemporary performances, there is much greater use of detailed scripts and rehearsed scenes, but performing these still depends on the ability to be able to execute set-piece actions and movements. What is more, audience appreciation of a performance, and of actors and actresses as performers, involves assessment and judgment of how well these actions and movements are executed.

Musical Instruments

Which musical instruments are used in traditional Chinese opera performances also varies to some degree from one form of opera to another. However, there are basically three types: percussion, string, and wind. For many kinds of regional opera, certain percussion and string instruments are the most important, with wind instruments tending to have an important but supplementary role. The key percussion instruments are drums, clappers, woodblocks, gongs, and cymbals. In some regional operas, such as Cantonese opera, the main percussionist leads the group of musicians—a little like the conductor of a Western orchestra—with rhythms played on the main woodblocks and drums. It is this percussionist's responsibility to watch the actors and coordinate the music with the actions of the drama. For any kind of *pihuang*-based regional opera, including Beijing and Cantonese operas, there is also an important melodic role given to one or other type of bowed fiddle, usually a *huqin* or an *erhu.* These are instruments like two-stringed violins without fingerboards and with much smaller but deeper round or hexagonal wooden sound boxes covered with snakeskin. Some regional operas also deploy plucked lute-like instruments such as the *pipa* or the *yueqin.* Wind instruments principally include different forms of transversal or end-blown flutes such as the *tizi* or *xiao* and double-reeded oboe-like instruments such as the harsh and very loud *suona* used to enhance ceremonial occasions and imperial entrances.

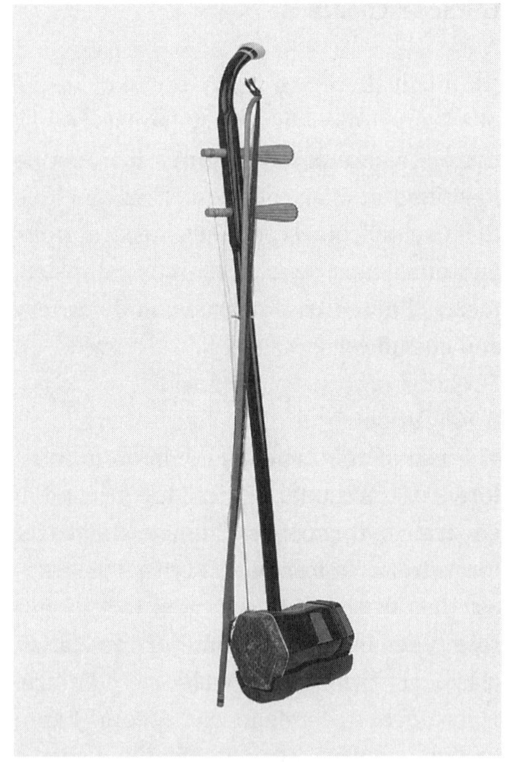

An *erhu*, a Chinese bowed, two-stringed instrument similar to a violin. (iStockPhoto.com)

Scenery and Costumes

The stage for traditional Chinese opera is often very simple. Historically, it deployed little more than a plain curtain backdrop with possibly a couple of chairs as stage props. This is also why set-piece actions and movements are so important in Chinese theatre for understanding what is going on. Without scenery or props to indicate doors, walls, sedan chairs, or horses, for instance, it is important to follow actors' gestures to understand fairly fundamental and basic issues such as whether people on the stage are in the same room or not and whether they are able to hear each other. In the twentieth century, some forms of regional opera—Cantonese opera probably more than any other—started breaking with convention and using painted scenery, more sophisticated and realistic stage props, and in some cases even special effects such as stroboscopic lighting, smoke machines or dry ice, and slide projection. However, most regional operas, particularly those performed in temporary rural contexts, are still performed with only very rudimentary scenery or props if any at all.

Given that almost without exception, all regional dramas relate historical stories about emperors, imperial scholar-officials, generals, and soldiers, all set in the imperial past—whether specifically identified historical facts or ambiguously imagined and imaginary scenes—traditional theatre costumes are all more or less loosely based on usually Ming dynasty imperial attire, from emperor's robes through officials' hats and gowns to more simple servants' clothes. If a particular story is very clearly and importantly set in another dynasty—such as the Manchu Qing dynasty, which had distinctive imperial dress codes—then some attention may be given to the historical detail of costumes. However, more often than not, historical accuracy or realism of costumes is of little major concern.

Performance Contexts

In contemporary China, as in the past, traditional theatre is performed in a number of different contexts, including commercial theatres, rural festivals, and amateur performances. Commercial theatre performances are now far fewer than in the past, reflecting the changing status of traditional theatre as a form of entertainment and social interaction. In the past, traditional Chinese theatre was the most popular form of leisure and entertainment activity in China. In contemporary urban China, it constitutes a relatively minor interest particularly enjoyed among older people and dedicated aficionados. Among the younger generations who have grown up with far greater access to cinema, television, home video, pop music, and now also the Internet, online gaming, and a whole range of other leisure and entertainment opportunities, there is little serious consideration of traditional Chinese theatre. Consequently, commercial theatre performances tend to be aimed at a relatively narrowly defined dedicated following of traditional theatre fans and, in the main cities such as Beijing and Shanghai, also tourists and foreign visitors.

Traditional theatre performances are still popular in the countryside, however. Indeed, given the lack of urban audiences, in recent decades, many of China's traditional theatre troupes—whether for Beijing opera or other regional opera forms—have relied upon rural performances to support themselves. The troupes themselves are usually based in relatively large towns

A Chinese opera performer in elaborate costume. The flags on his back indicate that this character is a military general, the flags representing his various armies. (Corel)

or cities, but they travel around the countryside setting up stage in small towns and villages for a few days, usually to celebrate special occasions or festivals and holidays. This kind of itinerant performance is nothing new to Chinese theatre, though. In fact, one of the most common traditional performance contexts has always been for temple festivals, when operas were staged in honor of the deity or deities of the temple. In communist China, at least until relatively recently in the reform period, temple festivals became a thing of the past as temples and religion were designated feudal superstition. Nonetheless, village performances of traditional theatre, with selected or rewritten politically acceptable stories, continued through the 1950s and 1960s up until the Cultural Revolution.

In the post-Mao period, the popularity of traditional opera performances in the countryside was reinvigorated by a context of greater artistic and cultural freedom, gradually relaxing political definitions of artistic production, and in many parts of the country also greater rural wealth, which meant that villagers had more money to invite troupes to come and perform. From the late 1980s and 1990s onward, however, theatre troupes were increasingly expected to rely upon the revenues that they raised and less on state subsidies, even though they generally continued to be state work units and actors were still state employees. Later in the 1990s, more troupes were also encouraged to become independent cooperatives, which meant even greater, if not complete, reliance upon their own revenues.

Two Contrasting Examples: Beijing Opera and Cantonese Opera

Beijing and Cantonese opera are two important forms of traditional Chinese theatre. Beijing opera is the nationally recognized form of traditional theatre and also has a strong cultural significance in northeast China in the locale of the capital after which it is named. Beijing opera is also the form of traditional theatre most often treated synonymously with "traditional Chinese theatre" and explanations of role types, acting, singing, music, and so on in both Chinese and foreign literature often take Beijing opera as their model.

Cantonese opera, by contrast, is the main form of regional opera performed in the southern province of Guangdong and neighboring Hong Kong. It also has a dedicated following among overseas Chinese communities in Southeast Asia, the United States, Canada, and other parts of the world. It is performed principally in Cantonese (the main dialect in Guangdong and Hong Kong), although musically it is based on the *pihuang* musical form, just like Beijing opera. Compared to Beijing opera, it has been far more affected over the years by Western theatrical influences—particularly in Hong Kong—and other media such as cinema. Consequently, it has transformed itself over the last century probably more than any other regional opera form.

Beijing opera really dates back to the late eighteenth century when a southern form of opera from Anhui Province became popular in the northern capital. Prior to that time, the popular opera in Beijing had been the elitist and intellectual *kunqu*, various forms of clapper opera largely from western and northwestern China, and some *yiyang qiang* opera. The new opera from the south was the first based on the *erhuang* and *xipi* musical forms to become popular in the capital, however. The new troupes that established themselves in the early nineteenth century were also popular for their impressive acrobatic displays, which was another new feature of this opera at the time. These features—*pihuang* music combined with acrobatics—not only were new then but are still distinctive features of Beijing opera today. Hence, we can see that *the* archetypal "traditional" Chinese theatre actually has a history in the capital, whose name it bears, of little more than 200 years.

Throughout the nineteenth century, the new form of Beijing opera flourished and also started to become popular throughout the country, becoming something starting to resemble a national theatrical form, even though other regional operas retained their local popularity. One of the features of the new Beijing opera was also the way that it appealed to audiences from across the social spectrum. In the past, *kunqu* was always the theatre of the elite and intellectuals, while the general populace was pleased by more bawdy and lively regional operas. Beijing opera, however, appealed to the population at large but also to wealthy, successful, and high-ranking people in society. Indeed, this popular regional genre flourished partly as a result of the patronage that leading actors managed to cultivate among the capital's ruling and influential classes.

Beijing opera has four broad categories of role types: the *sheng*, the *dan*, the *jing*, and the *chou*. The *sheng* roles are the male character roles: *wusheng* a leading military male role, *xiaosheng* the scholarly, romantic male role, and *laosheng* the old male character role, covering imperial officials, generals, and other older male figures. The *dan* roles are for female characters and include the leading female roles that play opposite the *wusheng* or *xiaosheng*. There are also military and civilian *dan* roles, with one of the most common being the civilian *dan* role known as the *qingyi* (literally "green clothes"), who is expected to be gentle, graceful, and demure. The *jing* role type, meanwhile, is the painted-face role type usually chosen for pictorial representations of Beijing opera because of its striking visual appearance. The *jing* role actor plays both military and civilian characters, including generals, warriors, imperial officials, gods, demons, and judges. However, *jing* actors are always notable for their strong, forceful characters and stage presence. They should speak with loud and penetrating voices, often use strong eye movements and facial expressions to enhance and exploit their facial make-up, and generally strike an imposing figure on the stage. Finally, the *chou* role type is for the comic, clown-like character. This is a lighter and less rigorously defined role, in the sense that *chou* characters can improvise more freely, are expected to tell and make jokes (often using dialect or some kind of local reference), and have much less arduous singing and acting repertoires to command. The *chou* character is usually immediately identifiable by a large, round white patch of make-up centered on the nose and covering some of the eyes and forehead.

Traditionally, at least up until the twentieth century, there were no female actors in Beijing opera troupes. This followed an imperial ban on mixed-gender troupes centuries back, when they were associated with immoral behavior. Consequently, all of the above roles used to be played by male actors, and some of the best-known and most acclaimed Beijing opera performers, such as Mei Lanfang (1894–1961) and Cheng Yanqiu (1904–1958), were men who played *dan* female roles. Fifth Generation film director Chen Kaige's famous 1990s cinematic depiction of the changing fortunes of a group of leading Beijing opera performers, *Farewell My Concubine*, gives a clear indication of such roles through the central character of Cheng Dieyi, the utterly dedicated homosexual *dan* actor played by award-winning Hong Kong actor Leslie Cheung.

Compared to Cantonese opera, as we will see below, Beijing opera has remained relatively loyal to its roots. Although there have clearly been innovations, developments, and changes over the years, Beijing opera today is still in many ways fundamentally similar to what was performed early in the twentieth century and even in the nineteenth century. Beijing opera performances still use minimal scenery and stage props. There is a relatively closely protected core of "classic" operas, arias, and scenes that remain favorites with actors and audiences alike. What has changed, though, are Beijing opera's audiences. Whereas a hundred years ago, and even fifty years ago, Beijing opera was incredibly popular among the general population of both the capital and many parts of the country in general, in the early 2000s, Beijing opera was followed by an ever dwindling core of increasingly elderly aficionados and enthusiasts while at the same time becoming the standard genre performed for tourists to represent classical Chinese culture. This has meant that the genre increasingly survives in a partly synthetic performance environment on

Scene from Chen Kaige's movie *Farewell My Concubine*, named after a classic opera. The movie gives a clear indication of the role of the *dan* through the central character of Cheng Dieyi. *Dan* roles are female character roles traditionally played by male actors. (Corbis)

the strength of its past glory, its cultural significance as a genre, and its ability to symbolize a traditional China that visitors from overseas are so often seeking.

Cantonese opera suffered a similar, if not worse, decline in audiences over the later decades of the twentieth century. However, this southern genre of performance also developed a split personality from 1949 onward. Until then, the cultural center of gravity for Cantonese opera performance was in the provincial capital Guangzhou (Canton). It was here that the Cantonese opera performers' guild, called the Bahe Association, was established. Until the Japanese occupation in the war years, it was also where the best and most appreciated performers generally preferred to perform. However, the disruption of the war years saw many performers flee first to Hong Kong and some then even farther overseas to escape the Japanese. Then, after the end of the civil war and with the founding of the People's Republic, the trajectory of Cantonese opera split into two increasingly contrasting directions. Within the PRC, Cantonese opera troupes, like Beijing opera and other theatre troupes, gradually became state work units—their productions were increasingly subject to political supervision and intervention, and their performers suffered greatly in the traumas of the Cultural Revolution. In the post-Mao era, there was some revival in the fate of troupes, and they increasingly found performance opportunities in the countryside, but until the late 1990s there was not even one commercial venue staging regular performances of Cantonese opera. Indeed, Cantonese opera performances were very few and far between.

In Hong Kong, by contrast, Cantonese opera picked up after the war where it had left off before it. The many eminent performers who ended up in the British colony were able to exploit a still-strong base of popular support for the genre that even in the 1930s and 1940s was still more widely attended than cinema. The 1950s became a new Cantonese opera heyday in the territory, particularly led by two actresses, Ren Jianhui and Bai Xuexian, who performed a number of new operas by playwright Tang Disheng that have since become the local "classics" of the genre. Cantonese opera in Hong Kong also saw its audiences decline in the late 1960s and 1970s as young people found new, more exciting and modern interests and as cinema, television, and pop music became more fashionable leisure pastimes. The genre managed to survive, despite virtually disappearing from local commercial theatres, as a result of continued temple festival performances and the regular airing of some of the hundreds of old black and white Cantonese opera films on Hong Kong television (see Latham 2000).

Cantonese opera, like Beijing opera, is based upon the *pihuang* musical systems. It also incorporates martial arts and acrobatics and deploys similar costumes, actions, and gestures. However, there are also distinct differences between the two genres that need pointing out. For one thing, the role-type system, although once very close to that of Beijing opera—in the early twentieth century, for instance—has evolved into its own distinct variation on the *sheng*, *dan*, *jing*, and *chou* formula. All four of these categories can be identified in Cantonese opera, but the role types are now generally considered to be six in number. These are the *wenwusheng*, the *xiaosheng*, the *zhengyin huadan*, the *erbang huadan*, the *wusheng*, and the *chousheng*. The *wenwusheng*, literally "civil-military man," is the leading male role character and incorporates features of what in Beijing opera are usually the separate civilian *xiaosheng* and military *wusheng* roles. Until the last few decades, *wenwusheng* were usually expected to demonstrate equally strong skills in singing, speaking, and acting on one hand and the more military skills of martial arts and acrobatics on the other. Since the 1980s, however, particularly in Hong Kong, Cantonese opera has been dominated by the more romantic scholarly official–type leading male role characters, similar to the *xiaosheng* of Beijing opera.

The *xiaosheng* in Cantonese opera, however, is differently defined from that in Beijing opera. In Cantonese opera, this role is effectively a more junior version of the *wenwusheng*, a hierarchical division that also distinguishes the leading female role, the *zhengyin huadan*, from the secondary female role *erbang huadan*. Again, unlike Beijing opera, these two female roles are not divided according to civilian or military characteristics so much as relative prominence and importance in the opera. However, unlike the leading male role equivalents, whereas most *xiaosheng* aim sooner or later to move up to *wenwusheng* roles, there are more female role performers who make their career specializing in the *erbang huadan* role type.

The two remaining Cantonese opera role types, *wusheng* and *chousheng*, are similar to the *jing* and *chousheng* roles in Beijing opera. The Cantonese opera *wusheng* is generally a bearded character used for older generals, emperors, senior imperial officials, and occasionally deities, usually also with a painted face, although the diversity of painted faces in Cantonese opera has diminished greatly over the years compared to Beijing opera. The Cantonese opera *chousheng*, like his Beijing opera namesake, is the clown-like role type and is generally similar to his Beijing opera counterpart, although costume and make-up may be more variable in the Cantonese version.

The other striking differences between Cantonese and Beijing opera performances are the use of scenery and stage props and the inclusion of Western musical instruments, again particularly, though not exclusively, in Hong Kong. Cantonese opera was in tough competition with cinema in the 1940s and 1950s, and with many Cantonese opera performers simultaneously becoming film stars, there was a lot of mutual interaction between the two entertainment genres. Consequently, Cantonese opera stage performances adopted film set–like scenery and props and eventually some special effects such as stroboscopic lighting as well—something virtually unheard of, and for many unimaginable, in Beijing opera. At the same time, the closer interaction with foreign musical and cinematic influences in both Hong Kong and Guangzhou from the 1930s onward saw Cantonese opera, which was constantly changing and transforming itself, adopt saxophones, electric and Hawaiian guitars, violins, and other Western musical instruments alongside their more traditional Chinese counterparts. These kinds of changes have led some people, particularly Beijing opera aficionados, to consider Cantonese opera as a more vulgar, lightweight, less culturally authentic, and even less "traditional" form of theatre than Beijing opera.

However, this requires some attention to what tradition in the two genres actually entails. Unlike Beijing opera, which has become relatively fossilized by the burden of national cultural heritage, Cantonese opera has historically thrived on a tradition of change through commercialism, innovation, creativity, flexibility, pastiche, and cross-cultural borrowing—whether from other Chinese opera forms, *Cinderella*, or the *Arabian Nights*. Yet even though in some senses the only thing that is enduring about Cantonese opera, at least in Hong Kong, is its rate of change, paradoxically it has not ceased to be taken as traditional. Elaborately costumed Cantonese opera performers have become a clichéd media symbol of traditional China. At the same time, performers, historians, musicians, and enthusiasts trace the genre back to its roots in Chinese theatrical forms centuries old. But it is this paradox of embodying tradition, though constantly changing, and the tension between a nostalgic grasping at the old alongside an unquenchable thirst for the new that lie at the heart of Cantonese opera as a living performance art in Hong Kong.

In Guangdong Province, by contrast, fifty years of Communist Party rule has bequeathed Cantonese opera a rather different history and a different relationship to tradition. For one thing, Cantonese opera was "revolutionized" along with other cultural and artistic forms under Mao so that operas had to relate to the socialist utopianism of the new order. During the Cultural Revolution, Cantonese opera performances were completely stopped as performers, like many other artists and intellectuals, were vilified and "struggled" against as representatives of the "four olds." Although troupes reformed in the 1970s and 1980s, crucially they lost their audience. In the late 1980s and early 1990s, it was almost impossible to see a performance of Cantonese opera in Guangzhou, the historical home of the genre, and troupes eked out a living by performing in the countryside or in Hong Kong. It was only in the late 1990s that one theatre in the city started commercial performances once again to new, limited (but enthusiastic) audiences. In the hi-tech environment of contemporary Guangzhou, however, Cantonese opera could not be thought of as new, as in its prewar heyday, and its rebirth became the reclamation of a traditional entertainment form.

Spoken Drama

In contrast to traditional drama, spoken drama has a much shorter history in China and was a foreign import. The first spoken dramas were performed in the late nineteenth century largely due to the influence of foreign missionaries. However, these were small-scale performances and of generally unremarkable quality. Nonetheless, a certain enthusiasm for spoken, or modern, drama soon arose, particularly among students, intellectuals, and left-wing activists in particular. At the beginning of the twentieth century, spoken drama became associated with the New Culture Movement and the May 4th literary movement, which sought to challenge tradition and raise the awareness of the Chinese population as to the injustices of society and the failings of the national character. Often inspired by foreign, socially motivated playwrights such as Henrik Ibsen and Anton Chekhov, young intellectual writers set about writing dramas for an increasingly large and hungry body of young actors and actresses.

At times, the demand from all the theatre troupes—most of which were amateur and noncommercial—was so great that there were not enough plays to go around (Mackerras 1975: 68). However, the interest in modern spoken drama was fairly narrowly defined. It was particularly centered in Shanghai, and although there were also movements to develop spoken drama in some of the other major cities it did not enjoy the success elsewhere that it did in Shanghai. At the same time, interest was generally concentrated among students and intellectuals involved in literary, film, or political movements rather than the populace as a whole. This meant that spoken drama was almost exclusively an urban activity.

Particularly in the 1920s, it was also common among left-leaning supporters of spoken drama to insist that troupes be made up of amateur performers in order to avoid what they saw as the overcommercialization of other forms of drama (Mackerras 1975: 67). To some degree, this also undermined the long-term stability of this genre of performance. However, particularly after the political split between the nationalist Kuomintang (KMT) government and the communists in 1927, there were more direct threats to spoken drama. The right-wing KMT government looked increasingly to crack down upon left-wing literary and cultural movements, and consequently various spoken drama troupes and dramatists were forced to stop their work. At least in Shanghai, left-wing actors, dramatists, and cultural associations did manage to find ways to continue their activities; however, these were politically dangerous times for them.

The kinds of plays written and performed at this time therefore often incorporated political and social messages. They sought to highlight and criticize social injustices, much in the way that social realist films of the 1930s and 1940s did (see Chapter 7). However, the relationship between drama and film was actually such that modern spoken stage drama provided the model that social realist film emulated and worked with. In fact, for decades, the most respected person in Chinese cinema production was not the director or the producer of a film but its screenplay writer. Film was seen as an extension of the spoken drama, only it could reach out to much larger audiences. Spoken dramas therefore regularly took current social issues such as prostitution, poverty, social inequality, and mistreatment of the disenfranchised, corruption, and injustice as their central themes.

Many commentators suggest that the Republican period represented a heyday for social realist drama. Despite the difficulties of being in a state at war, with the Japanese invasion and all the political turmoil of the times, spoken drama found itself in tune with wider intellectual and revolutionary movements abroad in society. In fact, the war against the Japanese proved to be a major source of inspiration for patriotic dramatists and theatre troupes. The Communist Party in particular organized and encouraged amateur drama troupes, many of them in rural areas, to stage patriotic anti-Japanese performances intended to provide morale-boosting propaganda in the unoccupied areas. In fact, a Party decree in 1943, following the spirit of Mao's 1942 Talks to the Yan'an Forum on Literature and Art, ordered that all plays not dealing with the war effort should be either stopped or revised. This was not popular with some dramatists and intellectuals who were still keen to have greater artistic independence, but it did not affect the number of performances or troupes. Indeed, in one province alone (Hubei) there were more than 1,000 active rural theatre troupes (Tung 1987: 2).

After the establishment of the People's Republic in 1949, spoken drama moved into a new phase of development. Like traditional opera, spoken drama benefited from the relative political, military, and social calm that came with the founding of the PRC and the end of the civil war. However, like cinema, spoken drama also had to comply more rigidly with the political understanding of art outlined by Mao in Yan'an. Like television in contemporary China, theatre in the Mao era was both blessed and dogged by its appeal to the Communist Party. Theatre was considered an extremely effective medium of political communication, which endeared it to the country's political leadership. However, that meant that it was potentially also very dangerous, should it be employed for communicating the wrong kind of political messages. Consequently, spoken drama flourished but, like other forms of art and literature, under strict politically defined conditions and limitations.

According to official figures, in 1953, state-owned theatre troupes alone performed to more than 45 million people at more than 41,000 performances, and this was at a time when there were also a large number of semiprivate theatre troupes. In 1954, performance and audience numbers were up more than 36 percent to 57,000 and 62.13 million, respectively. Of these performances, around 16 percent (9,300) were staged in factories and mines, 5.4 percent (3,100) were staged in the countryside, and 12.6 percent (7,200) were performed for the military (Tung 1987: 4–5).

The subject matter of spoken dramas also changed at this time. Anti-Japanese war propaganda became celebratory propaganda honoring the heroes of both the anti-Japanese conflict and the civil war. At the same time, the social realist dramas of the Republican period now became more rigidly dictated socialist realist dramas that were expected to reflect, support, and promote government and Party policy at any given time. This was achieved in particular through the organization and encouragement of amateur "outside-work" (*yeyu*) troupes, for whom short specially written plays were written on themes related to the latest government policy being promoted by the Party.

Over the first ten years of the PRC, there were continuing tensions between political cadres who saw theatre simply as a vehicle for propaganda and some actors, playwrights, and dramatists who regretted the heavy and at times heavy-handed political intervention in artistic production. Nonetheless, there was a lively intellectual theatre scene in China that saw complex and extended discussions of different dramatic theories. Some of the key influences on Chinese drama at this time also came from overseas, particularly with the dramatic theory of Stanislavsky coming both through the Soviet Union and in English translations via the United States (Sun 1987: 139). However, European figures who had influenced earlier Chinese social realist drama, such as Bertolt Brecht and Henrik Ibsen, continued to inform the development of Chinese dramatic performance. Although this on many occasions meant the production of originally Western plays, there were also ways in which Western dramatic theory mixed with indigenous conceptualizations of theatre. In particular, the work of one of China's best-known directors, Huang Zuoling, drew upon the work of Brecht, Konstantin Stanislavsky, and Mei Lanfang, the famous Beijing opera performer and drama theorist (Hsia 1987; Sun 1987).

However, despite a number of periods of relatively relaxed political pressure, the will of the Party always ultimately dominated theatre production. In the early 1960s, following the disasters of the Great Leap Forward, Mao and Communist Party hard-liners were pushed onto the back foot and there was a brief period of relative political openness. However, this was

Chinese actress Liu Dan in the Bertolt Brecht play *Threepenny Opera* in 1998. The performance, by an all-Chinese cast, was the first time the play, set in Victorian London, had been staged in China. (AP/Wide World Photos)

Cao Yü

Cao Yü was one of the most popular and also influential playwrights of the Republican period that lasted from 1911 to 1949. Many literary historians also consider him one of the greatest writers of Chinese spoken drama in the twentieth century. In the People's Republic, Cao became a high-ranking Party cadre charged with overseeing theatre and drama, although he was also subject to severe criticism and punishment in the Cultural Revolution.

Born in 1910, he was only twenty-three when he wrote his first and probably best-known play, *Thunderstorm* (*leiyü*). Like his other plays, and also in keeping with much of the contemporary May 4th literature, *Thunderstorm* reflected the enormous social, political, and cultural turmoil of his time, offering a critique of social inequalities and advancing the cause of the poor and downtrodden in society. Cao Yü's interest in drama developed during his school days when he attended one of Tianjin's most prestigious schools, the Nankai Middle School. There he was an active member of the school's drama society between 1926 and 1930 and participated in productions of plays by Ibsen and other foreign writers. Between 1931 and 1934, he studied English at the National Tsinghua University, one of the best and most prestigious in the country. It was there that he wrote *Thunderstorm.*

Thunderstorm tells the story of a coal mine manager named Zhou Puyuan and offers a critique of the traditional family and the capitalist exploitation of workers. In the play, one of Zhou's sons heads a labor movement in protests against his father's management of the mine, and the play reveals the tensions at the heart of the traditional Chinese patriarchal family. However, the long and complicated plot eventually sees Zhou bring tragedy on his family and consign himself to a lonely and miserable old age. *Thunderstorm* was first produced by an amateur theatre troupe at Shanghai's Fudan University and subsequently went on tour. It was a massive critical and commercial success and immediately established Cao Yü as a leading playwright, artist, and intellectual of his time. He then followed *Thunderstorm* with two more successful plays—*Sunrise* (*richu*) and *Wilderness* (or *The Wild*) (*yuanye*)—in 1936 and 1937, respectively.

Cao was always sympathetic to the left-wing cause, as evidenced in his writing, but he also insisted on maintaining his political independence in the Republican period and did not associate himself too closely with the Communist Party as such. In fact, it was not until 1956 that he became a Communist Party member. However, his joining the Party was indicative of the compromises and changes in his political attitudes after the founding of the PRC. From 1949 on, Cao held a range of important official and semi-official posts including the vice presidency of the Central Dramatic Institute, a directorship of the All-China Dramatic Association, and president of the Peking People's Artistic and Dramatic Institute. Cao's political and artistic survival under the new political system, like that of other artists, actors, and writers, meant complete submission to Mao and acceptance of the party line. Nonetheless, Cao, like many other leading writers and dramatists such as Lao She and Tian Han, was savagely criticized in the Cultural Revolution. After the Cultural Revolution, Cao Yü was restored to his previous respected position in the dramatic world, taking up several official positions including chairman of the Union of Chinese Dramatists and the president of the Chinese Society for Shakespearean Study.

followed by a gradual build-up of the pressure on all kinds of artistic production in the lead-up to the Cultural Revolution. Indeed, from 1964 on, the performance of almost all theatre other than the eight revolutionary model operas personally approved by Mao's wife Jiang Qing, herself a former actress, was banned until the end of the Cultural Revolution period in 1976.

Spoken drama re-emerged as a popular intellectual art form in the late 1970s and early 1980s at the beginning of the reform period. Once again, theatre was caught up in the political struggles between reformist and more conservative forces within the Communist Party. Despite several attempts by Party hard-liners to reimpose Maoist priorities, though, this time around the more liberal wing of the party—led by Deng Xiaoping, Zhao Ziyang, and Hu Yaobang—was able to prevail. Consequently, the 1980s started a whole new period of experimentation and artistic exploration in Chinese theatre.

The Revolutionary Stage

The politicization of Chinese theatre came to a height in the mid-1960s and lasted throughout the Cultural Revolution period until the death of Mao in 1976, the fall of the Gang of Four—one of whom was Jiang Qing—barely a month later, and the start of the post-Mao reform period. Although this period of highly politicized and tightly controlled drama was in many ways a tragic episode in the history of Chinese theatre, the Cultural Revolution was nonetheless responsible for the development of a new kind of theatre—the revolutionary model opera—that in the longer term has come to be recognized as an important theatrical genre in its own right.

As mentioned, from the late 1960s through 1976, the only theatre allowed to be performed was that represented by the eight revolutionary model operas: *Taking Tiger Mountain by Strategy*, *The Red Lantern*, *On the Docks*, *Song of the Dragon River*, *The Red Detachment of Women*, *A Surprise Attack on the White Tiger Regiment*, *Fighting on the Plain*, and *The Azalea Mountain*. These were also made into films circulated and watched repeatedly throughout the country. Consequently, by the early 1980s the Chinese people were generally tired and bored with this predictable diet of romanticized revolutionary melodrama, and for nearly two decades the model operas were barely performed. By the late 1990s and early 2000s, though, as the traumatic political associations of the dramas weakened, they started to be appreciated for their own unique artistic qualities, and new productions of the dramas were staged both in China and overseas.

Model operas are a hybrid dramatic form comprising elements from Beijing opera, modern spoken drama, Western-style opera and ballet, and formulaic Chinese socialist realist imagery, similar also to Soviet and other Eastern European socialist imagery. They emphasized positive, heroic characters fighting and making sacrifices for the revolution and the working people of China. They exalted the heroic efforts and good character of the "good" social classes—peasants, workers, and soldiers—while at the same time, in rather uncompromising terms, condemning the evil, selfish, exploitative, and cruel actions of "class enemies" such as landlords, KMT nationalists, capitalists, and entrepreneurs.

The idea of the revolutionary model operas was first outlined by Jiang Qing in February 1966 at the Forum on Literature and Art in the Armed Forces held in Shanghai (Mackerras 1983a: 167). Many of the principles of the production of model operas were familiar from other artistic contexts under Mao. Their underlying objective, for instance, was to reveal the workings of class antagonism in society and promote the cause of class struggle. They were to do this by working with the stories and experiences of ordinary people, from which they forged a heroic proletarian imagination that would inform and inspire the people to support the ongoing class revolution.

One of the best-known model operas was *Taking Tiger Mountain by Strategy.* Originally a Beijing opera adaptation of a novel, *Taking Tiger Mountain by Strategy* was revised on the command of Jiang Qing in 1963 and again over the following years before being recognized as a model opera in 1969 (Mackerras 1983a: 172). *Taking Tiger Mountain by Strategy* tells the fairly basic story of a People's Liberation Army (PLA) victory in the civil war against the KMT in Manchuria in the winter of 1946. PLA hero Yang Zirong infiltrates the enemy camp and enables a PLA attack on the KMT troops led by his commander Shao Jianbo while their leader is celebrating his birthday. The opera is clearly celebratory of the victory, but its ideological emphasis is placed on the heroic, selfless, and totally revolutionary character of the leading figures Yang and Shao and how their victory is facilitated by the impassioned support of the masses eager to be liberated from the evil ways of the KMT leader, known as the Vulture.

A poster for the revolutionary opera *Taking Tiger Mountain by Strategy.* This opera was one of the handful of operas approved by Jiang Qing for performance as a model opera during the Cultural Revolution period. The drama tells the story of a People's Liberation Army (PLA) victory in the civil war against the Kuomintang in Manchuria in the winter of 1946. (Library of Congress)

During the Cultural Revolution period, model operas such as *Taking Tiger Mountain by Strategy* were seen predominantly in ideological and propaganda terms. However, they were also seen by their proponents as the epitome of socialist drama, not only as propaganda but as a high cultural art form. Indeed, it is the highly stylized and dramatic nature of the model operas, along with the appeal of their romanticized melodrama, that has endeared them to more contemporary audiences. Unlike much of the propaganda of the Cultural Revolution period, model operas are likely to have a much longer lifetime and will find a new secure place for themselves in the repertoire of national Chinese theatrical performance.

Experimental Theatre of the 1980s and 1990s

From the beginning of the post-Mao period (late 1970s) through 1989, Chinese modern theatre underwent a revival and a transformation. The revival entailed the coming to life of critical, intellectual debates about drama, the production of new, experimental, and challenging drama, and a renewed interest among audiences—intellectuals in particular. Indeed, the early 1980s was a lively time for spoken drama in particular. The transformation entailed gradually unraveling the practices of decades of tight state and Party domination in this increasingly liberal intellectual environment.

In the first years after Mao, change was in some ways very slight. A small number of plays challenged some of the hitherto unquestionable practices of drama writing and production handed down from the Cultural Revolution period and before. These changes took the form of greater experimentation with plots and characters, although cautiously within perceived limits of political tolerance. For instance, whereas previously all plots and characters had to be rigidly conceived within the established frameworks of class and class conflict, in the early 1980s it started to become possible to work with alternative scenarios—love across class boundaries, the deployment of good characters from class backgrounds other than peasants, workers, or soldiers, and some acknowledgment of the political mistakes and suffering of the past in the Cultural Revolution or other earlier political campaigns. Experimental playwrights also experimented with form and new dramatic techniques and theories. In the words of Chinese drama scholar Henry Zhao, they tried "virtually anything that had not previously been seen in the mainstream 'realist' theatre" (2000: 6). For instance, experimental dramas resisted division into "acts" or "scenes" and experimented with theoretical ideas of narration and others such as the mutually related ideas of "hypotheticality" and "theatricism" (Zhao 2000: 43–49).

Hypotheticality, to use Zhao's term for the Chinese *jiadingxing* (2000: 46), is an idea that set out to problematize notions of realism and resemblance. It assumed that verisimilitude was not necessarily a good thing and so, through the use of pretense, metaphor, and synecdoche in a performance, would look to maximize the effect of the theatricality of the stage. Here, the related notion of "theatricism" (*juchangxing*) came into play. Theatricism was seen as stressing the particularity of theatre as an art form. "It foregrounds the artificiality of drama by intentionally mocking the efforts of covering the traces, thus renouncing effectively the supposition that what is being staged is a genuine simulation of reality" (Zhao 2000: 43).

Spoken drama also came to reflect some of the political battles going on within the Party itself between more conservative Maoist hard-liners and the modernizers led by Deng Xiaoping, Hu Yaobang, and Zhao Ziyang. This became clear in relation to a number of "modernizing" plays that were published or performed and then withdrawn and then performed again, reflecting the contrasting attitudes of different factions in authority. Plays that came in for criticism from conservative left-wing figures included *Bitter Love* (*kulian*) and *The Golden Lance of King Wu and the Sword of King Yue* (*wu wang jin ge yue wang jian*), written by army writer Bai Hua in 1979 and 1983, respectively; Bai Fengxi's *When the Bright Moon Shines* (*mingye chuzhao ren*), written in 1981; and Sha Yexin's *If I Were for Real* (*jiaru wo shi zhende*). Bai Hua and Sha Yexin in particular got some very public criticism that also attracted international attention. Perhaps the most famous of the experimental playwrights of the early 1980s, however, was Gao Xingjian, who later went on to win the Nobel Prize in literature in 2000.

Gao started his artistic career writing fiction, then in the early 1980s started writing plays, some based on his earlier works.

Gao Xingjian was the 2000 Nobel Literature Laureate. Gao started his artistic career writing fiction and plays in the 1980s. He relocated to Paris in 1987 where he wrote experimental plays free from the political limitations he had experienced in China. (© The Nobel Foundation)

He joined the Beijing People's Art Theatre in 1981, where his experimental work was to a large degree accepted and given a chance to develop under the patronage of Yu Shizhi, deputy head of the theatre. He wrote and staged his early successful work at the theatre, including the plays *Absolute Signal*, *Bus Stop*, and *Wild Man*. However, he was always treading a fine line between what he wanted to do with experimental theatre and what would be acceptable to the authorities. All of his early plays caused controversy, but he was to some degree protected by the open-minded administration of the theatre. However, he wanted to go much further than the system would tolerate and in 1985 left the Beijing People's Art Theatre before completing one of his most acclaimed works, *The Other Shore*, in the following year (Zhao 2000: 9). In 1987, he moved to Paris, where he continued to write experimental plays without the political limitations he had experienced in China.

One of the better-known of the controversial plays of this period also clearly demonstrated the tensions and deadlock between different political factions in the CCP relating to drama, literature, and the arts. *We* (*Women*) (also known as *WM*, taking the pinyin initials of the Chinese binome for "we"), written by Wang Peigong in the mid-1980s, tells the story, set in the military, of seven people between 1978 and 1984, illustrating their lives, desires, and frustrations in a realistic fashion. It focused more on the individuals and their dissatisfactions with society than with preconceived formulae of patriotism and self-sacrifice, even if the play nonetheless praises the soldiers' dedication and commitment to their country (Zhao 2000: 8). The play was to be staged by a respected military director, Wang Gui, in the summer of 1985. However, the performance was suddenly canceled without warning due to an intervention from more conservative-minded Party officials who were offended by the play's content. Wang Gui was also forced to step down from all his official positions in the Party and as director of the Spoken Drama Troupe of the Political Affairs Department of the People's Air Force. Similarly, Wang Peigong was demobilized with dishonor.

In this case, however, the story did not stop there. Wang Peigong, with other influential support, put up a defense of the play in journals and newspapers and even managed to get the play published in *Juben*, the official monthly journal of the Chinese Dramatists' Association, in September of that year. The movement snowballed; the play was staged by leading modernizing directors in Shanghai and later Beijing. There were again incidents where performances were suspended at the last minute but were restored a few days later (see Tung 1987: 18).

This kind of censorship and the potential consequences of political infighting within the CCP give an indication of the degree and nature of Chinese political liberalization in the arts. Although compared to the past, playwrights had much greater scope to use a variety of characters in different roles and settings, there were still clear, though often unstated, rules about what was acceptable to the authorities and what was not. Hence, it now became possible to have plays in which people of "good" and "bad" class backgrounds might fall in love or get married—something unthinkable in Mao-period drama—but it was not conceivable to portray any senior officials in plays negatively, for fear that it might be construed as a veiled criticism of the Party leadership.

In this way, critical drama was fairly tightly circumscribed and tended to be very indirect and deliberately ambiguous. Experimental theatre also composed no more than around 10 percent of total drama production and writing in the early 1980s (Zhao 2000: 6). Hence, playwrights and directors found various ways of introducing a political edge to their plays while still satisfying censors or alternatively of staging plays that would not run the risk of being seen as politically motivated. In the early 1980s, in particular, writers, directors, and actors were still very cautious about what they would write and perform. Such techniques of evasion therefore included staging foreign plays such as Arthur Miller's *Death of a Salesman*, Brecht's *Galileo*, and works by Ibsen, Jean-Paul Sartre, and other authors. Not all such performances were intended to be politically critical. In fact, many were staged as a way of gleaning inspiration from Western theatre. At the same time, however, the performance of Western plays—particularly something like *Galileo*, which has a strong antiauthoritarian theme—in a Chinese context could take on a whole different set of locally specific meanings and connotations from those traditionally associated with the play. Some playwrights also resorted to historical themes and settings for their work, hoping that this could deflect attention from potentially critical readings in the present. Given the long history of such a technique in Chinese drama and literature, however, its effectiveness was inevitably limited.

The early and mid-1980s was a flourishing period for experimental Chinese drama. However, in the latter part of the decade, what had become known as an experimental, postmodern, or avant-garde theatre movement (see Zhao 2000: 1–12) started to lose some of its vigor and then was in any case brought to an end with the events of 1989, which toughened official attitudes to all artistic production. In the 1990s, there were new kinds of experimental theatre that attracted new kinds of audiences. Spoken drama of the 1990s can broadly speaking be divided into two categories: popular dramas reflecting the changes taking place in Chinese society and other more obscure alternative forms of performance, in some ways carrying on the work of the 1980s experimentalists.

Much of the "popular" theatre was also labeled "experimental" (*shiyan*) and in the true sense of the word was not actually "popular." By the 1990s, the notion of experimental theatre had been broadened and diluted so that it came to refer in many cases to performances that, at least compared to the 1980s, were not particularly innovative, theoretically motivated, or intellectually challenging. Like many television dramas of recent years, these were dramas about "new," principally urban, middle-class social phenomenon that emerged in the reform period: individualism, consumerism, relationship breakdown, family separation, the undermining of moral values, money fetishism, gender equality and inequality, pressures of work, and so on. The subject matter of these dramas was also reflected in their "popularity." They were popular with urban middle-class, relatively wealthy, and educated young people. Among this group of new theatre-goers—to some extent replacing the previous intellectual bent of Chinese contemporary theatre—there was a strong following and interest in these plays, at least in part because they dealt with issues in this group of people's lives.

One of the most successful playwrights of this genre has been Zhang Xian, who has also written numerous successful film scripts. The titles of his plays and films—such as *Wife Back from America* (*meiguo laide qizi*), *Stock Craze* (*gufeng*), *The Woman Who Stayed Behind* (*liushou nü*), and *Freewheeling* (*dasaba*)—clearly reflect these concerns. Zhang's and other plays in this genre often experimented with minimalist use of props and sets to present lifestyles of luxury, consumption, and alienation, challenging China's emerging urban middle classes to reflect upon the pressures and forces guiding their lives. In these respects, these dramas were to some degree "experimental." However, some would argue that this theatre was not so much experimentally motivated as commercially motivated, using the "experimental" label as a marketing ploy (see, e.g., Huot 2000: 74). Claire Huot prefers to point to the work of artists and poets such as Mou Sen and Yu Jian as being truly experimental performance. One of Mou Sen's groundbreaking works, for instance, was *The Other Shore* (also known as *The Other Bank*), taking the name and some inspiration from Gao Xingjian's work. The performance took place in a classroom at the Beijing Film Institute and saw acting students from the Institute turned "into nimble, animal-like humans, able to cry, yell, laugh, speak, dance and jump" (Huot 2000: 78). The work plays with the very nature of the Chinese language and language itself, pushing also the limits of ideas of theatre, performance, and acting. These kinds of works are few in number, not popularly watched, and often inaccessible to the general public and appeal to a relatively small group of intellectuals. However, in the late 1990s and early 2000s some critics would argue that this was where the cutting edge of Chinese contemporary theatre was.

Theatre, Popular Culture, Politics, and Audiences

Theatre has for centuries been an important feature of China's popular cultural landscape. Whether in urban commercial performances, private performances for family celebrations of the wealthy, or either rural or urban temple festivals, traditional theatre was always one of the most popular and most spectacular forms of public or private entertainment. Theatre in China has also long been associated with politics. In imperial times, drama was often regarded with some suspicion for its potential to arouse trouble among the common people, and actors played key roles in some of the country's largest popular uprisings against imperial rule, such as the Taiping Rebellion of the mid- to late nineteenth century.

However, it was in the late nineteenth and early twentieth centuries that theatre truly entered into the political imagination. In the past, actors had been considered, among other things, as potential troublemakers, and there was always the potential for dramas to be politically critical of the imperial establishment (Mackerras 1983a: 92–118). However, in general the nature of traditional Chinese theatre performance and appreciation did not particularly lend itself to politically subversive activity. The stories often reflected the established moral values of Confucianism: filial piety, loyalty, righteousness, and humanity, for instance. Indeed, many commentators on Chinese theatre have attributed to it the role of maintaining and perpetuating Chinese cultural values underpinning Chinese society in Imperial times. At the same time, Chinese theatre is appreciated as much, if not more, for its artistic spectacle and the skills of the performers as for the story or "content" of the plays.

With modern, Western-influenced spoken drama, however, the emphasis shifted onto the script and ideological content. The twentieth century therefore saw a new kind of politicization of Chinese drama. However, this politicization has to be understood in relation to the broader context of the politicization of many aspects of life in China at this time and of many aspects of Chinese popular culture in particular. The politicization of drama was accompanied by the politicization of film, literature, visual arts, music, and other forms of cultural production. Drama with a political purpose in the early twentieth century was one part of a broader partial politicization of popular culture. There are two important things to note in relation to understanding the relation between politics and theatre in modern China. First, not all drama, and not all popular culture, was politicized, at least until the victory of the Communist Party and the founding of the People's Republic. As we noted with film in Chapter 7, there is a tendency for the history of Chinese media and popular culture to be written through the distorting lens of subsequent historical events, the political victory of the CCP in particular. As with film, so with drama, this partial perspective can tend to emphasize the importance of politically motivated—that is, left-wing—drama and neglect the existence of nonpolitical, or at least nonleftist, theatre.

It is therefore important to remember the broader context of drama within the contemporary popular cultural landscape and understand how its position in that landscape has changed over time. Compared to, say, television or newspapers neither traditional theatre nor modern spoken drama is particularly prominent in the contemporary Chinese popular cultural landscape, but they both have enormous historical significance and have to be considered if other areas of Chinese popular culture are to be fully understood.

The second issue in relation to theatre and politics is that of audiences. In some ways, the prominence (or otherwise) of drama in the Chinese popular cultural landscape is closely related to audiences. In the nineteenth and early twentieth centuries, traditional theatre commanded large audiences and enjoyed widespread popularity. Consequently, it was at the center of the Chinese popular cultural landscape. In the early decades of the PRC, both traditional and modern drama were given prominence by the CCP and at times constituted one of the few forms of entertainment open to people. However, in the post-Mao era, as we have discussed in other chapters of this volume, there arose a wide array of alternative forms of cultural production, entertainment, and leisure opportunities, from television to ten-pin bowling. Consequently, the audiences and general prominence of stage drama, whether traditional or modern, have both diminished considerably in recent years, even if some critics would argue that cutting-edge avant-garde drama like that of Gao Xingjian is at the forefront of critical Chinese cultural production. It is, however, difficult to justify the use of the term "popular," at least in the sense of pertaining to the general population, for this kind of drama. Indeed, some would argue that the main problem facing China's contemporary modern drama scene is its lack of general popularity with audiences.

Audiences and their reactions to drama are key for understanding the role of drama at any particular historical moment. In the Cultural Revolution period, for instance, audiences became tired and bored with the same restricted diet of revolutionary model operas. However, audiences were still large, given the lack of alternative entertainment and leisure opportunities and the political and social pressure to attend. Hence, theatre was an important part of the popular cultural landscape, though not necessarily particularly popular in the sense of being enjoyed by many. In recent years, contemporary avant-garde drama has pushed the limits of aesthetic and artistic understanding but failed to break far out of the realms of metropolitan intellectual interest.

A to Z

The Azalea Mountain. One of the eight revolutionary model operas from the Cultural Revolution period, written by Wang Shuyuan. Published in 1973, the play tells the story of a group of peasant fighters in the Hunan-Jiangxi border region in the late 1920s. The peasant partisans rescue a Communist Party leader, Ke Xiang, from nationalist KMT forces. Ke, a strong woman character, turns out to have the leadership skills that the disorderly, but dedicated, peasant fighters have been lacking. The opera ends with the fighters following Ke to join the Communist Party after defeating the nationalist troops.

Bangzi qiang. One of the three early systems of regional opera that emerged during the Ming dynasty (1368–1644), also known as clapper opera. *Bangzi qiang* has its roots in the Shanxi region of western China. Its distinctive characteristic was its rhythm, played with a wooden clapper. Unlike *yiyang qiang* and *kunqu*, *bangzi qiang* did not feature a chorus (Mackerras 1975: 16). Initially a local opera tradition, its popularity spread throughout the country.

Beijing opera. See *Jingju*.

Brecht, Bertolt. The famous German playwright and dramatist was himself strongly impressed by Chinese theatre and dramatic techniques after seeing Mei Lanfang perform on a visit to Europe. However, his relationship with Chinese drama has always been two-directional, with his own works popularly performed in China, particularly by left-wing actors and troupes, from the 1930s on. Brecht was particularly influential in the work of the leading 1950s Chinese dramatist Huang Zuoling.

Cao Yü. One of China's most famous playwrights of the 1930s and a leading figure in the world of Chinese spoken drama until the 1980s.

Chou. One of the main role types in traditional Chinese theatre. The *chou* role is a comic or clown role, usually identified in Beijing opera by a distinctive circle of white make-up in the middle of the face.

Dan. One of the main role types in traditional Chinese theatre. *Dan* roles are female character roles, although in many regional opera forms, including Beijing opera and until the 1930s also Cantonese opera, these were traditionally played by male actors. There are usually two or more subdivisions of *dan* role types.

Erhu. A traditional Chinese string instrument. The *erhu* is played with a bow that rests between the instrument's two strings. The small round or hexagonal sound box sits on the player's knee, with the neck of the instrument vertical. The *erhu* is one of the principal melodic instruments in many regional opera forms, including Cantonese opera.

Erhuang. One of the two principal musical systems, along with *xipi*, upon which many contemporary traditional theatre forms are based, including Beijing and Cantonese operas. *Erhuang* is generally used for more solemn or serious situations, while *xipi* is lighter and happier.

Fighting on the Plain (pingyuan zuozhan). One of the eight revolutionary model operas. Due to political restrictions, these were the only operas of any kind allowed to be performed for years during the Cultural Revolution period (1966–1976).

Gao Xingjian. Nobel Prize–winning experimental Chinese playwright who came to the fore in the 1980s with his work at the Beijing People's Art Theatre. His early successes included the plays *Absolute Signal*, *Bus Stop*, and *Wild Man*. However, his unorthodox, experimental style proved controversial in China, and in 1987 he emigrated to Paris, where he continued to write groundbreaking work strongly influenced by notions both from contemporary drama theory and Zen Buddhism (see Zhao 2000).

Huaju. Literally "speech plays," *huaju* is the Chinese term for modern spoken drama as opposed to forms of traditional Chinese opera which invariably include some kind of musical accompaniment and work with very different notions of performance, appreciation, realism, and art.

Huang Zuoling. One of China's leading intellectual playwrights from the 1940s and 1950s but one whose work has been recognized to the present day. Huang drew upon the work of Brecht, Stanislavsky, and Beijing opera performer and innovator Mei Lanfang for his dramatic inspiration. He has been dubbed by some as China's Brecht.

Huqin. A traditional Chinese string instrument. The *huqin* is held like a guitar and played by plucking the strings. It is one of the principal melodic instruments in many regional opera forms.

Ibsen, Henrik. Along with other leading Western dramatists including Brecht and Chekhov, Ibsen was a dominant foreign influence on much of the literary and drama movements of the May 4th period in the early twentieth century. Ibsen's plays, including *A Doll's House*, have maintained their popularity in Chinese intellectual circles to the present day.

Jing. One of the main role types in traditional Chinese theatre. *Jing* roles are painted-face male character roles, usually also bearded, reflecting the seniority of many of the characters. Common *jing* role characters include both military and civilian characters, including imperial officials, gods, demons, army generals, and judges.

Jingju. The Chinese term for Beijing (Peking) opera. *Jing* means "capital" and *ju* "opera." (Beijing literally means "northern capital.") *Jingju* as known today is the contemporary from of a dramatic tradition that developed and became popular in the Beijing area in the late Qing dynasty (late eighteenth and nineteenth centuries), although it is derived from southern regional dramatic styles. *Jingju* has become known as the national opera form.

Kunqu. One of the three early systems of regional opera that emerged during the Ming dynasty (1368–1644), along with *yiyang qiang* and *bangzi qiang* (clapper opera). *Kunqu* was particularly appreciated by the wealthy and educated sectors of the population and was considered a more refined or "higher" theatrical form than the coarser regional opera styles.

Lao She. One of China's leading twentieth-century writers and playwrights of the May 4th era. Lao She's most famous play, *Teahouse*, which exposes the inequalities and injustices of the old, feudal Chinese society, is considered a twentieth-century Chinese socialist realist classic. Lao She continued to be a dominant figure in Chinese drama following the foundation of the People's Republic but suffered severely and died during the Cultural Revolution at the hands of Mao's Red Guards.

Mei Lanfang. Probably China's most famous Beijing opera performer. He came to fame performing in Shanghai in the 1910s and continued to perform all his life except when living under Japanese occupation in Shanghai between 1941 and 1945. Mei played female character *dan* roles to much acclaim. He was in great demand throughout the country for his entire career and also toured overseas. He was also seen as an important Beijing opera reformer willing to experiment with traditional forms and styles.

Model operas. Model operas were designated by Jiang Qing, Mao's hard-line leftist wife, as the epitome of revolutionary artistic performance in the early 1960s, and in the Cultural Revolution period the eight approved model operas were for many years the only kind of theatrical performance permitted in China.

Mou Sen. An avant-garde playwright of the 1990s and 2000s, regarded by intellectual critics as being at the forefront of contemporary Chinese experimental theatre. Mou Sen picked up from the experimental theatre movements of the 1980s and has been much influenced by Gao Xingjian. His work is notorious for being inaccessible and difficult to understand, and his popularity is largely restricted to intellectual and drama circles.

Nanxi. Along with *zaju*, one of the two principal dramatic forms that emerged in the Yuan dynasty (AD 1271–1368) and which have since been seen as forming the roots of China's traditional literary dramatic tradition. *Nanxi* and *zaju* were the antecedents of three other regional opera forms: *yiyang qiang*, *bangzi qiang*, and *kunqu*. *Nanxi* was prevalent in southern China, compared to *zaju*'s popularity in the north.

On the Docks (haigang). A Beijing opera revised in 1972 to be recognized as one of the eight revolutionary model operas of the Cultural Revolution period.

The Other Shore (aka The Other Bank). The name of two experimental dramas by Gao Xingjian and Mou Sen, with the former being the inspiration for the latter. Gao's play, considered one of his principal works, was completed in 1986 just after he left the Beijing People's Art Theatre and before he moved to Paris. Mou Sen's play was performed at the Beijing Film Institute by students who imitated animal-human hybrids. The play investigates the fundamental nature of language.

Peking opera. See *Jingju*.

Pihuang. The shortened name given to forms of regional drama based on the *xipi* and *erhuang* musical systems.

Pipa. A traditional plucked string instrument often used as a solo performance instrument but also used for melodic rendition in some forms of traditional regional Chinese theatre.

Qiang. Literally "voice," *qiang* has various usages in relation to traditional Chinese theatre. It can be used as the name of kinds of opera music—for instance, *bangzi qiang*, "clapper opera." In Cantonese opera and some other regional operas, it is used to refer to the quality and different kinds of actors' voices.

The Red Detachment of Women (hongse niangzi jun). One of the eight revolutionary model operas of the Cultural Revolution period.

The Red Lantern (hongdeng ji). One of the best-known of the eight revolutionary model operas of the Cultural Revolution period. This was originally a Shanghai opera that was adapted for Beijing opera in the mid-1960s and was later revised again and recognized as a revolutionary model opera in 1970. The opera tells the story of three revolutionaries of different generations who live together and become embroiled in the fight against the Japanese. It is a story of revolutionary courage, strength, and tenacity of purpose.

Sheng. One of the main role types in traditional Chinese theatre. *Sheng* roles are the main male character roles. The precise organization and deployment of *sheng* roles varies from one form of regional opera to another (see text on the contrast between Beijing and Cantonese opera). However, *sheng* roles are often divided between military and civil, or scholarly, male protagonists.

Song of the Dragon River (longjiang song). One of the eight revolutionary model operas of the Cultural Revolution period.

Suona. A loud, double-reeded wind instrument like a short oboe with a flared trumpet-like end. The *suona* is a traditional instrument used in many kinds of Chinese folk music, including for wedding, funeral, and other ceremonial occasions and processions. It is also used as an instrument in many forms of regional opera, usually for grandiose ceremonial occasions or scenes of high tension such as battle or situations of panic and confusion.

A Surprise Attack on the White Tiger Regiment (qixi baihutuan). One of the eight revolutionary model operas of the Cultural Revolution period, revised and recognized as a model opera in September 1972.

Taking Tiger Mountain by Strategy (zhiqu weihushan). One of the best-known of the eight revolutionary model operas of the Cultural Revolution period, telling the story of a group of People's Liberation Army (PLA) soldiers fighting against the nationalists in the civil war period. This was the first revised Beijing opera, in 1969, to be adopted as a model opera in the Cultural Revolution period.

Thunderstorm (leiyü). The first and best-known play by one of China's leading twentieth-century playwrights, Cao Yü. Written while Cao was a student in the 1920s, it exposes the class tensions and inequalities of Republican period China.

Tizi. A kind of transverse flute used in traditional Chinese musical performance and some forms of regional opera.

Wang Peigong. Author of the controversial play *We* in the 1980s (see below).

We (Women). A controversial experimental play written by Wang Peigong in the mid-1980s. Also sometimes known as *WM*, taking the pinyin initials of the Chinese binome for "we." The play tells the story of seven soldiers in the late 1970s and early 1980s, focusing more on the individuals and their dissatisfactions with society than with preconceived formulae of patriotism and self-sacrifice as had been common in the past. The play was banned, and Wang Peigong and those performing the play, themselves in the military, were suspended from duties.

Xiao. A kind of flute used in traditional Chinese musical performance and some forms of regional opera.

Xipi. One of the two principal musical systems, along with *erhuang*, upon which many contemporary traditional theatre forms are based, including Beijing and Cantonese operas. *Erhuang* is generally used for more solemn or serious situations, while *xipi* is lighter and happier. Combined, the two forms are often referred to as *pihuang*.

Yiyang qiang. One of the three early systems of regional opera that emerged during the Ming dynasty (1368–1644) along with clapper opera, *bangzi qiang*, and the more refined and elitist *kunqu*. *Yiyang qiang* was originally a folk song tradition from Yiyang County in Jiangxi Province. It was distinctive for its use of a chorus in all its forms. Initially a local opera tradition, its popularity spread throughout the country.

Yueju. The Chinese name for Cantonese opera, *yue* being the Chinese character used to refer to Guangdong Province. Another *yueju*, with a different *yue* character and a different tone of pronunciation, refers to a relatively recent traditional form of Shanghainese opera also known as Shaohing opera, that dates back to the late nineteenth century.

Zaju. Along with *nanxi*, one of the two principal dramatic forms that emerged in the Yuan dynasty (AD 1271–1368) and which have since been seen as forming the roots of China's traditional literary dramatic tradition. *Nanxi* and *zaju* were the antecedents of three other regional opera forms: *yiyang qiang*, *bangzi qiang*, and *kunqu*. *Nanxi* was prevalent in southern China, compared to *zaju*'s popularity in the north.

Zhang Xian. Playwright of the 1980s and 1990s who came to fame for his plays dealing with issues at the heart of the transformations of urban life in post-Mao China including divorce, individualism, new wealth, foreign travel and study, business, and social alienation. His plays have proven very popular with the new, young middle classes.

References and Further Reading

Dolby, W. 1976. *A history of Chinese drama.* London: Elek.

Hsia, A. 1987. "Huang Zuoling's ideal of drama and Bertolt Brecht." In C. Tung & C. Mackerras (eds.) *Drama in the People's Republic of China.* New York: State University of New York Press.

Hu, J. Y. H. 1972. *Ts'ao Yü.* New York: Twayne Publishers, Inc.

Huot, C. 2000. *China's new cultural scene: A handbook of changes.* Durham, NC: Duke University Press.

Latham, K. 2000. "Consuming fantasies: Mediated stardom in Hong Kong Cantonese opera and cinema." *Modern China*, Vol. 26, No. 3 (July 2000), 309–347.

Mackerras, C. 1975. *The Chinese theatre in modern times: From 1840 to the present day.* London: Thames & Hudson.

———1983a. "Theater and the Masses." In C. Mackerras (ed.) *Chinese theater: From its origins to the present day.* Honolulu: University of Hawaii Press.

———1983b. "The drama of the Qing dynasty." In C. Mackerras (ed.) *Chinese theater: From its origins to the present day.* Honolulu: University of Hawaii Press.

———1987. "Modernisation and contemporary Chinese theater: Commercialiaztion and professionalization." In C. Tung & C. Mackerras (eds.) *Drama in the People's Republic of China.*

New York: State University of New York Press.

Sun, W. H. 1987. "Mei Lanfang, Stanislavsky and Brecht on China's state and their aesthetic significance." In C. Tung & C. Mackerras (eds.) *Drama in the People's Republic of China.* New York: State University of New York Press.

Tung, C. 1987. "Introduction." In C. Tung & C. Mackerras (eds.) *Drama in the People's Republic of China.* New York: State University of New York Press.

Tung, C. & Mackerras, C. 1987. *Drama in the People's Republic of China.* New York: State University of New York Press.

Yang, D. S. P. 1987. "Theater activities in post–Cultural Revolution China." In C. Tung & C. Mackerras (eds.) *Drama in the People's Republic of China.* New York: State University of New York Press.

Zhao, H. Y. H. 2000. *Towards a modern Zen theatre: Gao Xingjian and Chinese theatre experimentalism.* London: School of Oriental and African Studies Press.

14

Popular Music

China has a very long history of popular music going back several thousand years. Indeed, one of the best-known and most studied classical Chinese texts, *The Book of Songs*, is a collection of folk songs probably written and composed between 1000 and 700 BC. The collection, compiled around 600 BC, includes a large number of court songs written by nobles and used in court ceremonies of the Zhou dynasty (c. 1050–221 BC), but it also includes a range of other songs including love songs, work songs, ballads, seasonal songs, historical poems, and satirical poems, many of which appear to come from among the common people. One version of the book's history accounts for this variety by claiming the book was compiled when the Zhou king sent his officials out among the ordinary people of the kingdom to collect songs in order to understand their feelings, attitudes, and sentiments (see Waley 2005). The *Shijing*, as the book is known in Chinese, was subsequently adopted by Confucian scholars and became one of the main classical Chinese texts at the heart of the imperial exam system. For centuries, it was compulsory learning for would-be scholars and officials.

Popular music has also enjoyed a privileged place in more recent Chinese political history. Even before the foundation of the People's Republic of China in 1949, the Chinese Communist Party devoted considerable attention to popular songs and music. Indeed, in a twentieth-century version of the story of the compilation of the *Book of Songs*, the CCP sent hundreds of Party workers and soldiers out into the countryside to collect folk songs from the 1930s onward. Subsequently, many of these songs were then reworked into revolutionary songs to be sung by soldiers, workers, and peasants alike, as well as being recorded, worked into films, broadcast on radio, and taught in schools. Folk songs were seen as a way for the Party and the government to get closer to the people: to understand and appreciate their concerns and their interests, especially given the rural base of the Chinese revolution and the fact that the vast majority of the Chinese population was made up of peasant farmers. Many of these folk songs and revolutionary songs are still performed today in concerts and variety entertainment shows on television, not to mention in karaoke bars across the country. Although their political significance may have changed in the post-Mao era, they are nonetheless a prominent feature of the contemporary Chinese popular cultural scene.

The importance of popular music in contemporary Chinese cultural production is not restricted to either the distant imperial or the revolutionary past, however. From the 1980s onward, pop and rock music, particularly from Hong Kong and Taiwan, became increasingly popular with young Chinese people, who had been isolated from such music for decades. The popularity of Hong Kong and Taiwanese artists also inspired mainland Chinese artists to start writing, performing, and recording their own pop and rock music.

A division soon emerged between commercial popular music and rock music. Commercial pop music was largely either from Hong Kong and Taiwan or inspired by music from those territories, and rock music was more influenced by Western bands such as Nirvana and more politically engaged. There are dangers involved in simplifying distinctions between rock and pop music, and some authors have warned against using the dichotomy (see, e.g., Huot 2000: 155–156). One of these dangers is that it imports a set of preconceived ideas about what pop and rock music are about, drawing upon experiences in other parts of the world. Another problem is that it is at times difficult to draw a clear line between pop and rock, particularly in the commercial era from the early 1990s onward (see below). Nonetheless, the division does help with a broad conceptualization of some of the differences between rock and pop in China, and is also a commonly used distinction within the Chinese music industry.

The political side of Chinese rock came to the fore at the time of the 1989 Tiananmen Square demonstrations. Indeed, the suppression of the demonstrations spawned a new generation of rock bands, many of which wrote songs with various more or less veiled protest messages. Some such songs even appropriated revolutionary folk songs from the past in what were perceived by some to be potentially subversive ways. Hence, in one way or another popular music has found itself occupying a range of political positions in China, some supporting the political hegemony of the Communist Party and some standing opposed to it. Nonetheless, a good deal of Chinese popular music is also politically neutral—for instance, Hong Kong "Cantopop"-style love songs and ballads. However, what makes music political or not is also a matter of social and cultural context. Apparently controversial lyrics might make no impact whatsoever, while a seemingly innocuous love song could, in some circumstances, constitute an important social, cultural, or even political transformation. For this reason, it is important to consider not only the music, lyrics, or lives and motivations of pop and rock artists but the social and cultural contexts of popular music consumption—who is listening to it or buying it and how, when, and in what situations.

Kinds of Popular Music in Contemporary China

There is a wide range of popular music widely enjoyed in contemporary China. This includes pop and rock music, which we will deal with in greater detail below, but importantly also includes other kinds of popular music such as folk songs and folk music, revolutionary songs, and Chinese classical and Western classical music.

Folk Songs and Folk Music

Folk songs in China are generally locally specific. Although there are nationally known folk songs and melodies, this is in many cases due to their adoption and appropriation by the CCP, which used them for propaganda and entertainment purposes and their being adopted or rewritten as revolutionary songs (see below). The vast majority of Chinese folk songs, however, are known by a relatively small proportion of the national population in a relatively limited, often rural, geographical area.

Nonetheless, there is a strong folk music tradition that is rooted in broader cultural practices and customs. In particular, music is played to accompany weddings and funerals, to celebrate birthdays and other joyous occasions, and to commemorate traditional festivals such as Chinese New Year, the Dragon Boat Festival, and the mid-autumn festival. Ritual, ceremonial, and celebratory practices for weddings and funerals differ widely throughout the country, even if they often share common features. It is therefore very difficult to

A drummer keeps the beat as his team competes in the annual dragon boat races, which commemorate the death of Qu Yuan, a loyal poet who commited suicide in protest at corruption in the state of Chu on the fifth day of the fifth lunar month in 278 BC. (Corel)

generalize about the precise details of how such occasions are organized—however, traditional weddings and funerals usually involve some kind of procession which will be accompanied by music. This will usually be played by a small band of musicians with percussion and wind instruments dominated by the loud *suona* double-reed Chinese oboe-like instrument also used in traditional opera (see Chapter 13) and sometimes also vocal accompaniment (see Jones 2004 for a detailed introduction to ritual music and musicians past and present in rural Hebei Province, near Beijing).

In addition to this kind of ritual music, there are also hundreds of folk songs telling stories of love, work, the seasons, crops, fertility, and harvesting. In some parts of rural China, such as Yunnan in the southwest, there are also traditions of courting songs where young men and women exchange lines of song with each other, often with strong sexual connotations. Some rural communities in the past also performed songs, music, and dances in praise of local deities, to offer gratitude or ask for protection or good harvests, rain, fine weather, or other natural phenomena that would help them in their daily lives.

The so-called roots-seeking elements of 1980s intellectual movements seeking a deeper understanding of contemporary Chinese culture also engaged with Chinese folk music traditions. In the realm of popular culture in particular, the Fifth Generation films *Yellow Earth* and *Red Sorghum* (see Chapter 7) both offered clear examples of this. *Yellow Earth* in particular tells the story of a communist soldier sent out into the countryside of northeastern China, the historical and mythical birthplace of Chinese culture, to collect folk songs for the Party. The film is then peppered with scenes of mass dances with drumming, music, and singing calling upon the spirits to bring much-needed rain for the peasants' crops. In the film, directed by Chen Kaige with camerawork by Zhang Yimou, these scenes are highly choreographed and exploited for their striking visual and aural impact. However, they also push the viewer to make the link between popular music, dance, and the roots of Chinese culture. *Red Sorghum* by contrast uses the taunts of a bawdy folk song sung by the hired sedan bearers carrying Gong Li, the bride, to her arranged marriage, to set the scene for the film, which probes issues of Chinese gender relations, nationalism, self-sufficiency, and the weight of cultural traditions.

The folk song tradition in China is still very rich and very strong, even if in recent decades the distraction of other media, music, and leisure activities have diminished interest among younger generations. Now that even in rural areas people generally watch television and listen to recorded music and the radio and increasingly also use the Internet and other new media, clearly there are alternative forms of entertainment and leisure opportunities for young and old people alike, and the occasions on which people might spontaneously meet up and sing folk songs or play or listen to folk music are less common. Nonetheless, particularly in rural areas, there is still a strong faith in the importance of folk music traditions.

Revolutionary Songs

The important role of music in China's revolutionary tradition is clear. One only has to think of the revolutionary model operas (see Chapter 13) to realize the great significance attached to music by the CCP as part of its overall project of socialist transformation. As we have also seen, from its early days, the CCP attached great importance to folk songs for their ability to help them link up with and generate support among the general, largely rural, population. This became a particularly important strategy following the Long March of 1932 and the establishment of the Party's revolutionary base in Yan'an, in the remote province of Shaanxi. The Long March forced the CCP to focus its attention on rural rather than urban areas as the initial locus of the revolution, and given the largely urban history of the party and the fact that many of its early leaders were urban intellectuals and labor activists, there was a cultural and social gap that needed to be bridged between the party and the people they found themselves working with. Folk songs and music were seen as one of the best ways to achieve this.

Following the foundation of the PRC, the emphasis on music and folk songs was maintained. However, other revolutionary songs were written as well, including military marches and songs, adaptations of traditional opera, and appropriations of internationally recognized revolutionary songs such as "The Internationale," which was also sung by many demonstrating students in 1989. All kinds of revolutionary songs were taught to soldiers, workers, students, and schoolchildren and played regularly on the radio, on trains and buses, and in other public spaces throughout the Mao period. After Mao's death, they continued to be part of the national entertainment landscape where they have retained a place to the present day. Indeed, they are now even more widely accessible to those that want to listen to them, on CD, DVD, television, radio, and MP3. Importantly, however, these revolutionary songs generally have been transformed from political propaganda-entertainment to commercial, sometimes nostalgic popular cultural products.

Classical Chinese Music

There are many forms of classical Chinese music in addition to traditional Chinese opera. They are played solo, in small groups, and in larger, Western-style orchestra-like ensembles and are played on a wide range of traditional musical instruments. Some of the most popular traditional Chinese instruments, in addition to those used in Chinese opera (see Chapter 13), include the *pipa*, the *ruan*, the *guqin*, and the *zheng*.

The *pipa*, one of the best-known and most popular of traditional Chinese musical instruments, is a pear-shaped lute-like instrument with four strings and thirty frets. It is played rather like a guitar, but with five plectra strapped to the fingers. Usually employed as a solo instrument, the *pipa* is used to play very expressive music. The *pipa* is descended from the older but similar instrument the *ruan*, which is a round, lute-like instrument, also with four strings and a fretted neck. The *ruan*, which used to be known as the *pipa*, is strictly speaking a family of instruments with small, medium, and large versions. As the contemporary form of the *pipa* took over that name, the older version became known as the *ruan* after a third-century BC scholar named Ruan Xian, who was one of the early masters of the instrument.

The *guqin* is one of the oldest classical Chinese instruments, with a history stretching back more than 3,000 years. Reputedly, Confucius, in the seventh century BC, was an aficionado and accomplished player of the *guqin*. It is a zither-type

Children in traditional costume holding traditional musical instruments, ca. 1919. The child on the left is holding a *pipa* and the one in the center an *erhu*. (Library of Congress)

instrument with seven strings. Partly for its antiquity and partly because it was also considered the instrument of scholars, imperial officials, and ladies of the gentry families, the *guqin* is often considered a symbol of Chinese high culture. Another ancient zither-like instrument is the *zheng* or *guzheng*, with *gu* as in *guqin* meaning old or ancient. The *guzheng* is used in small ensemble classical Chinese music or as a solo instrument. It has movable bridges that can be placed along the length of the wooden sound-board. The instrument now usually has between twenty-one and twenty-five strings, although the early versions of the instrument had only five. Like the *pipa*, the *guzheng* is plucked using plectra strapped to the fingers. The *yangqin* is another commonly seen classical Chinese dulcimer with a square board of strings played with two lightly held bamboo sticks used to hit the strings.

Classical Chinese music is particularly popular with the older generations and the more highly educated. However, there is still a following among ordinary people, and many young people also learn traditional Chinese instruments in their school years. As with Chinese opera singing, there are amateur groups, often of retired people, who meet to play classical Chinese music in parks and other public spaces if not at home. Classical Chinese music concerts are staged regularly in the concert halls of the large cities but also in other towns and cities throughout the country. Classical Chinese music CDs and DVDs are also widely available.

Western Classical Music

Western classical music also enjoys a strong following in China. It is a minority following, as is that for classical Chinese music, but it nonetheless constitutes a significant part of China's contemporary popular cultural scene. The country's first Western symphony orchestra was founded in 1879, and there are very highly respected classical music conservatories in Shanghai and Beijing. China has also produced countless internationally recognized classical musicians and soloists who play around the world. Western-style classical music is studied in schools, broadcast on radio and television, and increasingly valued among China's emerging middle classes who are keen to see their children learn the piano, the violin, or some other Western classical musical instrument.

Western classical music first came to China with foreign missionaries, including the Italian Jesuit missionary Matteo Ricci, who introduced the Ming emperor Wanli (1563–1620) to the clavichord. In the Qing dynasty (1644–1911), two emperors in particular, Kangxi and Qianlong, both learned Western classical music from missionaries and promoted it within the court. In the late nineteenth and early twentieth centuries, Western classical music went hand in hand with many of the modernizing trends of the times, finding support among late Qing and May 4th intellectuals and military warlords alike. In 1927, the country's first music conservatory was set up in Shanghai, clearly establishing the city as the center of China's Western classical musical excellence. What is more, with the exception of the Cultural Revolution years, Western classical music has also been widely accepted throughout the People's Republic period. As we have discussed, Western ballet was also one of the various influences on Chinese revolutionary model operas.

In 2001, the Chinese authorities officially started construction work on the new National Grand Theatre in the center of Beijing near Tiananmen Square and the Forbidden City. The controversial egg-shaped building, sitting in the middle of a large pool of water, makes a stunning addition to the Beijing scenery but also symbolizes the importance attached to Western classical music and dance—which will be among the principal forms of performance at the theatre—in contemporary China.

Hence, although Western classical music is foreign in origin, in many ways Chinese people have made it their own. Not only do millions of families pay for music lessons for their children and millions of people buy and listen to Western classical music recordings and attend live concerts, there are many accomplished Chinese composers who write their music using the Western musical scale, nomenclature, and instruments. Sometimes they incorporate

Chinese musical instruments into the orchestra or use them as solo instruments, and sometimes they incorporate both Chinese and Western traditions into one piece of music. For many Chinese, in fact, there is no strong sense that Western-style classical music, particularly that written and performed by Chinese, is "foreign" or for foreigners—it is one kind of music among others in the spectrum of popular music commonly found in China.

Gangtai and Mainland Chinese Pop Music

The Mandarin for Hong Kong is *xianggang*, from which the phrase *gangtai* is derived, combining the names for Hong Kong and Taiwan. The phrase is used widely for many things originating from or characteristic of the two territories. Hence, Chinese media, politicians, and ordinary people regularly talk about *gangtai* policies, *gangtai* trade, *gangtai* relations, and so on. The word is also widely used to refer to popular cultural products—films, television, music, books, games, magazines, newspapers, and so on. Within this frame of reference, it is also commonly used to talk about Hong Kong and Taiwan pop music.

Hong Kong and Taiwan both have long established popular music industries, and Hong Kong and Taiwanese singers have been recording and performing in both territories, as well as farther afield in Southeast Asia, for decades. There is therefore a well-established tradition of Hong Kong and Taiwanese pop stars with large fan bases. However, although the popular music industries in the two territories have long been interlinked, with singers and musicians regularly moving between Hong Kong and Taiwan and cultivating a following in both places, in the postwar period up until the 1980s, Hong Kong and Taiwanese popular cultural products were not allowed into China and existed in quite separate media, production, and distribution domains. All this started to change in the late 1970s and 1980s in the era of the post-Mao economic reforms and Deng Xiaoping's open-door policy. Nonetheless, one of the first major impacts of *gangtai* music in post-Mao China was through the illegal circulation of pirated cassettes.

From the late 1970s, *gangtai* cassettes started being smuggled into China, illegally copied and sold either through networks of friends or on stalls on the newly emerging "free markets" (*ziyou shichang*) that allowed individual entrepreneurs to sell goods privately for a personal profit for the first time in decades. Certain Hong Kong and Taiwanese pop stars rapidly became the new unofficial superstars of the People's Republic. The best-known of these was a female Taiwanese singer named Deng Lijun (also known as Teresa Teng), whose songs and cassettes enjoyed enormous popularity throughout China in the 1980s and have retained a position in China's popular cultural landscape to the present day.

Alongside Deng Lijun, there were the "four heavenly kings" of Cantonese pop music, as they became known due to their immense popularity in Hong Kong and overseas and their domination of the "Cantopop" scene for years, even decades. These were four male singers: Andy Lau, Leon Lai, Jacky Cheung, and Aaron Kwok. All four came to fame in the 1980s through a mixture of film, television

Hong Kong Cantopop singer Jacky Cheung performing on stage. In the 1980s he became known as one of the "four heavenly kings" of Cantopop music, gaining immense popularity with fans throughout Greater China. (AFP/Getty Images)

acting, and singing. Between them, they have starred in hundreds of Hong Kong films and made dozens of albums over the years. They have also managed to maintain their popularity, to varying degrees, up to the present day, both in Hong Kong and in mainland China, where they have all performed live concerts at different times.

Deng's songs and music, along with that of other *gangtai* artists, caused a major upheaval in the Chinese popular music scene. However, Deng's music was in stark contrast to what is usually considered groundbreaking in Western popular music contexts. From Elvis Presley through punk and heavy metal to rap, house, and other contemporary Western popular music, rebellious popular music has so often attempted to be either louder and more raucous or more provocative and more outrageous than whatever went before it. Deng Lijun's music, however, was classic Taiwan and Hong Kong pop predominantly consisting of sweet, gentle love songs and ballads. From a Western point of view or even from a contemporary Chinese point of view, the lyrics and music of *gangtai* pop are singularly unremarkable. However, as with so many areas of popular culture, understanding pop music in 1980s China requires thinking about the social, political, and cultural contexts as well as the immediate history of the times. Mainland Chinese people, especially younger generations who had grown up during the People's Republic period, were totally unaccustomed to listening to this kind of nonpolitical, personal, and expressive music. Writing on the subject of Chinese pop music in the 1980s, Andrew Jones quotes a mainland Chinese musician and songwriter, Jia Ding, explaining how he felt when he heard Deng Lijun's songs for the first time:

> The first time I heard Deng Lijun's songs was in 1978. I just stood there listening for a whole afternoon. I never knew before that the world had such good music. I felt such pain. I cried. (Jones 1992: 16)

The rapid spread and popularity of *gangtai* pop music in the 1980s and 1990s was due to the convergence of several factors. On one hand, there was rapid technological development combined with increasing consumer spending power and disposable income. Hence, Chinese people were suddenly able to buy or look forward to buying radios, cassette players, televisions, and videocassette recorders. This facilitated the circulation of pirated cassettes and made possible listening to music not carried by the mainstream media. Anthropologist Tom Gold (1993) has also pointed to other social structural changes going on in China at the time that facilitated the rise of *gangtai* popular culture in general, and pop music in particular. These included improved standards of living, the single-child policy, increasing knowledge of and interest in the world outside of mainland China, changing tastes associated with improved education, and inbound tourism as well as the cultural vacuum created following the destruction of the Cultural Revolution.

One must not overlook the importance of the combination of familiarity and difference in *gangtai* pop music. As the quote above shows, the new imported music was utterly different from that to which Chinese people were used to listening. However, it was nonetheless in Chinese. Even if most output from Hong Kong was in Cantonese, which most Chinese people do not speak, they could still read the lyrics and soon started to understand the songs through listening. Meanwhile, music from Taiwan was sung in Mandarin and was therefore immediately accessible to most of the mainland Chinese population. The cultural and linguistic familiarity of *gangtai* pop music, combined with its freshness and difference from what people were used to, even if it did hark back to pre-1949 sentimental popular music styles (Baranovitch 2003: 14), made it attractive to mainland Chinese people and gave it a clear advantage over other international pop music in other languages and coming from unfamiliar cultural and social backgrounds.

Gangtai pop music has also had a broader fundamental influence on the mainland Chinese pop music scene since the late 1970s. On one hand, Chinese people have become regular, and increasingly economically important, consumers of Hong Kong and Taiwanese pop music. *Gangtai* singers continue to target the mainland Chinese market, and stars like Miriam Yeung, Eason Chan, Canadian-born hip-hop vocalist Edison Chen, Joey Yung, Taiwanese Fish Leong, and many more contemporary *gangtai* stars have a popular following throughout mainland China. Just as significant is the effect that *gangtai* pop music has had on mainland pop music composers and artists. *Gangtai* pop music has shaped mainstream Chinese pop music up to the present day. Since the early days of the 1980s, countless mainland Chinese artists have made names for themselves through their own work and music. However, much of China's popular pop music still fits the mold of the love song. In fact, although there was a number of intervening popular fads such as for the so-called northeast wind music or "prison songs" (see Baranovitch 2003: 18–30), from the 1990s onward the influence of *gangtai* popular music on the mainland Chinese music scene was strengthened. This was due to a combination of factors. To start with, post-Tiananmen China moved ever more firmly from politicization to commercialization, and *gangtai* music is nothing if not commercial. In addition, the large international music companies with whom most Hong Kong and Taiwan artists were signed had all by the 1990s started to look more seriously toward the Chinese market. It was by this time no longer bootleg recordings and pirated copies that were driving the market—although they have remained a dominant feature of the Chinese music scene—but commercially produced and distributed music. The commerciality of the *gangtai* music industries moved full-force into China. Other important factors included the continued improvement of and access to new technologies from karaoke systems to CDs and eventually MP3 players.

Chinese Rock Music

The heyday of Chinese rock music was in the late 1980s and early 1990s. Nonetheless, the genre is still of considerable significance in China's popular cultural landscape, for several reasons. First, not only has it been the most politically engaged and transgressive of popular music genres in China, but it has been one of the most transgressive forms of Chinese popular culture more generally. Second, partly as a consequence of this political engagement, rock music has drawn more international attention than any other form of Chinese popular music. Third, and once again related to the other two points, rock music has also been linked with the more intellectual end of the Chinese popular cultural spectrum, being compared with avant-garde literature, poetry, and art (see, e.g., Huot 2000: 154–181; Baranovitch 2003; Barmé 1999: 127–136; Jones 1992), even if some note how rock music is one of those popular cultural genres that cuts across the intellectual high culture and commercialized mass culture distinction (see, e.g., Barmé 1999: 129). For some analysts, Chinese rock music became a new voice for the country's disaffected intellectuals of the 1980s and 1990s.

Yet despite its general significance, Chinese rock music, even at its peak, had a narrower and more restricted following than mainstream pop music. *Gangtai* and *gangtai*-influenced Chinese pop music may have started out as an illicit popular cultural product, but it very soon became openly accepted and recognized and in the 1990s moved into commercial overdrive. Chinese rock, by contrast, enjoyed a similar rise in popularity in the late 1980s through the circulation of more or less legal audio cassettes. Following the political upheavals of 1989 and rock's close associations with the student protests, however, it was subsequently more tightly controlled by the authorities. Rock was not allowed on television, it was restricted on radio, and live performances were also reined in. According to Chinese rock music scholar Jeroen de Kloet, China's rock music scene is also characterized by divisions, rivalries, and some lack of internal coordination (de Kloet 2002).

That said, the "subversive" nature of rock music should not be overstated. The late 1980s was a time of economic, social, political, and cultural experimentation, when Chinese people were rediscovering the possibilities of alternatives to state-imposed popular culture. In their own ways, art, literature, films, and even to some degree television were all challenging what had previously been clearly defined limits of what was acceptable to the government and the Party and what was not. Some rock musicians pushed a little further than others. However, for the main part, they did not become outright political "dissidents."

Although they were real and had real effects on the consumption of rock music, one should also not overstate the limitations placed on rock music. Probably the most consequential limitation was on television and radio broadcasts, since these potentially reached the largest audiences. However, in the late 1980s and early 1990s, Chinese rock musicians, including those that upset the Chinese authorities, still managed to perform in major concerts, including in the Beijing area.

One of the first major concerts that put Chinese rock on the popular cultural map was in fact an officially organized popular, or *tongsu*, music concert staged in 1986. The transformation of the usage of the term *tongsu* in itself was interesting in the 1980s. *Tongsu*, which means "popular" or "common," also had connotations of vulgarity, as it was used in the late 1970s and early 1980s by the Chinese authorities to refer to imported pop music. *Gangtai* pop music, with its love-song, individual- centered lyrics, was often considered decadent by still relatively conservative Communist officials at this time. By 1986, however, *tongsu* pop music had become officially recognized. It could be broadcast on television and radio, it became a category of performance in officially sanctioned singing competitions (Baranovitch 2003: 18), and *tongsu* music concerts were permitted for the first time.

It was one of these concerts that helped put Chinese rock music on the country's popular cultural map. In May 1986, there was a large, officially approved *tongsu* concert staged in Beijing, with more than a hundred artists performing. One of these was the man who was to become China's most famous rock star, Cui Jian. Cui Jian broke onto China's music scene with his own songs and lyrics that, like much Western rock music, simultaneously promoted individualism, self-expression, and a rebellious attitude toward different forms of authority. Like all forms of protest in China, Cui Jian's songs and music had to make compromises with government restrictions. Had the singer openly criticized Chinese

Cui Jian, China's godfather of rock music, performs during the opening of the Shanghai Travel Festival, September 2003. Cui, who played in Tiananmen Square before the military moved in to crush the student protests in 1989, was at one time banned by the Chinese government from playing live. (AFP/Getty Images)

leaders or the CCP or directly called for any kind of confrontation with the authorities, he would have been severely punished and certainly not allowed to continue with his career. Consequently, his songs, in a time-honored Chinese style, used connotation, implicit satire, or ambiguous interpretative possibilities to voice his protests. He also appropriated revolutionary songs such as "Nanniwan," a Chinese communist song from the 1940s, and wrote more or less veiled political attacks on different political subjects (see, e.g., Huot 2000: 160–161).

According to China popular music scholar Nimrod Baranovitch, it was Cui's version of "Nanniwan" that upset the Chinese authorities in 1987 and consequently led to the singer being banned from public performance for two years (Baranovitch 2003: 51–52). However, once performing again in 1989, Cui was in the middle of the upheavals surrounding the Tiananmen Square student protests. He performed live in the square in May, and his songs were soon adopted by many of the students as anthems for the protests. After 1989, Cui naturally found himself out of favor with the Chinese authorities once again. Still performing live in the 2000s, Cui Jian's appeal to mainland Chinese, overseas Chinese, and other international audiences has endured, making him one of the longest-surviving Chinese popular music stars of the 1980s.

It is also arguable that the special position that rock music enjoys in the history of Chinese popular music owes much to its associations with antiestablishment attitudes in general and the student protests and democracy movement of 1989 in particular. Indeed, the protests of that year seemed to prompt clusters of new rock groups to form, particularly in the Beijing area. In some ways, rock seemed to function, for a short period, as a cathartic release for the pent-up anger and frustration both of protesters in the time leading up to June 4 and of Beijing youth more generally in the following months. That year saw the launch of several prominent rock bands, including one with the name "1989." Others included Breathing (*huxi*) and girl-band Cobra, two of the most successful rock bands of the late 1980s and early 1990s. The late 1980s also saw the emergence of several other bands that were to dominate the Chinese rock scene for several years, including Tang Dynasty and Black Panther, both of which came to be known to some degree internationally as well as within China itself. In February 1990, many of these bands played in what was at the time China's biggest rock concert ever, the 1990 Modern Music Concert.

The 1990 Modern Music Concert attracted around 20,000 people on each of two consecutive nights and saw performances by Cui Jian, Tang Dynasty, Cobra, Breathing, and 1989. Later in the year, Cui Jian also performed in a concert commemorating the Eleventh Asian Games, which were being held in Beijing, in what some have seen as a compromise intended to ingratiate himself with the Chinese authorities (see, e.g., Barmé 1999: 130). From 1990 onward, rock and roll, or *yaogun*—literally "rock roll"—as it had become known in Chinese, was an established feature of the Chinese popular cultural scene. Cui Jian's partial rapprochement with the Chinese authorities also marked the start of a period of greater political neutrality and commercialization—even if Chinese officials have always remained wary of rock music's potential for subversion. In the 1990s, rock music became big business. The leading bands and artists all signed up with large record companies—many of them international labels such as EMI, Sony, BMG, RCA, Polygram, and Warner Music (Huot 2000: 170).

Despite increasing commercialization, or some might say because of it, after 1993, rock music started to lose its popular edge. This was due to a combination of factors. For one thing, both Chinese and foreign recording labels were by now becoming much more efficient in their marketing and distribution in mainland China, and their core emphasis was on the politically safer, unrestricted, and more broadly popular *gangtai* and *gangtai*-style pop music. At the same time, rock music had lost much of its novelty for the general public, and it became ever more a specialized music subcategory with a strong but limited following. Artists like Cui Jian were already starting to be considered "old," particularly by the new generation that had grown up in the 1980s (de Kloet 2002: 102). Even if age has not proven a problem for many Hong Kong pop stars, such as Andy Lau, who have managed to maintain their superstar status for decades, somehow it was more important for China's rockers, partly because of their close associations with the intellectual movements of the 1980s. At the same time, however, the Chinese authorities also started taking a tougher line with rock music and rock musicians from around 1993 onward. De Kloet (2002: 96) identifies piracy, cheap and easy home-recording technologies, the Asian financial crisis, and state intervention as key factors making circumstances difficult for rock music in the late 1990s. Restrictions on television broadcasts of rock music remained in place throughout the early 1990s, but in 1993 the Chinese authorities also started imposing more stringent conditions and restrictions on live performances. Baranovitch (2003: 46) has also suggested that the spread of karaoke technologies contributed to the decline in rock music's popularity in the mid- to late 1990s, given that much rock music was not suitable for singing along to, unlike its *gangtai* counterparts.

Another problem for rock music, compared to other pop music genres, was its close affiliation with and to a large degree also location in the capital. Rock music in China has been very much a Beijing affair—many of the most successful bands came from Beijing, played in Beijing, to some degree sang about Beijing, and in their more politically aware moments engaged with the politics of Beijing. Many of China's rock fans were also to be found among Beijing youth, epitomized in Zhang Yuan's Sixth Generation film *Beijing Bastards*, also featuring Cui Jian. In the late 1980s and even early 1990s, this association with the capital was an asset. However, as rock's popularity started to decline, it also started to seem ever more localized, distant from other parts of the country and relatively narrow in focus, following, and performance.

Chinese Pop and Rock Lyrics

Here it is only possible to give a brief indication of Chinese pop and rock lyrics (for a fuller discussion, see Huot 2000: 154–181; Baranovitch 2003; de Kloet 2002). Understandably, these lyrics cover a wide spectrum of different styles, complexities, and motivations. At one end of the spectrum, there are very simple expressions of love, while at the other there is abstract imagery and more or less direct political satire. *Gangtai* love songs are well exemplified by the lyrics of Deng Lijun's "The Moon Represents My Heart" (cited in Baranovitch 2003: 10):

> You asked me how deep is my love for you
> How strong is my love for you?
> My feelings are true
> My love is also true
> The moon represents my heart . . .
> One gentle kiss
> Already moved my heart
> A short time of deep emotions
> Made me long until now . . . .
> (Anonymous lyrics, performed by Deng Lijun)

The vast majority of *gangtai* pop music is similar to this kind of relatively simple love ballad. There are differences in language between Hong Kong and Taiwanese songs, with the former generally sung in Cantonese and the latter in Mandarin. In actual fact, however, few Cantonese songs actually use a lot of truly colloquial Cantonese and are often written in standard written Chinese, more akin to Mandarin than Cantonese, sung with a Cantonese pronunciation. Occasionally, lyrics use classical Chinese-style poetry. As the mainland Chinese market became ever more important for Hong Kong artists from the 1990s onward, however, they also started producing more recordings in Mandarin or even producing the same songs and albums in both Mandarin and Cantonese versions. In the late 1990s and early 2000s, as *gangtai* pop music became more influenced by other international popular music such as hip-hop and rap, some *gangtai* lyrics became more expressive of youth dissatisfaction, alienation, attitudes, and beliefs. Nonetheless, the majority of *gangtai* output is still in the love ballad mold.

Chinese rock music lyrics are in this sense more complex and more interesting. Indeed, it is rock lyrics that have attracted most scholarly attention in relation to youth alienation, political criticism, and antiestablishment and anti-authority attitudes. The most widely discussed rock lyrics are those of Cui Jian. Some of Cui's lyrics clearly come very close to outright criticism of the Chinese Communist Party. For instance, in his song "A Piece of Red Cloth" (cited in Huot 2000: 162) he wrote:

> That day you took a piece of red cloth, covered my eyes and covered the sky.
> You asked me what I saw, I said I saw happiness.
> This feeling makes me feel good, it makes me forget I've got no place to live.
> You ask what else I want, I say I want to walk your road.
> (Written and performed by Cui Jian)

Cui Jian's song "Opportunists," which the singer performed live in Tiananmen Square in 1989, famously became an anthem for the student demonstrators with its refrain "Oh, we have an opportunity, let's show our desires, Oh, we have an opportunity, let's show our power."

Cui was not alone, however, and other early 1990s rock bands wrote similarly provocative lyrics. An early 1990s Black Panthers song, "No Place to Hide," lamented:

> I don't believe anymore, don't believe in any reasoning . . .
> I don't look back anymore, don't look back at any past.
> I'm not the one I used to be.
> (Cited in Huot 2000: 171)

Ironically, as China gradually became more open and in some ways more politically relaxed, and as the Internet and other new media and popular cultural opportunities presented Chinese people with an ever greater range of kinds and sources of information, many rock lyrics became far more bland and mainstream, themselves succumbing to the pull of love songs and ballads (Huot 2000: 171).

Recent Trends: Technology and Diversification

For China's popular music scene, the second half of the 1990s was characterized by increasing commercialization and diversification. Rock music became more commercial; China's home-grown pop stars became ever more widely known and popular; *gangtai* artists, supported by their recording companies, consolidated and built upon their already significant presence in the mainland market; and the march of new technological developments—compact discs, karaoke, and satellite and cable television—all contributed to transforming China's popular music scene.

Gangtai and *gangtai*-style love songs, ballads, light rock, and easy listening songs and music have remained at the core of Chinese pop music over the last three decades. New artists have come and gone—both in the mainland and in Hong Kong and Taiwan—but at the same time, some of the *gangtai* pop stars who enjoyed early mainland fame in the 1980s and 1990s were still at the top in the early 2000s. However, the pop music scene has continued to transform itself gradually over the years. For example, from the late 1990s onward there has been a gradual shift in popularity away from Cantonese pop music ("Cantopop"), which has dominated the Hong Kong music scene for decades, to Mandarin pop music. This reflects broader social, cultural, and political changes that have taken place in both Hong Kong and the mainland. While Hong Kong society, since its return to Chinese sovereignty in 1997, has moved progressively toward greater use of Mandarin in many areas of public life, mainland Chinese pop music consumers have become ever less dependent upon whatever Hong Kong might supply them with, as in the past, and ever more able to dictate market demand for themselves. Consequently, even Hong Kong musicians increasingly produce Mandarin pop music to remain competitive.

Chinese pop music has also diversified and become more adventurous and experimental in recent years, leaving the China rock music heritage largely in the past. Chinese pop artists experiment with a range of club and dance music, including hip-hop, electronica, techno, and house styles, as well as punk and thrash. The range is ever broadening, even if Chinese music industry professionals in the 2000s often lamented the lack of creative talent and originality in the industry that would see it move away from its rooting in *gangtai*-style ballads.

It is not simply artists and music producers that are transforming China's popular music scene, however. From the late 1990s onward, but particularly in the 2000s, technology has played an important role in shaping the contemporary Chinese music industry. Given that illegally copied cassettes have been a fundamental part of China's music landscape since the late 1970s, piracy is nothing new to the industry; however, the growing popularity of home personal computing and the ability to copy CDs and DVDs with ease has not helped the Chinese authorities or the music industry to tackle the problem. In the early 2000s, the spread of Internet technologies worsened matters. Most notably, illegal music download sites, including peer-to-peer (P2P) file-sharing sites, offering free MP3 files have transformed the way that many young Chinese people in particular think about popular music. The idea of an album is for some becoming anachronistic when MP3 players and personal computers make it easy for almost anyone to put together their own personal collection of favorite music tracks. Given the easy access to illegal, but free, music downloads, the idea of paying for one's music is also kept at a distance by some Chinese consumers.

The level of legal music sales plummeted in the decade from the early 1990s to the early 2000s. Record companies went from counting sales in the millions to sales in the tens, or at best hundreds, of thousands. Much of this is due to the impact of new forms of online piracy rather than the industrial piracy that saw illegal copies of CDs produced in their thousands.

The mobile phone has also acquired an important role in establishing the success of popular music tracks through ringtone downloads. Illegal downloading aside, the cellphone ringtone download market was worth tens of millions of dollars a month

A computer downloading music. Illegal music download and file-sharing sites offering free MP3 files have transformed the way that many young Chinese people in particular think about and acquire popular music. (iStockPhoto.com)

in 2005–2006, and pop songs are often among the most popular downloads. In this way, the mobile phone not only has become a new source of revenue for the music industry but has taken on a new role in music marketing and promotion.

Online technology, however, has also opened up a new noncommercial DIY popular music market in China. Popular Web sites in China offer musicians the chance to upload their music to be downloaded for free by potential fans. Some such music tracks were reportedly downloaded hundreds of millions of times in 2005–2006. Many of the mainly young artists that upload their tracks are hopeful of being discovered by an established record label and moving into the mainstream music industry. The legal free-download market that they have helped create with their dreams has opened up new avenues for both established and would-be Chinese pop stars.

In 2005, the "democratization" of the pop music industry took another giant leap forward when a televised talent contest attracted hundreds of millions of viewers all over the country (see the sidebar, "Reality TV and *Supergirl's Voice*," Chapter 3). The winner of the contest, Li Yuchun, subsequently became a household name and, along with several of the runners-up, soon found herself signing a recording contract. The show was an unexpected runaway success and produced a massive popular response, particularly among young female fans.

Fans celebrate after Li Yuchun was declared winner of the 2005 *Supergirl's Voice* contest finals in Shanghai on August 27, 2005. Li won more than 3.52 million votes from mobile phone text messages in the finals of the *American Idol*–type pop star contest on Hunan Satellite Television. (Corbis)

Situating Popular Music

Understanding popular music in China's cultural landscape requires more than just attention to the kinds of music, artists, songs, and lyrics that are popular. It is also important to consider the social, political, and historical contexts and situations in which different kinds of music have been successful or become important. We have already seen examples of why this is the case.

For instance, in the 1980s, rock music drew a lot of scholarly and intellectual attention because of the veiled political criticisms carried by its lyrics. In many ways, however, the more important and groundbreaking development in 1980s popular music was the relatively innocuous-seeming earlier arrival of *gangtai* love songs and ballads like those of Deng Lijun. To outsiders, Deng's lyrics may seem politically vacuous. However, in the context of early 1980s China, where the public expression of individual desires was still an unfamiliar experience, this music, *including* its lyrics, took on tremendous political, social, and cultural significance. This music, particularly considering the extent of its popularity, was for many Chinese people individually liberating and in a sense politically radical at that time for that reason. Even in the 1990s, when there was nothing politically significant about *gangtai*-style pop, it was nonetheless at least as important as the more political Chinese rock music because of its widespread popularity, its strong attraction for consumers, its popularity on television and radio, and its contribution to the country's entertainment markets. Rock music, by contrast, experienced low media visibility, was strongly associated with Beijing, and had a relatively niche following compared to *gangtai* pop with its much greater appeal to the general populace.

The performance locations of *gangtai*-influenced pop, compared to those of Chinese rock music, were also distinct. Rock music, even in its late 1980s and early 1990s heyday, was often to be found in relatively narrowly defined contexts. As Baranovitch described it, "The main venue for rock performances . . . was still informal, small-scale, underground rock parties, called 'party(s)' in English, which enabled musicians to perform, earn some money, socialize, and establish a rock community that provided the individuals who participated a desired identity of exclusive anti-mainstream and anti-officialdom fraternity" (2003: 39). Mainstream pop, by contrast, was on television, radio, and in the newspapers. It was often performed in large stadiums or concert halls to massive audiences—particularly when famous Hong Kong or Taiwanese pop stars were involved—and pop was also widely heard on buses, trains, and airplanes, in restaurants, on karaoke machines, and in other public spaces.

In relation to classical music—both traditional Chinese and Western—context and situation are once again important. Many of China's major cities have built their own concert halls, largely in order to stage classical music concerts, and these have become popular entertainment venues particularly for China's burgeoning middle classes as well as intellectuals. Although associating classical music with the middle classes and intellectuals may seem unsurprising from a Western perspective, in China this is significant. Certainly, classical Chinese music has a history of association with the elite gentry classes in China—those who had the leisure time and educational opportunities to appreciate it. In pre-1949 China, classical music was also associated with intellectuals and the middle classes. Given the heavy politicization of all cultural production in the Mao era, however, the association of classical music with economic class was undermined. Indeed, classical musicians were often heavily criticized and mistreated in the Cultural Revolution period for their bourgeois practices. Yet, in post-Mao China, classical music has become one of the ways that some of China's emerging middle classes have come to identify themselves through cultural taste and consumption. Classical music connotes a degree of education, refinement, and higher cultural level.

The contexts of traditional Chinese music performances have also come to play a key role marking different kinds of ethnic identities. This happens in many different ways. For instance, Chinese classical music concerts, particularly in Beijing, Shanghai, and to a lesser degree Guangzhou, are also popular attractions for foreign tourists. In this context, the music is often thought of by audiences and presented by performers not only as forms of performance art but specifically as *Chinese* performance art. For many tourists, there is an aspect of discovery of the "other" and of the exotic in attending such concerts, fueled by the curiosity to know what "traditional" Chinese music is like as much as to appreciate the skills of particular performers, some of which tourists unfamiliar with the musical genres are unlikely to be able to assess. It is not only foreign tourists who associate music with ethnic identity, however.

Singing and dancing, usually to folk music, but also at times forms of pop music, are among the most common official and unofficial ethnic markers of minority peoples in China. Whether in performances for Chinese or foreign tourists, on national or local television, at festivals and other public celebrations, or in regional promotional materials and advertising, China's fifty-five officially recognized minority nationality peoples are routinely to be found singing and dancing in colorful traditional costumes. In such situations, complicated questions about "authenticity" have to be asked, given that many such performances are never performed for any purpose other than to represent the particular minority people involved in the context of tourism or mediated consumption. Some of them are entirely devised, even if perhaps on the basis of traditional folk songs, precisely for such purposes. Authenticity aside, the majority of Han Chinese, and many minority peoples also, see such performances as a marker of ethnic identity (see Baranovitch 2003: 54–108 for a detailed discussion of the relation between ethnicity and popular music of different kinds).

As we have discussed, technology has also played a key role in shaping where, when, and how Chinese popular music has been listened to and appreciated. The spread of relatively cheap, easily copied audio and video cassettes in the 1980s made the phenomenal rise of artists like Deng Lijun possible. Audio and video piracy—even if it is illegal—has also played a major part in opening up the various different worlds of popular music to new listeners throughout the country. Similarly, the television ban on rock music, which has now been applied for decades, has strongly influenced the spread and influence of different kinds of popular music. Whereas rock has remained relatively specialized and with a strong regional focus, *gangtai*-influenced pop music, including Cantonese pop music not easily understood by the majority of Chinese people but which has suffered far fewer media restrictions, has become the country's popular music mainstream.

The latest technological developments to greatly affect popular music consumption include the Internet and MP3 players. In the early 2000s, with the expansion of the Internet in China, particularly among urban youth, music downloading, often illegally, became an increasingly popular way of obtaining recordings of popular music. Yet as long as Chinese people could listen to downloaded music only on their computers, the effect on the overall popular music market was bound to be limited. Around 2003, however, other technologies started to amplify the effects of music availability on the Internet. More and more Chinese people acquired computers with writable CD, and later DVD, drives, which meant that they could listen to downloaded music on conventional CD players. Shortly after that, MP3 players became a popular phenomenon, among young people in particular. Consequently, downloaded music could be listened to just about anywhere, CD sales started to level off, and the MP3 format became an increasingly important way for Chinese people to enjoy their music. With third-generation multimedia-capable mobile phones now increasingly becoming part of China's popular technological landscape, the importance and popularity of downloaded music will only increase.

The digitalization of popular music has also clearly affected the transferability of music. Although the cassettes of the past could always be copied, MP3 files make the process that much quicker, easier, and more flexible. However, it has also led to new ways in which music is popularized, most notably through the cellphone ringtone. From the early 2000s, as in many other parts of the world, young people in particular became enthusiastic ringtone downloaders, and although not all ringtones are pop songs, many of them are. Consequently, the mobile phone became an important medium through which people found out about, listened to, familiarized themselves with, and transferred popular music files, even if in simplified or abbreviated forms.

Popular Music and Popular Culture: History, Technology, and Identity

Popular music has historically enjoyed a special place in the Chinese popular cultural landscape, particularly over the last half a century but also before. Popular music not only marked and accompanied many of the major historical events and transformations of the twentieth century in China, it importantly participated in them, shaped them, and contributed to making them happen. From the CCP's enthusiasm for the collection, appropriation, and promotion of folk songs to the internationally recognized role of Cui Jian's rock music in the 1989 student demonstrations, popular music has been a prominent and important feature of not only China's popular cultural landscape but its popular political landscape.

Popular music has also played a part in forming, shaping, and maintaining various Chinese identities. That is to say, people's identifications with different kinds of popular music at different times have shaped the way they think about themselves and others. Popular music came to identify political and class identities in the Mao era through folk songs and folk music as well as revolutionary model operas. In the post-Mao era, a whole new range of personal and individual identifications became possible, starting with imported *gangtai* pop music and subsequently incorporating mainland Chinese pop, rock, and to some degree foreign popular music. Similarly, popular music, in the form of folk music, has figured in the perpetuation and construction of local and ethnic identities for centuries.

In the political and commercial climate of the early 2000s, popular music lost much of its political significance. Some songwriters still write songs expressing some dissatisfaction, but they are still denied access to any substantial audience. Recording companies would not risk the penalties that could follow from producing anything possibly construed as politically sensitive, and broadcasters are even more cautious. At the same time, music has become a large highly commercialized business, with key roles played by large transnational music and media companies. Meanwhile, audiences have changed dramatically. The sheltered or isolated consumers of the early 1980s, for whom the music of Deng Lijun could constitute a personal revolution and even political transgression, are largely a thing of the past. As we have seen in other chapters, Chinese consumers in the twenty-first century are very media-wise, often well-informed, and cognizant of music, media, and popular cultural trends both within China and overseas.

In China's popular music and popular cultural scenes there is still an important factor to be reckoned with, one whose potential to shape the future is enormous: technology. As we have seen, technology has had a crucial role to play in the development of Chinese popular music over the last three decades and will clearly continue to do so in the future. Importantly, the Internet, despite strong controls which can be very effective (see Chapter 8), gives Chinese people access to a vast array of music, an array that they will not necessarily find in their local music store. Similarly, runaway music piracy, as with film, has made a mockery of efforts to control music content and availability. Most Chinese people are not actively looking for banned or subversive music. Indeed, the vast majority of the music-consuming population is content with the mainstream popular music that is readily available and has no political motivation behind its music choices. The key issue is that new technologies regularly create new opportunities and enhance the potential for unofficial music consumption whatever its motivation.

Politics aside, technology is still likely to be one of the key factors to shape the future development of popular music in China. Musical tastes are likely to continue to diversify, and technology is likely to make it increasingly possible to meet the diversified and ever more personalized demands that result. From mobile phones to MP3 players, mobile accessibility of popular music will increase. Specialized, niche music markets will become a feature of the future music scene. At the same time, file-sharing and Internet downloading will continue to eat into the conventional music CD market. With the spread of broadband Internet use, the development of data storage and digital recording technologies, and television, telecommunications, and computing network convergence, the enjoyment and production of all different kinds of popular music will be enhanced and transformed once again with greater access to music videos, online music on demand, and the ability to enjoy music across a range of technological platforms.

A to Z

AK-47. A heavy rock band using strong electronic sounds, effects, and sampling. The band was launched in 2000 by lead singer Zhang Zhiyong along with guitarists Zhang Wei and Li Siwei, with Lu Wei on drums and Meng Qingwang on electronic effects.

Black Panther (hei pao). One of the leading Chinese rock bands of the 1990s.

The Book of Songs (Shijing). One of the five so-called Confucian Classics, by some accounts compiled by Confucius himself around 600 BC. The *Shijing* is an ancient collection of song lyrics, including ceremonial court songs and folk songs detailing everyday life at the time.

Butterfly Lovers Violin Concerto. One of the best-known and loved pieces of Chinese-written Western-style classical music. The piece was written by He Zhanhao and Chen Gang, two students of the Shanghai Conservatory, in 1959. The concerto started to become widely popular in the 1970s.

Cantopop. The colloquial abbreviation often used to refer to Cantonese pop music almost exclusively originating from Hong Kong but very popular in mainland China also since the 1980s. "Cantopop" is renowned for its gentle, easy-listening love songs and ballads.

Cobra. One of China's best-known 1990s rock bands, even if one of its less musically productive. Also known as *The Females Rock Band*—a direct translation of its Chinese name—*Cobra* was China's first and best-known all-girl rock band in a male-dominated music scene.

Cui Jian. China's best-known rock singer and writer, whose career has spanned two decades—from the 1980s to the present day. Cui is often thought of in relation to his prominent involvement in the 1989 student demonstrations in Tiananmen Square.

Deng Lijun. Also known as Teresa Teng, Taiwanese-born Deng Lijun was one of the leading *gangtai* pop stars from the 1980s until her untimely death in 1995. Her music swept mainland China in the 1980s and was for many young Chinese their first encounter with the very different pop music scene outside the PRC.

Folk songs and folk music. These have a special place in Chinese popular cultural history because of the CCP's attention to collecting folk songs from the 1930s onward as a way of trying to get close to the people, peasant farmers in particular. Folk music also features prominently on many ritual and festival occasions.

Gangtai. The colloquial abbreviation for music and other things originating from or associated with Hong Kong and Taiwan. The term combines elements of the Chinese name for Hong Kong (*Xianggang*) and "Taiwan."

Guqin. One of the oldest classical Chinese instruments, with a history stretching back more than 3,000 years. It is a zither-type instrument with seven strings traditionally associated with being the instrument of scholars, imperial officials, and ladies of the gentry families and hence often a symbol of Chinese high culture.

Hang on the Box. A Chinese punk band based in Beijing and recording in the early 2000s. The band was known for its heavy sound and lyrics dealing with sex, youth alienation, and personal politics, often spattered with English phrases. One of its best-known albums is called *For Every Punk Bitch and Arsehole.*

Huxi (Breathing). One of China's leading rock bands of the early 1990s.

Li Yuchun. The 2005 winner of Hunan Satellite Television's *Supergirl's Voice* reality TV talent contest. The program reeled in audiences in excess of 400 million nationwide and launched the twenty-one-year-old Sichuan-born Li to instant stardom.

Mandopop. The colloquial abbreviation sometimes used to refer to Mandarin pop music generally originating from Taiwan.

No. The name of a 1990s rock band noted for its discordant guitar-based sound. The group's best-known song "No Solution" (*wujie*), which describes how the different limbs of the singer's body have all lost awareness of each other, is often seen as a parody of a well-known Cui Jian track (see Huot 2000: 166–167).

Pipa. A traditional plucked stringed instrument, often used as a solo performance instrument but also used for melodic rendition in some forms of traditional regional Chinese theatre.

Piracy. Illegal copying of cassettes, videos, CDs, and DVDs as well as more recent illegal downloading of MP3 music files constitutes one of the greatest threats to the Chinese music industry.

Revolutionary model operas. Model operas were designated by Jiang Qing, Mao's hard-line leftist wife, as the epitome of revolutionary artistic performance in the early 1960s. For many years in the Cultural Revolution period, the eight approved model operas were the only kind of theatrical performance permitted in China.

Shijing. See *The Book of Songs.*

Suona. A loud, double-reeded wind instrument like a short oboe with a flared, trumpet-like end. The *suona* is a traditional instrument used in many kinds of Chinese folk music, including for weddings, funerals, and other ceremonial occasions and processions. It is also used as an instrument in many forms of regional opera, usually for grandiose ceremonial occasions or scenes of high tension such as battle or situations of panic and confusion.

Tang Dynasty. One of China's best-known and internationally recognized rock bands of the 1990s.

Teresa Teng. See *Deng Lijun.*

Xiang Xiang. One of China's first "Internet pop stars" to draw widespread attention in 2005 following the launch of her *Song of Pig* on a free music download site. She subsequently signed a conventional commercial recording contract. Xiang Xiang's success reflects the changing nature of the Chinese music industry as new communications technologies are developed.

Yangqin. A commonly seen classical Chinese dulcimer with a square board of strings and played with two lightly held bamboo sticks used to hit the strings.

Yellow River Cantata/Piano Concerto. *The Yellow River Cantata* was a famous piece of Chinese Communist propaganda music written in Yan'an in 1939 by composer Xian Xinghai. The piece was arranged for piano as a four-movement piano concerto by composer Yin Chengzong and became one of the best-known pieces of Western-style classical Chinese music along with *The Butterfly Lovers Violin Concerto.*

Yeung, Miriam. One of the most popular Hong Kong pop singers of the late 1990s and early 2000s.

Zheng* or *guzheng. An ancient musical instrument used in small ensemble classical Chinese music or as a solo instrument. It has movable bridges that can be placed along the length of the wooden sound-board. The contemporary *zheng* usually has between twenty-one and twenty-five strings, although the early versions of the instrument had only five. Like the *pipa*, the *guzheng* is plucked using plectra strapped to the fingers.

References and Further Reading

Baranovitch, N. 2003. *China's new voices: Popular music, ethnicity, gender and politics, 1978–1997.* Berkeley, CA: University of California Press.

Barmé, G. 1999. *In the red: On contemporary Chinese culture.* New York: Columbia University Press.

de Kloet, J. 2002. "Rock in a hard place: Commercial fantasies in China's music industry." In S. Hemelryk Donald, M. Keane, and Y. Hong (eds.) *Media in China: Consumption, content, and crisis.* London: RoutledgeCurzon.

Gold, T. 1993. "Go with your feelings: Hong Kong and Taiwan popular culture in Greater China." *China Quarterly,* No. 136 (December 1993).

Huot, C. 2000. *China's new cultural scene: A handbook of changes.* Durham and London: Duke University Press.

Jones, A. 1992. *Like a knife: Ideology and genre in contemporary Chinese popular music.* Cornell East Asia Series. Ithaca, NY: Cornell University Press.

Jones, S. 2002. "Rock in a hard place: Commercial fantasies in China's music industry." In S. H. Donald, M. Keane, & Hong Y. (eds.) *Media in China: Consumption, content and crisis.* London: RoutledgeCurzon.

———2004. *Plucking the winds: Lives of village musicians in old and new China.* Leiden: CHIME Foundation.

Kraus, R. C. 1989. *Pianos and politics in China: Middle-class ambitions and the struggle over Western music.* Oxford: Oxford University Press.

Melvin, S. & Cai, J. 2004. *Rhapsody in red: How Western classical music became Chinese.* New York: Algora Publishing.

Mittler, B. 1997. *Dangerous tunes: The politics of Chinese music in Hong Kong, Taiwan and the People's Republic of China since 1949.* Wiesbaden: Harrassowitz.

Waley, A. 2005 (1952). *The book of songs.* Translated from the Chinese by Arthur Waley. London: Routledge.

15

Afterword: Looking to the Future of Chinese Popular Culture

Foretelling the future in an area such as Chinese popular culture is a risky endeavor. China, as a country, an economy, a political entity, and above all a society, is changing at a terrific pace. The rate of change is such that people who visited China's major cities as little as ten to fifteen years ago may hardly recognize them today. Social and cultural change and development depends on a host of factors including government policies, economic factors, demographic factors, the development of new technologies, the cost and accessibility of new technologies, and constantly evolving relations with the rest of the world. In all of these areas, there are significant uncertainties that make precisely predicting the future very difficult if not impossible.

That does not mean that we have no idea of what the future might look like. At the very least, we can identify the key issues and drivers of change and the key factors that are likely to have bearing on Chinese popular culture. Many of these have already been introduced in the individual chapters of this book. For instance, the key factors to take into consideration have to include those of technology, globalization, government policies and politics, the economy, and social-demographic factors.

As we have seen through the chapters of this book, technology and technological innovation has played a fundamental role in the development of Chinese popular culture over the last century, whether it be with the arrival of cinema in the early twentieth century; the development of wired radio or the deployment of mobile cinema units in the 1950s and 1960s; the explosion of television, video, and audio recording in the 1980s; or the emergence of cable television networks, satellite broadcasting, the Internet, and mobile phones in the 1990s. Technology is not all-determining, but the range and direction of social and cultural development can certainly be influenced by the deployment, popularity, and availability of new forms of technology. Contemporary popular culture in many parts of the world is now unimaginable without television, radio, film, and increasingly new technologies such as the Internet and the mobile phone.

Predicting the future is more complex than simply looking at what new technologies are being developed, but thinking about which technologies are likely to be important in the near to medium term is one way of trying to comprehend what things may be like. In relation to Chinese popular culture, there are several technological developments occurring now that will shape the future in one way or another. For instance, China's Internet users are switching more and more to broadband, third-generation mobile phones are likely to come into widespread use from 2008 onward, and cellphone television and Internet protocol television (IPTV) are changing the ways that Chinese people watch television programs. These will become ever more popular and widespread forms of media consumption. At the same time, direct-to-home satellite television is starting to bring more channel choice and better picture quality to ever more remote and rural areas. MP3 and MP4 players are changing the ways people select, buy, and listen to popular music and other information services, while ever more powerful computers and software are enabling the development of increasingly sophisticated online and video games. All of these technologies will play an important part in the immediate future development of Chinese popular culture.

Globalization is a contentious term that can be understood and conceptualized in a number of quite different ways. For present purposes, however, we can think of globalization as the increasing degree to which China plays a part in the everyday lives of people in other parts of the world and the increasing degree to which people's everyday lives in China have to be understood in relation to what is going on in the rest of the world. It is important to remember that globalization is not unidirectional but refers to an array of complex processes of interaction. Clearly China's open-door policy from the 1980s onward has played an important part in opening up China and its people to external cultural, political, and commercial interests and activities. The last ten to fifteen years has also seen China increasingly playing an important role in the world economy both as an opening market in itself and as a crucial production base for other markets around the world. The fact that China produces consumer goods for the rest of the world has meant that Chinese people are increasingly aware of international consumer tastes. Chinese television, radio, newspapers, and Web sites offer a wide spectrum of news and information about the rest of the world, a spectrum unimaginable in the Mao period. At the same time, the ever greater numbers of foreign businesspeople, students, and tourists coming to China and of Chinese businesspeople, students, and tourists traveling around the world mean both that Chinese people are becoming increasingly visible and active in international contexts and that Chinese people in China are increasingly in contact with people, ideas, and technologies from other parts of the world.

Some areas of the relationship between contemporary Chinese popular culture and globalization are clear, whether it be from the millions of Chinese who watch European soccer or North American basketball every week, the presence of Chinese versions of international fashion magazines on Chinese newsstands, or the declaration "Made in China" commonly found on consumer goods bought and sold both in China and around the world. This makes clear the extent to which China is now fully embroiled in broader global economic systems but also how globalization will become an ever more important factor shaping Chinese popular cultural and other social landscapes.

The case of the open-door policy and the extent to which it opened up new popular cultural and other horizons to China and its people is a clear example of how government policy and politics play a crucial role in shaping popular cultural practices. Throughout this book we have also mentioned plenty of other examples. In the early PRC period, for instance, government and Party policy stipulated that all cultural production had to be political. Media production in China, past and present, cannot be understood without reference to government policy, and government attitudes toward the use and operation of the Internet and other new technologies have been fundamental to the way that they have developed in the country.

It is almost unimaginable that China will return to any kind of rigid political control like that seen in the Mao period, and the signs are that the gradual process of opening up and relaxation of rules governing different areas of popular cultural production will continue. However, there is still plenty of scope for government policy to mold the future shape of Chinese popular culture. Government policy has gradually depoliticized many areas of media production, but there are still clear and strictly enforced constraints on what kind of content is acceptable. Government policy is also clearly important for shaping the country's relation to both technology and globalization as well as the economy and social-demographic issues discussed below.

It goes without saying that the state of the economy will affect the development of Chinese popular culture. To start with, as we have seen, many areas of popular cultural production are now subject to market forces and the vagaries of supply and demand. At the same time, many areas of Chinese popular culture are now areas of popular mass consumption. This means that they are also subject to fundamental economic factors such as the size of salaries and the cost of housing, food, and other basic goods and services. The more that popular cultural products and services depend upon commercial consumption, the more they depend upon levels of disposable income, which is generally linked to the strength of the overall economy.

Given that the Chinese economy grew on average by more than 9 percent per annum between 1978 and 2005, and in 2006 employment was still rising by as much as 1 million per year, there is every reason to believe that the Chinese economic boom is set to continue for some years to come. It therefore seems reasonable to assume that economic growth is likely to support the further expansion of China's consumerism into less developed and more rural areas, which will bring with it the kinds of entertainment and leisure opportunities that have become popular in recent years.

Social-demographic factors will be fundamentally important in the development of Chinese popular cultural practices. Indeed, at present, many areas of popular culture help to demarcate significant social-demographic distinctions. One of the easiest ways to see this is in relation to China's growing digital divide, which broadly maps onto several axes: urban-rural, east-west, rich-poor, and young-old. There are no clear-cut boundaries between the poles of any of these axes, and they are better thought of as heuristic spectra rather than absolute categories. Nonetheless, one can generally say that Chinese people who would find themselves nearer to any of the urban, east, rich, or young ends of these spectra are more likely to have access to and regularly use new technologies, to be more familiar with latest trends and developments in media, entertainment, and popular culture, and to live lives in which popular culture is an experience rather than an aspiration. Popular cultural practices are also gendered, in the sense, for instance, that Internet users are more likely to be male than female, as are soccer fans, but the gender divide does not map neatly onto these other social-demographic spectra. Media images, for instance, which often tend to fix upon pretty, young female models, clearly make men's and women's relations to visual popular culture quite different and feed into complex understandings of sexuality (see, e.g., Evans 1996), but many of these issues equally affect men and women of different ages, in different parts of the country, and of different economic groups and labor categories.

In the 2000s, the Chinese government has become increasingly concerned about the east-west and rural-urban divisions in China and similarly the technological or digital divide that is being laid over them. Despite prominent campaigns to try to redress the problem, the signs have generally been that the digital—and we might add popular cultural—divides are gradually widening rather than narrowing. This will be important for the development of popular culture in China. Already much of what is discussed in this book is urban popular culture, and one could already argue that one ought to distinguish between urban and rural popular cultural practices. This argument will become all the more pressing if the social-demographic divisions emerging in the country are not addressed effectively in the near future, something that does not seem likely to happen.

In the individual chapters in this book, I have given indications of likely future developments of the different aspects of popular culture dealt with in each case, and there is no need to repeat those considerations here. However, we can identify some other broad trends and possibilities that are likely to be important in Chinese popular culture in the future. For instance, the commercialization of Chinese popular culture is likely to continue, and the relationship between popular culture and technology is likely to expand and intensify. At the same time, there is a general trend in China away from the notion of mass culture toward an emphasis on individual likes and preferences expressed or satisfied through more personalized and customized consumption. Again, technology—for instance, through mobile-phone downloads, broadband video-on-demand, and personal Web space—is playing a large part in making this possible.

Consequently, Chinese popular culture is likely to be increasingly fragmented and niche-oriented. The digitization of television, for instance, has already moved the industry toward specialized subscription channels, and video-on-demand will make selective viewing even easier and more popular. There are also other niche popular cultural practices that we have come across in this volume and that illustrate this trend. For instance, different forms of arts theatre, particularly in large cities like Beijing and Shanghai, have relatively small but dedicated followings. Among intellectuals and students, there is a strong interest in literature, including new forms of online literary publishing, discussion, and interaction. There are also many regional and local popular cultural niches, from forms of regional traditional opera to gourmet cuisine.

There are other important new trends in leisure consumption emerging that are likely to have profound effects on Chinese popular cultural practices but also on Chinese society more generally. Most notable among these is the emergence in recent years of Chinese tourism, both within China and overseas. The combination of an emerging middle class with reasonable levels of disposable income, along with the falling cost of international tourism and an ever more open attitude on the part of the Chinese government to travel, means that hundreds of millions of Chinese are starting to enjoy vacations away from home. For many, this will involve traveling within China to Beijing, Shanghai, or the other major cities. For others, it will mean exploring the more remote and ethnically diverse parts of the country such as Tibet. Significantly, however, international travel and package vacations are increasingly options for Chinese tourists. At the lower end of the budget spectrum, destinations such as Thailand and Malaysia are popular for beach getaways, while at the other end of the spectrum Chinese tour groups are increasingly heading for Europe, Australia, and the United States. This emerging trend will have profound effects on international tourism but also on Chinese social attitudes and self-understanding.

Finally, there is one more broad trend that is clear and of great significance. The contents of this book have shown the breadth and depth of contemporary Chinese popular cultural practices, how they are intricately embroiled in the daily lives of hundreds of millions of Chinese people, and how they are increasingly significant features of everyday Chinese social interaction and cultural production and increasingly important for understanding contemporary Chinese society and culture more generally. We may have discussions about the different ways of defining popular culture and, as noted in Chapter 1, this raises issues that are not necessarily easily resolved. However, even taking a simplistic—and hence restricted—definition of popular culture as commercial mass consumer culture and media, the importance of popular culture in understanding contemporary China is undeniable. Much of Chinese people's everyday lives—including those in the more remote, rural, and less developed parts of the country—is mediated in one way or another, hundreds of millions of Chinese participate daily in the country's consumer culture, and new forms of social and cultural interaction arising out of new media and technologies emerge with consistent regularity. One may argue as to whether popular culture should or should not be differentiated from Chinese culture more generally, but one thing is for certain: However they are categorized and understood, the cultural practices discussed in this book play a fundamental role in shaping contemporary China and Chinese society and will continue to do so for years and decades to come.

References and Further Reading

Evans, H. 1996. *Women and sexuality in China: Dominant discourses of female sexuality and gender since 1949*. Oxford: Polity.

Index

About the Author

Dr. Kevin Latham is a Lecturer at the Department of Anthropology and Sociology at the School of Oriental and African Studies of the University of London. His research focuses on Chinese media with particular attention to journalists working in newspapers and television in Guangzhou. His earlier research on Chinese theatre (Cantonese opera in particular) dealt extensively with audiences, practices of appreciation and the production of different kinds of knowledge. He has written on Chinese practices of consumption, consumerism and popular culture.